François Rabelais, Thomas Urquhart, Peter Antony Motteux

Five Books of the Lives, Heroic deeds and Sayings of Gargantua and his Son Pantagruel

Vol. I

François Rabelais, Thomas Urquhart, Peter Antony Motteux

Five Books of the Lives, Heroic deeds and Sayings of Gargantua and his Son Pantagruel
Vol. I

ISBN/EAN: 9783337193485

Printed in Europe, USA, Canada, Australia, Japan

Cover: Foto ©ninafisch / pixelio.de

More available books at **www.hansebooks.com**

François Rablais

J. Sarrabat fecit et excudit   Se vend à Paris ... S.t Louis proche le Palais à la Toison d'Or.

Master Francis Rabelais

FIVE BOOKS OF THE LIVES, HEROIC DEEDS AND SAYINGS OF GARGANTUA AND HIS SON PANTAGRUEL

TRANSLATED INTO ENGLISH BY
SIR THOMAS URQUHART OF CROMARTY
AND
PETER ANTONY MOTTEUX

WITH AN INTRODUCTION BY
ANATOLE DE MONTAIGLON

ILLUSTRATIONS BY LOUIS CHALON

VOLUME I

LONDON: LAWRENCE AND BULLEN
16, HENRIETTA STREET, W.C.
1892

CHISWICK PRESS:—C. WHITTINGHAM AND CO., TOOKS COURT,
CHANCERY LANE, LONDON.

PUBLISHERS' NOTICE.

HE text of the first Two Books of Rabelais has been reprinted from the first edition (1653) of Urquhart's translation. Footnotes initialled "M" are drawn from the Maitland Club edition (1838); other footnotes are by the translator. Urquhart's translation of Book III. appeared posthumously in 1693, with a new edition of Books I. and II., under Motteux's editorship. Motteux's rendering of Books IV. and V. followed in 1708. Occasionally (as the footnotes indicate) passages omitted by Motteux have been restored from the 1738 copy edited by Ozell.

We have pleasure in announcing that M. Anatole de Montaiglon is preparing for us a volume of Notes on Rabelais.

22nd November, 1892.

Contents.

	PAGE
INTRODUCTION	xv

The First Book.

	PAGE
J. De la Salle, to the Honoured, Noble Translator of Rabelais	3
Rablophila	6
The Author's Prologue to the First Book	9
Rabelais to the Reader	13
Chapter I. Of the Genealogy and Antiquity of Gargantua	15
II. The Antidoted Fanfreluches: or, a Galimatia of extravagant Conceits found in an ancient Monument	17
III. How Gargantua was carried eleven months in his mother's belly	20
IV. How Gargamelle, being great with Gargantua, did eat a huge deal of tripes	22
V. The Discourse of the Drinkers	23
VI. How Gargantua was born in a strange manner	27
VII. After what manner Gargantua had his name given him, and how he tippled, bibbed, and curried the can	29
VIII. How they apparelled Gargantua	30
IX. The colours and liveries of Gargantua	33
X. Of that which is signified by the colours white and blue	36
XI. Of the youthful age of Gargantua	39
XII. Of Gargantua's wooden horses	41
XIII. How Gargantua's wonderful understanding became known to his father Grangousier, by the invention of a torchecul or wipebreech	43
XIV. How Gargantua was taught Latin by a Sophister	47
XV. How Gargantua was put under other schoolmasters	49
XVI. How Gargantua was sent to Paris, and of the huge great mare that he rode on; how she destroyed the oxflies of the Beauce	51

CONTENTS.

	PAGE
CHAPTER XVII. How Gargantua paid his welcome to the Parisians, and how he took away the great bells of Our Lady's Church	52
XVIII. How Janotus de Bragmardo was sent to Gargantua to recover the great bells	54
XIX. The oration of Master Janotus de Bragmardo for recovery of the bells	55
XX. How the Sophister carried away his cloth, and how he had a suit in law against the other masters	57
XXI. The study of Gargantua, according to the discipline of his schoolmasters the Sophisters	59
XXII. The games of Gargantua	61
XXIII. How Gargantua was instructed by Ponocrates, and in such sort disciplinated, that he lost not one hour of the day	66
XXIV. How Gargantua spent his time in rainy weather	72
XXV. How there was great strife and debate raised betwixt the cake-bakers of Lerné, and those of Gargantua's country, whereupon were waged great wars	74
XXVI. How the inhabitants of Lerné, by the commandment of Picrochole their king, assaulted the shepherds of Gargantua unexpectedly and on a sudden	76
XXVII. How a monk of Sevillé saved the close of the abbey from being ransacked by the enemy	78
XXVIII. How Picrochole stormed and took by assault the rock Clermond, and of Grangousier's unwillingness and aversion from the undertaking of war	83
XXIX. The tenour of the letter which Grangousier wrote to his son Gargantua	85
XXX. How Ulric Gallet was sent unto Picrochole	86
XXXI. The speech made by Gallet to Picrochole	87
XXXII. How Grangousier, to buy peace, caused the cakes to be restored	89
XXXIII. How some statesmen of Picrochole, by hairbrained counsel, put him in extreme danger	92
XXXIV. How Gargantua left the city of Paris to succour his country, and how Gymnast encountered with the enemy	96
XXXV. How Gymnast very souply and cunningly killed Captain Tripet and others of Picrochole's men	98
XXXVI. How Gargantua demolished the castle at the ford of Vede, and how they passed the ford	100
XXXVII. How Gargantua, in combing his head, made the great cannon-balls fall out of his hair	102
XXXVIII. How Gargantua did eat up six pilgrims in a salad	104
XXXIX. How the Monk was feasted by Gargantua, and of the jovial discourse they had at supper	106
XL. Why monks are the outcasts of the world; and wherefore some have bigger noses than others	109

CONTENTS.

		PAGE
CHAPTER XLI.	How the Monk made Gargantua sleep, and of his hours and breviaries	111
XLII.	How the Monk encouraged his fellow-champions, and how he hanged upon a tree	113
XLIII.	How the scouts and fore-party of Picrochole were met with by Gargantua, and how the Monk slew Captain Drawforth, and then was taken prisoner by his enemies	115
XLIV.	How the Monk rid himself of his keepers, and how Picrochole's forlorn hope was defeated	118
XLV.	How the Monk carried along with him the Pilgrims, and of the good words that Grangousier gave them	120
XLVI.	How Grangousier did very kindly entertain Touchfaucet his prisoner	122
XLVII.	How Grangousier sent for his legions, and how Touchfaucet slew Rashcalf, and was afterwards executed by the command of Picrochole	125
XLVIII.	How Gargantua set upon Picrochole within the rock Clermond, and utterly defeated the army of the said Picrochole	127
XLIX.	How Picrochole in his flight fell into great misfortunes, and what Gargantua did after the battle	130
L.	Gargantua's speech to the vanquished	131
LI.	How the victorious Gargantuists were recompensed after the battle	134
LII.	How Gargantua caused to be built for the Monk the Abbey of Theleme	136
LIII.	How the abbey of the Thelemites was built and endowed	138
LIV.	The inscription set upon the great gate of Theleme	140
LV.	What manner of dwelling the Thelemites had	143
LVI.	How the men and women of the religious order of Theleme were apparelled	145
LVII.	How the Thelemites were governed, and of their manner of living	147
LVIII.	A prophetical Riddle	149

The Second Book.

FOR THE READER		155
MR. HUGH SALEL TO RABELAIS		157
THE AUTHOR'S PROLOGUE		159
CHAPTER I.	Of the original and antiquity of the great Pantagruel	163
II.	Of the nativity of the most dread and redoubted Pantagruel	168
III.	Of the grief wherewith Gargantua was moved at the decease of his wife Badebec	171
IV.	Of the infancy of Pantagruel	173

CONTENTS.

		PAGE
CHAPTER V.	Of the acts of the noble Pantagruel in his youthful age	176
VI.	How Pantagruel met with a Limousin, who too affectedly did counterfeit the French language	179
VII.	How Pantagruel came to Paris, and of the choice books of the Library of St. Victor	181
VIII.	How Pantagruel, being at Paris, received letters from his father Gargantua, and the copy of them	187
IX.	How Pantagruel found Panurge, whom he loved all his lifetime	192
X.	How Pantagruel judged so equitably of a controversy, which was wonderfully obscure and difficult, that, by reason of his just decree therein, he was reputed to have a most admirable judgment	196
XI.	How the Lords of Kissbreech and Suckfist did plead before Pantagruel without an attorney	200
XII.	How the Lord of Suckfist pleaded before Pantagruel	204
XIII.	How Pantagruel gave judgment upon the difference of the two lords	208
XIV.	How Panurge related the manner how he escaped out of the hands of the Turks	210
XV.	How Panurge showed a very new way to build the walls of Paris	215
XVI.	Of the qualities and conditions of Panurge	219
XVII.	How Panurge gained the pardons, and married the old women, and of the suit in law which he had at Paris	224
XVIII.	How a great scholar of England would have argued against Pantagruel, and was overcome by Panurge	227
XIX.	How Panurge put to a nonplus the Englishman that argued by signs	232
XX.	How Thaumast relateth the virtues and knowledge of Panurge	235
XXI.	How Panurge was in love with a lady of Paris	237
XXII.	How Panurge served a Parisian lady a trick that pleased her not very well	240
XXIII.	How Pantagruel departed from Paris, hearing news that the Dipsodes had invaded the land of the Amaurots; and the cause wherefore the leagues are so short in France	243
XXIV.	A letter which a messenger brought to Pantagruel from a lady of Paris, together with the exposition of a posy written in a gold ring	244
XXV.	How Panurge, Carpalin, Eusthenes, and Epistemon, the gentlemen attendants of Pantagruel, vanquished and discomfited six hundred and threescore horsemen very cunningly	247
XXVI.	How Pantagruel and his company were weary in eating still salt meats; and how Carpalin went a-hunting to have some venison	249
XXVII.	How Pantagruel set up one trophy in memorial of their valour, and Panurge another in remembrance of the hares. How	

CONTENTS.

	PAGE
Pantagruel likewise with his farts begat little men, and with his fisgs little women; and how Panurge broke a great staff over two glasses	252
CHAPTER XXVIII. How Pantagruel got the victory very strangely over the Dipsodes and the Giants	255
XXIX. How Pantagruel discomfited the three hundred giants armed with freestone, and Loupgarou their captain	259
XXX. How Epistemon, who had his head cut off, was finely healed by Panurge, and of the news which he brought from the devils, and of the damned people in hell	264
XXXI. How Pantagruel entered into the city of the Amaurots, and how Panurge married King Anarchus to an old lantern-carrying hag, and made him a crier of green sauce	270
XXXII. How Pantagruel with his tongue covered a whole army, and what the author saw in his mouth	272
XXXIII. How Pantagruel became sick, and the manner how he was recovered	275
XXXIV. The conclusion of this present book, and the excuse of the author	277

The Third Book.

FRANCIS RABELAIS TO THE SOUL OF THE DECEASED QUEEN OF NAVARRE	283
THE AUTHOR'S PROLOGUE	285
CHAPTER I. How Pantagruel transported a colony of Utopians into Dipsody	295
II. How Panurge was made Laird of Salmigondin in Dipsody, and did waste his revenue before it came in	299
III. How Panurge praiseth the debtors and borrowers	303
IV. Panurge continueth his discourse in the praise of borrowers and lenders	307
V. How Pantagruel altogether abhorreth the debtors and borrowers	311
VI. Why new married men were privileged from going to the wars	313
VII. How Panurge had a flea in his ear, and forbore to wear any longer his magnificent codpiece	316
VIII. Why the codpiece is held to be the chief piece of armour amongst warriors	319
IX. How Panurge asketh counsel of Pantagruel whether he should marry, yea or no	322
X. How Pantagruel representeth unto Panurge the difficulty of giving advice in the matter of marriage; and to that purpose mentioneth somewhat of the Homeric and Virgilian lotteries	325

CONTENTS.

CHAPTER XI. How Pantagruel showeth the trial of one's fortune by the throwing of dice to be unlawful 329

XII. How Pantagruel doth explore by the Virgilian lottery what fortune Panurge shall have in his marriage 331

XIII. How Pantagruel adviseth Panurge to try the future good or bad luck of his marriage by dreams 335

LIST OF PLATES IN VOL. I.

PORTRAIT OF RABELAIS . . . . *Frontispiece*

To face page

BOOK I., CHAPTER VII. If he did weep, if he did cry, and what grievous quarter soever he kept, in bringing him some drink he would be instantly pacified 30

BOOK I., CHAPTER XVII. And they pressed so hard upon him that he was constrained to rest himself upon the towers of Our Lady's Church . . 53

BOOK I., CHAPTER LI. At the taking up of the table he distributed amongst them his whole cupboard of plate 135

BOOK I., CHAPTER LV. Before the said lodging of the ladies . . . were placed . . . the theatre or public playhouse, and natatory or place to swim in 143

BOOK I., CHAPTER LVII. In all their rule and strictest tie of their order was but this one clause to be observed, Do WHAT THOU WILT 147

BOOK II., CHAPTER XXIII. She could find no remedy but to retire unto her house, which was a palace. Thither she went, and the dogs after her 242

BOOK II., CHAPTER XXXII. At last I came into his mouth . . . I walked there . . . and saw there great rocks 273

BOOK III., CHAPTER XI. He had no sooner spoke these words than the works of Virgil were brought in 330

Introduction.

AD Rabelais never written his strange and marvellous romance, no one would ever have imagined the possibility of its production. It stands outside other things—a mixture of mad mirth and gravity, of folly and reason, of childishness and grandeur, of the commonplace and the out-of-the-way, of popular verve and polished humanism, of mother-wit and learning, of baseness and nobility, of personalities and broad generalization, of the comic and the serious, of the impossible and the familiar. Throughout the whole there is such a force of life and thought, such a power of good sense, a kind of assurance so authoritative, that he takes rank with the greatest; and his peers are not many. You may like him or not, may attack him or sing his praises, but you cannot ignore him. He is of those that die hard. Be as fastidious as you will; make up your mind to recognize only those who are, without any manner of doubt, beyond and above all others; however few the names you keep, Rabelais' will always remain.

We may know his work, may know it well, and admire it more every time we read it. After being amused by it, after having enjoyed it, we may return again to study it and to enter more fully into its meaning. Yet there is no possibility of knowing his own life in the same fashion. In spite of all the efforts, often successful, that have been made to throw light on it, to bring forward a fresh document, or some obscure mention in a forgotten book, to add some little fact, to fix a date more precisely, it remains nevertheless full of uncertainty and of gaps. Besides, it has been burdened and sullied by all kinds of wearisome stories and foolish anecdotes, so that really there is more to weed out than to add.

INTRODUCTION.

This injustice, at first wilful, had its rise in the sixteenth century, in the furious attacks of a monk of Fontevrault, Gabriel de Puy-Herbault, who seems to have drawn his conclusions concerning the author from the book, and, more especially, in the regrettable satirical epitaph of Ronsard, piqued, it is said, that the Guises had given him only a little *pavillon* in the Forest of Meudon, whereas the presbytery was close to the chateau. From that time legend has fastened on Rabelais, has completely travestied him, till, bit by bit, it has made of him a buffoon, a veritable clown, a vagrant, a glutton, and a drunkard.

PORTRAIT FROM THE CHRONOLOGIE COLLÉE.

The likeness of his person has undergone a similar metamorphosis. He has been credited with a full moon of a face, the rubicund nose of an incorrigible toper, and thick coarse lips always apart because always laughing. The picture would have surprised his friends no less than himself. There have been portraits painted of Rabelais; I have seen many such. They are all of the seventeenth century, and the greater number are conceived in this jovial and popular style.

As a matter of fact there is only one portrait of him that counts, that has more than the merest chance of being authentic, the one in the *Chronologie collée* or *coupée*. Under this double name is known and cited a large sheet divided by lines and cross lines into little squares, containing about a hundred heads of illustrious Frenchmen. This sheet was stuck on pasteboard for hanging on the wall, and was cut in little pieces, so that the portraits might be sold separately. The majority of the portraits are of known persons and can therefore be verified. Now it can be seen that these have been selected with care, and taken from the most authentic sources; from statues, busts, medals, even stained glass, for the persons of most distinction, from earlier engravings for the others. Moreover, those of which no other copies exist, and which are therefore the most valuable, have each an individuality very distinct, in the features, the hair, the beard, as well as in the costume. Not one of them is like another. There has been no tampering with them, no forgery. On the contrary, there is in each a difference, a very marked personality. Leonard Gaultier, who published this engraving towards the end of the sixteenth century, reproduced a great many portraits besides from chalk drawings, in the style of his master, Thomas de Leu. It must have been such drawings that were the originals of those portraits which he alone has issued, and which may therefore be as authentic and reliable as the others whose correctness we are in a position to verify.

Now Rabelais has here nothing of the Roger Bontemps of low degree about him. His features are strong, vigorously cut, and furrowed with deep wrinkles; his beard is short and scanty; his cheeks are thin and already worn-looking. On his head he wears the square cap of the doctors and the clerks, and his dominant expression, somewhat rigid and severe, is that of a physician and a scholar. And this is the only portrait to which we need attach any importance.

This is not the place for a detailed biography, nor for an exhaustive study. At most this introduction will serve as a framework on which to fix a few certain dates, to hang some general observations. The date of Rabelais' birth is very doubtful. For long it was placed as far back as 1483: now scholars are disposed to put it forward to about 1495. The reason, a good one, is that all those whom he has mentioned as his friends, or in any real sense his contemporaries, were born at the very end of the fifteenth century. And, indeed, it is in the references in his romance to names, persons, and places, that the most certain and valuable evidence is to be found of his intercourse, his patrons, his friendships, his sojournings, and his travels: his own work is the best and richest mine in which to search for the details of his life.

Like Descartes and Balzac, he was a native of Touraine, and Tours and Chinon have only done their duty in each of them erecting in recent years a statue to his honour, a twofold homage reflecting credit both on the province and on the town. But the precise facts about his birth are nevertheless vague. Huet speaks of the village of Benais, near Bourgueil, of whose vineyards Rabelais makes mention. As the little vineyard of La Devinière, near Chinon, and familiar to all his readers, is supposed to have belonged to his father, Thomas Rabelais, some would have him born there. It is better to hold to the earlier general opinion that Chinon was his native town; Chinon, whose praises he sang with such heartiness and affection. There he might well have been born in the Lamproie house, which belonged to his father, who, to judge from this circumstance, must have been in easy circumstances, with the position of a well-to-do citizen. As La Lamproie in the seventeenth century was a hostelry, the father of Rabelais has been set down as an innkeeper. More probably he was an apothecary, which would fit in with the medical profession adopted by his son in after years. Rabelais had brothers, all older than himself. Perhaps because he was the youngest, his father destined him for the Church.

The time he spent while a child with the Benedictine monks at Seuillé is uncertain. There he might have made the acquaintance of the prototype of his Friar John, a brother of the name of Buinart, afterwards Prior of Sermaize. He was longer at the Abbey of the Cordeliers at La Baumette, half a mile from Angers, where he became a novice. As the brothers Du Bellay, who were later his Mæcenases, were then studying at the University of Angers, where it is certain he was not a student, it is doubtless from this youthful period that his acquaintance and alliance with them should date. Voluntarily, or induced by his family, Rabelais now embraced the ecclesiastical profession, and entered the monastery of the Franciscan Cordeliers at Fontenay-le-Comte, in Lower Poitou, which was honoured by his long sojourn at the vital period of his life when his powers were ripening. There it was he began to study and to think, and there also began his troubles.

In spite of the wide-spread ignorance among the monks of that age, the encyclopædic movement of the Renaissance was attracting all the lofty minds. Rabelais threw himself into it with enthusiasm, and Latin antiquity was not enough for him. Greek, a study discountenanced by the Church, which looked on it as dangerous and tending to freethought and heresy, took possession of him. To it he owed the warm friendship of Pierre Amy and of the celebrated Guillaume Budé. In fact, the Greek letters of the latter are the best source of information concerning this period of Rabelais' life. It was at Fontenay-le-Comte also that he became acquainted with the Brissons and the great jurist André Tiraqueau, whom he never mentions but with admiration and deep affection. Tiraqueau's treatise, *De legibus connubialibus*, published for the first time in 1513, has an important bearing on the life of Rabelais. There we learn that, dissatisfied with the incomplete translation of Herodotus by Laurent Valla, Rabelais had retranslated into Latin the first book of the History. That translation unfortunately is lost, as so many other of his scattered works. It is probably in this direction that the hazard of fortune has most discoveries and surprises in store for the lucky searcher. Moreover, as in this law treatise Tiraqueau attacked women in a merciless fashion, President Amaury Bouchard published in 1522 a book in their defence, and Rabelais, who was a friend of both the antagonists, took the side of Tiraqueau. It should be observed also in passing, that there are several pages of such audacious plain-speaking, that Rabelais, though he did not copy these in his Marriage of Panurge, has there been, in his own fashion, as outspoken as Tiraqueau. If such freedom of language could be permitted in a grave treatise of law, similar liberties were certainly, in the same century, more natural in a book which was meant to amuse.

The great reproach always brought against Rabelais is not the want of reserve of his language merely, but his occasional studied coarseness, which is enough to spoil his whole work, and which lowers its value. La Bruyère, in the chapter *Des ouvrages de l'esprit*, not in the first edition of the *Caractères*, but in the fifth, that is to say in 1690, at the end of the great century, gives us on this subject his own opinion and that of his age

"Marot and Rabelais are inexcusable in their habit of scattering filth about their writings. Both of them had genius enough and wit enough to do without any such expedient, even for the amusement of those persons who look more to the laugh to be got out of a book than to what is admirable in it. Rabelais especially is incomprehensible. His book is an enigma,—one may say inexplicable. It is a Chimera; it is like the face of a lovely woman with the feet and the tail of a reptile, or of some creature still more loathsome. It is a monstrous confusion of fine and rare morality with filthy corruption. Where it is bad, it goes beyond the worst; it is the delight of the basest of men Where it is good, it reaches the exquisite, the very best; it ministers to the most delicate tastes."

Putting aside the rather slight connection established between two men of whom one is of very little importance compared with the other, this is otherwise very admirably said, and the judgment is a very just one, except with regard to one point—the misunderstanding of the atmosphere in which the book was created, and the ignoring of the examples of a similar tendency furnished by literature as well as by the popular taste. Was it not the Ancients that began it? Aristophanes, Catullus, Petronius, Martial, flew in the face of decency in their ideas as well as in the words they used, and they dragged after them in this direction not a few of the Latin poets of the Renaissance, who believed themselves bound to imitate them. Is Italy without fault in this respect? Her story-tellers in prose lie open to easy accusation. Her *Capitoli* in verse go to incredible lengths; and the astonishing success of Aretino must not be forgotten, nor the licence of the whole Italian comic theatre of the sixteenth century. The *Calandra* of Bibbiena, who was afterwards a Cardinal, and the *Mandragola* of Machiavelli, are evidence enough, and these were played before Popes, who were not a whit embarrassed. Even in England the drama went very far for a time, and the comic authors of the reign of Charles II., evidently from a reaction, and to shake off the excess and the wearisomeness of Puritan prudery and affectation, which sent them to the opposite extreme, are not exactly noted for their reserve. But we need not go beyond France. Slight indications, very easily verified, are all that may be set down here; a formal and detailed proof would be altogether too dangerous.

Thus, for instance, the old Fabliaux—the Farces of the fifteenth century, the story-tellers of the sixteenth—reveal one of the sides, one of the veins, so to speak, of our literature. The art that addresses itself to the eye had likewise its share of this coarseness. Think of the sculptures on the capitals and the modillions of churches, and the crude frankness of certain painted windows of the fifteenth century. Queen Anne was, without any doubt, one of the most virtuous women in the world. Yet she used to go up the staircase of her chateau at Blois, and her eyes were not offended at seeing at the foot of a bracket a not very decent carving of a monk and a nun. Neither did she tear out of her book of Hours the large miniature of the winter month, in which, careless of her neighbours' eyes, the mistress of the house, sitting before her great fireplace, warms herself in a fashion which it is not advisable that dames of our age should imitate. The statue of Cybele by the Tribolo, executed for Francis I., and placed, not against a wall, but in the middle of Queen Claude's chamber at Fontainebleau, has behind it an attribute which would have been more in place on a statue of Priapus, and which was the symbol of generativeness. The tone of the conversations was ordinarily of a surprising coarseness, and the Précieuses, in spite of their absurdities, did a very good work in setting themselves in opposition to it. The worthy Chevalier de La-Tour-Landry, in his Instructions to his own daughters, without a thought of harm, gives examples which are singular indeed, and in Caxton's translation these are not omitted. The *Adevineaux Amoureux*, printed at Bruges by Colard Mansion, are astonishing indeed when one considers that they were the little society diversions of the Duchesses of Burgundy and of the great ladies of a court more luxurious and more refined than the French court, which revelled in the *Cent Nouvelles* of good King Louis XI. Rabelais' pleasantry about the woman *folle à la messe* is exactly in the style of the *Adevineaux*.

A later work than any of his, the *Novelle* of Bandello, should be kept in mind—for the writer was Bishop of Agen, and his work was translated into French—as also the *Dames Galantes* of Brantôme. Read the *Journal* of Heroard, that honest doctor, who day by day wrote down the details concerning the health of Louis XIII. from his birth, and you will understand the tone of the conversation of Henry IV. The jokes at a country wedding are trifles compared with this royal coarseness. *Le Moyen de Parvenir* is nothing but a tissue and a mass of filth, and the too celebrated *Cabinet Satyrique* proves what, under Louis XIII., could be written, printed, and read. The collection of songs formed by Clairambault shows that the seventeenth and eighteenth centuries were no purer than the sixteenth. Some of the most ribald songs are actually the work of Princesses of the royal House.

It is, therefore, altogether unjust to make Rabelais the scapegoat, to charge him alone with the sins of everybody else. He spoke as those of his time used to speak; when amusing them he used their language to make himself understood, and to slip in his *asides*, which without this sauce would never have been accepted, would have found neither eyes nor ears. Let us blame not him, therefore, but the manners of his time.

Besides, his gaiety, however coarse it may appear to us—and how rare a thing is gaiety!—has, after all, nothing unwholesome about it; and this is too often overlooked. Where does he tempt one to stray from duty? Where, even indirectly, does he give pernicious advice? Whom has he led to evil ways? Does he ever inspire feelings that breed misconduct and vice, or is he ever the apologist of these? Many poets and romance writers, under cover of a fastidious style, without one coarse expression, have been really and actively hurtful; and of that it is impossible to accuse Rabelais. Women in particular quickly revolt from him, and turn away repulsed at once by the archaic form of the language and by the outspokenness of the words. But if he be read aloud to them, omitting the rougher parts and modernizing the pronunciation, it will be seen that they too are impressed by his lively wit as by the loftiness of his thought. It would be possible, too, to extract, for young persons, without modification, admirable passages of incomparable force. But those who have brought out expurgated editions of him, or who have thought to improve him by trying to rewrite him in modern French, have been fools for their pains, and their insulting attempts have had, and always will have, the success they deserve.

His dedications prove to what extent his whole work was accepted. Not to speak of his epistolary relations with Budé, with the Cardinal d'Armagnac and with Pellissier, the ambassador of Francis I. and Bishop of Maguelonne, or of his dedication to Tiraqueau of his Lyons edition of the *Epistolæ Medicinales* of Giovanni Manardi of Ferrara, of the one addressed to the President Amaury Bouchard of the two legal texts which he believed antique, there is still the evidence of his other and more important dedications. In 1532 he dedicated his Hippocrates and his Galen to Geoffroy d'Estissac, Bishop of Maillezais, to whom in 1535 and 1536 he addressed from Rome the three news letters, which alone have been preserved; and in 1534 he dedicated from Lyons his edition of the Latin book of Marliani on the topography of Rome to Jean du Bellay (at that time Bishop of Paris) who was raised to the Cardinalate in 1535. Beside these dedications we must set the privilege of Francis I. of September, 1545, and the new privilege granted by Henry II. on August 6th, 1550, Cardinal de Châtillon present, for the third book, which was dedicated, in an eight-lined stanza, to the Spirit of the Queen of Navarre. These privileges, from the praises and eulogies they express in terms very personal and very exceptional, are as important in Rabelais' life as were, in connection with other matters, the Apostolic Pastorals in his favour. Of course, in these the popes had not to introduce his books of diversions, which, nevertheless, would have seemed in their eyes but very venial sins. The *Sciomachie* of 1549, an account of the festivities arranged at Rome by Cardinal du Bellay in honour of the birth of the second son of Henry II., was addressed to Cardinal de Guise, and in 1552 the fourth book was dedicated, in a new prologue, to Cardinal de Châtillon, the brother of Admiral de Coligny.

These are no unknown or insignificant personages, but the greatest lords and princes of the Church. They loved and admired and protected Rabelais, and put no restrictions in his way. Why should we be more fastidious and severe than they were? Their high contemporary appreciation gives much food for thought.

There are few translations of Rabelais in foreign tongues; and certainly the task is no light one, and demands more than a familiarity with ordinary French. It would have been easier in Italy than anywhere else. Italian, from its flexibility and its analogy to French, would have lent itself admirably to the purpose; the instrument was ready, but the hand was not forthcoming. Neither is there any Spanish translation, a fact which can be more easily understood. The Inquisition would have been a far more serious opponent than the Paris' Sorbonne, and no one ventured on the experiment. Yet Rabelais forces comparison with Cervantes, whose precursor he was in reality, though the two books and the two minds are very different. They have only one point in common, their attack and ridicule of the romances of chivalry and of the wildly improbable adventures of knight-errants. But in *Don Quixote* there is not a single detail which would suggest that Cervantes knew Rabelais' book or owed anything to it whatsoever, even the starting-point of his subject. Perhaps it was better he should not have been influenced by him, in however slight a degree; his originality is the more intact and the more genial.

On the other hand, Rabelais has been several times translated into German. In the present century Regis published at Leipsic, from 1831 to 1841, with copious notes, a close and faithful translation. The first one cannot be so described, that of Johann Fischart, a native of Mainz or Strasburg, who died in 1614. He was a Protestant controversialist, and a satirist of fantastic and abundant imagination. In 1575 appeared his translation of Rabelais' first book, and in 1590 he published the comic catalogue of the library of Saint Victor, borrowed from the second book. It is not a translation, but a recast in the boldest style, full of alterations and of exaggerations, both as regards the coarse expressions which he took upon himself to develop and to add to, and in the attacks on the Roman Catholic Church. According to Jean Paul Richter, Fischart is much superior to Rabelais in style and in the fruitfulness of his ideas, and his equal in erudition and in the invention of new expressions after the manner of Aristophanes. He is sure that his work was successful, because it was often reprinted during his lifetime; but this enthusiasm of Jean Paul would hardly carry conviction in France. Who treads in another's footprints must follow in the rear. Instead of a creator, he is but an imitator. Those who take the ideas of others to modify them, and make of them creations of their own, like Shakespeare in England, Molière and La Fontaine in France, may be superior to those who have served them with suggestions; but then the new works must be altogether different, must exist by themselves. Shakespeare and the others, when they imitated, may be said always to have destroyed their models. Those copyists, if we call them so, created such works of genius that the only pity is they are so rare. This is not the case with Fischart, but it would be none the less curious were some one thoroughly familiar with German to translate Fischart for us, or at least, by long extracts from him, give an idea of the vagaries of German taste when it thought it could do better than Rabelais. It is dangerous to tamper with so great a work, and he who does so runs a great risk of burning his fingers.

England has been less daring, and her modesty and discretion have brought her success. But, before speaking of Urquhart's translation, it is but right to mention the English-French Dictionary of Randle Cotgrave, the first edition of which dates from 1611. It is in every way exceedingly valuable, and superior to that of Nicot, because instead of keeping to the plane of classic and Latin French, it showed an acquaintance with and mastery of the popular tongue as well as of the written and learned language. As a foreigner, Cotgrave is a little behind in his information. He is not aware of all the changes and novelties of the passing fashion. The *Pleiad* School he evidently knew nothing of, but kept to the writers of the fifteenth and the first half of the sixteenth century. Thus words out of Rabelais, which he always translates with admirable skill, are frequent, and he attaches to them their author's name. So Rabelais had already crossed the Channel, and was read in his own tongue. Somewhat later, during the full sway of the Commonwealth—and Maître Alcofribas Nasier must have been a surprising apparition in the midst of Puritan severity—Captain Urquhart undertook to translate him and to naturalize him completely in England.

Thomas Urquhart belonged to a very old family of good standing in the North of Scotland. After studying in Aberdeen he travelled in France, Spain, and Italy, where his sword was as active as that intelligent curiosity of his which is evidenced by his familiarity with three languages and the large library which he brought back, according to his own account, from sixteen countries he had visited.

On his return to England he entered the service of Charles I., who knighted him in 1641. Next year, after the death of his father, he went to Scotland to set his family affairs in order, and to redeem his house in Cromarty. But, in spite of another sojourn in foreign lands, his efforts to free himself from pecuniary embarrassments were unavailing. At the king's death his Scottish loyalty caused him to side with those who opposed the Parliament. Formally proscribed in 1649, taken prisoner at the defeat of Worcester in 1651, stripped of all his belongings, he was brought to London, but was released on parole at Cromwell's recommendation. After receiving permission to spend five months in Scotland to try once more to settle his affairs, he came back to London to escape from his creditors. And there he must have died, though the date of his death is unknown. It probably took place after 1653, the date of the publication of the two first books, and after having written the translation of the third, which was not printed from his manuscript till the end of the seventeenth century.

His life was therefore not without its troubles, and literary activity must have been almost his only consolation. His writings reveal him as the strangest character, fantastic, and full of a naïve vanity, which, even at the time he was translating the genealogy of Gargantua—surely well calculated to cure any pondering on his own—caused him to trace his unbroken descent from Adam, and to state that his family name was derived from his ancestor Esormon, Prince of Achaia, 2139 B.C., who was surnamed Ουροχαρτος, that is to say the Fortunate and the Well-beloved. A Gascon could not have surpassed this.

Gifted as he was, learned in many directions, an enthusiastic mathematician, master of several languages, occasionally full of wit and humour, and even good sense, yet he gave his books the strangest titles, and his ideas were no less whimsical. His style is mystic, fastidious, and too often of a wearisome length and obscurity; his verses rhyme anyhow, or not at all; but vivacity, force and heat are never lacking, and the Maitland Club did well in reprinting, in 1834, his various works, which are very rare. Yet, in spite of their curious interest, he owes his real distinction and the survival of his name to his translation of Rabelais.

The first two books appeared in 1653. The original edition, exceedingly scarce, was carefully reprinted in 1838, only a hundred copies being issued, by an English bibliophile, T[heodore] M[artin], whose interesting preface I regret to sum up so cursorily. At the end of the seventeenth century, in 1693, a French refugee, Peter Antony Motteux, whose English verses and whose plays are not without value, published in a little octavo volume a reprint, very incorrect as to the text, of the first two books, to which he added the third, from the manuscript found amongst Urquhart's papers. The success which attended this venture suggested to Motteux the idea of completing the work, and a second edition, in two volumes, appeared in 1708, with the translation of the fourth and fifth books, and notes. Nineteen years after his death, John Ozell, translator on a large scale of French, Italian, and Spanish authors, revised Motteux's edition, which he published in five volumes in 1737, adding Le Duchat's notes; and this version has often been reprinted since.

The continuation by Motteux, who was also the translator of *Don Quixote*, has merits of its own. It is precise, elegant, and very faithful. Urquhart's, without taking liberties with Rabelais like Fischart, is not always so closely literal and exact. Nevertheless, it is much superior to Motteux's. If Urquhart does not constantly adhere to the form of the expression, if he makes a few slight additions, not only has he an understanding of the original, but he feels it, and renders the sense with a force and a vivacity full of warmth and brilliancy. His own learning made the comprehension of the work easy to him, and his anglicization of words fabricated by Rabelais is particularly successful. The necessity of keeping to his text prevented his indulgence in the convolutions and divagations dictated by his exuberant fancy when writing on his own account. His style, always full of life and vigour, is here balanced, lucid, and picturesque. Never elsewhere did he write so well. And thus the translation reproduces the very accent of the original, besides possessing a very remarkable character of its own. Such a literary tone and such literary qualities are rarely found in a translation. Urquhart's, very useful for the interpretation of obscure passages, may, and indeed should be read as a whole, both for Rabelais and for its own merits.

Holland, too, possesses a translation of Rabelais. They knew French in that country in the seventeenth century better than they do to-day, and there Rabelais' works were reprinted when no editions were appearing in France. This Dutch translation was published at Amsterdam in 1682, by J. Tenhoorn. The name attached to it, *Claudio Gallitalo* (Claudius French-Italian) must certainly be a pseudonym. Only a Dutch scholar could identify the translator, and state the value to be assigned to his work.

Rabelais' style has many different sources. Besides its force and brilliancy, its gaiety, wit, and dignity, its abundant richness is no less remarkable. It would be impossible and useless to compile a glossary of Voltaire's words. No French writer has used so few, and all of them are of the simplest. There is not one of them that is not part of the common speech, or which demands a note or an explanation. Rabelais' vocabulary, on the other hand, is of an astonishing variety. Where does it all come from? As a fact, he had at his command something like three languages, which he used in turn, or which he mixed according to the effect he wished to produce.

First of all, of course, he had ready to his hand the whole speech of his time, which had no secrets for him. Provincials have been too eager to appropriate him, to make of him a local author, the pride of some village, in order that their district might have the merit of being one of the causes, one of the factors of his genius. Every neighbourhood where he ever lived has declared that his distinction was due to his knowledge of its popular speech. But these dialect-patriots have fallen out among themselves. To which dialect was he indebted? Was it that of Touraine, or Berri, or Poitou, or Paris? It is too often forgotten, in regard to French patois—leaving out of count the languages of the South—that the words or expressions that are no longer in use to-day are but a survival, a still living trace of the tongue and the pronunciation of other days. Rabelais, more than any other writer, took advantage of the happy chances and the richness of the popular speech, but he wrote in French, and nothing but French. That is why he remains so forcible, so lucid, and so living, more living even—speaking only of his style out of charity to the others—than any of his contemporaries.

It has been said that great French prose is solely the work of the seventeenth century. There were nevertheless, before that, two men, certainly very different and even hostile, who were its initiators and its masters, Calvin on the one hand, on the other Rabelais.

Rabelais had a wonderful knowledge of the prose and the verse of the fifteenth century: he was familiar with Villon, *Pathelin*, the *Quinze Joies de Mariage*, the *Cent Nouvelles*, the chronicles and the romances, and even earlier works, too, such as the *Roman de la Rose*. Their words, their turns of expression came naturally to his pen, and added a piquancy and, as it were, a kind of gloss of antique novelty to his work. He fabricated words, too, on Greek and Latin models, with great ease, sometimes audaciously and with needless frequency. These were for him so many means, so many elements of variety. Sometimes he did this in mockery, as in the humorous discourse of the Limousin scholar, for which he is not a little indebted to Geoffroy Tory in the *Champfleury*; sometimes, on the contrary, seriously, from a habit acquired in dealing with classical tongues.

Again, another reason of the richness of his vocabulary was that he invented and forged words for himself. Following the example of Aristophanes, he coined an enormous number of interminable words, droll expressions, sudden and surprising constructions. What had made Greece and the Athenians laugh was worth transporting to Paris.

With an instrument so rich, resources so endless, and the skill to use them, it is no wonder that he could give voice to anything, be as humorous as he could be serious, as comic as he could be grave, that he could express himself and everybody else, from the lowest to the highest. He had every colour on his palette, and such skill was in his fingers that he could depict every variety of light and shade.

We have evidence that Rabelais did not always write in the same fashion. The *Chronique Gargantuaine* is uniform in style and quite simple, but cannot with certainty be attributed to him. His

TITLE-PAGE OF THE 1532 (?) EDITION OF "PANTAGRUEL."

sa pōme. Et ce faict Pātagruel se pforce de rēdre sa gorge/ ¢ facillemēt les mist dehors/¢ ne mōstroiēt en sa guorge en plus quūg pet en sa bostre/¢ la sortirēt hors d se˜s pillules ioyeusemēt. Il me souuenoit quand les Gregeoys sortirēt du cheual en Troye. Et p ce moyen fut guery ¢ reduyt a sa pmiere cōualescēce. Et de ces pillules daratn en auez vne en Orleās sus le clochier de seglise de saincte Croyx.

OR messieurs vous auez ouy vng cōmencemēt de lhistoire horrificque de mō maistre ¢ seigñr Pātagruel. Icy ie feray fin a ce pmier liure: car la teste me faict vng peu de mal/¢ sens biē q̄ les registres de mon ceruau sōt ālque peu brouillez de ceste puree de Septēbre.

Vous aurez le reste de lhistoire a ces foires de Frācfort prochainemēt venātes:¢ la vo9 verrez cōment il trouua la pierre philosophalle/cōmēt il passa les mōts Caspies/cō¬ mēt il nauiga p la mer Athlātich ¢ deffit les Caniballes ¢ cōq̄sta les isles de Perlas. Cōmēt il espousa la fille du roy de Inde dit Prestre Iehā. Cōment il cōbatit cōtre les diables/¢ feist bruller cinq chābres dēfer/et rōpit. iiii. dētz a Lucifer ¢ vne corne au cul. Cōmēt il visita les regiōs de la lune/pour scauoir si a la verite la lune nestoit pas entie¬ re:mais q̄ les femmes en auoiēt. iii. cartiers en la teste. Et mille aultres petites ioyeusettez toutes veritables: ce sōt beaulx textes deuāgilles en frācoys. Bō soir messieurs/ pardōnate my/¢ ne pēsez pas tāt a mes faultes q̄ vous ne pēsez biē es vostres.

¶Finis.

LAST PAGE OF THE 1532 (?) EDITION OF "PANTAGRUEL."

letters are bombastic and thin; his few attempts at verse are heavy, lumbering, and obscure, altogether lacking in harmony, and quite as bad as those of his friend, Jean Bouchet. He had no gift of poetic form, as indeed is evident even from his prose. And his letters from Rome to the Bishop of Maillezais, interesting as they are in regard to the matter, are as dull, bare, flat, and dry in style as possible. Without his signature no one would possibly have thought of attributing them to him. He is only a literary artist when he wishes to be such; and in his romance he changes the style completely every other moment: it has no constant character or uniform manner, and therefore unity is almost entirely wanting in his work, while his endeavours after contrast are unceasing. There is throughout the whole the evidence of careful and conscious elaboration.

Hence, however lucid and free be the style of his romance, and though its flexibility and ease seem at first sight to have cost no trouble at all, yet its merit lies precisely in the fact that it succeeds in concealing the toil, in hiding the seams. He could not have reached this perfection at a first attempt. He must have worked long at the task, revised it again and again, corrected much, and added rather than cut away. The aptness of form and expression has been arrived at by deliberate means, and owes nothing to chance. Apart from the toning down of certain bold passages, to soften their effect, and appease the storm—for these were not literary alterations, but were imposed on him by prudence—one can see how numerous are the variations in his text, how necessary it is to take account of them, and to collect them. A good edition, of course, would make no attempt at amalgamating these. That would give a false impression and end in confusion; but it should note them all, and show them all, not combined, but simply as variations.

After Le Duchat, all the editions, in their care that nothing should be lost, made the mistake of collecting and placing side by side things which had no connection with each other, which had even been substituted for each other. The result was a fabricated text, full of contradictions naturally. But since the edition issued by M. Jannet, the well-known publisher of the Bibliothèque Elzevirienne, who was the first to get rid of this patchwork, this mosaic, Rabelais' latest text has been given, accompanied by all the earlier variations, to show the changes he made, as well as his suppressions and additions. It would also be possible to reverse the method. It would be interesting to take his first text as the basis, noting the later modifications. This would be quite as instructive and really worth doing. Perhaps one might then see more clearly with what care he made his revisions, after what fashion he corrected, and especially what were the additions he made.

No more striking instance can be quoted than the admirable chapter about the shipwreck. It was not always so long as Rabelais made it in the end: it was much shorter at first. As a rule, when an author recasts some passage that he wishes to revise, he does so by rewriting the whole, or at least by interpolating passages at one stroke, so to speak. Nothing of the kind is seen here. Rabelais suppressed nothing, modified nothing; he did not change his plan at all. What he did was to make insertions, to slip in between two clauses a new one. He expressed his meaning in a lengthier way, and the former clause is found in its integrity along with the additional one, of which it forms, as it were, the warp. It was by this method of touching up the smallest details, by making here and there such little noticeable additions, that he succeeded in heightening the effect without either change or loss. In the end it looks as if he had altered nothing, added nothing new, as if it had always been so from the first, and had never been meddled with.

The comparison is most instructive, showing us to what an extent Rabelais' admirable style was due to conscious effort, care, and elaboration, a fact which is generally too much overlooked, and how instead of leaving any trace which would reveal toil and study, it has on the contrary a marvellous cohesion, precision, and brilliancy. It was modelled and remodelled, repaired, touched up, and yet it has all the appearance of having been created at a single stroke, or of having been run like molten wax into its final form.

Something should be said here of the sources from which Rabelais borrowed. He was not the first in France to satirize the romances of chivalry. The romance in verse by Baudouin de Sebourc, printed in recent years, was a parody of the *Chansons de Geste*. In the *Moniage Guillaume*, and especially in the *Moniage Rainouart*, in which there is a kind of giant, and occasionally a comic giant, there are situations and scenes which remind us of Rabelais. The kind of Fabliaux in mono-rhyme quatrains of the old Aubery anticipate his coarse and popular jests. But all that is beside the question; Rabelais did not know these. Nothing is of direct interest save what was known to him, what fell under his eyes, what lay to his hand—as the *Facetiæ* of Poggio, and the last *sermonnaires*. In the course of one's reading one may often enough come across the origin of some of Rabelais' witticisms; here and there we may discover how he has developed a situation. While gathering his materials wherever he could find them, he was nevertheless profoundly original.

On this point much research and investigation might be employed. But there is no need why these researches should be extended to the region of fancy. Gargantua has been proved by some to be of Celtic origin. Very often he is a solar myth, and the statement that Rabelais only collected popular traditions and gave new life to ancient legends is said to be proved by the large number of megalithic monuments to which is attached the name of Gargantua. It was, of course, quite right to make a list of these, to draw up, as it were, a chart of them, but the conclusion is not justified. The name, instead of being earlier, is really later, and is a witness, not to the origin, but to the success and rapid popularity of his novel. No one has ever yet produced a written passage or any ancient testimony to prove the existence of the name before Rabelais. To place such a tradition on a sure basis, positive traces must be forthcoming; and they cannot be adduced even for the most celebrated of these monuments, since he mentions himself the great menhir near Poitiers, which he christened by the name of Passe-lourdin. That there is something in the theory is possible. Perrault found the subjects of his stories in the tales told by mothers and nurses. He fixed them finally by writing them down. Floating about vaguely as they were, he seized them, worked them up, gave them shape, and yet of scarcely any of them is there to be found before his time a single trace. So we must resign ourselves to know just as little of what Gargantua and Pantagruel were before the sixteenth century.

In a book of a contemporary of Rabelais, the *Légende de Pierre Faifeu* by the Angevin, Charles de Bourdigné, the first edition of which dates from 1526 and the second 1531—both so rare and so forgotten that the work is only known since the eighteenth century by the reprint of Custelier—in the introductory ballad which recommends this book to readers, occur these lines in the list of popular books which Faifeu would desire to replace:

> " Laissez ester Caillette le folastre,
> Les quatre filz Aymon vestuz de bleu,
> Gargantua qui a cheveux de plastre."

He has not "cheveux de plastre" in Rabelais. If the rhyme had not suggested the phrase—and the exigencies of the strict form of the ballade and its forced repetitions often imposed an idea which had its whole origin in the rhyme—we might here see a dramatic trace found nowhere else. The name of Pantagruel is mentioned too, incidentally, in a Mystery of the fifteenth century. These are the only references to the names which up till now have been discovered, and they are, as one sees, of but little account.

On the other hand, the influence of Aristophanes and of Lucian, his intimate acquaintance with nearly all the writers of antiquity, Greek as well as Latin, with whom Rabelais is more permeated even than Montaigne, were a mine of inspiration. The proof of it is everywhere. Pliny especially was his encyclopædia, his constant companion. All he says of the Pantagruelian herb, though he amply developed it for himself, is taken from Pliny's chapter on flax. And there is a great deal more of this kind to be discovered, for Rabelais does not always give it as quotation. On the other hand, when he writes, "Such an one says," it would be difficult enough to find who is meant, for the "such an one" is a fictitious writer. The method is amusing, but it is curious to account for it.

The question of the *Chronique Gargantuaine* is still undecided. Is it by Rabelais or by someone else? Both theories are defensible, and can be supported by good reasons. In the *Chronique* everything is heavy, occasionally meaningless, and nearly always insipid. Can the same man have written the *Chronique* and *Gargantua*, replaced a book really commonplace by a masterpiece, changed the facts and incidents, transformed a heavy icy pleasantry into a work glowing with wit and life, made it no longer a mass of laborious trifling and cold-blooded exaggerations but a satire on human life of the highest genius. Still there are points common to the two. Besides, Rabelais wrote other things; and it is only in his romance that he shows literary skill. The conception of it would have entered his mind first only in a bare and summary fashion. It would have been taken up again, expanded, developed, metamorphosed. That is possible, and, for my part, I am of those who, like Brunet and Nodier, are inclined to think that the *Chronique*, in spite of its inferiority, is really a first attempt, condemned as soon as the idea was conceived in another form. As its earlier date is incontestable, we must conclude that if the *Chronique* is not by him, his *Gargantua* and its continuation would not have existed without it. This would be a great obligation to stand under to some unknown author, and in that case it is astonishing that his enemies did not reproach him during his lifetime with being merely an imitator and a plagiarist. So there are reasons for and against his authorship of it, and it would be dangerous to make too bold an assertion.

One fact which is absolutely certain and beyond all controversy, is that Rabelais owed much to one of his contemporaries, an Italian, to the *Histoire Macaronique* of Merlin Coccaie. Its author, Theophilus Folengo, who was also a monk, was born in 1491, and died only a short time before Rabelais, in 1544. But his burlesque poem was published in 1517. It was in Latin verse, written in an elaborately fabricated style. It is not dog Latin, but Latin ingeniously italianized, or rather Italian, even Mantuan, latinized. The contrast between the modern form of the word and its Roman garb produces the most amusing effect. In the original it is sometimes difficult to read, for Folengo has no objection to using the most colloquial words and phrases.

The subject is quite different. It is the adventures of Baldo, son of Guy de Montauban, the very lively history of his youth, his trial, imprisonment and deliverance, his journey in search of his father, during which he visits the Planets and Hell. The narration is constantly interrupted by incidental adventures. Occasionally they are what would be called to-day very naturalistic, and sometimes they are madly extravagant.

But Fracasso, Baldo's friend, is a giant; another friend, Cingar, who delivers him, is Panurge exactly, and quite as much given to practical joking. The women in the senile amour of the old Tognazzo, the judges, and the poor sergeants, are no more gently dealt with by Folengo than by the monk of the Iles d'Hyères. If Dindenaut's name does not occur, there are the sheep. The tempest is there, and the invocation to all the saints. Rabelais improves all he borrows, but it is from Folengo he starts. He does not reproduce the words, but, like the Italian, he revels in drinking scenes, junkettings, gormandizing, battles, scuffles, wounds and corpses, magic, witches, speeches, repeated enumerations, lengthiness, and a solemnly minute precision of impossible dates and numbers. The atmosphere, the tone, the methods are the same, and to know Rabelais well, you must know Folengo well too.

Detailed proof of this would be too lengthy a matter; one would have to quote too many passages, but on this question of sources nothing is more interesting than a perusal of the *Opus Macaronicorum*. It was translated into French only in 1606—Paris, Gilley Robinot. This translation of course cannot reproduce all the many amusing forms of words, but it is useful, nevertheless, in showing more clearly the points of resemblance between the two works,—how far in form, ideas, details, and phrases Rabelais was permeated by Folengo. The anonymous translator saw this quite well, and said so in his title, " Histoire macaronique de Merlin Coccaie, prototype of Rabelais." It is nothing but the truth, and Rabelais, who does not hide it from himself, on more than one occasion mentions the name of Merlin Coccaie.

Besides, Rabelais was fed on the Italians of his time as on the Greeks and Romans. Panurge, who owes much to Cingar, is also not free from obligations to the miscreant Margutte in the *Morgante Maggiore* of Pulci. Had Rabelais in his mind the tale from the Florentine Chronicles, how in the Savonarola riots, when the Piagnoni and the Arrabiati came to blows in the church of the Dominican convent of San-Marco, Fra Pietro in the scuffle broke the heads of the assailants with the bronze crucifix he had taken from the altar? A well-handled cross could so readily be used as a weapon, that probably it has served as such more than once, and other and even quite modern instances might be quoted.

But other Italian sources are absolutely certain. There are few more wonderful chapters in Rabelais than the one about the drinkers. It is not a dialogue: those short exclamations exploding from every side, all referring to the same thing, never repeating themselves, and yet always varying the same theme. At the end of the *Novelle* of Gentile Sermini of Siena, there is a chapter called *Il Giuoco della pugna*, the Game of Battle. Here are the first lines of it: " Apre, apre, apre. Chi gioca, chi gioca—uh, uh!—A Porrione, a Porrione.—Vielà, vielà; date a ognuno.—Alle mantella, alle mantella.—Oltre di corsa; non vi fermate.—Voltate qui; ecco costoro; fate veli innanzi.—Vielà, vielà; date costi.—Chi la fà? Io—Ed io.—Dagli; ah, ah, buona fu.— Or cosi; alla mascella, al fianco.—Dagli basso; di punta, di punta.— Ah, ah, buon gioco, buon gioco."

Grāds Annales ou croniques Tresueritables

des Gestes merueilleux du grand Gargantua & Pantagruel son filz. Roý des Diplodes: enchronicquez par feu Maistre Alcofribas: abstracteur de quinte essence.

1 5 4 2

A.i.

And thus it goes on with fire and animation for pages. Rabelais probably translated or directly imitated it. He changed the scene; there was no *giuocco della pugna* in France. He transferred to a drinking-bout this clatter of exclamations which go off by themselves, which cross each other and get no answer. He made a wonderful thing of it. But though he did not copy Sermini, yet Sermini's work provided him with the form of the subject, and was the theme for Rabelais' marvellous variations.

Who does not remember the fantastic quarrel of the cook with the poor devil who had flavoured his dry bread with the smoke of the roast, and the judgment of Seyny John, truly worthy of Solomon? It comes from the *Cento Novelle Antiche*, rewritten from tales older than Boccaccio, and moreover of an extreme brevity and dryness. They are only the framework, the notes, the skeleton of tales. The subject is often wonderful, but nothing is made of it: it is left unshaped. Rabelais wrote a version of one, the ninth. The scene takes place, not at Paris, but at Alexandria in Egypt among the Saracens, and the cook is called Fabrac. But the surprise at the end, the sagacious judgment by which the sound of a piece of money was made the price of the smoke, is the same. Now the first dated edition of the *Cento Novelle* (which were frequently reprinted) appeared at Bologna in 1525, and it is certain that Rabelais had read the tales. And there would be much else of the same kind to learn if we knew Rabelais' library.

A still stranger fact of this sort may be given to show how nothing came amiss to him. He must have known, and even copied the Latin Chronicle of the Counts of Anjou. It is accepted, and rightly so, as an historical document, but that is no reason for thinking that the truth may not have been manipulated and adorned. The Counts of Anjou were not saints. They were proud, quarrelsome, violent, rapacious, and extravagant, as greedy as they were charitable to the Church, treacherous and cruel. Yet their anonymous panegyrist has made them patterns of all the virtues. In reality it is both a history and in some sort a romance; especially is it a collection of examples worthy of being followed, in the style of the *Cyropædia*, our Juvenal of the fifteenth century, and a little like Fénelon's *Télémaque*. Now in it there occurs the address of one of the counts to those who rebelled against him and who were at his mercy. Rabelais must have known it, for he has copied it, or rather, literally translated whole lines of it in the wonderful speech of Gargantua to the vanquished. His contemporaries, who approved of his borrowing from antiquity, could not detect this one, because the book was not printed till much later. But Rabelais lived in Maine. In Anjou, which often figures among the localities he names, he must have met with and read the Chronicles of the Counts in manuscript, probably in some monastery library, whether at Fontenay-le-Comte or elsewhere it matters little. There is not only a likeness in the ideas and tone, but in the words too, which cannot be a mere matter of chance. He must have known the Chronicles of the Counts of Anjou, and they inspired one of his finest pages. One sees, therefore, how varied were the sources whence he drew, and how many of them must probably always escape us.

When, as has been done for Molière, a critical bibliography of the works relating to Rabelais is drawn up—which, by the bye, will entail a very great amount of labour—the easiest part will certainly be the bibliography of the old editions.[1] That is the section that has been most satisfactorily and most completely worked out. M. Brunet said the last word on the subject in his *Researches* in 1852, and in the important article in the fifth edition of his *Manuel du Libraire* (iv., 1863, pp. 1037-1071).

The facts about the fifth book cannot be summed up briefly. It was printed as a whole at first, without the name of the place, in 1564, and next year at Lyons by Jean Martin. It has given, and even still gives rise to two contradictory opinions. Is it Rabelais' or not?

First of all, if he had left it complete, would sixteen years have gone by before it was printed? Then, does it bear evident marks of his workmanship? Is the hand of the master visible throughout? Antoine Du Verdier in the 1605 edition of his *Prosopographie* writes: "[Rabelais'] misfortune has been that everybody has wished to 'pantagruelize!' and several books have appeared under his name, and have been added to his works, which are not by him, as, for instance, *l'Ile Sonnante*, written by a certain scholar of Valence and others."

The scholar of Valence might be Guillaume des Autels, to whom with more certainty can be ascribed the authorship of a dull imitation

---

[1] The bibliography will be treated hereafter in the volume of *Notes* that I am preparing.

of Rabelais, the *History of Fanfreluche and Gaudichon*, published in 1578, which, to say the least of it, is very much inferior to the fifth book.

Louis Guyon, in his *Diverses Leçons*, is still more positive: "As to the last book which has been included in his works, entitled *l'Ile Sonnante*, the object of which seems to be to find fault with and laugh at the members and the authorities of the Catholic Church, I protest that he did not compose it, for it was written long after his death. I was at Paris when it was written, and I know quite well who was its author; he was not a doctor." That is very emphatic, and it is impossible to ignore it.

Yet everyone must recognize that there is a great deal of Rabelais in the fifth book. He must have planned it and begun it. Remembering that in 1548 he had published, not as an experiment, but rather as a bait and as an announcement, the first eleven chapters of the fourth book, we may conclude that the first sixteen chapters of the fifth book published by themselves nine years after his death, in 1562, represent the remainder of his definitely finished work. This is the more certain because these first chapters, which contain the Apologue of the Horse and the Ass and the terrible Furred Lawcats, are markedly better than what follows them. They are not the only ones where the master's hand may be traced, but they are the only ones where no other hand could possibly have interfered.

In the remainder the sentiment is distinctly Protestant. Rabelais was much struck by the vices of the clergy and did not spare them. Whether we are unable to forgive his criticisms because they were conceived in a spirit of raillery, or whether, on the other hand, we feel admiration for him on this point, yet Rabelais was not in the least a sectary. If he strongly desired a moral reform, indirectly pointing out the need of it in his mocking fashion, he was not favourable to a political reform. Those who would make of him a Protestant altogether forget that the Protestants of his time were not for him, but against him. Henri Estienne, for instance, Ramus, Théodore de Bèze, and especially Calvin, should know how he was to be regarded. Rabelais belonged to what may be called the early reformation, to that band of honest men in the beginning of the sixteenth century, precursors of the later one perhaps, but, like Erasmus, between the two extremes. He was neither Lutheran nor Calvinist, neither German nor Genevese, and it is quite natural that his work was not reprinted in Switzerland, which would certainly have happened had the Protestants looked on him as one of themselves.

That Rabelais collected the materials for the fifth book, had begun it, and got on some way, there can be no doubt : the excellence of a large number of passages prove it, but—taken as a whole—the fifth book has not the value, the verve, and the variety of the others. The style is quite different, less rich, briefer, less elaborate, drier, in parts even wearisome. In the first four books Rabelais seldom repeats himself. The fifth book contains from the point of view of the vocabulary really the least novelty. On the contrary, it is full of words and expressions already met with, which is very natural in an imitation, in a copy, forced to keep to a similar tone, and to show by such reminders and likenesses that it is really by the same pen. A very striking point is the profound difference in the use of anatomical terms. In the other books they are most frequently used in a humorous sense, and nonsensically, with a quite other meaning than their own ; in the fifth they are applied correctly. It was necessary to include such terms to keep up the practice, but the writer has not thought of using them to add to the comic effect : one cannot always think of everything. Trouble has been taken, of course, to include enumerations, but there are much fewer fabricated and fantastic words. In short, the hand of the maker is far from showing the same suppleness and strength.

A eulogistic quatrain is signed *Nature quite*, which, it is generally agreed, is an anagram of Jean Turquet. Did the adapter of the fifth book sign his work in this indirect fashion ? He might be of the Genevese family to whom Louis Turquet and his son Theodore belonged, both well-known, and both strong Protestants. The obscurity relating to this matter is far from being cleared up, and perhaps never will be.

It fell to my lot—here, unfortunately, I am forced to speak of a personal matter—to print for the first time the manuscript of the fifth book. At first it was hoped it might be in Rabelais' own hand ; afterwards that it might be at least a copy of his unfinished work. The task was a difficult one, for the writing, extremely flowing and rapid, is execrable, and most difficult to decipher and to transcribe accurately. Besides, it often happens in the sixteenth and the end of the fifteenth century, that manuscripts are much less correct than the printed versions, even when they have not been copied by clumsy and ignorant hands. In this case, it is the writing of a clerk executed as quickly as possible. The farther it goes the more incorrect it becomes, as if the writer were in haste to finish.

What is really the origin of it? It has less the appearance of notes or fragments prepared by Rabelais than of a first attempt at revision. It is not an author's rough draft; still less is it his manuscript. If I had not printed this enigmatical text with scrupulous and painful fidelity, I would do it now. It was necessary to do it so as to clear the way. But as the thing is done, and accessible to those who may be interested, and who wish to critically examine it, there is no further need of reprinting it. All the editions of Rabelais continue, and rightly, to reproduce the edition of 1564. It is not the real Rabelais, but however open to criticism it may be, it was under that form that the fifth book appeared in the sixteenth century, under that form it was accepted. Consequently it is convenient and even necessary to follow and keep to the original edition.

The first sixteen chapters may, and really must be, the text of Rabelais, in the final form as left by him, and found after his death; the framework, and a number of the passages in the continuation, the best ones, of course, are his, but have been patched up and tampered with. Nothing can have been suppressed of what existed; it was evidently thought that everything should be admitted with the final revision; but the tone was changed, additions were made, and "improvements." Adapters are always strangely vain.

In the seventeenth century, the French printing-press, save for an edition issued at Troyes in 1613, gave up publishing Rabelais, and the work passed to foreign countries. Jean Fuet reprinted him at Antwerp in 1602. After the Amsterdam edition of 1659, where for the first time appears "The Alphabet of the French Author," comes the Elzevir edition of 1663. The type, an imitation of what made the reputation of the little volumes of the Gryphes of Lyons, is charming, the printing is perfect, and the paper, which is French —the development of paper-making in Holland and England did not take place till after the Revocation of the Edict of Nantes—is excellent. They are pretty volumes to the eye, but, as in all the reprints of the seventeenth century, the text is full of faults and most untrustworthy.

LA PLAISANTE,
ET IOYEVSE
hiſtoyre du grand
Geatit Gargantua.

Prochainement reueuë & de beaucoup
augmentée par l'Autheur meſmes.

A Valence,
Chés Claude La Ville.
1547

France, through a representative in a foreign land, however, comes into line again in the beginning of the eighteenth century, and in a really serious fashion, thanks to the very considerable learning of a French refugee, Jacob Le Duchat, who died in 1748. He had a most thorough knowledge of the French prose-writers of the sixteenth century, and he made them accessible by his editions of the *Quinze Joies du Mariage*, of Henri Estienne, of Agrippa d'Aubigné, of L'Etoile, and of the *Satyre Ménippée*. In 1711 he published an edition of Rabelais at Amsterdam, through Henry Bordesius, in five duodecimo volumes. The reprint in quarto which he issued in 1741, seven years before his death, is, with its engravings by Bernard Picot, a fine library edition. Le Duchat's is the first of the critical editions. It takes account of differences in the texts, and begins to point out the variations. His very numerous notes are remarkable, and are still worthy of most serious consideration. He was the first to offer useful elucidations, and these have been repeated after him, and with good reason will continue to be so. The Abbé de Massy's edition of 1752, also an Amsterdam production, has made use of Le Duchat's, but does not take its place. Finally, at the end of the century, Cazin printed Rabelais in his little volume, in 1782, and Bartiers issued two editions (of no importance) at Paris in 1782 and 1798. Fortunately the nineteenth century has occupied itself with the great "Satyrique" in a more competent and useful fashion.

In 1820 L'Aulnaye published through Desoer his three little volumes, printed in exquisite style, and which have other merits besides. His volume of annotations, in which, that nothing might be lost of his own notes, he has included many things not directly relating to Rabelais, is full of observations and curious remarks which are very useful additions to Le Duchat. One fault to be found with him is his further complication of the spelling. This he did in accordance with a principle that the words should be referred to their real etymology. Learned though he was, Rabelais had little care to be so etymological, and it is not his theories but those of the modern scholar that have been ventilated.

Somewhat later, from 1823 to 1826, Esmangart and Johanneau issued a variorum edition in nine volumes, in which the text is often encumbered by notes which are really too numerous, and, above all, too long. The work was an enormous one, but the best part of it is Le Duchat's, and what is not his is too often absolutely hypothetical and beside the truth. Le Duchat had already given too much importance to the false historical explanation. Here it is constantly coming in, and it rests on no evidence. In reality, there is no need of the key to Rabelais by which to discover the meaning of subtle allusions. He is neither so complicated nor so full of riddles. We know how he has scattered the names of contemporaries about his work, sometimes of friends, sometimes of enemies, and without disguising them under any mask. He is no more Panurge than Louis XII. is Gargantua or Francis I. Pantagruel. Rabelais says what he wants, all he wants, and in the way he wants. There are no mysteries below the surface, and it is a waste of time to look for knots in a bulrush. All the historical explanations are purely imaginary, utterly without proof, and should the more emphatically be looked on as baseless and dismissed. They are radically false, and therefore both worthless and harmful.

In 1840 there appeared in the Bibliothèque Charpentier the Rabelais in a single duodecimo volume, begun by Charles Labiche, and, after his death, completed by M. Paul Lacroix, whose share is the larger. The text is that of L'Aulnaye; the short footnotes, with all their brevity, contain useful explanations of difficult words. Amongst the editions of Rabelais this is one of the most important, because it brought him many readers and admirers. No other has made him so well and so widely known as this portable volume, which has been constantly reprinted. No other has been so widely circulated, and the sale still goes on. It was, and must still be looked on as a most serviceable edition.

The edition published by Didot in 1857 has an altogether special character. In the biographical notice M. Rathery for the first time treated as they deserve the foolish prejudices which have made Rabelais misunderstood, and M. Burgaud des Marets set the text on a quite new base. Having proved, what of course is very evident, that in the original editions the spelling, and the language too, were of the simplest and clearest, and were not bristling with the nonsensical and superfluous consonants which have given rise to the idea that Rabelais is difficult to read, he took the trouble first of all to note the spelling of each word. Whenever in a single instance he found it in accordance with modern spelling, he made it the same throughout. The task was a hard one, and Rabelais certainly gained in clearness, but over-zeal is often fatal to a reform. In respect to its precision and the value of its notes, which are short and very judicious, Burgaud des Marets' edition is valuable, and is amongst those which should be known and taken into account.

Since Le Duchat all the editions have a common fault. They are not exactly guilty of fabricating, but they set up an artificial text in the sense that, in order to lose as little as possible, they have collected and united what originally were variations—the revisions, in short, of the original editions. Guided by the wise counsels given by Brunet in 1852 in his *Researches* on the old editions of Rabelais, Pierre Jannet published the first three books in 1858; then, when the publication of the Bibliothèque Elzévirienne was discontinued, he took up the work again and finished the edition in Picard's blue library, in little volumes, each book quite distinct. It was M. Jannet who in our days first restored the pure and exact text of Rabelais, not only without retouching it, but without making additions or insertions, or juxtaposition of things that were not formerly found together. For each of the books he has followed the last edition issued by Rabelais, and all the earlier differences he gives as variations. It is astonishing that a thing so simple and so fitting should not have been done before, and the result is that this absolutely exact fidelity has restored a lucidity which was not wanting in Rabelais' time, but which had since been obscured. All who have come after Jannet have followed in his path, and there is no reason for straying from it.

FRANCIS RABELAIS.

The first BOOK
Of the WORKS of
Mr. *FRANCIS RABELAIS,*
Doctor In
Physick:
Containing five Books of the Lives, Heroick Deeds, and Sayings of
GARGANTUA,
And his Sonne
PANTAGRUEL.
TOGETHER
With the *Pantagrueline* Prognostication, the Oracle of the divine *Bachuc*, and response of the bottle.

Hereunto are annexed the Navigations unto the founding Isle, and the Isle of the *Apedefts*: as likewise the Philosophical cream with a Limosin Epistle. All done by Mr. Francis Rabelais, in the *French* Tongue, and now faithfully translated into *English*.

Ἐυνοεῖ εὐλόγε ᷇ εὐπαρίε.

LONDON, Printed for *Richard Baddeley*, within the middle *Temple*-gate. 1653.

To the
Honoured, Noble
Translator of Rabelais.

ABELAIS, *whose wit prodigiously was made,*
All men, professions, actions to invade,
With so much furious vigour, as if it
Had lived o'er each of them, and each had quit,
Yet with such happy sleight and careless skill,
As, like the serpent, doth with laughter kill;
So that although his noble leaves appear
Antic and Gottish, and dull souls forbear
To turn them o'er, lest they should only find
Nothing but savage monsters of a mind,—
No shapen beauteous thoughts; yet when the wise
Seriously strip him of his wild disguise,
Melt down his dross, refine his massy ore,
And polish that which seem'd rough-cast before,
Search his deep sense, unveil his hidden mirth,
And make that fiery which before seem'd earth
(Conquering those things of highest consequence,
What's difficult of language or of sense),
He will appear some noble table writ
In the old Egyptian hieroglyphic wit;
Where, though you monsters and grotescoes see,
You meet all mysteries of philosophy.
For he was wise and sovereignly bred

TO THE TRANSLATOR.

To know what mankind is, how't may be led:
He stoop'd unto them, like that wise man, who
Rid on a stick, when's children would do so.
For we are easy sullen things, and must
Be laugh'd aright, and cheated into trust;
Whilst a black piece of phlegm, that lays about
Dull menaces, and terrifies the rout,
And cajoles it, with all its peevish strength
Piteously stretch'd and botch'd up into length,
Whilst the tired rabble sleepily obey
Such opiate talk, and snore away the day,
By all his noise as much their minds relieves,
As caterwauling of wild cats frights thieves.

  But RABELAIS *was another thing, a man*
Made up of all that art and nature can
Form from a fiery genius,—he was one
Whose soul so universally was thrown
Through all the arts of life, who understood
Each stratagem by which we stray from good;
So that he best might solid virtue teach,
As some 'gainst sins of their own bosoms preach:
He from wise choice did the true means prefer,
In the fool's coat acting th' philosopher.

  Thus hoary Æsop's beasts did mildly tame
Fierce man, and moralize him into shame;
Thus brave romances, while they seem to lay
Great trains of lust, platonic love display;
Thus would old Sparta, if a seldom chance
Show'd a drunk slave, teach children temperance;
Thus did the later poets nobly bring
The scene to height, making the fool the king.

  And, noble sir, you vigorously have trod
In this hard path, unknown, un-understood
By its own countrymen, 'tis you appear
Our full enjoyment which was our despair,
Scattering his mists, cheering his cynic frowns
(For radiant brightness now dark RABELAIS *crowns),*
Leaving your brave heroic cares, which must
Make better mankind and embalm your dust,

TO THE TRANSLATOR.

So undeceiving us, that now we see
All wit in Gascon and in Cromarty,
Besides that Rabelais *is convey'd to us,*
And that our Scotland is not barbarous.

J. DE LA SALLE.

Rablophila.

The First Decade.

The Commendation.

USA! canas nostrorum in testimonium Amorum,
Et GARGANTUEAS perpetuato faces,
Utque homini tali resultet nobilis ECCHO:
Quicquid Fama canit, PANTAGRUELIS erit.

The Argument.

Here I intend mysteriously to sing
With a pen pluck'd from Fame's own wing.
Of Garagantua that learn'd breech-wiping king.

Decade the First.

I.

Help me, propitious stars; a mighty blaze
Benumbs me! I must sound the praise
Of him hath turn'd this crabbed work in such heroic phrase.

II.

What wit would not court martyrdom to hold
Upon his head a laurel of gold,
Where for each rich conceit a Pumpion-pearl is told:

III.

And such a one is this, art's masterpiece,
    A thing ne'er equall'd by old Greece :
A thing ne'er match'd as yet, a real Golden Fleece.

IV.

Vice is a soldier fights against mankind;
    Which you may look but never find :
For 'tis an envious thing, with cunning interlined.

V.

And thus he rails at drinking all before 'em,
    And for lewd women does be-whore 'em,
And brings their painted faces and black patches to th' quorum.

VI.

To drink he was a furious enemy
    Contented with a six-penny—
(With diamond hatband, silver spurs, six horses.) pie—

VII.

And for tobacco's pate-rotunding smoke,
    Much had he said, and much more spoke,
But 'twas not then found out, so the design was broke.

VIII.

Muse! Fancy! Faith! come now arise aloud,
    Assembled in a blue-vein'd cloud,
And this tall infant in angelic arms now shroud.

IX.

To praise it further I would now begin
    Were 't now a thoroughfare and inn,
It harbours vice, though 't be to catch it in a gin.

X.

Therefore, my Muse, draw up thy flowing sail,
    And acclamate a gentle hail
With all thy art and metaphors, which must prevail.

Jam prima Oceani pars est præterita nostri.
  Imparibus restat danda secunda modis.
Quam si præstiterit mentem Dæmon malus addam,
  Cùm sapiens totus prodierit RABELAIS.

MALEVOLUS.

Reader, the ERRATA, *which in this book are not a few, are casually lost; and therefore the Translator, not having leisure to collect them again, craves thy pardon for such as thou may'st meet with.*

The Author's Prologue to the First Book.

OST noble and illustrious drinkers, and you thrice precious pockified blades (for to you, and none else, do I dedicate my writings), Alcibiades, in that dialogue of Plato's, which is entitled The Banquet, whilst he was setting forth the praises of his schoolmaster Socrates (without all question the prince of philosophers), amongst other discourses to that purpose, said that he resembled the Silenes. Silenes of old were little boxes, like those we now may see in the shops of apothecaries, painted on the outside with wanton toyish figures, as harpies, satyrs, bridled geese, horned hares, saddled ducks, flying goats, thiller harts, and other such-like counterfeited pictures at discretion, to excite people unto laughter, as Silenus himself, who was the foster-father of good Bacchus, was wont to do; but within those capricious caskets were carefully preserved and kept many rich jewels and fine drugs, such as balm, ambergris, amomon, musk, civet, with several kinds of precious stones, and other things of great price. Just such another thing was Socrates. For to have eyed his outside, and esteemed of him by his exterior appearance, you would not have given the peel of an onion for him, so deformed he was in body, and ridiculous in his gesture. He had a sharp pointed nose, with the look of a bull, and countenance of a fool: he was in his carriage simple, boorish in his apparel, in fortune poor, unhappy in his wives, unfit for all offices in the commonwealth, always laughing, tippling,

and merrily carousing to everyone, with continual gibes and jeers, the better by those means to conceal his divine knowledge. Now, opening this box you would have found within it a heavenly and inestimable drug, a more than human understanding, an admirable virtue, matchless learning, invincible courage, unimitable sobriety, certain contentment of mind, perfect assurance, and an incredible misregard of all that for which men commonly do so much watch, run, sail, fight, travel, toil and turmoil themselves.

Whereunto (in your opinion) doth this little flourish of a preamble tend? For so much as you, my good disciples, and some other jolly fools of ease and leisure, reading the pleasant titles of some books of our invention, as Gargantua, Pantagruel, Whippot,[1] the Dignity of Codpieces, of Pease and Bacon with a Commentary, &c., are too ready to judge that there is nothing in them but jests, mockeries, lascivious discourse, and recreative lies; because the outside (which is the title) is usually, without any farther inquiry, entertained with scoffing and derision. But truly it is very unbeseeming to make so slight account of the works of men, seeing yourselves avouch that it is not the habit makes the monk, many being monasterially accoutred, who inwardly are nothing less than monachal, and that there are of those that wear Spanish capes, who have but little of the valour of Spaniards in them. Therefore is it, that you must open the book, and seriously consider of the matter treated in it. Then shall you find that it containeth things of far higher value than the box did promise; that is to say, that the subject thereof is not so foolish as by the title at the first sight it would appear to be.

And put the case, that in the literal sense you meet with purposes merry and solacious enough, and consequently very correspondent to their inscriptions, yet must not you stop there as at the melody of the charming syrens, but endeavour to interpret that in a sublimer sense which possibly you intended to have spoken in the jollity of your heart. Did you ever pick the lock of a cupboard to steal a bottle of wine out of it? Tell me truly, and, if you did, call to mind the countenance which then you had. Or, did you ever see a dog with a marrowbone in his mouth,—the beast of all other, says Plato, lib. 2, de Republica, the most philosophical? If you have seen him, you might have remarked with what devotion and circumspectness he wards and watcheth it: with what care he keeps it:

[1] Fessepinte.

how fervently he holds it : how prudently he gobbets it : with what affection he breaks it : and with what diligence he sucks it. To what end all this? What moveth him to take all these pains? What are the hopes of his labour? What doth he expect to reap thereby? Nothing but a little marrow. True it is, that this little is more savoury and delicious than the great quantities of other sorts of meat, because the marrow (as Galen testifieth, 5. facult. nat. & 11. de usu partium) is a nourishment most perfectly elaboured by nature.

In imitation of this dog, it becomes you to be wise, to smell, feel and have in estimation these fair goodly books, stuffed with high conceptions, which, though seemingly easy in the pursuit, are in the cope and encounter somewhat difficult. And then, like him, you must, by a sedulous lecture, and frequent meditation, break the bone, and suck out the marrow,—that is, my allegorical sense, or the things I to myself propose to be signified by these Pythagorical symbols, with assured hope, that in so doing you will at last attain to be both well-advised and valiant by the reading of them : for in the perusal of this treatise you shall find another kind of taste, and a doctrine of a more profound and abstruse consideration, which will disclose unto you the most glorious sacraments and dreadful mysteries, as well in what concerneth your religion, as matters of the public state, and life economical.

Do you believe, upon your conscience, that Homer, whilst he was a-couching his Iliads and Odysses, had any thought upon those allegories, which Plutarch, Heraclides Ponticus, Eustathius, Cornutus squeezed out of him, and which Politian filched again from them? If you trust it, with neither hand nor foot do you come near to my opinion, which judgeth them to have been as little dreamed of by Homer, as the Gospel sacraments were by Ovid in his Metamorphoses, though a certain gulligut friar[1] and true bacon-picker would have undertaken to prove it, if perhaps he had met with as very fools as himself, (and as the proverb says) a lid worthy of such a kettle.

If you give no credit thereto, why do not you the same in these jovial new chronicles of mine? Albeit when I did dictate them, I thought upon no more than you, who possibly were drinking the whilst as I was. For in the composing of this lordly book, I never lost nor bestowed any more, nor any other time than what was

[1] Frère Lubin croquelardon.

appointed to serve me for taking of my bodily refection, that is, whilst I was eating and drinking. And indeed that is the fittest and most proper hour wherein to write these high matters and deep sciences: as Homer knew very well, the paragon of all philologues, and Ennius, the father of the Latin poets, as Horace calls him, although a certain sneaking jobernol alleged that his verses smelled more of the wine than oil.

So saith a turlupin or a new start-up grub of my books, but a turd for him. The fragrant odour of the wine, O how much more dainty, pleasant, laughing,[1] celestial and delicious it is, than that smell of oil! And I will glory as much when it is said of me, that I have spent more on wine than oil, as did Demosthenes, when it was told him, that his expense on oil was greater than on wine. I truly hold it for an honour and praise to be called and reputed a Frolic Gualter and a Robin Goodfellow; for under this name am I welcome in all choice companies of Pantagruelists. It was upbraided to Demosthenes by an envious surly knave, that his Orations did smell like the sarpler or wrapper of a foul and filthy oil-vessel. For this cause interpret you all my deeds and sayings in the perfectest sense; reverence the cheese-like brain that feeds you with these fair billevezees and trifling jollities, and do what lies in you to keep me always merry. Be frolic now, my lads, cheer up your hearts, and joyfully read the rest, with all the ease of your body and profit of your reins. But hearken, joltheads, you viedazes, or dickens take ye, remember to drink a health to me for the like favour again, and I will pledge you instantly, *Tout ares-metys.*

[1] Riant, priant, friant.

Rabelais to the Reader.

GOOD friends, my Readers, who peruse this Book,
Be not offended, whilst on it you look:
Denude yourselves of all depraved affection,
For it contains no badness, nor infection:
'Tis true that it brings forth to you no birth
Of any value, but in point of mirth;
Thinking therefore how sorrow might your mind
Consume, I could no apter subject find;
One inch of joy surmounts of grief a span;
Because to laugh is proper to the man.

Rabelais.

CHAPTER I.

Of the Genealogy and Antiquity of Gargantua.

I MUST refer you to the great chronicle of Pantagruel for the knowledge of that genealogy and antiquity of race by which Gargantua is come unto us. In it you may understand more at large how the giants were born in this world, and how from them by a direct line issued Gargantua, the father of Pantagruel: and do not take it ill, if for this time I pass by it, although the subject be such, that the oftener it were remembered, the more it would please your worshipful Seniorias; according to which you have the authority of Plato in Philebo and Gorgias; and of Flaccus, who says that there are some kinds of purposes (such as these are without doubt), which, the frequentlier they be repeated, still prove the more delectable.

Would to God everyone had as certain knowledge of his genealogy since the time of the ark of Noah until this age. I think many are at this day emperors, kings, dukes, princes, and popes on the earth, whose extraction is from some porters and pardon-pedlars; as, on the contrary, many are now poor wandering beggars, wretched and miserable, who are descended of the blood and lineage of great kings and emperors, occasioned, as I conceive it, by the transport and revolution of kingdoms and empires, from the Assyrians to the Medes, from the Medes to the Persians, from the Persians to the Macedonians, from the Macedonians to the Romans, from the Romans to the Greeks, from the Greeks to the French.

And to give you some hint concerning myself, who speaks unto you, I cannot think but I am come of the race of some rich king or prince in former times; for never yet saw you any man that had a greater desire to be a king, and to be rich, than I have, and that only that I may make good cheer, do nothing, nor care for anything, and plentifully enrich my friends, and all honest and learned men. But herein do I comfort myself, that in the other world I shall be so, yea and greater too than at this present I dare wish. As for you, with the same or a better conceit consolate yourselves in your distresses, and drink fresh if you can come by it.

To return to our wethers, I say that by the sovereign gift of heaven, the antiquity and genealogy of Gargantua hath been reserved for our use more full and perfect than any other except that of the Messias, whereof I mean not to speak; for it belongs not unto my purpose, and the devils, that is to say, the false accusers and dissembled gospellers, will therein oppose me. This genealogy was found by John Andrew in a meadow, which he had near the pole-arch, under the olive-tree, as you go to Narsay: where, as he was making cast up some ditches, the diggers with their mattocks struck against a great brazen tomb, and unmeasurably long, for they could never find the end thereof, by reason that it entered too far within the sluices of Vienne. Opening this tomb in a certain place thereof, sealed on the top with the mark of a goblet, about which was written in Etrurian letters HIC BIBITUR, they found nine flagons set in such order as they use to rank their kyles in Gascony, of which that which was placed in the middle had under it a big, fat, great, grey, pretty, small, mouldy, little pamphlet, smelling stronger, but no better than roses. In that book the said genealogy was found written all at length, in a chancery hand, not in paper, not in parchment, nor in wax, but in the bark of an elm-tree, yet so worn with the long tract of time, that hardly could three letters together be there perfectly discerned.

I (though unworthy) was sent for thither, and with much help of those spectacles, whereby the art of reading dim writings, and letters that do not clearly appear to the sight, is practised, as Aristotle teacheth it, did translate the book as you may see in your Pantagruelizing, that is to say, in drinking stiffly to your own heart's desire, and reading the dreadful and horrific acts of Pantagruel. At the end of the book there was a little treatise entitled the Antidoted Fanfreluches, or a Galimatia of extravagant conceits. The rats and moths, or (that I may not lie) other wicked beasts, had nibbled off the beginning: the rest I have hereto subjoined, for the reverence I bear to antiquity.

CHAP. II.

The Antidoted Fanfreluches: or, a Galimatia of extravagant Conceits found in an ancient Monument.

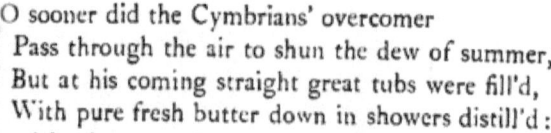

NO sooner did the Cymbrians' overcomer
Pass through the air to shun the dew of summer,
But at his coming straight great tubs were fill'd,
With pure fresh butter down in showers distill'd:
Wherewith when water'd was his grandam, Hey,
Aloud he cried, Fish it, sir, I pray y';
Because his beard is almost all beray'd;
Or, that he would hold to 'm a scale, he pray'd.

To lick his slipper, some told was much better,
Than to gain pardons, and the merit greater.
In th' interim a crafty chuff approaches,
From the depth issued, where they fish for roaches;
Who said, Good sirs, some of them let us save,
The eel is here, and in this hollow cave
You'll find, if that our looks on it demur,
A great waste in the bottom of his fur.

To read this chapter when he did begin,
Nothing but a calf's horns were found therein;
I feel, quoth he, the mitre which doth hold
My head so chill, it makes my brains take cold.
Being with the perfume of a turnip warm'd,
To stay by chimney hearths himself he arm'd,
Provided that a new thill-horse they made
Of every person of a hair-brain'd head.

They talked of the bunghole of Saint Knowles,
Of Gilbathar and thousand other holes,

If they might be reduced t' a scarry stuff,
Such as might not be subject to the cough:
Since ev'ry man unseemly did it find,
To see them gaping thus at ev'ry wind:
For, if perhaps they handsomely were closed,
For pledges they to men might be exposed.

In this arrest by Hercules the raven
Was flayed at her [his] return from Lybia haven.
Why am not I, said Minos, there invited?
Unless it be myself, not one's omitted:
And then it is their mind, I do no more
Of frogs and oysters send them any store:
In case they spare my life and prove but civil,
I give their sale of distaffs to the devil.

To quell him comes Q. B., who limping frets
At the safe pass of tricksy crackarets:
The boulter, the grand Cyclops' cousin, those
Did massacre, whilst each one wiped his nose:
Few ingles in this fallow ground are bred,
But on a tanner's mill are winnowed.
Run thither all of you, th' alarms sound clear,
You shall have more than you had the last year.

Short while thereafter was the bird of Jove
Resolved to speak, though dismal it should prove;
Yet was afraid, when he saw them in ire,
They should o'erthrow quite flat down dead th' empire.
He rather choosed the fire from heaven to steal,
To boats where were red herrings put to sale;
Than to be calm 'gainst those, who strive to brave us,
And to the Massorets' fond words enslave us.

All this at last concluded gallantly,
In spite of Ate and her hern-like thigh,
Who, sitting, saw Penthesilea ta'en,
In her old age, for a cress-selling quean.

Each one cried out, Thou filthy collier toad,
Doth it become thee to be found abroad?
Thou hast the Roman standard filch'd away,
Which they in rags of parchment did display.

Juno was born, who, under the rainbow,
Was a-bird-catching with her duck below:
When her with such a grievous trick they plied
That she had almost been bethwacked by it.
The bargain was, that, of that throatful, she
Should of Proserpina have two eggs free;
And if that she thereafter should be found,
She to a hawthorn hill should be fast bound.

Seven months thereafter, lacking twenty-two,
He, that of old did Carthage town undo,
Did bravely midst them all himself advance,
Requiring of them his inheritance;
Although they justly made up the division,
According to the shoe-welt-law's decision,
By distributing store of brews and beef
To these poor fellows that did pen the brief.

But th' year will come, sign of a Turkish bow,
Five spindles yarn'd, and three pot-bottoms too,
Wherein of a discourteous king the dock
Shall pepper'd be under an hermit's frock.
Ah! that for one she hypocrite you must
Permit so many acres to be lost!
Cease, cease, this vizard may become another,
Withdraw yourselves unto the serpent's brother.

'Tis in times past, that he who is shall reign
With his good friends in peace now and again.
No rash nor heady prince shall then rule crave.
Each good will its arbitrement shall have;
And the joy, promised of old as doom
To the heaven's guests, shall in its beacon come.

Then shall the breeding mares, that benumb'd were,
Like royal palfreys ride triumphant there.

And this continue shall from time to time,
Till Mars be fetter'd for an unknown crime;
Then shall one come, who others will surpass,
Delightful, pleasing, matchless, full of grace.
Cheer up your hearts, approach to this repast,
All trusty friends of mine; for he's deceased,
Who would not for a world return again,
So highly shall time past be cried up then.

He who was made of wax shall lodge each member
Close by the hinges of a block of timber.
We then no more shall Master, master, whoot,
The swagger, who th' alarum bell holds out;
Could one seize on the dagger which he bears,
Heads would be free from tingling in the ears,
To baffle the whole storehouse of abuses.
And thus farewell Apollo and the Muses.

CHAP. III.

How Gargantua was carried eleven months in his mother's belly.

GRANGOUSIER was a good fellow in his time, and notable jester; he loved to drink neat, as much as any man that then was in the world, and would willingly eat salt meat. To this intent he was ordinarily well furnished with gammons of bacon, both of Westphalia, Mayence and Bayonne, with store of dried neat's tongues, plenty of links, chitterlings and puddings in their season; together with salt beef and mustard, a good deal of hard roes of powdered mullet called botargos, great provision of sausages, not of Bolonia (for he feared the Lombard Boccone), but of Bigorre, Longaulnay, Brene, and Rouargue. In the vigour of his age he married Gargamelle, daughter to the King of the Parpaillons,

a jolly pug, and well-mouthed wench. These two did oftentimes do the two-backed beast together, joyfully rubbing and frotting their bacon 'gainst one another, in so far, that at last she became great with child of a fair son, and went with him unto the eleventh month; for so long, yea longer, may a woman carry her great belly, especially when it is some masterpiece of nature, and a person predestinated to the performance, in his due time, of great exploits. As Homer says, that the child, which Neptune begot upon the nymph, was born a whole year after the conception, that is, in the twelfth month. For, as Aulus Gellius saith, lib. 3, this long time was suitable to the majesty of Neptune, that in it the child might receive his perfect form. For the like reason Jupiter made the night, wherein he lay with Alcmena, last forty-eight hours, a shorter time not being sufficient for the forging of Hercules, who cleansed the world of the monsters and tyrants wherewith it was suppressed. My masters, the ancient Pantagruelists, have confirmed that which I say, and withal declared it to be not only possible, but also maintained the lawful birth and legitimation of the infant born of a woman in the eleventh month after the decease of her husband. Hypocrates, *lib. de alimento.* Plinius, *lib.* 7, *cap.* 5. Plautus, in his *Cistelleria.* Marcus Varro, in his satire inscribed *The Testament*, alleging to this purpose the authority of Aristotle. Censorinus, *lib. de die natali.* Arist. *lib.* 7, *cap.* 3 & 4, *de natura animalium.* Gellius, *lib.* 3, *cap.* 16. Servius, in his exposition upon this verse of Virgil's eclogues, *Matri longa decem, &c.*, and a thousand other fools, whose number hath been increased by the lawyers *ff. de suis, et legit l. intestato. paragrapho. fin.* and in *Auth. de restitut. et ea quæ parit in xi mense.* Moreover upon these grounds they have foisted in their Robidilardic, or Lapiturolive law. Gallus *ff. de lib. et posth. l. sept. ff. de stat. hom.*, and some other laws, which at this time I dare not name. By means whereof the honest widows may without danger play at the close buttock game with might and main, and as hard as they can, for the space of the first two months after the decease of their husbands. I pray you, my good lusty springal lads, if you find any of these females, that are worth the pains of untying the cod-piece-point, get up, ride upon them, and bring them to me; for, if they happen within the third month to conceive, the child shall be heir to the deceased, if, before he died, he had no other children, and the mother shall pass for an honest woman.

When she is known to have conceived, thrust forward boldly, spare her not, whatever betide you, seeing the paunch is full. As Julia, the daughter of the Emperor Octavian, never prostituted herself to her belly-bumpers, but when she found herself with child, after the manner of ships, that receive not their steersman till they have their ballast and lading. And if any blame them for this their rataconniculation, and reiterated lechery upon their pregnancy and big-belliedness, seeing beasts, in the like exigent of their fulness, will never suffer the male-masculant to encroach them, their answer will be, that those are beasts, but they are women, very well skilled in the pretty vales and small fees of the pleasant trade and mysteries of superfetation: as Populia heretofore answered, according to the relation of Macrobius, *lib. 2. Saturnal.* If the devil will not have them to bag, he must wring hard the spigot, and stop the bung-hole.

CHAP. IV.

How Gargamelle, being great with Gargantua, did eat a huge deal of tripes.

THE occasion and manner how Gargamelle was brought to bed, and delivered of her child, was thus: and, if you do not believe it, I wish your bum-gut fall out and make an escapade. Her bum-gut, indeed, or fundament escaped her in an afternoon, on the third day of February, with having eaten at dinner too many godebillios. Godebillios are the fat tripes of coiros. Coiros are beeves fattened at the cratch in ox-stalls, or in the fresh guimo meadows. Guimo meadows are those that for their fruitfulness may be mowed twice a year. Of those fat beeves they had killed three hundred sixty-seven thousand and fourteen, to be salted at Shrovetide, that in the entering of the spring they might have plenty of powdered beef, wherewith to season their mouths at the beginning of their meals, and to taste their wine the better.

They had abundance of tripes, as you have heard, and they were so delicious, that everyone licked his fingers. But the mischief was this, that, for all men could do, there was no possibility to keep them long in that relish; for in a very short while they would have stunk, which had been an undecent thing. It was therefore concluded, that they should be all of them gulched up, without losing anything. To this effect they invited all the burghers of Sainais, of Suillé, of the Roche-Clermaud, of Vaugaudry, without omitting the Coudray, Monpensier, the Gué de Véde, and other their neighbours, all stiff drinkers, brave fellows, and good players at the kyles. The good man Grangousier took great pleasure in their company, and commanded there should be no want nor pinching for anything. Nevertheless he bade his wife eat sparingly, because she was near her time, and that these tripes were no very commendable meat. They would fain, said he, be at the chewing of ordure, that would eat the case wherein it was. Notwithstanding these admonitions, she did eat sixteen quarters, two bushels, three pecks and a pipkin full. O the fair fecality wherewith she swelled, by the ingrediency of such shitten stuff!

After dinner they all went out in a hurl to the grove of the willows, where, on the green grass, to the sound of the merry flutes and pleasant bagpipes, they danced so gallantly, that it was a sweet and heavenly sport to see them so frolic.

CHAP. V.

The Discourse of the Drinkers.

THEN did they fall upon the chat of victuals and some belly furniture to be snatched at in the very same place. Which purpose was no sooner mentioned, but forthwith began flagons to go, gammons to trot, goblets to fly, great bowls to ting, glasses to ring. Draw, reach, fill, mix, give it me without water. So, my friend, so, whip me off this glass neatly, bring me hither some claret, a full weeping glass till it run over. A cessation and truce with thirst. Ha, thou false fever, wilt thou not be gone? By my figgins, godmother, I cannot as yet enter in the humour of being merry, nor drink so currently as I would. You have catched a cold, gammer? Yea, forsooth, sir. By the belly of Sanct Buff, let us talk of our drink: I never drink but at my hours, like the Pope's mule. And I never drink but in my breviary, like a fair father guardian. Which was first, thirst or drinking? Thirst, for who in the time of innocence would have drunk without being athirst? Nay, sir, it was drinking; for *privatio præsupponit habitum*. I am learned, you see: *Fœcundi calices quem non fecere disertum?* We poor innocents drink but too much without thirst. Not I truly, who am a sinner, for I never drink without thirst, either present or future. To prevent it, as you know, I drink for the thirst to come. I drink eternally. This is to me an eternity of drinking, and drinking of eternity. Let us sing, let us drink, and tune up our roundelays. Where is my funnel? What, it seems I do not drink but by an attorney? Do you wet yourselves to dry, or do you dry to wet you? Pish, I understand not the rhetoric (theoric, I should say), but I help myself somewhat by the practice. *Baste!* enough! I sup, I wet, I humect, I moisten my gullet, I drink, and all for fear of dying. Drink always and you shall never die. If I drink not, I am a-ground, dry, gravelled and spent. I am stark dead without drink, and my soul ready to fly into some marsh amongst frogs; the soul never dwells in a dry place, drouth kills it. O you butlers, creators of new forms, make me of no drinker a drinker, a perennity and everlastingness of sprinkling and bedewing me through these my parched and sinewy bowels. He drinks in vain that feels not the pleasure of it. This entereth into my veins, —the pissing tools and urinal vessels shall have nothing of it. I would willingly wash the tripes of the calf which I apparelled this morning. I have pretty well now ballasted my stomach and stuffed my paunch. If the papers of my bonds and bills could drink as well as I do, my creditors would not want for wine when they come to see me, or when they are to make any formal exhibition of their rights to what of me they can demand. This hand of yours spoils your nose. O how many other such will enter here before this go out! What, drink so shallow? It is enough to break both girds and petrel. This is called a cup of dissimulation, or flagonal hypocrisy.

What difference is there between a bottle and a flagon. Great difference; for the bottle is stopped and shut up with a stopple, but the flagon with a vice.[1] Bravely and well played upon the words! Our fathers drank lustily, and emptied their cans. Well cacked,

---

[1] La bouteille est fermée à bouchon, et le flaccon à vis.

well sung! Come, let us drink: will you send nothing to the river? Here is one going to wash the tripes. I drink no more than a sponge. I drink like a Templar knight. And I, *tanquam sponsus*. And I, *sicut terra sine aqua*. Give me a synonymon for a gammon of bacon. It is the compulsory of drinkers: it is a pulley. By a pulley-rope wine is let down into a cellar, and by a gammon into the stomach. Hey! now, boys, hither, some drink, some drink. There is no trouble in it. *Respice personam, pone pro duos, bus non est in usu.* If I could get up as well as I can swallow down, I had been long ere now very high in the air.

Thus became Tom Tosspot rich,—thus went in the tailor's stitch. Thus did Bacchus conquer th' Inde—thus Philosophy, Melinde. A little rain allays a great deal of wind: long tippling breaks the thunder. But if there came such liquor from my ballock, would you not willingly thereafter suck the udder whence it issued? Here, page, fill! I prithee, forget me not when it comes to my turn, and I will enter the election I have made of thee into the very register of my heart. Sup, Guillot, and spare not, there is somewhat in the pot. I appeal from thirst, and disclaim its jurisdiction. Page, sue out my appeal in form. This remnant in the bottom of the glass must follow its leader. I was wont heretofore to drink out all, but now I leave nothing. Let us not make too much haste; it is requisite we carry all along with us. Heyday, here are tripes fit for our sport, and, in earnest, excellent godebillios of the dun ox (you know) with the black streak. O, for God's sake, let us lash them soundly, yet thriftily. Drink, or I will,—No, no, drink, I beseech you.[1] Sparrows will not eat unless you bob them on the tail, nor can I drink if I be not fairly spoke to. The concavities of my body are like another Hell for their capacity. Lagonædatera.[2] There is not a corner, nor coney-burrow in all my body, where this wine doth not ferret out my thirst. Ho, this will bang it soundly. But this shall banish it utterly. Let us wind our horns by the sound of flagons and bottles, and cry aloud, that whoever hath lost his thirst come not hither to seek it. Long clysters of drinking are to be voided without doors. The great God made the planets, and we make the platters neat. I have the word of the gospel in my mouth,

---

[1] Ou je vous, je vous prie.
[2] λαγὼν *lateris cavitas:* αἰένης *orcus:* and ἕτερος *alter.*

Sitio. The stone called asbestos is not more unquenchable than the thirst of my paternity. Appetite comes with eating, says Angeston, but the thirst goes away with drinking. I have a remedy against thirst, quite contrary to that which is good against the biting of a mad dog. Keep running after a dog, and he will never bite you; drink always before the thirst, and it will never come upon you. There I catch you, I awake you. Argus had a hundred eyes for his sight, a butler should have (like Briareus) a hundred hands wherewith to fill us wine indefatigably. Hey now, lads, let us moisten ourselves, it will be time to dry hereafter. White wine here, wine, boys! Pour out all in the name of Lucifer, fill here, you, fill and fill (peascods on you) till it be full. My tongue peels. Lans trinque; to thee, countryman, I drink to thee, good fellow, comrade to thee, lusty, lively! Ha, la, la, that was drunk to some purpose, and bravely gulped over. *O lachryma Christi*, it is of the best grape! I'faith, pure Greek, Greek! O the fine white wine! upon my conscience, it is a kind of taffetas wine,—hin, hin, it is of one ear, well wrought, and of good wool. Courage, comrade, up thy heart, billy! We will not be beasted at this bout, for I have got one trick. *Ex hoc in hoc.* There is no enchantment nor charm there, every one of you hath seen it. My 'prenticeship is out, I am a free man at this trade. I am prester mast,[1] Prish, Brum! I should say, master past. O the drinkers, those that are a-dry, O poor thirsty souls! Good page, my friend, fill me here some, and crown the wine, I pray thee. Like a cardinal! *Natura abhorret vacuum.* Would you say that a fly could drink in this? This is after the fashion of Switzerland. Clear off, neat, supernaculum! Come, therefore, blades, to this divine liquor and celestial juice, swill it over heartily, and spare not! It is a decoction of nectar and ambrosia.

[1] Prestre macé, maistre passé.

CHAP. VI.

How Gargantua was born in a strange manner.

WHILST they were on this discourse and pleasant tattle of drinking, Gargamelle began to be a little unwell in her lower parts; whereupon Grangousier arose from off the grass, and fell to comfort her very honestly and kindly, suspecting that she was in travail, and told her that it was best for her to sit down upon the grass under the willows, because she was like very shortly to see young feet, and that therefore it was convenient she should pluck up her spirits, and take a good heart of new at the fresh arrival of her baby; saying to her withal, that although the pain was somewhat grievous to her, it would be but of short continuance, and that the succeeding joy would quickly remove that sorrow, in such sort that she should not so much as remember it. On, with a sheep's courage! quoth he. Despatch this boy, and we will speedily fall to work for the making of another. Ha! said she, so well as you speak at your own ease, you that are men! Well, then, in the name of God, I'll do my best, seeing that you will have it so, but would to God that it were cut off from you! What? said Grangousier. Ha, said she, you are a good man indeed, you understand it well enough. What, my member? said he. By the goat's blood, if it please you, that shall be done instantly; cause bring hither a knife. Alas, said she, the Lord forbid, and pray Jesus to forgive me! I did not say it from my heart, therefore let it alone, and do not do it neither more nor less any kind of harm for my speaking so to you. But I am like to have work enough to do to-day and all for your member, yet God bless you and it.

Courage, courage, said he, take you no care of the matter, let the four foremost oxen do the work. I will yet go drink one whiff more, and if in the mean time anything befall you that may require my presence, I will be so near to you, that, at the first whistling in your fist, I shall be with you forthwith. A little while after she began to groan, lament, and cry. Then suddenly came the midwives from all quarters, who groping her below, found some peloderies, which was a certain filthy stuff, and of a taste truly bad enough.

This they thought had been the child, but it was her fundament, that was slipped out with the mollification of her straight entrail, which you call the bum-gut, and that merely by eating of too many tripes, as we have showed you before. Whereupon an old ugly trot in the company, who had the repute of an expert she-physician, and was come from Brisepaille, near to Saint Genou, three score years before, made her so horrible a restrictive and binding medicine, and whereby all her *larris*, arse-pipes, and conduits were so oppilated, stopped, obstructed, and contracted, that you could hardly have opened and enlarged them with your teeth, which is a terrible thing to think upon; seeing the Devil at the mass at Saint Martin's was puzzled with the like task, when with his teeth he had lengthened out the parchment whereon he wrote the tittle-tattle of two young mangy whores. By this inconvenient the cotyledons of her matrix were presently loosed, through which the child sprang up and leaped, and so, entering into the hollow vein, did climb by the diaphragm even above her shoulders, where the vein divides itself into two, and from thence taking his way towards the left side, issued forth at her left ear. As soon as he was born, he cried not as other babes use to do, *Miez, miez, miez, miez*, but with a high, sturdy, and big voice shouted about, Some drink, some drink, some drink, as inviting all the world to drink with him. The noise hereof was so extremely great, that it was heard in both the countries at once of Beauce and Bibarois. I doubt me, that you do not thoroughly believe the truth of this strange nativity. Though you believe it not, I care not much: but an honest man, and of good judgment, believeth still what is told him, and that which he finds written.

Is this beyond our law or our faith—against reason or the holy Scripture? For my part, I find nothing in the sacred Bible that is against it. But tell me, if it had been the will of God, would you say that he could not do it? Ha, for favour sake, I beseech you, never emberlucock or inpulregafize your spirits with these vain thoughts and idle conceits; for I tell you, it is not impossible with God, and, if he pleased, all women henceforth should bring forth their children at the ear. Was not Bacchus engendered out of the very thigh of Jupiter? Did not Roquetaillade come out at his mother's heel, and Crocmoush from the slipper of his nurse? Was not Minerva born of the brain, even through the ear of Jove? Adonis, of the bark of a myrrh tree; and Castor and Pollux of the doupe of that egg which was laid and hatched by Leda? But you would wonder more, and with far greater amazement, if I should now present you with that chapter of Plinius, wherein he treateth of strange births, and contrary to nature, and yet am not I so impudent a liar as he was. Read the seventh book of his Natural History, chap. 3, and trouble not my head any more about this.

CHAP. VII.

After what manner Gargantua had his name given him, and how he tippled, bibbed, and curried the can.

THE good man Grangousier, drinking and making merry with the rest, heard the horrible noise which his son had made as he entered into the light of this world, when he cried out, Some drink, some drink, some drink ; whereupon he said in French, *Que grand tu as et souple le gousier!* that is to say, How great and nimble a throat thou hast. Which the company hearing, said that verily the child ought to be called Gargantua ; because it was the first word that after his birth his father had spoke, in imitation, and at the example of the ancient Hebrews ; whereunto he condescended, and his mother was very well pleased therewith. In the meanwhile, to quiet the child, they gave him to drink a tirelaregot, that is, till his throat was like to crack with it ; then was he carried to the font, and there baptized, according to the manner of good Christians.

Immediately thereafter were appointed for him seventeen thousand, nine hundred, and thirteen cows of the towns of Pautille and Brehemond, to furnish him with milk in ordinary, for it was impossible to find a nurse sufficient for him in all the country, considering the great quantity of milk that was requisite for his nourishment ; although there were not wanting some doctors of the opinion of Scotus, who affirmed that his own mother gave him suck, and that she could draw out of her breasts one thousand, four hundred, two pipes, and nine pails of milk at every time.

Which indeed is not probable, and this point hath been found duggishly scandalous and offensive to tender ears, for that it savoured a little of heresy. Thus was he handled for one year and ten months; after which time, by the advice of physicians, they began to carry him, and then was made for him a fine little cart drawn with oxen, of the invention of Jan Denio, wherein they led him hither and thither with great joy; and he was worth the seeing, for he was a fine boy, had a burly physiognomy, and almost ten chins. He cried very little, but beshit himself every hour: for, to speak truly of him, he was wonderfully phlegmatic in his posteriors, both by reason of his natural complexion and the accidental disposition which had befallen him by his too much quaffing of the Septembral juice. Yet without a cause did not he sup one drop; for if he happened to be vexed, angry, displeased, or sorry, if he did fret, if he did weep, if he did cry, and what grievous quarter soever he kept, in bringing him some drink, he would be instantly pacified, reseated in his own temper, in a good humour again, and as still and quiet as ever. One of his governesses told me (swearing by her fig), how he was so accustomed to this kind of way, that, at the sound of pints and flagons, he would on a sudden fall into an ecstasy, as if he had then tasted of the joys of paradise; so that they, upon consideration of this, his divine complexion, would every morning, to cheer him up, play with a knife upon the glasses, on the bottles with their stopples, and on the pottle-pots with their lids and covers, at the sound whereof he became gay, did leap for joy, would loll and rock himself in the cradle, then nod with his head, monochordizing with his fingers, and barytonizing with his tail.

CHAP. VIII.

How they apparelled Gargantua.

BEING of this age, his father ordained to have clothes made to him in his own livery, which was white and blue. To work then went the tailors, and with great expedition were those clothes made, cut, and sewed, according to the fashion that was then in request. I find by the ancient records or pancarts, to be seen in the chamber of accounts, or court of the exchequer at Montsoreau, that he was accoutred in manner as followeth. To make him every shirt of his were taken

up nine hundred ells of Chasteleraud linen, and two hundred for the gussets, in manner of cushions, which they put under his armpits. His shirt was not gathered nor plaited, for the plaiting of shirts was not found out till the seamstresses (when the point of their needle [1] was broken) began to work and occupy with the tail. There were taken up for his doublet, eight hundred and thirteen ells of white satin, and for his points fifteen hundred and nine dogs' skins and a half. Then was it that men began to tie their breeches to their doublets, and not their doublets to their breeches : for it is against nature, as hath most amply been showed by Ockham upon the exponibles of Master Haultechaussade.

For his breeches were taken up eleven hundred and five ells and a third of white broadcloth. They were cut in the form of pillars, chamfered, channelled and pinked behind that they might not overheat his reins : and were, within the panes, puffed out with the lining of as much blue damask as was needful : and remark, that he had very good leg-harness, proportionable to the rest of his stature.

For his codpiece were used sixteen ells and a quarter of the same cloth, and it was fashioned on the top like unto a triumphant arch, most gallantly fastened with two enamelled clasps, in each of which was set a great emerald, as big as an orange ; for, as says Orpheus, *lib. de lapidibus,* and Plinius, *libro ultimo,* it hath an erective virtue and comfortative of the natural member. The exiture, outjecting or outstanding, of his codpiece was of the length of a yard, jagged and pinked, and withal bagging, and strutting out with the blue damask lining, after the manner of his breeches. But had you seen the fair embroidery of the small needlework purl, and the curiously interlaced knots, by the goldsmith's art set out and trimmed with rich diamonds, precious rubies, fine turquoises, costly emeralds, and Persian pearls, you would have compared it to a fair cornucopia, or horn of abundance, such as you see in antiques, or as Rhea gave to the two nymphs, Amalthea and Ida, the nurses of Jupiter.

And, like to that horn of abundance, it was still gallant, succulent, droppy, sappy, pithy, lively, always flourishing, always fructifying, full of juice, full of flower, full of fruit, and all manner of delight. I avow God, it would have done one good to have seen him, but I will tell you more of him in the book which I have made of the dignity of

---

[1] *Beiongner du cul,* Englished *The eye of the needle.*

codpieces. One thing I will tell you, that as it was both long and large, so was it well furnished and victualled within, nothing like unto the hypocritical codpieces of some fond wooers and wench-courtiers, which are stuffed only with wind, to the great prejudice of the female sex.

For his shoes were taken up four hundred and six ells of blue crimson-velvet, and were very neatly cut by parallel lines, joined in uniform cylinders. For the soling of them were made use of eleven hundred hides of brown cows, shapen like the tail of a keeling.

For his coat were taken up eighteen hundred ells of blue velvet, dyed in grain, embroidered in its borders with fair gilliflowers, in the middle decked with silver purl, intermixed with plates of gold and store of pearls, hereby showing that in his time he would prove an especial good fellow and singular whipcan.

His girdle was made of three hundred ells and a half of silken serge, half white and half blue, if I mistake it not. His sword was not of Valentia, nor his dagger of Saragossa, for his father could not endure these *hidalgos borrachos maranisados como diablos:* but he had a fair sword made of wood, and the dagger of boiled leather, as well painted and gilded as any man could wish.

His purse was made of the cod of an elephant, which was given him by Herr Pracontal, proconsul of Lybia.

For his gown were employed nine thousand six hundred ells, wanting two-thirds, of blue velvet, as before, all so diagonally purled, that by true perspective issued thence an unnamed colour, like that you see in the necks of turtle-doves or turkey-cocks, which wonderfully rejoiced the eyes of the beholders. For his bonnet or cap were taken up three hundred, two ells and a quarter of white velvet, and the form thereof was wide and round, of the bigness of his head; for his father said that the caps of the Marrabaise fashion, made like the cover of a pasty, would one time or other bring a mischief on those that wore them. For his plume, he wore a fair great blue feather, plucked from an onocrotal of the country of Hircania the wild, very prettily hanging down over his right ear. For the jewel or brooch which in his cap he carried, he had in a cake of gold, weighing three score and eight marks, a fair piece enamelled, wherein was portrayed a man's body with two heads, looking towards one another, four arms, four feet, two arses, such as Plato, *in Symposio,* says was the mystical beginning of man's nature;

and about it was written in Ionic letters, Ἀγάπη οὐ ζητεῖ τὰ ἑαυτῆς, or rather, Ἀνὴρ καὶ γυνὴ ζυγάδα ἄνθρωπος ἰδιαίτατα, that is, *Vir et mulier junctim propriissime homo.* To wear about his neck, he had a golden chain, weighing twenty-five thousand and sixty-three marks of gold, the links thereof being made after the manner of great berries, amongst which were set in work green jaspers engraven and cut dragon-like, all environed with beams and sparks, as king Nicepsos of old was wont to wear them: and it reached down to the very bust of the rising of his belly, whereby he reaped great benefit all his life long, as the Greek physicians know well enough. For his gloves were put in work sixteen otters' skins, and three of the loup-garous, or men-eating wolves, for the bordering of them: and of this stuff were they made, by the appointment of the Cabalists of Sanlouand. As for the rings which his father would have him to wear, to renew the ancient mark of nobility, he had on the forefinger of his left hand a carbuncle as big as an ostrich's egg, enchased very daintily in gold of the fineness of a Turkey seraph. Upon the middle finger of the same hand he had a ring made of four metals together, of the strangest fashion that ever was seen; so that the steel did not crash against the gold, nor the silver crush the copper. All this was made by Captain Chappuys, and Alcofribas his good agent. On the medical finger of his right hand he had a ring made spire-wise, wherein was set a perfect Balas ruby, a pointed diamond, and a Physon emerald, of an inestimable value. For Hans Carvel, the king of Melinda's jeweller, esteemed them at the rate of threescore nine millions, eight hundred ninety-four thousand, and eighteen French crowns of Berry, and at so much did the Foucres of Augsburg prize them.

CHAP. IX.

The colours and liveries of Gargantua.

GARGANTUA'S colours were white and blue, as I have showed you before, by which his father would give us to understand that his son to him was a heavenly joy; for the white did signify gladness, pleasure, delight, and rejoicing, and the blue, celestial things. I know well enough that, in reading this, you laugh at the old drinker, and hold this exposition of colours to be very extravagant, and utterly disagreeable to reason, because white is said to signify faith, and blue constancy. But without moving, vexing, heating, or putting you in a chafe (for the weather is dangerous), answer me, if it please you; for no other compulsory way of arguing will I use towards you, or any else; only now and then I will mention a word or two of my bottle. What is it that induceth you, what stirs you up to believe, or who told you that white signifieth faith, and blue constancy? An old paltry book, say you, sold by the hawking pedlars and balladmongers, entitled The Blason of Colours. Who made it? Whoever it was, he was wise in that he did not set his name to it. But, besides, I know not what I should rather admire in him, his presumption or his sottishness. His presumption and overweening, for that he should without reason, without cause, or without any appearance of truth, have dared to prescribe, by his private authority, what things should be denotated and signified by the colour: which is the custom of tyrants, who will have their will to bear sway in stead of equity, and not of the wise and learned, who with the evidence of reason satisfy their readers. His sottishness and want of spirit, in that he thought that, without any other demonstration or sufficient argument, the world would be pleased to make his blockish and ridiculous impositions the rule of their devices. In effect, according to the proverb, To a shitten tail fails never ordure, he hath found, it seems, some simple ninny in those rude times of old, when the wearing of high round bonnets was in fashion, who gave some trust to his writings, according to which they carved and engraved their apophthegms and mottoes, trapped and caparisoned their mules and sumpter-horses, apparelled their pages, quartered their breeches, bordered their gloves, fringed the curtains and valances of their beds, painted their ensigns, composed songs, and, which is worse, placed many deceitful jugglings and unworthy base tricks undiscoveredly amongst the very chastest matrons and most reverend sciences. In the like darkness and mist of ignorance are wrapped up these vain-glorious courtiers and name-transposers, who, going about in their impresas to signify *esperance* (that is, hope), have portrayed a sphere—and birds' pennes for pains—*l'ancholie* (which is the flower colombine) for melancholy—a waning moon or crescent, to show the increasing or rising of one's fortune—a bench rotten and broken, to signify bankrupt—*non* and a *corslet* for *non dur habit* (otherwise *non durabit*, it shall not last), *un lit sans ciel*, that is, a bed without a tester, for *un licencié*, a graduated person, as bachelor in divinity or utter barrister-at-law; which are equivocals so absurd and witless, so barbarous and clownish, that a fox's tail should be fastened to the neck-piece of, and a vizard made of a cowsherd given to everyone that henceforth should offer, after the restitution of learning, to make use of any such fopperies in France.

By the same reasons (if reasons I should call them, and not ravings rather, and idle triflings about words), might I cause paint a pannier, to signify that I am in pain—a mustard-pot, that my heart tarries much for't—one pissing upwards for a bishop—the bottom of a pair of breeches for a vessel full of fart-hings—a codpiece for the office of the clerks of the sentences, decrees, or judgments, or rather, as the English bears it, for the tail of a codfish—and a dog's turd for the dainty turret wherein lies the love of my sweetheart. Far otherwise did heretofore the sages of Egypt, when they wrote by letters, which they called hieroglyphics, which none understood who were not skilled in the virtue, property, and nature of the things represented by them. Of which Orus Apollon hath in Greek composed two books, and Polyphilus, in his Dream of Love, set down more. In France you have a taste of them in the device or impresa of my Lord Admiral, which was carried before that time by Octavian Augustus. But my little skiff alongside these unpleasant gulfs and shoals will sail no further, therefore must I return to the port from whence I came. Yet do I hope one day to write more at large of these things, and to show both by philosophical arguments and authorities, received and approved of by and from all antiquity, what, and how many colours there are in nature, and what may be signified by every one of them, if God save the mould of my cap, which is my best wine-pot, as my grandam said.

CHAP. X.

Of that which is signified by the colours white and blue.

HE white therefore signifieth joy, solace, and gladness, and that not at random, but upon just and very good grounds: which you may perceive to be true, if laying aside all prejudicate affections, you will but give ear to what presently I shall expound unto you.

Aristotle saith that, supposing two things contrary in their kind, as good and evil, virtue and vice, heat and cold, white and black, pleasure and pain, joy and grief,—and so of others,—if you couple them in such manner that the contrary of one kind may agree in reason with the contrary of the other, it must follow by consequence that the other contrary must answer to the remanent opposite to that wherewith it is conferred. As, for example, virtue and vice are contrary in one kind, so are good and evil. If one of the contraries of the first kind be consonant to one of those of the second, as virtue and goodness, for it is clear that virtue is good, so shall the other two contraries, which are evil and vice, have the same connection, for vice is evil.

This logical rule being understood, take these two contraries, joy and sadness; then these other two, white and black, for they are physically contrary. If so be, then, that black do signify grief, by good reason then should white import joy. Nor is this signification instituted by human imposition, but by the universal consent of the world received, which philosophers call Jus Gentium, the Law of Nations, or an uncontrollable right of force in all countries whatsoever. For you know well enough that all people, and all languages and nations, except the ancient Syracusans and certain Argives, who had cross and thwarting souls, when they mean outwardly to give evidence of their sorrow, go in black; and all mourning is done with black. Which general consent is not without some argument and reason in nature, the which every man may by himself very suddenly comprehend, without the instruction of any—and this we call the law of nature. By virtue of the same natural instinct we know that by white all the world hath understood joy, gladness, mirth, pleasure, and delight. In former times the Thracians and Cretans did mark their good, propitious, and fortunate days with white stones, and their sad, dismal, and unfortunate ones with black. Is not the night mournful, sad, and melancholic? It is black and dark by the privation of light. Doth not the light comfort all the world? And it is more white than anything else. Which to prove, I could direct you to the book of Laurentius Valla against Bartolus; but an evangelical testimony I hope will content you. Matth. 17 it is said that, at the transfiguration of our Lord, *Vestimenta ejus facta sunt alba sicut lux*, his apparel was made white like the light. By which lightsome whiteness he gave his three apostles to understand the idea and figure of the eternal joys; for by the light are all men comforted, according to the word of the old woman, who, although she had never a tooth in her head, was wont to say, *Bona lux*. And Tobit, chap. 5, after he had lost his sight, when Raphael saluted him, answered, *What joy can I have, that do not see the light of Heaven?* In that colour did the angels testify the joy of the whole world at the resurrection of our Saviour, John 20, and at his ascension, Acts 1. With the like colour of vesture did St. John the Evangelist, Apoc. 4. 7, see the faithful clothed in the heavenly and blessed Jerusalem.

Read the ancient, both Greek and Latin histories, and you shall find that the town of Alba (the first pattern of Rome) was founded and so named by reason of a white sow that was seen there. You shall likewise find in those stories, that when any man, after he had vanquished his enemies, was by decree of the senate to enter into Rome triumphantly, he usually rode in a chariot drawn by white horses: which in the ovation triumph was also the custom; for by no sign or colour would they so significantly express the joy of their coming as by the white. You shall there also find, how Pericles, the general of the Athenians, would needs have that part of his army unto whose lot befell the white beans, to spend the whole day in mirth, pleasure, and ease, whilst the rest were a-fighting. A thousand other examples and places could I allege to this purpose, but that it is not here where I should do it.

By understanding hereof, you may resolve one problem, which Alexander Aphrodiseus hath accounted unanswerable: why the lion, who with his only cry and roaring affrights all beasts, dreads and feareth only a white cock? For, as Proclus saith, *Libro de Sacrificio et Magia*, it is because the presence of the virtue of the sun, which is the organ and promptuary of all terrestrial and sidereal light, doth more symbolize and agree with a white cock, as well in regard of that colour, as of his property and specifical quality, than with a lion. He saith, furthermore, that devils have been often seen in the shape of lions, which at the sight of a white cock have presently vanished. This is the cause why Galli or Gallices (so are the Frenchmen called, because they are naturally white as milk, which the Greeks call Gala,) do willingly wear in their caps white feathers, for by nature they are of a candid disposition, merry, kind, gracious, and well-beloved, and for their cognizance and arms have the whitest flower of any, the Flower de luce or Lily.

If you demand how, by white, nature would have us understand joy and gladness, I answer, that the analogy and uniformity is thus. For, as the white doth outwardly disperse and scatter the rays of the sight, whereby the optic spirits are manifestly dissolved, according to the opinion of Aristotle in his problems and perspective treatises; as you may likewise perceive by experience, when you pass over mountains covered with snow, how you will complain that you cannot see well; as Xenophon writes to have happened to his men, and as Galen very largely declareth, *lib*. 10, *de usu partium:* just so the heart with excessive joy is inwardly dilated, and suffereth a manifest resolution of the vital spirits, which may go so far on that it may thereby be deprived of its nourishment, and by consequence of life itself, by this perichary or extremity of gladness, as Galen saith, *lib*. 12, *method, lib*. 5, *de locis affectis, and lib*. 2, *de symptomatum causis*. And as it hath come to pass in former times, witness Marcus Tullius, *lib*. 1, *Quæst. Tuscul*., Verrius, Aristotle, Titus Livius, in his relation of the battle of Cannæ, Plinius, *lib*. 7, *cap*. 32 *and* 34, A. Gellius, *lib*. 3, *c*. 15, and many other writers,—to Diagoras the Rhodian, Chilon, Sophocles, Dionysius the tyrant of Sicily, Philippides, Philemon, Polycrates, Philistion, M. Juventi, and others who died with joy. And as Avicen speaketh, *in* 2 *canon et lib. de virib. cordis*, of the saffron, that it doth so rejoice the heart that, if you take of it excessively, it will by a superfluous resolution and dilation deprive it altogether of life. Here peruse Alex. Aphrodiseus, *lib* 1, *Probl*., *cap*. 19, and that for a cause. But what? It seems I am entered further into this point than I intended at the first. Here, therefore, will I strike sail, referring the rest to that book of mine which handleth this matter to the full. Meanwhile, in a word I will tell you, that blue doth certainly signify heaven and heavenly things, by the same very tokens and symbols that white signifieth joy and pleasure.

CHAP. XI.

Of the youthful age of Gargantua.

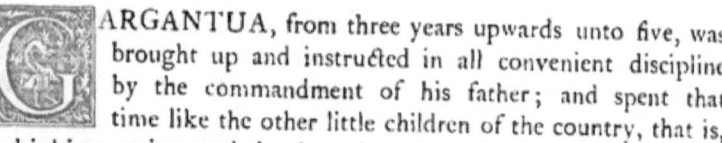ARGANTUA, from three years upwards unto five, was brought up and instructed in all convenient discipline by the commandment of his father; and spent that time like the other little children of the country, that is, in drinking, eating, and sleeping: in eating, sleeping, and drinking: and in sleeping, drinking, and eating. Still he wallowed and rolled up and down himself in the mire and dirt—he blurred and sullied his nose with filth—he blotted and smutched his face with any kind of scurvy stuff—he trod down his shoes in the heel—at the flies he did oftentimes yawn, and ran very heartily after the butterflies, the empire whereof belonged to his father. He pissed in his shoes, shit in his shirt, and wiped his nose on his sleeve—he did let his snot and snivel fall in his pottage, and dabbled, paddled, and slobbered everywhere—he would drink in his slipper, and ordinarily rub his belly against a pannier. He sharpened his teeth with a top, washed his hands with his broth, and combed his head with a bowl. He would sit down betwixt two stools, and his arse to the ground—would cover himself with a wet sack, and drink in eating of his soup. He did eat his cake sometimes without bread, would bite in laughing, and laugh in biting. Oftentimes did he spit in the basin, and fart for fatness, piss against the sun, and hide himself in the water for fear of rain. He would strike out of the cold iron, be often in the dumps, and frig and wriggle it. He would flay the fox, say the ape's paternoster, return to his sheep, and turn the hogs to the hay. He would beat the dogs before the lion, put the plough before the oxen, and claw where it did not itch. He would pump one to draw somewhat out of him, by griping all would hold fast nothing, and always eat his white bread first. He shoed the geese, kept a self-tickling to make himself laugh, and was very steadable in the kitchen:

made a mock at the gods, would cause sing Magnificat at matins, and found it very convenient so to do. He would eat cabbage, and shite beets,—knew flies in a dish of milk, and would make them lose their feet. He would scrape paper, blur parchment, then run away as hard as he could. He would pull at the kid's leather, or vomit up his dinner, then reckon without his host. He would beat the bushes without catching the birds, thought the moon was made of green cheese, and that bladders are lanterns. Out of one sack he would take two moultures or fees for grinding; would act the ass's part to get some bran, and of his fist would make a mallet. He took the cranes at the first leap, and would have the mail-coats to be made link after link. He always looked a given horse in the mouth, leaped from the cock to the ass, and put one ripe between two green. By robbing Peter he paid Paul, he kept the moon from the wolves, and hoped to catch larks if ever the heavens should fall. He did make of necessity virtue, of such bread such pottage, and cared as little for the peeled as for the shaven. Every morning he did cast up his gorge, and his father's little dogs eat out of the dish with him, and he with them. He would bite their ears, and they would scratch his nose—he would blow in their arses, and they would lick his chaps.

But hearken, good fellows, the spigot ill betake you, and whirl round your brains, if you do not give ear! This little lecher was always groping his nurses and governesses, upside down, arsiversy, topsyturvy, harri bourriquet, with a Yacco haick, hyck gio! handling them very rudely in jumbling and tumbling them to keep them going; for he had already begun to exercise the tools, and put his codpiece in practice. Which codpiece, or braguette, his governesses did every day deck up and adorn with fair nosegays, curious rubies, sweet flowers, and fine silken tufts, and very pleasantly would pass their time in taking you know what between their fingers, and dandling it, till it did revive and creep up to the bulk and stiffness of a suppository, or street magdaleon, which is a hard rolled-up salve spread upon leather. Then did they burst out in laughing, when they saw it lift up its ears, as if the sport had liked them. One of them would call it her little dille, her staff of love, her quillety, her faucetin, her dandilolly. Another, her peen, her jolly kyle, her bableret, her membretoon, her quickset imp: another again, her branch of coral, her female adamant, her placket-racket, her Cyprian sceptre, her jewel for ladies. And some of the other women would give it these names,—my bunguetee, my stopple too, my bush-rusher, my gallant wimble, my pretty borer, my coney-burrow-ferret, my little piercer, my augretine, my dangling hangers, down right to it, stiff and stout, in and to, my pusher, dresser, pouting stick, my honey pipe, my pretty pillicock, linky pinky, futilletie, my lusty andouille, and crimson chitterling, my little couille bredouille, my pretty rogue, and so forth. It belongs to me, said one. It is mine, said the other. What, quoth a third, shall I have no share in it? By my faith, I will cut it then. Ha, to cut it, said the other, would hurt him. Madam, do you cut little children's things? Were his cut off, he would be then *Monsieur sans queue*, the curtailed master. And that he might play and sport himself after the manner of the other little children of the country, they made him a fair weather whirl-jack of the wings of the windmill of Myrebalais.

CHAP. XII.

Of Gargantua's wooden horses.

AFTERWARDS, that he might be all his lifetime a good rider, they made to him a fair great horse of wood, which he did make leap, curvet, jerk out behind, and skip forward, all at a time: to pace, trot, rack, gallop, amble, to play the hobby, the hackney-gelding: go the gait of the camel, and of the wild ass. He made him also change his colour of hair, as the monks of Coultibo (according to the variety of their holidays) use to do their clothes, from bay brown, to sorrel, dapple-grey, mouse-dun, deer-colour, roan, cow-colour, gingioline, skewed colour, piebald, and the colour of the savage elk.

Himself of a huge big post made a hunting nag, and another for daily service of the beam of a vinepress: and of a great oak made up a mule, with a footcloth, for his chamber. Besides this, he had ten or twelve spare horses, and seven horses for post; and all these were lodged in his own chamber, close by his bedside. One day the Lord of Breadinbag[1] came to visit his father in great bravery, and

[1] Painensac.

with a gallant train : and, at the same time, to see him came likewise the Duke of Freemeal and the Earl of Wetgullet.[1] The house truly for so many guests at once was somewhat narrow, but especially the stables; whereupon the steward and harbinger of the said Lord Breadinbag, to know if there were any other empty stable in the house, came to Gargantua, a little young lad, and secretly asked him where the stables of the great horses were, thinking that children would be ready to tell all. Then he led them up along the stairs of the castle, passing by the second hall unto a broad great gallery, by which they entered into a large tower, and as they were going up at another pair of stairs, said the harbinger to the steward, This child deceives us, for the stables are never on the top of the house. You may be mistaken, said the steward, for I know some places at Lyons, at the Basmette, at Chaisnon, and elsewhere, which have their stables at the very tops of the houses : so it may be that behind the house there is a way to come to this ascent. But I will question with him further. Then said he to Gargantua, My pretty little boy, whither do you lead us? To the stable, said he, of my great horses. We are almost come to it; we have but these stairs to go up at. Then leading them alongst another great hall, he brought them into his chamber, and, opening the door, said unto them, This is the stable you ask for; this is my jennet; this is my gelding; this is my courser, and this is my hackney, and laid on them with a great lever. I will bestow upon you, said he, this Friesland horse ; I had him from Frankfort, yet will I give him you; for he is a pretty little nag, and will go very well, with a tessel of goshawks, half a dozen of spaniels, and a brace of greyhounds: thus are you king of the hares and partridges for all this winter. By St. John, said they, now we are paid, he hath gleeked us to some purpose, bobbed we are now for ever. I deny it, said he,—he was not here above three days. Judge you now, whether they had most cause, either to hide their heads for shame, or to laugh at the jest. As they were going down again thus amazed, he asked them, Will you have a whimwham ?[2] What is that, said they? It is, said he, five turds to make you a muzzle. To-day, said the steward, though we happen to be roasted, we shall not be burnt, for we are pretty well quipped and larded, in my opinion. O my jolly dapper boy, thou hast given us a gudgeon ; I hope to see thee Pope before I die. I think so, said he, myself;

---

[1] Francrepas. Mouillevent.   [2] Aubeliere.

and then shall you be a puppy, and this gentle popinjay a perfect papelard, that is, dissembler. Well, well, said the harbinger. But, said Gargantua, guess how many stitches there are in my mother's smock. Sixteen, quoth the harbinger. You do not speak gospel, said Gargantua, for there is cent before, and cent behind, and you did not reckon them ill, considering the two under holes. When? said the harbinger. Even then, said Gargantua, when they made a shovel of your nose to take up a quarter of dirt, and of your throat a funnel, wherewith to put it into another vessel, because the bottom of the old one was out. Cocksbod, said the steward, we have met with a prater. Farewell, master tattler, God keep you, so goodly are the words which you come out with, and so fresh in your mouth, that it had need to be salted.

Thus going down in great haste, under the arch of the stairs they let fall the great lever, which he had put upon their backs; whereupon Gargantua said, What a devil! you are, it seems, but bad horsemen, that suffer your bilder to fail you when you need him most. If you were to go from hence to Cahusac, whether had you rather, ride on a gosling or lead a sow in a leash? I had rather drink, said the harbinger. With this they entered into the lower hall, where the company was, and relating to them this new story, they made them laugh like a swarm of flies.

CHAP. XIII.

How Gargantua's wonderful understanding became known to his father Grangousier, by the invention of a torcheul or wipebreech.

ABOUT the end of the fifth year, Grangousier returning from the conquest of the Canarians, went by the way to see his son Gargantua. There was he filled with joy, as such a father might be at the sight of such a child of his: and whilst he kissed and embraced him, he asked many childish questions of him about divers matters, and drank very freely with him and with his governesses, of whom in great earnest he asked, amongst other things, whether they had been careful to keep him clean and sweet. To this Gargantua answered,

that he had taken such a course for that himself, that in all the country there was not to be found a cleanlier boy than he. How is that? said Grangousier. I have, answered Gargantua, by a long and curious experience, found out a means to wipe my bum, the most lordly, the most excellent, and the most convenient that ever was seen. What is that? said Grangousier, how is it? I will tell you by-and-by, said Gargantua. Once I did wipe me with a gentlewoman's velvet mask, and found it to be good; for the softness of the silk was very voluptuous and pleasant to my fundament. Another time with one of their hoods, and in like manner that was comfortable. At another time with a lady's neckerchief, and after that I wiped me with some ear-pieces of hers made of crimson satin, but there was such a number of golden spangles in them (turdy round things, a pox take them) that they fetched away all the skin of my tail with a vengeance. Now I wish St. Antony's fire burn the bum-gut of the goldsmith that made them, and of her that wore them! This hurt I cured by wiping myself with a page's cap, garnished with a feather after the Switzers' fashion.

Afterwards, in dunging behind a bush, I found a March-cat, and with it I wiped my breech, but her claws were so sharp that they scratched and exulcerated all my perinee. Of this I recovered the next morning thereafter, by wiping myself with my mother's gloves, of a most excellent perfume and scent of the Arabian Benin. After that I wiped me with sage, with fennel, with anet, with marjoram, with roses, with gourd-leaves, with beets, with colewort, with leaves of the vine-tree, with mallows, wool-blade, which is a tail-scarlet, with lettuce, and with spinach leaves. All this did very great good to my leg. Then with mercury, with parsley, with nettles, with comfrey, but that gave me the bloody flux of Lombardy, which I healed by wiping me with my braguette. Then I wiped my tail in the sheets, in the coverlet, in the curtains, with a cushion, with arras hangings, with a green carpet, with a table-cloth, with a napkin, with a handkerchief, with a combing-cloth; in all which I found more pleasure than do the mangy dogs when you rub them. Yea, but, said Grangousier, which torchecul did you find to be the best? I was coming to it, said Gargantua, and by-and-by shall you hear the *tu autem*, and know the whole mystery and knot of the matter. I wiped myself with hay, with straw, with thatch-rushes, with flax, with wool, with paper, but,

Who his foul tail with paper wipes,
Shall at his ballocks leave some chips.

What, said Grangousier, my little rogue, hast thou been at the pot, that thou dost rhyme already? Yes, yes, my lord the king, answered Gargantua, I can rhyme gallantly, and rhyme till I become hoarse with rheum. Hark, what our privy says to the skiters:

> Shittard,
> Squirtard,
> Crackard,
>   Turdous,
> Thy bung
> Hath flung
> Some dung
>   On us:
> Filthard,
> Cackard,
> Stinkard,
>   St. Antony's fire seize on
>   thy toane [bone?],
> If thy
> Dirty
> Dounby
>   Thou do not wipe, ere
>   thou be gone.

Will you have any more of it? Yes, yes, answered Grangousier. Then, said Gargantua,

A ROUNDELAY.

> In shitting yes'day I did know
> The sess I to my arse did owe:
> The smell was such came from that slunk,
> That I was with it all bestunk:
> O had but then some brave Signor
> Brought her to me I waited for,
>   In shitting!

I would have cleft her watergap,
And join'd it close to my flipflap,
Whilst she had with her fingers guarded
My foul nockandrow, all bemerded
In shitting.

Now say that I can do nothing! By the Merdi, they are not of my making, but I heard them of this good old grandam, that you see here, and ever since have retained them in the budget of my memory.

Let us return to our purpose, said Grangousier. What, said Gargantua, to skite? No, said Grangousier, but to wipe our tail. But, said Gargantua, will not you be content to pay a puncheon of Breton wine, if I do not blank and gravel you in this matter, and put you to a non-plus? Yes, truly, said Grangousier.

There is no need of wiping one's tail, said Gargantua, but when it is foul; foul it cannot be, unless one have been a-skiting; skite then we must before we wipe our tails. O my pretty little waggish boy, said Grangousier, what an excellent wit thou hast? I will make thee very shortly proceed doctor in the jovial quirks of gay learning, and that, by G—, for thou hast more wit than age. Now, I prithee, go on in this torcheculative, or wipe-bummatory discourse, and by my beard I swear, for one puncheon, thou shalt have threescore pipes, I mean of the good Breton wine, not that which grows in Britain, but in the good country of Verron. Afterwards I wiped my bum, said Gargantua, with a kerchief, with a pillow, with a pantoufle, with a pouch, with a pannier, but that was a wicked and unpleasant torchecul; then with a hat. Of hats, note that some are shorn, and others shaggy, some velveted, others covered with taffeties, and others with satin. The best of all these is the shaggy hat, for it makes a very neat abstersion of the fecal matter.

Afterwards I wiped my tail with a hen, with a cock, with a pullet, with a calf's skin, with a hare, with a pigeon, with a cormorant, with an attorney's bag, with a montero, with a coif, with a falconer's lure. But, to conclude, I say and maintain, that of all torcheculs, arsewisps, bumfodders, tail-napkins, bunghole cleansers, and wipe-breeches, there is none in the world comparable to the neck of a goose, that is well downed, if you hold her head betwixt your legs. And believe me therein upon mine honour, for you will thereby feel in your nockhole a most wonderful pleasure, both in regard of the softness of the said down and of the temperate heat of the goose, which is easily communicated to the bum-gut and the rest of the inwards, in so far as to come even to the regions of the heart and brains. And think not that the felicity of the heroes and demigods in the Elysian fields consisteth either in their asphodel, ambrosia, or nectar, as our old women here used to say; but in this, according to my judgment, that they wipe their tails with the neck of a goose, holding her head betwixt their legs, and such is the opinion of Master John of Scotland, alias Scotus.

CHAP. XIV.

How Gargantua was taught Latin by a Sophister.

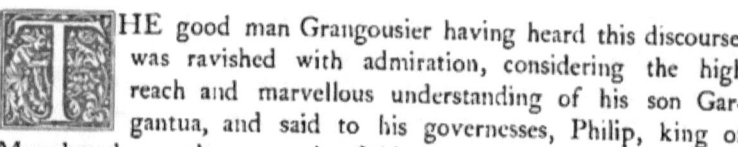

THE good man Grangousier having heard this discourse, was ravished with admiration, considering the high reach and marvellous understanding of his son Gargantua, and said to his governesses, Philip, king of Macedon, knew the great wit of his son Alexander by his skilful managing of a horse; for his horse Bucephalus was so fierce and unruly that none durst adventure to ride him, after that he had given to his riders such devilish falls, breaking the neck of this man, the other man's leg, braining one, and putting another out of his jawbone. This by Alexander being considered, one day in the hippodrome (which was a place appointed for the breaking and managing of great horses), he perceived that the fury of the horse proceeded merely from the fear he had of his own shadow, whereupon getting on his back, he run him against the sun, so that the shadow fell behind, and by that means tamed the horse and brought him to his hand. Whereby his father, knowing the divine judgment that was in him, caused him most carefully to be instructed by Aristotle, who at that time was highly renowned above all the philosophers of Greece. After the same manner I tell you, that by this only discourse, which now I have here had before you with my son Gargantua, I know that his understanding doth participate of some divinity, and that, if he be well taught, and have that education which is fitting, he will attain to a supreme degree of wisdom.

Therefore will I commit him to some learned man, to have him indoctrinated according to his capacity, and will spare no cost. Presently they appointed him a great sophister-doctor, called Master Tubal Holofernes, who taught him his A B C so well, that he could say it by heart backwards; and about this he was five years and three months. Then read he to him Donat, Le Facet, Theodolet, and Alanus *in parabolis*. About this he was thirteen years, six months, and two weeks. But you must remark that in the mean time he did learn to write in Gothic characters, and that he wrote all his books—for the art of printing was not then in use—and did ordinarily carry a great pen and inkhorn, weighing about seven thousand quintals (that is, 700,000 pound weight), the penner whereof was as big and as long as the great pillars of Enay, and the horn was hanging to it in great iron chains, it being of the wideness of a tun of merchant ware. After that he read unto him the book *de modis significandi*, with the commentaries of Hurtbise, of Fasquin, of Tropdieux, of Gualhaut, of John Calf, of Billonio, of Berlinguandus, and a rabble of others; and herein he spent more than eighteen years and eleven months, and was so well versed in it that, to try masteries in school disputes with his condisciples, he would recite it by heart backwards, and did sometimes prove on his finger-ends to his mother, *quod de modis significandi non erat scientia*. Then did he read to him the compost for knowing the age of the moon, the seasons of the year, and tides of the sea, on which he spent sixteen years and two months, and that justly at the time that his said preceptor died of the French pox, which was in the year one thousand four hundred and twenty. Afterwards he got an old coughing fellow to teach him, named Master Jobelin Bridé, or muzzled dolt, who read unto him Hugutio, Hebrard['s] *Grecism*, the Doctrinal, the Parts, the *Quid est*, the *Supplementum*, Marmotretus, *De moribus in mensa servandis*, Seneca *de quatuor virtutibus cardinalibus*, Passavantus *cum commento*, and *Dormi secure* for the holidays, and some other of such like mealy stuff, by reading whereof he became as wise as any we ever since baked in an oven.

CHAP. XV.

How Gargantua was put under other schoolmasters.

AT the last his father perceived that indeed he studied hard, and that, although he spent all his time in it, he did nevertheless profit nothing, but which is worse, grew thereby foolish, simple, doted, and blockish, whereof making a heavy regret to Don Philip of Marays, Viceroy or Deputy King of Papeligosse, he found that it were better for him to learn nothing at all, than to be taught such-like books, under such schoolmasters; because their knowledge was nothing but brutishness, and their wisdom but blunt foppish toys, serving only to bastardize good and noble spirits, and to corrupt all the flower of youth. That it is so, take, said he, any young boy of this time who hath only studied two years,—if he have not a better judgment, a better discourse, and that expressed in better terms than your son, with a completer carriage and civility to all manner of persons, account me for ever hereafter a very clounch and bacon-slicer of Brene. This pleased Grangousier very well, and he commanded that it should be done. At night at supper, the said Des Marays brought in a young page of his, of Ville-gouges, called Eudemon, so neat, so trim, so handsome in his apparel, so spruce, with his hair in so good order, and so sweet and comely in his behaviour, that he had the resemblance of a little angel more than of a human creature. Then he said to Grangousier, Do you see this young boy? He is not as yet full twelve years old. Let us try, if it please you, what difference there is betwixt the knowledge of the doting Mateologians of old time and the young lads that are now. The trial pleased Grangousier, and he commanded the page to begin. Then Eudemon, asking leave of the vice-king his master so to do, with his cap in his hand, a clear and open countenance, beautiful and ruddy lips, his eyes steady, and his looks fixed upon Gargantua with a youthful modesty, standing up straight on his feet, began very gracefully to commend him; first, for his virtue and good manners; secondly, for his knowledge; thirdly, for his nobility; fourthly, for his bodily accomplishments; and, in the fifth place, most sweetly exhorted him to reverence his father with all due observancy, who was so careful to have him well brought up. In the end he prayed him, that he would vouchsafe to admit of him amongst the least of his servants; for other favour at that time desired he none of heaven, but that he might do him some grateful and acceptable service. All this was by him delivered with such proper gestures, such distinct pronunciation, so pleasant a delivery, in such exquisite fine terms, and so good Latin, that he seemed rather a Gracchus, a Cicero, an Æmilius of the time past, than a youth of this age. But all the countenance that Gargantua kept was, that he fell to crying like a cow, and cast down his face, hiding it with his cap, nor could they possibly draw one word from him, no more than a fart from a dead ass. Whereat his father was so grievously vexed that he would have killed Master Jobelin, but the said Des Marays withheld him from it by fair persuasions, so that at length he pacified his wrath. Then Grangousier commanded he should be paid his wages, that they should whittle him up soundly, like a sophister, with good drink, and then give him leave to go to all the devils in hell. At least, said he, to-day shall it not cost his host much if by chance he should die as drunk as a Switzer. Master Jobelin being gone out of the house, Grangousier consulted with the Viceroy what schoolmaster they should choose for him, and it was betwixt them resolved that Ponocrates, the tutor of Eudemon, should have the charge, and that they should go altogether to Paris, to know what was the study of the young men of France at that time.

CHAP. XVI.

How Gargantua was sent to Paris, and of the huge great mare that he rode on; how she destroyed the oxflies of the Beauce.

IN the same season Fayoles, the fourth King of Numidia, sent out of the country of Africa to Grangousier the most hideously great mare that ever was seen, and of the strangest form, for you know well enough how it is said that Africa always is productive of some new thing. She was as big as six elephants, and had her feet cloven into fingers, like Julius Cæsar's horse, with slouch-hanging ears, like the goats in Languedoc, and a little horn on her buttock. She was of a burnt sorrel hue, with a little mixture of dapple-grey spots, but above all she had a horrible tail; for it was little more or less than every whit as great as the steeple-pillar of St. Mark beside Langes: and squared as that is, with tuffs and ennicroches or hair-plaits wrought within one another, no otherwise than as the beards are upon the ears of corn.

If you wonder at this, wonder rather at the tails of the Scythian rams, which weighed above thirty pounds each; and of the Surian sheep, who need, if Tenaud say true, a little cart at their heels to bear up their tail, it is so long and heavy. You female lechers in the plain countries have no such tails. And she was brought by sea in three carricks and a brigantine unto the harbour of Olone in Thalmondois. When Grangousier saw her, Here is, said he, what is fit to carry my son to Paris. So now, in the name of God, all will be well. He will in times coming be a great scholar. If it were not, my masters, for the beasts, we should live like clerks. The next morning—after they had drunk, you must understand—they took their journey; Gargantua, his pedagogue Ponocrates, and his train, and with them Eudemon, the young page. And because the weather was fair and temperate, his father caused to be made for him a pair of dun boots,—Babin calls them buskins. Thus did they merrily pass their time in travelling on their high way, always making good cheer, and were very pleasant till they came a little above Orleans, in which place there was a forest of five-and-thirty leagues long, and seventeen in breadth, or thereabouts. This forest was most horribly fertile and copious in dorflies, hornets, and wasps, so that it was a very purgatory for the poor mares, asses, and horses. But Gargantua's mare did avenge herself handsomely of all the outrages therein committed upon beasts of her kind, and that by a trick whereof they had no suspicion. For as soon as ever they were entered into the said forest, and that the wasps had given the assault, she drew out and unsheathed her tail, and therewith skirmishing, did so sweep them that she overthrew all the wood alongst and athwart, here and there, this way and that way, longwise and sidewise, over and under, and felled everywhere the wood with as much ease as a mower doth the grass, in such sort that never since hath there been there neither wood nor dorflies: for all the country was thereby reduced to a plain champaign field. Which Gargantua took great pleasure to behold, and said to his company no more but this: *Je trouve beau ce* (I find this pretty); whereupon that country hath been ever since that time called Beauce. But all the breakfast the mare got that day was but a little yawning and gaping, in memory whereof the gentlemen of Beauce do as yet to this day break their fast with gaping, which they find to be very good, and do spit the better for it. At last they came to Paris, where Gargantua refreshed himself two or three days, making very merry with his folks, and inquiring what men of learning there were then in the city, and what wine they drunk there.

CHAP. XVII.

How Gargantua paid his welcome to the Parisians, and how he took away the great bells of Our Lady's Church.

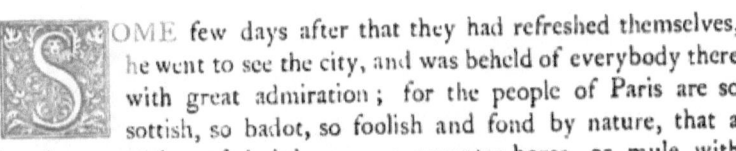OME few days after that they had refreshed themselves, he went to see the city, and was beheld of everybody there with great admiration; for the people of Paris are so sottish, so badot, so foolish and fond by nature, that a juggler, a carrier of indulgences, a sumpter-horse, or mule with cymbals or tinkling bells, a blind fiddler in the middle of a cross

lane, shall **draw a greater confluence of people together than an** evangelical preacher. And they pressed so hard upon him that he was constrained **to rest himself upon** the towers of Our Lady's Church. At which place, seeing so many about him, he said with a loud voice, **I believe that** these buzzards will have me to pay them here my welcome hither, and my *Proficiat*. It is but good reason. I will now give them their wine, but it shall be only in sport. Then smiling, he untied his fair braguette, and drawing out his mentul into the open air, he so bitterly all-to-bepissed them, that he drowned two hundred and sixty thousand, four hundred and eighteen, besides **the women and** little children. Some, nevertheless, of the company escaped this piss-flood by **mere speed** of foot, who, when they were at the higher end of the university, sweating, coughing, spitting, and out of breath, they began to swear and curse, some in good hot earnest, and others in jest. Carimari, carimara : golynoly, golynolo. By my sweet Sanctess, we are washed in sport, a sport truly to laugh at ;—in French, *Par ris*, for which that city hath been ever since called Paris; whose name formerly was Leucotia, as Strabo testifieth, *lib. quarto*, from **the Greek word** λευκότης, whiteness,—because of the white thighs of the ladies of that place. And forasmuch as, at **this imposition of a** new name, all the people that were there swore everyone by the Sancts of his parish, the Parisians, which are **patched up of all** nations and all pieces of countries, are by nature **both good jurors and good jurists, and somewhat overweening ;** whereupon Joanninus de Barrauco, *libro de copiositate reverentiarum*, thinks that they are called Parisians from the Greek word παρρησία, **which signifies** boldness and liberty in speech. This done, he considered the great bells, which were in the said towers, and made **them sound very** harmoniously. Which whilst he was doing, it came into his mind that they would serve very well for tingling tantans and ringing campanels to hang about his mare's neck when she should be sent back to his father, as he intended to do, loaded with Brie cheese and fresh herring. And indeed he forthwith carried them to **his** lodging. In the meanwhile there came a master beggar of the friars of St. Anthony to demand in his canting way the usual benevolence of some hoggish stuff, who, that he might be heard afar off, and to make **the** bacon he **was in quest** of shake in the very chimneys, made account to filch them away privily. Nevertheless, he left them behind **very honestly, not** for that they were too hot, but that they were somewhat too heavy for his carriage. This was not he of Bourg, for he was too good a friend of mine. All the city was risen up in sedition, they being, as you know, upon any slight occasion, so ready to uproars and insurrections, that foreign nations wonder at the patience of the kings of France, who do not by good justice restrain them from such tumultuous courses, seeing the manifold inconveniences which thence arise from day to day. Would to God I knew the shop wherein are forged these divisions and factious combinations, that I might bring them to light in the confraternities of my parish! Believe for a truth, that the place wherein the people gathered together, were thus sulphured, hopurymated, moiled, and bepissed, was called Nesle, where then was, but now is no more, the oracle of Leucotia. There was the case proposed, and the inconvenience showed of the transporting of the bells. After they had well ergoted pro and con, they concluded in baralipton, that they should send the oldest and most sufficient of the faculty unto Gargantua, to signify unto him the great and horrible prejudice they sustain by the want of those bells. And notwithstanding the good reasons given in by some of the university why this charge was fitter for an orator than a sophister, there was chosen for this purpose our Master Janotus de Bragmardo.

CHAP. XVIII.

How Janotus de Bragmardo was sent to Gargantua to recover the great bells.

MASTER JANOTUS, with his hair cut round like a dish *à la Cæsarine*, in his most antique accoutrement liripipionated with a graduate's hood, and having sufficiently antidoted his stomach with oven-marmalades, that is, bread and holy water of the cellar, transported himself to the lodging of Gargantua, driving before him three red-muzzled beadles, and dragging after him five or six artless masters, all thoroughly bedaggled with the mire of the streets. At their entry Ponocrates met them, who was afraid, seeing them so disguised, and thought they had been some masquers out of their wits, which moved him

to inquire of one of the said artless masters of the company what this mummery meant. It was answered him, that they desired to have their bells restored to them. As soon as Ponocrates heard that, he ran in all haste to carry the news unto Gargantua, that he might be ready to answer them, and speedily resolve what was to be done. Gargantua being advertised hereof, called apart his schoolmaster Ponocrates, Philotimus, steward of his house, Gymnastes, his esquire, and Eudemon, and very summarily conferred with them, both of what he should do and what answer he should give. They were all of opinion that they should bring them unto the goblet-office, which is the buttery, and there make them drink like roysters and line their jackets soundly. And that this cougher might not be puffed up with vain-glory by thinking the bells were restored at his request, they sent, whilst he was chopining and plying the pot, for the mayor of the city, the rector of the faculty, and the vicar of the church, unto whom they resolved to deliver the bells before the sophister had propounded his commission. After that, in their hearing, he should pronounce his gallant oration, which was done; and they being come, the sophister was brought in full hall, and began as followeth, in coughing.

CHAP. XIX.

The oration of Master Janotus de Bragmardo for recovery of the bells.

HEM, hem, gud-day, sirs, gud-day. *Et vobis*, my masters. It were but reason that you should restore to us our bells; for we have great need of them. Hem, hem, aihfuhash. We have oftentimes heretofore refused good money for them of those of London in Cahors, yea and those of Bourdeaux in Brie, who would have bought them for the substantific quality of the elementary complexion, which is intronificated in the terrestreity of their quidditative nature, to extraneize the blasting mists and whirlwinds upon our vines, indeed not ours, but these round about us. For if we lose the piot and liquor of the grape, we lose all, both sense and law. If you restore them unto us at my request, I shall gain by it six basketfuls of sausages and a fine pair of breeches, which will do my legs a great deal of good, or else they will not keep their promise to me. Ho by gob, *Domine*, a pair of breeches is good, *et vir sapiens non abhorrebit eam.* Ha, ha, a pair of breeches is not so easily got; I have experience of it myself. Consider, *Domine*, I have been these eighteen days in matagrabolizing this brave speech. *Reddite quæ sunt Cæsaris, Cæsari, et quæ sunt Dei, Deo. Ibi jacet lepus.* By my faith, *Domine*, if you will sup with me in *cameris*, by cox body, *charitatis, nos faciemus bonum cherubin. Ego occiditunum porcum, et ego habet bonum vino:* but of good wine we cannot make bad Latin. Well, *de parte Dei date nobis bellas nostras.* Hold, I give you in the name of the faculty a *Sermones de Utino*, that *utinam* you would give us our bells. *Vultis etiam pardonos? Per diem vos habebitis, et nihil payabitis.* O sir, *Domine, bellagivaminor nobis;* verily, *est bonum vobis.* They are useful to everybody. If they fit your mare well, so do they do our faculty; *quæ comparata est jumentis insipientibus, et similis facta est eis, Psalmo nescio quo.* Yet did I quote it in my note-book, *et est unum bonum* Achilles, a good defending argument. Hem, hem, hem, haikhash! For I prove unto you, that you should give me them. *Ego sic argumentor. Omnis bella bellabilis in bellerio bellando, bellans bellativo, bellare facit, bellabiliter bellantes. Parisius habet bellas. Ergo gluc,* Ha, ha, ha. This is spoken to some purpose. It is *in tertio primæ*, in *Darii*, or elsewhere. By my soul, I have seen the time that I could play the devil in arguing, but now I am much failed, and henceforward want nothing but a cup of good wine, a good bed, my back to the fire, my belly to the table, and a good deep dish. Hei, *Domine*, I beseech you, *in nomine Patris, Filii, et Spiritûs sancti, Amen,* to restore unto us our bells: and God keep you from evil, and our Lady from health, *qui vivit et regnat per omnia secula seculorum, Amen.* Hem, hashchehhawksash, qzrchremhemhash.

Verum enim vero, quandoquidem, dubio procul. Edepol, quoniam, ita certe, medius fidius; a town without bells is like a blind man without a staff, an ass without a crupper, and a cow without cymbals. Therefore be assured, until you have restored them unto us, we will never leave crying after you, like a blind man that hath lost his staff, braying like an ass without a crupper, and making a noise like a cow without cymbals. A certain latinisator, dwelling near the hospital, said since, producing the authority of one Taponnus,—I lie, it was one Pontanus the secular poet,—who wished those bells had been made of feathers, and the clapper of a foxtail, to the end they might have begot a chronicle in the bowels of his brain, when he was about the composing of his carminiformal lines. But nac petetin petetac, tic, torche lorgne, or rot kipipur kipipot put pantse malf, he was declared an heretic. We make them as of wax. And no more saith the deponent. *Valete et plaudite. Calepinus recensui.*

CHAP. XX.

How the Sophister carried away his cloth, and how he had a suit in law against the other masters.

THE sophister had no sooner ended, but Ponocrates and Eudemon burst out in a laughing so heartily, that they had almost split with it, and given up the ghost, in rendering their souls to God: even just as Crassus did, seeing a lubberly ass eat thistles; and as Philemon, who, for seeing an ass eat those figs which were provided for his own dinner, died with force of laughing. Together with them Master Janotus fell a-laughing too as fast as he could, in which mood of laughing they continued so long, that their eyes did water by the vehement concussion of the substance of the brain, by which these lachrymal humidities, being pressed out, glided through the optic nerves, and so to the full represented Democritus Heraclitizing and Heraclitus Democritizing.

When they had done laughing, Gargantua consulted with the prime of his retinue what should be done. There Ponocrates was of opinion that they should make this fair orator drink again; and seeing he had showed them more pastime, and made them laugh more than a natural soul could have done, that they should give him ten baskets full of sausages, mentioned in his pleasant speech, with a pair of hose, three hundred great billets of logwood, five-and-twenty hogsheads of wine, a good large down-bed, and a deep capacious dish, which he said were necessary for his old age. All this

I

was done as they did appoint: only Gargantua, doubting that they could not quickly find out breeches fit for his wearing, because he knew not what fashion would best become the said orator, whether the martingale fashion of breeches, wherein is a spunghole with a drawbridge for the more easy caguing: or the fashion of the mariners, for the greater solace and comfort of his kidneys: or that of the Switzers, which keeps warm the bedondaine or belly-tabret: or round breeches with straight cannions, having in the seat a piece like a cod's tail, for fear of over-heating his reins:—all which considered, he caused to be given him seven ells of white cloth for the linings. The wood was carried by the porters, the masters of arts carried the sausages and the dishes, and Master Janotus himself would carry the cloth. One of the said masters, called Jousse Bandouille, showed him that it was not seemly nor decent for one of his condition to do so, and that therefore he should deliver it to one of them. Ha, said Janotus, baudet, baudet, or blockhead, blockhead, thou dost not conclude *in modo et figura*. For lo, to this end serve the suppositions and *parva logicalia*. *Pannus, pro quo supponit? Confusè*, said Bandouille, *et distributive*. I do not ask thee, said Janotus, blockhead, *quomodo supponit*, but *pro quo?* It is, blockhead, *pro tibiis meis*, and therefore I will carry it, *Egomet, sicut suppositum portat appositum*. So did he carry it away very close and covertly, as Patelin the buffoon did his cloth. The best was, that when this cougher, in a full act or assembly held at the Mathurins, had with great confidence required his breeches and sausages, and that they were flatly denied him, because he had them of Gargantua, according to the informations thereupon made, he showed them that this was gratis, and out of his liberality, by which they were not in any sort quit of their promises. Notwithstanding this, it was answered him that he should be content with reason, without expectation of any other bribe there. Reason? said Janotus. We use none of it here. Unlucky traitors, you are not worth the hanging. The earth beareth not more arrant villains than you are. I know it well enough; halt not before the lame. I have practised wickedness with you. By God's rattle, I will inform the king of the enormous abuses that are forged here and carried underhand by you, and let me be a leper, if he do not burn you alive like sodomites, traitors, heretics and seducers, enemies to God and virtue.

Upon these words they framed articles against him: he on the other side warned them to appear. In sum, the process was retained by the court, and is there as yet. Hereupon the magisters made a vow never to decrott themselves in rubbing off the dirt of either their shoes or clothes: Master Janotus with his adherents vowed never to blow or snuff their noses, until judgment were given by a definitive sentence.

By these vows do they continue unto this time both dirty and snotty; for the court hath not garbled, sifted, and fully looked into all the pieces as yet. The judgment or decree shall be given out and pronounced at the next Greek kalends, that is, never. As you know that they do more than nature, and contrary to their own articles. The articles of Paris maintain that to God alone belongs infinity, and nature produceth nothing that is immortal; for she putteth an end and period to all things by her engendered, according to the saying, *Omnia orta cadunt, &c.* But these thick mist-swallowers make the suits in law depending before them both infinite and immortal. In doing whereof, they have given occasion to, and verified the saying of Chilo the Lacedæmonian, consecrated to the oracle at Delphos, that misery is the inseparable companion of law-debates; and that pleaders are miserable; for sooner shall they attain to the end of their lives, than to the final decision of their pretended rights.

CHAP. XXI.

The study of Gargantua, according to the discipline of his schoolmasters the Sophisters.

THE first day being thus spent, and the bells put up again in their own place, the citizens of Paris, in acknowledgment of this courtesy, offered to maintain and feed his mare as long as he pleased, which Gargantua took in good part, and they sent her to graze in the forest of Biere. I think she is not there now. This done, he with all his heart submitted his study to the discretion of Ponocrates; who for the beginning appointed that he should do as he was accustomed, to the end he might understand by what means, in so long time, his old masters

had made him so sottish and ignorant. He disposed therefore of his time in such fashion, that ordinarily he did awake betwixt eight and nine o'clock, whether it was day or not, for so had his ancient governors ordained, alleging that which David saith, *Vanum est vobis ante lucem surgere.* Then did he tumble and toss, wag his legs, and wallow in the bed some time, the better to stir up and rouse his vital spirits, and apparelled himself according to the season: but willingly he would wear a great long gown of thick frieze, furred with fox-skins. Afterwards he combed his head with an Almain comb, which is the four fingers and the thumb. For his preceptor said that to comb himself otherwise, to wash and make himself neat, was to lose time in this world. Then he dunged, pissed, spewed, belched, cracked, yawned, spitted, coughed, yexed, sneezed and snotted himself like an archdeacon, and, to suppress the dew and bad air, went to breakfast, having some good fried tripes, fair rashers on the coals, excellent gammons of bacon, store of fine minced meat, and a great deal of sippet brewis, made up of the fat of the beef-pot, laid upon bread, cheese, and chopped parsley strewed together. Ponocrates showed him that he ought not to eat so soon after rising out of his bed, unless he had performed some exercise beforehand. Gargantua answered, What! have not I sufficiently well exercised myself? I have wallowed and rolled myself six or seven turns in my bed before I rose. Is not that enough? Pope Alexander did so, by the advice of a Jew his physician, and lived till his dying day in despite of his enemies. My first masters have used me to it, saying that to breakfast made a good memory, and therefore they drank first. I am very well after it, and dine but the better. And Master Tubal, who was the first licenciate at Paris, told me that it was not enough to run apace, but to set forth betimes: so doth not the total welfare of our humanity depend upon perpetual drinking in a ribble rabble, like ducks, but on drinking early in the morning; *unde versus*,

> To rise betimes is no good hour,
> To drink betimes is better sure.

After that he had thoroughly broke his fast, he went to church, and they carried to him, in a great basket, a huge impantoufled or thick-covered breviary, weighing, what in grease, clasps, parchment and cover, little more or less than eleven hundred and six pounds.

There he heard six-and-twenty or thirty masses. This while, to the same place came his orison-mutterer impaletocked, or lapped up about the chin like a tufted whoop, and his breath pretty well antidoted with store of the vine-tree-syrup. With him he mumbled all his kiriels and dunsical breborions, which he so curiously thumbed and fingered, that there fell not so much as one grain to the ground. As he went from the church, they brought him, upon a dray drawn with oxen, a confused heap of paternosters and aves of St. Claude, every one of them being of the bigness of a hat-block; and thus walking through the cloisters, galleries, or garden, he said more in turning them over than sixteen hermits would have done. Then did he study some paltry half-hour with his eyes fixed upon his book; but, as the comic saith, his mind was in the kitchen. Pissing then a full urinal, he sat down at table; and because he was naturally phlegmatic, he began his meal with some dozens of gammons, dried neat's tongues, hard roes of mullet, called botargos, andouilles or sausages, and such other forerunners of wine. In the meanwhile, four of his folks did cast into his mouth one after another continually mustard by whole shovelfuls. Immediately after that, he drank a horrible draught of white wine for the ease of his kidneys. When that was done, he ate according to the season meat agreeable to his appetite, and then left off eating when his belly began to strout, and was like to crack for fulness. As for his drinking, he had in that neither end nor rule. For he was wont to say, That the limits and bounds of drinking were, when the cork of the shoes of him that drinketh swelleth up half a foot high.

CHAP. XXII.

The games of Gargantua.

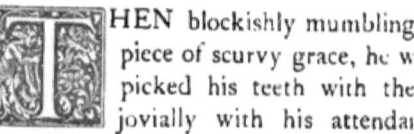

THEN blockishly mumbling with a set on countenance a piece of scurvy grace, he washed his hands in fresh wine, picked his teeth with the foot of a hog, and talked jovially with his attendants. Then the carpet being spread, they brought plenty of cards, many dice, with great store and abundance of chequers and chessboards.

There he played.

At flush.
At primero.
At the beast.
At the rifle.
At trump.
At the prick and spare not.
At the hundred.
At the peeny.
At the unfortunate woman.
At the fib.
At the pass ten.
At one-and-thirty.
At post and pair, or even and sequence.
At three hundred.
At the unlucky man.
At the last couple in hell.
At the hock.
At the surly.
At the lansquenet.
At the cuckoo.
At puff, or let him speak that hath it.
At take nothing and throw out.
At the marriage.
At the frolic or jackdaw.
At the opinion.
At who doth the one, doth the other.
At the sequences.
At the ivory bundles.
At the tarots.
At losing load him.
At he's gulled and *esto*.
At the torture.
At the handruff.
At the click.
At honours.
At love.
At the chess.
At Reynard the fox.
At the squares.
At the cows.
At the lottery.
At the chance or mumchance.
At three dice or maniest bleaks.
At the tables.
At ninivinack.
At the lurch.
At doublets or queen's game.
At the faily.
At the French trictrac.
At the long tables or ferkeering.
At feldown.
At tod's body.
At needs must.
At the dames or draughts.
At bob and mow.
At primus secundus.
At mark-knife.
At the keys.
At span-counter.
At even or odd.
At cross or pile.
At ball and huckle-bones.
At ivory balls.
At the billiards.
At bob and hit.
At the owl.
At the charming of the hare.
At pull yet a little.
At trudgepig.
At the magatapies.
At the horn.
At the flowered or Shrovetide ox.
At the madge-owlet.

At pinch without laughing.
At prickle me tickle me.
At the unshoeing of the ass.
At the cocksess.
At hari hohi.
At I set me down.
At earl beardy.
At the old mode.
At draw the spit.
At put out.
At gossip lend me your sack.
At the ramcod ball.
At thrust out the harlot.
At Marseilles figs.
At nicknamry.
At stick and hole.
At boke or him, or flaying the fox.
At the branching it.
At trill madam, or grapple my lady.
At the cat selling.
At blow the coal.
At the re-wedding.
At the quick and dead judge.
At unoven the iron.
At the false clown.
At the flints, or at the nine stones.
At to the crutch hulch back.
At the Sanct is found.
At hinch, pinch and laugh not.
At the leek.
At bumdockdousse.
At the loose gig.
At the hoop.
At the sow.
At belly to belly.
At the dales or straths.
At the twigs.
At the quoits.
At I'm for that.
At tilt at weeky.
At ninepins.
At the cock quintin.
At tip and hurl.
At the flat bowls.
At the veer and turn.
At rogue and ruffian.
At bumbatch touch.
At the mysterious trough.
At the short bowls.
At the dapple-grey.
At cock and crank it.
At break-pot.
At my desire.
At twirly whirlytrill.
At the rush bundles.
At the short staff.
At the whirling gig.
At hide and seek, or are you all hid?
At the picket.
At the blank.
At the pilferers.
At the caveson.
At prison bars.
At have at the nuts.
At cherry-pit.
At rub and rice.
At whiptop.
At the casting top.
At the hobgoblins.
At the O wonderful.
At the soily smutchy.
At fast and loose.
At scutchbreech.
At the broom-besom.
At St. Cosme, I come to adore thee.
At the lusty brown boy.

At I take you napping.
At fair and softly passeth Lent.
At the forked oak.
At truss.
At the wolf's tail.
At bum to buss, or nose in breech.
At Geordie, give me my lance.
At swaggy, waggy or shoggyshou.
At stook and rook, shear and threave.
At the birch.
At the muss.
At the dilly dilly darling.
At ox moudy.
At purpose in purpose.
At nine less.
At blind-man-buff.
At the fallen bridges.
At bridled nick.
At the white at butts.
At thwack swinge him.
At apple, pear, plum.
At murngi.
At the toad.
At cricket.
At the pounding stick.
At jack and the box.
At the queens.
At the trades.
At heads and points.
At the vine-tree hug.
At black be thy fall.
At ho the distaff.
At Joan Thomson.
At the bolting cloth.
At the oat's seed.
At greedy glutton.
At the morris dance.
At feeby.
At the whole frisk and gambol.
At battabum, or riding of the wild mare.
At Hind the ploughman.
At the good mawkin.
At the dead beast.
At climb the ladder, Billy.
At the dying hog.
At the salt doup.
At the pretty pigeon.
At barley break.
At the bavine.
At the bush leap.
At crossing.
At bo-peep.
At the hardit arsepursy.
At the harrower's nest.
At forward hey.
At the fig.
At gunshot crack.
At mustard peel.
At the gome.
At the relapse.
At jog breech, or prick him forward.
At knockpate.
At the Cornish c[h]ough.
At the crane-dance.
At slash and cut.
At bobbing, or the flirt on the nose.
At the larks.
At fillipping.

After he had thus well played, revelled, past and spent his time, it was thought fit to drink a little, and that was eleven glassfuls the man, and, immediately after making good cheer again, he would stretch himself upon a fair bench, or a good large bed, and there sleep two or three hours together, without thinking or speaking any hurt. After he was awakened he would shake his ears a little. In the mean time they brought him fresh wine. There he drank better than ever. Ponocrates showed him that it was an ill diet to drink so after sleeping. It is, answered Gargantua, the very life of the patriarchs and holy fathers; for naturally I sleep salt, and my sleep hath been to me in stead of so many gammons of bacon. Then began he to study a little, and out came the paternosters or rosary of beads, which the better and more formally to despatch, he got upon an old mule, which had served nine kings, and so mumbling with his mouth, nodding and doddling his head, would go see a coney ferreted or caught in a gin. At his return he went into the kitchen to know what roast meat was on the spit, and what otherwise was to be dressed for supper. And supped very well, upon my conscience, and commonly did invite some of his neighbours that were good drinkers, with whom carousing and drinking merrily, they told stories of all sorts from the old to the new. Amongst others he had for domestics the Lords of Fou, of Gourville, of Griniot, and of Marigny. After supper were brought in upon the place the fair wooden gospels and the books of the four kings, that is to say, many pairs of tables and cards—or the fair flush, one, two, three—or at all, to make short work; or else they went to see the wenches thereabouts, with little small banquets, intermixed with collations and rear-suppers. Then did he sleep, without unbridling, until eight o'clock in the next morning.

CHAP. XXIII.

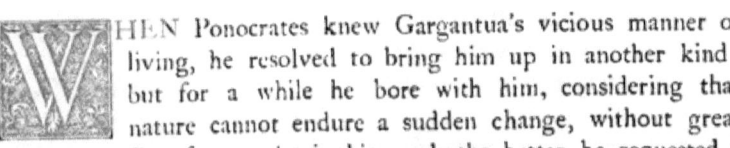
How Gargantua was instructed by Ponocrates, and in such sort disciplinated, that he lost not one hour of the day.

WHEN Ponocrates knew Gargantua's vicious manner of living, he resolved to bring him up in another kind; but for a while he bore with him, considering that nature cannot endure a sudden change, without great violence. Therefore, to begin his work the better, he requested a learned physician of that time, called Master Theodorus, seriously to perpend, if it were possible, how to bring Gargantua into a better course. The said physician purged him canonically with Anticyrian hellebore, by which medicine he cleansed all the alteration and perverse habitude of his brain. By this means also Ponocrates made him forget all that he had learned under his ancient preceptors, as Timotheus did to his disciples, who had been instructed under other musicians. To do this the better, they brought him into the company of learned men, which were there, in whose imitation he had a great desire and affection to study otherwise, and to improve his parts. Afterwards he put himself into such a road and way of studying, that he lost not any one hour in the day, but employed all his time in learning and honest knowledge. Gargantua awaked, then, about four o'clock in the morning. Whilst they were in rubbing of him, there was read unto him some chapter of the holy Scripture aloud and clearly, with a pronunciation fit for the matter, and hereunto was appointed a young page born in Basché, named Anagnostes. According to the purpose and argument of that lesson, he oftentimes gave himself to worship, adore, pray, and send up his supplications to that good God, whose Word did show his majesty and marvellous judgment. Then went he unto the secret places to make excretion of his natural digestions. There his master repeated what had been read, expounding unto him the most obscure and difficult points. In returning, they considered the face of the sky, if it was such as they had observed it the night before, and into what signs the sun was entering, as also the moon for that day. This done, he was apparelled, combed, curled, trimmed, and perfumed, during which time they repeated to him the lessons of the day before. He himself said them by heart, and upon them would ground some practical cases concerning the estate of man, which he would prosecute sometimes two or three hours, but ordinarily they ceased as soon as he was fully clothed. Then for three good hours he had a lecture read unto him. This done, they went forth, still conferring of the substance of the lecture, either unto a field near the university called the Brack, or unto the meadows, where they played at the ball, the long-tennis, and at the piletrigone (which is a play wherein we throw a triangular piece of iron at a ring, to pass it), most gallantly exercising their bodies, as formerly they had done their minds. All their play was but in liberty, for they left off when they pleased, and that was commonly when they did sweat over all their body, or were otherwise weary. Then were they very well wiped and rubbed, shifted their shirts, and, walking soberly, went to see if dinner was ready. Whilst they stayed for that, they did clearly and eloquently pronounce some sentences that they had retained of the lecture. In the meantime Master Appetite came, and then very orderly sat they down at table. At the beginning of the meal there was read some pleasant history of the warlike actions of former times, until he had taken a glass of wine. Then, if they thought good, they continued reading, or began to discourse merrily together; speaking first of the virtue, propriety, efficacy, and nature of all that was served in at the table; of bread, of wine, of water, of salt, of fleshes, fishes, fruits, herbs, roots, and of their dressing. By means whereof he learned in a little time all the passages competent for this that were to be found in Pliny, Athenæus, Dioscorides, Julius Pollux, Galen, Porphyry, Oppian, Polybius, Heliodore, Aristotle, Ælian, and others. Whilst they talked of these things, many times, to be the more certain, they caused the very books to be brought to the table, and so well and perfectly did he in his memory retain the things above said, that in that time there was not a physician that knew half so much as he did. Afterwards they conferred of the lessons read in the morning, and, ending their repast with some conserve or marmalade of quinces, he picked his teeth with mastic tooth-pickers, washed his hands and eyes with fair fresh water, and gave thanks unto God in some fine cantiques, made in praise of the divine bounty and munificence. This done, they brought in cards, not to play, but to learn a thousand pretty tricks and new inventions, which were all grounded upon arithmetic. By this means he fell in love with that numerical science, and every day after dinner and supper he passed his time in it as pleasantly as he was wont to do at cards and dice; so that at last he understood so well both the theory and practical part thereof, that Tunstall the Englishman, who had written very largely of that purpose, confessed that verily in comparison of him he had no skill at all. And not only in that, but in the other mathematical sciences, as geometry, astronomy, music, &c. For in waiting on the concoction and attending the digestion of his food, they made a thousand pretty instruments and geometrical figures, and did in some measure practise the astronomical canons.

After this they recreated themselves with singing musically, in four or five parts, or upon a set theme or ground at random, as it best pleased them. In matter of musical instruments, he learned to play upon the lute, the virginals, the harp, the Almain flute with nine holes, the viol, and the sackbut. This hour thus spent, and digestion finished, he did purge his body of natural excrements, then betook himself to his principal study for three hours together, or more, as well to repeat his matutinal lectures as to proceed in the book wherein he was, as also to write handsomely, to draw and form the antique and Roman letters. This being done, they went out of their house, and with them a young gentleman of Touraine, named the Esquire Gymnast, who taught him the art of riding. Changing then his clothes, he rode a Naples courser, a Dutch roussin, a Spanish jennet, a barded or trapped steed, then a light fleet horse, unto whom he gave a hundred carieres, made him go the high saults, bounding in the air, free the ditch with a skip, leap over a stile or pale, turn short in a ring both to the right and left hand. There he broke not his lance; for it is the greatest foolery in the world to say, I have broken ten lances at tilts or in fight. A carpenter can do even as much. But it is a glorious and praiseworthy action with one lance to break and overthrow ten enemies. Therefore, with a sharp, stiff, strong, and well-steeled lance would he usually force up a door, pierce a harness, beat down a tree, carry away the ring, lift up a cuirassier saddle, with the mail-coat and gauntlet. All this he did in complete arms from head to foot. As for the prancing flourishes and smacking popisms for the better cherishing of the horse, commonly used in riding, none did them better than he. The cavallerize of Ferrara was but as an ape compared to him. He was singularly skilful in leaping nimbly from one horse to another without putting foot to ground, and these horses were called desultories. He could likewise from either side, with a lance in his hand, leap on horseback without stirrups, and rule the horse at his pleasure without a bridle, for such things are useful in military engagements. Another day he exercised the battle-axe, which he so dexterously wielded, both in the nimble, strong, and smooth management of that weapon, and that in all the feats practicable by it, that he passed knight of arms in the field, and at all essays.

Then tossed he the pike, played with the two-handed sword, with the backsword, with the Spanish tuck, the dagger, poniard, armed, unarmed, with a buckler, with a cloak, with a target. Then would he hunt the hart, the roebuck, the bear, the fallow deer, the wild boar, the hare, the pheasant, the partridge, and the bustard. He played at the balloon, and made it bound in the air, both with fist and foot. He wrestled, ran, jumped—not at three steps and a leap, called the hops, nor at clochepied, called the hare's leap, nor yet at the Almains; for, said Gymnast, these jumps are for the wars altogether unprofitable, and of no use—but at one leap he would skip over a ditch, spring over a hedge, mount six paces upon a wall, ramp and grapple after this fashion up against a window of the full height of a lance. He did swim in deep waters on his belly, on his back, sideways, with all his body, with his feet only, with one hand in the air, wherein he held a book, crossing thus the breadth of the river of Seine without wetting it, and dragged along his cloak with his teeth, as did Julius Cæsar; then with the help of one hand he entered forcibly into a boat, from whence he cast himself again headlong into the water, sounded the depths, hollowed the rocks, and plunged into the pits and gulfs. Then turned he the boat about, governed it, led it swiftly or slowly with the stream and against the stream, stopped it in his course, guided it with one hand, and with the other laid hard about him with a huge great oar, hoisted the sail, hied up along the mast by the shrouds, ran upon the edge of the decks, set the compass in order, tackled the bowlines, and steered the helm. Coming out of the water, he ran furiously up against a hill, and with the same alacrity and swiftness ran down again. He climbed up at trees like a cat, and leaped from the one to the other like a squirrel. He did pull down the great boughs and branches like another Milo; then with two sharp well-steeled daggers and two tried bodkins would he run up by the wall to the very top of a house like a rat; then suddenly came down from the top to the bottom, with such an even composition of members that by the fall he would catch no harm.

He did cast the dart, throw the bar, put the stone, practise the javelin, the boar-spear or partisan, and the halbert. He broke the strongest bows in drawing, bended against his breast the greatest crossbows of steel, took his aim by the eye with the hand-gun, and shot well, traversed and planted the cannon, shot at butt-marks, at the papgay from below upwards, or to a height from above downwards, or to a descent; then before him, sideways, and behind him, like the Parthians. They tied a cable-rope to the top of a high tower, by one end whereof hanging near the ground he wrought himself with his hands to the very top; then upon the same track came down so sturdily and firm that you could not on a plain meadow have run with more assurance. They set up a great pole fixed upon two trees. There would he hang by his hands, and with them alone, his feet touching at nothing, would go back and fore along the foresaid rope with so great swiftness that hardly could one overtake him with running; and then, to exercise his breast and lungs, he would shout like all the devils in hell. I heard him once call Eudemon from St. Victor's gate to Montmartre. Stentor had never such a voice at the siege of Troy. Then for the strengthening of his nerves or sinews they made him two great sows of lead, each of them weighing eight thousand and seven hundred quintals, which they called alteres. Those he took up from the ground, in each hand one, then lifted them up over his head, and held them so without stirring three quarters of an hour and more, which was an inimitable force. He fought at barriers with the stoutest and most vigorous champions; and when it came to the cope, he stood so sturdily on his feet that he abandoned himself unto the strongest, in case they could remove him from his place, as Milo was wont to do of old. In whose imitation, likewise, he held a pomegranate in his hand, to give it unto him that could take it from him. The time being thus bestowed, and himself rubbed, cleansed, wiped, and refreshed with other clothes, he returned fair and softly; and passing through certain meadows, or other grassy places, beheld the trees and plants, comparing them with what is written of them in the books of the ancients, such as Theophrast, Dioscorides, Marinus, Pliny, Nicander, Macer, and Galen, and carried home to the house great handfuls of them, whereof a young page called Rizotomos had charge; together with little mattocks, pickaxes, grubbing-hooks, cabbies, pruning-knives, and other instruments requisite for herborizing. Being come to their lodging, whilst supper was making ready, they repeated certain passages of that which hath been read, and sat down to table. Here remark, that his dinner was sober and thrifty, for he did then eat only to prevent the gnawings of his stomach, but his supper was copious and large, for he took then as much as was fit to maintain and nourish him; which, indeed, is the true diet prescribed by the art of good and sound physic, although a rabble of loggerheaded physicians, nuzzeled in the brabbling shop of sophisters, counsel the contrary. During that repast was continued the lesson read at dinner as long as they thought good; the rest was spent in good discourse, learned and profitable. After that they had given thanks, he set himself to sing vocally, and play upon harmonious instruments, or otherwise passed his time at some pretty sports, made with cards or dice, or in practising the feats of legerdemain with cups and balls. There they stayed some nights in frolicking thus, and making themselves merry till it was time to go to bed; and on other nights they would go make visits unto learned men, or to such as had been travellers in strange and remote countries. When it was full night before they retired themselves, they went unto the most open place of the house to see the face of the sky, and there beheld the comets, if any were, as likewise the figures, situations, aspects, oppositions, and conjunctions of both the fixed stars and planets.

Then with his master did he briefly recapitulate, after the manner of the Pythagoreans, that which he had read, seen, learned, done, and understood in the whole course of that day.

Then prayed they unto God the Creator, in falling down before him, and strengthening their faith towards him, and glorifying him for his boundless bounty; and, giving thanks unto him for the time that was past, they recommended themselves to his divine clemency for the future. Which being done, they went to bed, and betook themselves to their repose and rest.

CHAP. XXIV.

How Gargantua spent his time in rainy weather.

F it happened that the weather were anything cloudy, foul, and rainy, all the forenoon was employed, as before specified, according to custom, with this difference only, that they had a good clear fire lighted to correct the distempers of the air. But after dinner, instead of their wonted exercitations, they did abide within, and, by way of apotherapy (that is, a making the body healthful by exercise), did recreate themselves in bottling up of hay, in cleaving and sawing of wood, and in threshing sheaves of corn at the barn. Then they studied the art of painting or carving; or brought into use the antique play of tables, as Leonicus hath written of it, and as our good friend Lascaris playeth at it. In playing they examined the passages of ancient authors wherein the said play is mentioned or any metaphor drawn from it. They went likewise to see the drawing of metals, or the casting of great ordnance; how the lapidaries did work; as also the goldsmiths and cutters of precious stones. Nor did they omit to visit the alchemists, money-coiners, upholsters, weavers, velvet-workers, watchmakers, looking-glass framers, printers, organists, and other such kind of artificers, and, everywhere giving them somewhat to drink, did learn and consider the industry and invention of the trades. They went also to hear the public lectures, the solemn commencements, the repetitions, the acclamations, the pleadings of the gentle lawyers, and sermons of evangelical preachers. He went through the halls and places appointed for fencing, and there played against the masters themselves at all weapons, and showed them by experience that he knew as much in it as, yea more than, they. And, instead of herborizing, they visited the shops of druggists, herbalists, and apothecaries, and diligently considered the fruits, roots, leaves, gums, seeds, the grease and ointments of some foreign parts, as also how they did adulterate them. He went to see the jugglers, tumblers, mountebanks, and quacksalvers, and considered their cunning, their shifts, their somersaults and smooth tongue,

especially of those of Chauny in Picardy, who are naturally great praters, and brave givers of fibs, in matter of green apes.

At their return they did eat more soberly at supper than at other times, and meats more desiccative and extenuating; to the end that the intemperate moisture of the air, communicated to the body by a necessary confinitive, might by this means be corrected, and that they might not receive any prejudice for want of their ordinary bodily exercise. Thus was Gargantua governed, and kept on in this course of education, from day to day profiting, as you may understand such a young man of his age may, of a pregnant judgment, with good discipline well continued. Which, although at the beginning it seemed difficult, became a little after so sweet, so easy, and so delightful, that it seemed rather the recreation of a king than the study of a scholar. Nevertheless Ponocrates, to divert him from this vehement intension of the spirits, thought fit, once in a month, upon some fair and clear day, to go out of the city betimes in the morning, either towards Gentilly, or Boulogne, or to Montrouge, or Charanton bridge, or to Vanves, or St. Clou, and there spend all the day long in making the greatest cheer that could be devised, sporting, making merry, drinking healths, playing, singing, dancing, tumbling in some fair meadow, unnestling of sparrows, taking of quails, and fishing for frogs and crabs. But although that day was passed without books or lecture, yet was it not spent without profit; for in the said meadows they usually repeated certain pleasant verses of Virgil's agriculture, of Hesiod and of Politian's husbandry, would set a-broach some witty Latin epigrams, then immediately turned them into roundelays and songs for dancing in the French language. In their feasting they would sometimes separate the water from the wine that was therewith mixed, as Cato teacheth, *De re rustica*, and Pliny with an ivy cup would wash the wine in a basinful of water, then take it out again with a funnel as pure as ever. They made the water go from one glass to another, and contrived a thousand little automatory engines, that is to say, moving of themselves.

CHAP. XXV.

How there was great strife and debate raised betwixt the cake-bakers of Lerné, and those of Gargantua's country, whereupon were waged great wars.

AT that time, which was the season of vintage, in the beginning of harvest, when the country shepherds were set to keep the vines, and hinder the starlings from eating up the grapes, as some cake-bakers of Lerné happened to pass along in the broad highway driving into the city ten or twelve horses loaded with cakes, the said shepherds courteously entreated them to give them some for their money, as the price then ruled in the market. For here it is to be remarked, that it is a celestial food to eat for breakfast hot fresh cakes with grapes, especially the frail clusters, the great red grapes, the muscadine, the verjuice grape, and the laskard, for those that are costive in their belly, because it will make them gush out, and squirt the length of a hunter's staff, like the very tap of a barrel; and oftentimes, thinking to let a squib, they did all-to-besquatter and conskite themselves, whereupon they are commonly called the vintage thinkers. The bun-sellers or cake-makers were in nothing inclinable to their request; but, which was worse, did injure them most outrageously, calling them prattling gabblers, lickorous gluttons, freckled bittors, mangy rascals, shite-a-bed scoundrels, drunken roysters, sly knaves, drowsy loiterers, slapsauce fellows, slabberdegullion druggels, lubberly louts, cozening foxes, ruffian rogues, paltry customers, sycophant-varlets, drawlatch hoydens, flouting milksops, jeering companions, staring clowns, forlorn snakes, ninny lobcocks, scurvy sneaksbies, fondling fops, base loons, saucy coxcombs, idle lusks, scoffing braggarts, noddy meacocks, blockish grutnols, doddipol-joltheads, jobbernol goosecaps, foolish loggerheads, flutch calf-lollies, grouthead gnat-snappers, lob-dotterels, gaping changelings, codshead loobies, woodcock slangams, ninny-hammer flycatchers, noddypeak simpletons, turdy gut, shitten shepherds, and other suchlike defamatory epithets; saying further, that it was not for them to eat of these dainty cakes, but might very well content themselves with the coarse

unranged bread, or to eat of the great brown household loaf. To which provoking words, one amongst them, called Forgier, an honest fellow of his person and a notable springal, made answer very calmly thus: How long is it since you have got horns, that you are become so proud? Indeed formerly you were wont to give us some freely, and will you not now let us have any for our money? This is not the part of good neighbours, neither do we serve you thus when you come hither to buy our good corn, whereof you make your cakes and buns. Besides that, we would have given you to the bargain some of our grapes, but, by his zounds, you may chance to repent it, and possibly have need of us at another time, when we shall use you after the like manner, and therefore remember it. Then Marquet, a prime man in the confraternity of the cake-bakers, said unto him, Yea, sir, thou art pretty well crest-risen this morning, thou didst eat yesternight too much millet and bolymong. Come hither, sirrah, come hither, I will give thee some cakes. Whereupon Forgier, dreading no harm, in all simplicity went towards him, and drew a sixpence out of his leather satchel, thinking that Marquet would have sold him some of his cakes. But, instead of cakes, he gave him with his whip such a rude lash overthwart the legs, that the marks of the whipcord knots were apparent in them, then would have fled away; but Forgier cried out as loud as he could, O, murder, murder, help, help, help! and in the meantime threw a great cudgel after him, which he carried under his arm, wherewith he hit him in the coronal joint of his head, upon the crotaphic artery of the right side thereof, so forcibly, that Marquet fell down from his mare more like a dead than living man. Meanwhile the farmers and country swains, that were watching their walnuts near to that place, came running with their great poles and long staves, and laid such load on these cake-bakers, as if they had been to thresh upon green rye. The other shepherds and shepherdesses, hearing the lamentable shout of Forgier, came with their slings and slackies following them, and throwing great stones at them, as thick as if it had been hail. At last they overtook them, and took from them about four or five dozen of their cakes. Nevertheless they paid for them the ordinary price, and gave them over and above one hundred eggs and three baskets full of mulberries. Then did the cake-bakers help to get up to his mare Marquet, who was most shrewdly wounded, and forthwith returned to Lerné, changing the resolution they had to go to Pareillé, threatening very sharp and boisterously the cowherds, shepherds, and farmers of Sevillé and Sinays. This done, the shepherds and shepherdesses made merry with these cakes and fine grapes, and sported themselves together at the sound of the pretty small pipe, scoffing and laughing at those vainglorious cake-bakers, who had that day met with a mischief for want of crossing themselves with a good hand in the morning. Nor did they forget to apply to Forgier's leg some fair great red medicinal grapes, and so handsomely dressed it and bound it up that he was quickly cured.

CHAP. XXVI.

How the inhabitants of Lerné, by the commandment of Picrochole their king, assaulted the shepherds of Gargantua unexpectedly and on a sudden.

THE cake-bakers, being returned to Lerné, went presently, before they did either eat or drink, to the Capitol, and there before their king, called Picrochole, the third of that name, made their complaint, showing their panniers broken, their caps all crumpled, their coats torn, their cakes taken away, but, above all, Marquet most enormously wounded, saying that all that mischief was done by the shepherds and herdsmen of Grangousier, near the broad highway beyond Sevillé. Picrochole incontinent grew angry and furious; and, without asking any further what, how, why, or wherefore, commanded the ban and arrière ban to be sounded throughout all his country, that all his vassals of what condition soever should, upon pain of the halter, come, in the best arms they could, unto the great place before the castle, at the hour of noon, and, the better to strengthen his design, he caused the drum to be beat about the town. Himself, whilst his dinner was making ready, went to see his artillery mounted upon the carriage, to display his colours, and set up the great royal standard, and loaded wains with store of ammunition both for the field and the belly, arms and victuals. At dinner he despatched his commissions, and by his express edict my Lord Shagrag was

appointed to command the vanguard, wherein were numbered sixteen thousand and fourteen arquebusiers or firelocks, together with thirty thousand and eleven volunteer adventurers. The great Touquedillon, master of the horse, had the charge of the ordnance, wherein were reckoned nine hundred and fourteen brazen pieces, in cannons, double cannons, basilisks, serpentines, culverins, bombards or murderers, falcons, bases or passevolins, spirols, and other sorts of great guns. The rearguard was committed to the Duke of Scrapegood. In the main battle was the king and the princes of his kingdom. Thus being hastily furnished, before they would set forward, they sent three hundred light horsemen, under the conduct of Captain Swillwind, to discover the country, clear the avenues, and see whether there was any ambush laid for them. But, after they had made diligent search, they found all the land round about in peace and quiet, without any meeting or convention at all; which Picrochole understanding, commanded that everyone should march speedily under his colours. Then immediately in all disorder, without keeping either rank or file, they took the fields one amongst another, wasting, spoiling, destroying, and making havoc of all wherever they went, not sparing poor nor rich, privileged or unprivileged places, church nor laity, drove away oxen and cows, bulls, calves, heifers, wethers, ewes, lambs, goats, kids, hens, capons, chickens, geese, ganders, goslings, hogs, swine, pigs, and such like; beating down the walnuts, plucking the grapes, tearing the hedges, shaking the fruit-trees, and committing such incomparable abuses, that the like abomination was never heard of. Nevertheless, they met with none to resist them, for everyone submitted to their mercy, beseeching them that they might be dealt with courteously in regard that they had always carried themselves as became good and loving neighbours, and that they had never been guilty of any wrong or outrage done upon them, to be thus suddenly surprised, troubled, and disquieted, and that, if they would not desist, God would punish them very shortly. To which expostulations and remonstrances no other answer was made, but that they would teach them to eat cakes.

CHAP. XXVII.

How a monk of Seville saved the close of the abbey from being ransacked by the enemy.

SO much they did, and so far they went pillaging and stealing, that at last they came to Sevillé, where they robbed both men and women, and took all they could catch : nothing was either too hot or too heavy for them. Although the plague was there in the most part of all the houses, they nevertheless entered everywhere, then plundered and carried away all that was within, and yet for all this not one of them took any hurt, which is a most wonderful case. For the curates, vicars, preachers, physicians, chirurgeons, and apothecaries, who went to visit, to dress, to cure, to heal, to preach unto and admonish those that were sick, were all dead of the infection, and these devilish robbers and murderers caught never any harm at all. Whence comes this to pass, my masters? I beseech you think upon it. The town being thus pillaged, they went unto the abbey with a horrible noise and tumult, but they found it shut and made fast against them. Whereupon the body of the army marched forward towards a pass or ford called the Gué de Véde, except seven companies of foot and two hundred lancers, who, staying there, broke down the walls of the close, to waste, spoil, and make havoc of all the vines and vintage within that place. The monks (poor devils) knew not in that extremity to which of all their sancts they should vow themselves. Nevertheless, at all adventures they rang the bells *ad capitulum capitulantes*. There it was decreed that they should make a fair procession, stuffed with good lectures, prayers, and litanies *contra hostium insidias*, and jolly responses *pro pace*.

There was then in the abbey a claustral monk, called Friar John of the funnels and gobbets, in French *des entoumeures*, young, gallant, frisk, lusty, nimble, quick, active, bold, adventurous, resolute, tall, lean, wide-mouthed, long-nosed, a fair despatcher of morning prayers, unbridler of masses, and runner over of vigils; and, to conclude summarily in a word, a right monk, if ever there was any, since the monking world monked a monkery: for the rest, a clerk even to the teeth in matter of breviary. This monk, hearing the noise that the enemy made within the enclosure of the vineyard, went out to see what they were doing; and perceiving that they were cutting and gathering the grapes, whereon was grounded the foundation of all their next year's wine, returned unto the choir of the church where the other monks were, all amazed and astonished like so many bell-melters. Whom when he heard sing, im, nim, pe, ne, ne, ne, ne, nene, tum, ne, num, num, ini, i mi, co, o, no, o, o, neno, ne, no, no, no, rum, nenum, num : It is well shit, well sung, said he. By the virtue of God, why do not you sing, Panniers, farewell, vintage is done? The devil snatch me, if they be not already within the middle of our close, and cut so well both vines and grapes, that, by God's body, there will not be found for these four years to come so much as a gleaning in it. By the belly of Sanct James, what shall we poor devils drink the while? Lord God! *da mihi potum.* Then said the prior of the convent : What should this drunken fellow do here? let him be carried to prison for troubling the divine service. Nay, said the monk, the wine service, let us behave ourselves so that it be not troubled; for you yourself, my lord prior, love to drink of the best, and so doth every honest man. Never yet did a man of worth dislike good wine, it is a monastical apophthegm. But these responses that you chant here, by G- -, are not in season. Wherefore is it, that our devotions were instituted to be short in the time of harvest and vintage, and long in the advent, and all the winter? The late friar, Massepelosse, of good memory, a true zealous man, or else I give myself to the devil, of our religion, told me, and I remember it well, how the reason was, that in this season we might press and make the wine, and in winter whiff it up. Hark you, my masters, you that love the wine, Cop's body, follow me ; for Sanct Anthony burn me as freely as a faggot, if they get leave to taste one drop of the liquor that will not now come and fight for relief of the vine. Hog's belly, the goods of the church! Ha, no, no. What the devil, Sanct Thomas of England was well content to die for them ; if I died in the same cause, should not I be a sanct likewise? Yes. Yet shall not I die there for all this, for it is I that must do it to others and send them a-packing.

As he spake this he threw off his great monk's habit, and laid hold upon the staff of the cross, which was made of the heart of a sorbapple-tree, it being of the length of a lance, round, of a full grip, and a little powdered with lilies called flower de luce, the workmanship whereof was almost all defaced and worn out. Thus went he out in a fair long-skirted jacket, putting his frock scarfwise athwart his breast, and in this equipage, with his staff, shaft or truncheon of the cross, laid on so lustily, brisk, and fiercely upon his enemies, who, without any order, or ensign, or trumpet, or drum, were busied in gathering the grapes of the vineyard. For the cornets, guidons, and ensign-bearers had laid down their standards, banners, and colours by the wall sides: the drummers had knocked out the heads of their drums on one end to fill them with grapes: the trumpeters were loaded with great bundles of bunches and huge knots of clusters: in sum, everyone of them was out of array, and all in disorder. He hurried, therefore, upon them so rudely, without crying gare or beware, that he overthrew them like hogs, tumbled them over like swine, striking athwart and alongst, and by one means or other laid so about him, after the old fashion of fencing, that to some he beat out their brains, to others he crushed their arms, battered their legs, and bethwacked their sides till their ribs cracked with it. To others again he unjointed the spondyles or knuckles of the neck, disfigured their chaps, gashed their faces, made their cheeks hang flapping on their chin, and so swinged and belammed them that they fell down before him like hay before a mower. To some others he spoiled the frame of their kidneys, marred their backs, broke their thigh-bones, pashed in their noses, poached out their eyes, cleft their mandibles, tore their jaws, dung in their teeth into their throat, shook asunder their omoplates or shoulder-blades, sphacelated their shins, mortified their shanks, inflamed their ankles, heaved off of the hinges their ishies, their sciatica or hip-gout, dislocated the joints of their knees, squattered into pieces the boughts or pestles of their thighs, and so thumped, mauled and belaboured them everywhere, that never was corn so thick and threefold threshed upon by ploughmen's flails as were the pitifully disjointed members of their mangled bodies under the merciless baton of the cross. If any offered to hide himself amongst the thickest of the vines, he laid him squat as a flounder, bruised the ridge of his back, and dashed his reins like a dog. If any thought by flight to escape, he made his head to fly in pieces by the lambdoidal commissure, which is a seam in the hinder part of the skull. If anyone did scramble up into a tree, thinking there to be safe, he rent up his perinee, and impaled him in at the fundament. If any of his old acquaintance happened to cry out, Ha, Friar John, my friend Friar John, quarter, quarter, I yield myself to you, to you I render myself! So thou shalt, said he, and must, whether thou wouldst or no, and withal render and yield up thy soul to all the devils in hell; then suddenly gave them dronos, that is, so many knocks, thumps, raps, dints, thwacks, and bangs, as sufficed to warn Pluto of their coming and despatch them a-going. If any was so rash and full of temerity as to resist him to his face, then was it he did show the strength of his muscles, for without more ado he did transpierce him, by running him in at the breast, through the mediastine and the heart. Others, again, he so quashed and bebumped, that, with a sound bounce under the hollow of their short ribs, he overturned their stomachs so that they died immediately. To some, with a smart souse on the epigaster, he would make their midriff swag, then, redoubling the blow, gave them such a homepush on the navel that he made their puddings to gush out. To others through their ballocks he pierced their bumgut, and left not bowel, tripe, nor entrail in their body that had not felt the impetuosity, fierceness, and fury of his violence. Believe, that it was the most horrible spectacle that ever one saw. Some cried unto Sanct Barbe, others to St. George. O the holy Lady Nytouch, said one, the good Sanctess; O our Lady of Succours, said another, help, help! Others cried, Our Lady of Cunaut, of Loretto, of Good Tidings, on the other side of the water St. Mary Over. Some vowed a pilgrimage to St. James, and others to the holy handkerchief at Chamberry, which three months after that burnt so well in the fire that they could not get one thread of it saved. Others sent up their vows to St. Cadouin, others to St. John d'Angely, and to St. Eutropius of Xaintes. Others again invoked St. Mesmes of Chinon, St. Martin of Candes, St. Clouaud of Sinays, the holy relics of Laurezay, with a thousand other jolly little sancts and santrels. Some died without speaking, others spoke without dying; some died in speaking, others spoke in dying. Others shouted as loud as they could Confession, Confession, *Confiteor*, *Miserere*, *In manus!* So great was the cry of the wounded, that the prior of the abbey with all his monks came forth, who, when they saw these poor wretches so slain amongst the vines, and wounded to death, confessed some of them. But whilst the priests were busied in confessing them, the little monkies ran all to the place where Friar John was, and asked him wherein he would be pleased to require their assistance. To which he answered that they should cut the throats of those he had thrown down upon the ground. They presently, leaving their outer habits and cowls upon the rails, began to throttle and make an end of those whom he had already crushed. Can you tell with what instruments they did it? With fair gullies, which are little hulchbacked demi-knives, the iron tool whereof is two inches long, and the wooden handle one inch thick, and three inches in length, wherewith the little boys in our country cut ripe walnuts in two while they are yet in the shell, and pick out the kernel, and they found them very fit for the expediting of that weasand-slitting exploit. In the meantime Friar John, with his formidable baton of the cross, got to the breach which the enemies had made, and there stood to snatch up those that endeavoured to escape. Some of the monkitos carried the standards, banners, ensigns, guidons, and colours into their cells and chambers to make garters of them. But when those that had been shriven would have gone out at the gap of the said breach, the sturdy monk quashed and felled them down with blows, saying, These men have had confession and are penitent souls; they have got their absolution and gained the pardons: they go into paradise as straight as a sickle, or as the way is to Faye (like Crooked-Lane at Eastcheap). Thus by his prowess and valour were discomfited all those of the army that entered into the close of the abbey, unto the number of thirteen thousand, six hundred, twenty and two, besides the women and little children, which is always to be understood. Never did Maugis the Hermit bear himself more valiantly with his bourdon or pilgrim's staff against the Saracens, of whom is written in the Acts of the four sons of Aymon, than did this monk against his enemies with the staff of the cross.

CHAP. XXVIII.

How Picrochole stormed and took by assault the rock Clermond, and of Grangousier's unwillingness and aversion from the undertaking of war.

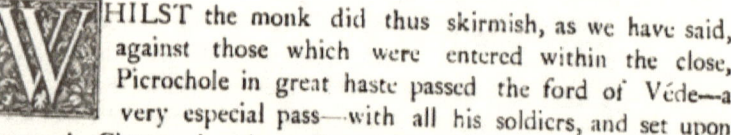HILST the monk did thus skirmish, as we have said, against those which were entered within the close, Picrochole in great haste passed the ford of Véde—a very especial pass—with all his soldiers, and set upon the rock Clermond, where there was made him no resistance at all; and, because it was already night, he resolved to quarter himself and his army in that town, and to refresh himself of his pugnative choler. In the morning he stormed and took the bulwarks and castle, which afterwards he fortified with rampiers, and furnished with all ammunition requisite, intending to make his retreat there, if he should happen to be otherwise worsted; for it was a strong place, both by art and nature, in regard of the stance and situation of it. But let us leave them there, and return to our good Gargantua, who is at Paris very assiduous and earnest at the study of good letters and athletical exercitations, and to the good old man Grangousier his father, who after supper warmeth his ballocks by a good, clear, great fire, and, waiting upon the broiling of some chestnuts, is very serious in drawing scratches on the hearth, with a stick burnt at the one end, wherewith they did stir up the fire, telling to his wife and the rest of the family pleasant old stories and tales of former times.

Whilst he was thus employed, one of the shepherds which did keep the vines, named Pillot, came towards him, and to the full related the enormous abuses which were committed, and the excessive spoil that was made by Picrochole, King of Lerné, upon his lands and territories, and how he had pillaged, wasted, and ransacked all the country, except the enclosure at Sevillé, which Friar John des Entoumeures to his great honour had preserved; and that at the same present time the said king was in the rock Clermond, and there, with great industry and circumspection, was strengthening himself and his whole army. Halas, halas, alas! said Grangousier, what is this, good people? Do I dream, or is it true that they tell me? Picrochole, my ancient friend of old time, of my own kindred and alliance, comes he to invade me? What moves him? What provokes him? What sets him on? What drives him to it? Who hath given him this counsel? Ho, ho, ho, ho, ho, my God, my Saviour, help me, inspire me, and advise me what I shall do! I protest, I swear before thee, so be thou favourable to me, if ever I did him or his subjects any damage or displeasure, or committed any the least robbery in his country; but, on the contrary, I have succoured and supplied him with men, money, friendship, and counsel, upon any occasion wherein I could be steadable for the improvement of his good. That he hath therefore at this nick of time so outraged and wronged me, it cannot be but by the malevolent and wicked spirit. Good God, thou knowest my courage, for nothing can be hidden from thee. If perhaps he be grown mad, and that thou hast sent him hither to me for the better recovery and re-establishment of his brain, grant me power and wisdom to bring him to the yoke of thy holy will by good discipline. Ho, ho, ho, ho, my good people, my friends and my faithful servants, must I hinder you from helping me? Alas, my old age required henceforward nothing else but rest, and all the days of my life I have laboured for nothing so much as peace; but now I must, I see it well, load with arms my poor, weary, and feeble shoulders, and take in my trembling hand the lance and horseman's mace, to succour and protect my honest subjects. Reason will have it so; for by their labour am I entertained, and with their sweat am I nourished, I, my children and my family. This notwithstanding, I will not undertake war, until I have first tried all the ways and means of peace: that I resolve upon.

Then assembled he his council, and proposed the matter as it was indeed. Whereupon it was concluded that they should send some discreet man unto Picrochole, to know wherefore he had thus suddenly broken the peace and invaded those lands unto which he had no right nor title. Furthermore, that they should send for Gargantua, and those under his command, for the preservation of the country, and defence thereof now at need. All this pleased Grangousier very well, and he commanded that so it should be done. Presently therefore he sent the Basque his lackey to fetch Gargantua with all diligence, and wrote to him as followeth.

CHAP. XXIX.

The tenour of the letter which Grangousier wrote to his son Gargantua.

THE fervency of thy studies did require that I should not in a long time recall thee from that philosophical rest thou now enjoyest, if the confidence reposed in our friends and ancient confederates had not at this present disappointed the assurance of my old age. But seeing such is my fatal destiny, that I should be now disquieted by those in whom I trusted most, I am forced to call thee back to help the people and goods which by the right of nature belong unto thee. For even as arms are weak abroad, if there be not counsel at home, so is that study vain and counsel unprofitable which in a due and convenient time is not by virtue executed and put in effect. My deliberation is not to provoke, but to appease—not to assault, but to defend—not to conquer, but to preserve my faithful subjects and hereditary dominions, into which Picrochole is entered in a hostile manner without any ground or cause, and from day to day pursueth his furious enterprise with that height of insolence that is intolerable to freeborn spirits. I have endeavoured to moderate his tyrannical choler, offering him all that which I thought might give him satisfaction; and oftentimes have I sent lovingly unto him to understand wherein, by whom, and how he found himself to be wronged. But of him could I obtain no other answer but a mere defiance, and that in my lands he did pretend only to the right of a civil correspondency and good behaviour, whereby I knew that the eternal God hath left him to the disposure of his own free will and sensual appetite—which cannot choose but be wicked, if by divine grace it be not continually guided—and to contain him within his duty, and bring him to know himself, hath sent him hither to me by a grievous token. Therefore, my beloved son, as soon as thou canst, upon sight of these letters, repair hither with all diligence, to succour not me so much, which nevertheless by natural piety thou oughtest to do, as thine own people, which by reason thou mayest save and preserve. The exploit shall

be done with as little effusion of blood as may be. And, if possible, by means far more expedient, such as military policy, devices, and stratagems of war, we shall save all the souls, and send them home as merry as crickets unto their own houses. My dearest son, the peace of Jesus Christ our Redeemer be with thee. Salute from me Ponocrates, Gymnastes, and Eudemon. The twentieth of September.

Thy Father Grangousier.

CHAP. XXX.

How Ulric Gallet was sent unto Picrochole.

THE letters being dictated, signed, and sealed, Grangousier ordained that Ulric Gallet, master of the requests, a very wise and discreet man, of whose prudence and sound judgment he had made trial in several difficult and debateful matters, [should] go unto Picrochole, to show what had been decreed amongst them. At the same hour departed the good man Gallet, and having passed the ford, asked at the miller that dwelt there in what condition Picrochole was: who answered him that his soldiers had left him neither cock nor hen, that they were retired and shut up into the rock Clermond, and that he would not advise him to go any further for fear of the scouts, because they were enormously furious. Which he easily believed, and therefore lodged that night with the miller.

The next morning he went with a trumpeter to the gate of the castle, and required the guards he might be admitted to speak with the king of somewhat that concerned him. These words being told unto the king, he would by no means consent that they should open the gate; but, getting upon the top of the bulwark, said unto the ambassador, What is the news, what have you to say? Then the ambassador began to speak as followeth.

CHAP. XXXI.

The speech made by Gallet to Picrochole.

THERE cannot arise amongst men a juster cause of grief than when they receive hurt and damage where they may justly expect for favour and good will; and not without cause, though without reason, have many, after they had fallen into such a calamitous accident, esteemed this indignity less supportable than the loss of their own lives, in such sort that, if they have not been able by force of arms nor any other means, by reach of wit or subtlety, to stop them in their course and restrain their fury, they have fallen into desperation, and utterly deprived themselves of this light. It is therefore no wonder if King Grangousier, my master, be full of high displeasure and much disquieted in mind upon thy outrageous and hostile coming; but truly it would be a marvel if he were not sensible of and moved with the incomparable abuses and injuries perpetrated by thee and thine upon those of his country, towards whom there hath been no example of inhumanity omitted. Which in itself is to him so grievous, for the cordial affection wherewith he hath always cherished his subjects, that more it cannot be to any mortal man; yet in this, above human apprehension, is it to him the more grievous that these wrongs and sad offences have been committed by thee and thine, who, time out of mind, from all antiquity, thou and thy predecessors have been in a continual league and amity with him and all his ancestors; which, even until this time, you have as sacred together inviolably preserved, kept, and entertained, so well, that not he and his only, but the very barbarous nations of the Poictevins, Bretons, Manceaux, and those that dwell beyond the isles of the Canaries, and that of Isabella, have thought it as easy to pull down the firmament, and to set up the depths above the clouds, as to make a breach in your alliance; and have been so afraid of it in their enterprises that they have never dared to provoke, incense, or endamage the one for fear of the other. Nay, which is more, this sacred league hath so filled the world, that there are few nations at this day inhabiting throughout all the continent and isles of the ocean, who have not ambitiously aspired to be received into it, upon your own covenants and conditions, holding your joint confederacy in as high esteem as their own territories and dominions, in such sort, that from the memory of man there hath not been either prince or league so wild and proud that durst have offered to invade, I say not your countries, but not so much as those of your confederates. And if, by rash and heady counsel, they have attempted any new design against them, as soon as they heard the name and title of your alliance, they have suddenly desisted from their enterprises. What rage and madness, therefore, doth now incite thee, all old alliance infringed, all amity trod under foot, and all right violated, thus in a hostile manner to invade his country, without having been by him or his in anything prejudiced, wronged, or provoked? Where is faith? Where is law? Where is reason? Where is humanity? Where is the fear of God? Dost thou think that these atrocious abuses are hidden from the eternal spirit and the supreme God who is the just rewarder of all our undertakings? If thou so think, thou deceivest thyself; for all things shall come to pass as in his incomprehensible judgment he hath appointed. Is it thy fatal destiny, or influences of the stars, that would put an end to thy so long enjoyed ease and rest? For that all things have their end and period, so as that, when they are come to the superlative point of their greatest height, they are in a trice tumbled down again, as not being able to abide long in that state. This is the conclusion and end of those who cannot by reason and temperance moderate their fortunes and prosperities. But if it be predestinated that thy happiness and ease must now come to an end, must it needs be by wronging my king,—him by whom thou wert established? If thy house must come to ruin, should it therefore in its fall crush the heels of him that set it up? The matter is so unreasonable, and so dissonant from common sense, that hardly can it be conceived by human understanding, and altogether incredible unto strangers, till by the certain and undoubted effects thereof it be made apparent that nothing is either sacred or holy to those who, having emancipated themselves from God and reason, do merely follow the perverse affections of their own depraved nature. If any wrong had been done by us to thy subjects and dominions—if we had favoured thy ill-willers—if we had not assisted thee in thy need—if thy name and reputation had been wounded by us—or, to speak more truly, if the calumniating spirit, tempting to induce thee to evil, had, by false illusions and deceitful fantasies, put into thy conceit the impression of a thought that we had done unto thee anything unworthy of our ancient correspondence and friendship, thou oughtest first to have inquired out the truth, and afterwards by a seasonable warning to admonish us thereof; and we should have so satisfied thee, according to thine own heart's desire, that thou shouldst have had occasion to be contented. But, O eternal God, what is thy enterprise? Wouldst thou, like a perfidious tyrant, thus spoil and lay waste my master's kingdom? Hast thou found him so silly and blockish, that he would not—or so destitute of men and money, of counsel and skill in military discipline, that he cannot withstand thy unjust invasion? March hence presently, and to-morrow, some time of the day, retreat unto thine own country, without doing any kind of violence or disorderly act by the way; and pay withal a thousand besans of gold (which, in English money, amounteth to five thousand pounds), for reparation of the damages thou hast done in this country. Half thou shalt pay to-morrow, and the other half at the ides of May next coming, leaving with us in the mean time, for hostages, the Dukes of Turnbank, Lowbuttock, and Smalltrash, together with the Prince of Itches and Viscount of Snatchbit.[1]

CHAP. XXXII

How Grangousier, to buy peace, caused the cakes to be restored.

WITH that the good man Gallet held his peace, but Picrochole to all his discourse answered nothing but Come and fetch them, come and fetch them,—they have ballocks fair and soft,—they will knead and provide some cakes for you. Then returned he to Grangousier, whom he found upon his knees bareheaded, crouching in a little corner of his cabinet, and humbly praying unto God that he would vouchsafe to

[1] Tournemoule, Bas-de-fesses, Menuail, Gratelles, Morpiaille.

assuage the choler of Picrochole, and bring him to the rule of reason without proceeding by force. When the good man came back, he asked him, Ha, my friend, my friend, what news do you bring me? There is neither hope nor remedy, said Gallet; the man is quite out of his wits, and forsaken of God. Yea, but, said Grangousier, my friend, what cause doth he pretend for his outrages? He did not show me any cause at all, said Gallet, only that in a great anger he spoke some words of cakes. I cannot tell if they have done any wrong to his cake-bakers. I will know, said Grangousier, the matter thoroughly, before I resolve any more upon what is to be done. Then sent he to learn concerning that business, and found by true information that his men had taken violently some cakes from Picrochole's people, and that Marquet's head was broken with a slacky or short cudgel; that, nevertheless, all was well paid, and that the said Marquet had first hurt Forgier with a stroke of his whip athwart the legs. And it seemed good to his whole council, that he should defend himself with all his might. Notwithstanding all this, said Grangousier, seeing the question is but about a few cakes, I will labour to content him; for I am very unwilling to wage war against him. He inquired then what quantity of cakes they had taken away, and understanding that it was but some four or five dozen, he commanded five cartloads of them to be baked that same night; and that there should be one full of cakes made with fine butter, fine yolks of eggs, fine saffron, and fine spice, to be bestowed upon Marquet, unto whom likewise he directed to be given seven hundred thousand and three Philips [that is, at three shillings the piece, one hundred five thousand pounds and nine shillings of English money], for reparation of his losses and hindrances, and for satisfaction of the chirurgeon that had dressed his wound; and furthermore settled upon him and his for ever in freehold the apple-orchard called La Pomardière. For the conveyance and passing of all which was sent Gallet, who by the way as they went made them gather near the willow-trees great store of boughs, canes, and reeds, wherewith all the carriers were enjoined to garnish and deck their carts, and each of them to carry one in his hand, as himself likewise did, thereby to give all men to understand that they demanded but peace, and that they came to buy it.

Being come to the gate, they required to speak with Picrochole from Grangousier. Picrochole would not so much as let them in, nor go to speak with them, but sent them word that he was busy, and that they should deliver their mind to Captain Touquedillon, who was then planting a piece of ordnance upon the wall. Then said the good man unto him, My lord, to ease you of all this labour, and to take away all excuses why you may not return unto our former alliance, we do here presently restore unto you the cakes upon which the quarrel arose. Five dozen did our people take away: they were well paid for: we love peace so well that we restore unto you five cartloads, of which this cart shall be for Marquet, who doth most complain. Besides, to content him entirely, here are seven hundred thousand and three Philips, which I deliver to him, and, for the losses he may pretend to have sustained, I resign for ever the farm of the Pomardière, to be possessed in fee-simple by him and his for ever, without the payment of any duty, or acknowledgment of homage, fealty, fine, or service whatsoever, and here is the tenour of the deed. And, for God's sake, let us live henceforward in peace, and withdraw yourselves merrily into your own country from within this place, unto which you have no right at all, as yourselves must needs confess, and let us be good friends as before. Touquedillon related all this to Picrochole, and more and more exasperated his courage, saying to him, These clowns are afraid to some purpose. By G—, Grangousier conskites himself for fear, the poor drinker. He is not skilled in warfare, nor hath he any stomach for it. He knows better how to empty the flagons,—that is his art. I am of opinion that it is fit we send back the carts and the money, and, for the rest, that very speedily we fortify ourselves here, then prosecute our fortune. But what! Do they think to have to do with a ninny-whoop, to feed you thus with cakes? You may see what it is. The good usage and great familiarity which you have had with them heretofore hath made you contemptible in their eyes. Anoint a villain, he will prick you: prick a villain, and he will anoint you.[1]

Sa, sa, sa, said Picrochole, by St. James you have given a true character of them. One thing I will advise you, said Touquedillon. We are here but badly victualled, and furnished with mouth-harness very slenderly. If Grangousier should come to besiege us, I would go presently, and pluck out of all your soldiers' heads and mine own all the teeth, except three to each of us, and with them alone

---

[1] Ungentem pungit, pungentem rusticus ungit.

we should make an end of our provision but too soon. We shall have, said Picrochole, but too much sustenance and feeding-stuff. Came we hither to eat or to fight? To fight, indeed, said Touquedillon; yet from the paunch comes the dance, and where famine rules force is exiled. Leave off your prating, said Picrochole, and forthwith seize upon what they have brought. Then took they money and cakes, oxen and carts, and sent them away without speaking one word, only that they would come no more so near, for a reason that they would give them the morrow after. Thus, without doing anything, returned they to Grangousier, and related the whole matter unto him, subjoining that there was no hope left to draw them to peace but by sharp and fierce wars.

CHAP. XXXIII.

How some statesmen of Picrochole, by hairbrained counsel, put him in extreme danger.

THE carts being unloaded, and the money and cakes secured, there came before Picrochole the Duke of Smalltrash, the Earl Swashbuckler, and Captain Dirttail,[1] who said unto him, Sir, this day we make you the happiest, the most warlike and chivalrous prince that ever was since the death of Alexander of Macedonia. Be covered, be covered, said Picrochole. Gramercy, said they, we do but our duty. The manner is thus. You shall leave some captain here to have the charge of this garrison, with a party competent for keeping of the place, which, besides its natural strength, is made stronger by the rampiers and fortresses of your devising. Your army you are to divide into two parts, as you know very well how to do. One part thereof shall fall upon Grangousier and his forces. By it shall he be easily at the very first shock routed, and then shall you get money by heaps, for the clown hath store of ready coin. Clown we call him, because a noble and generous prince hath never a penny, and that to hoard up treasure is but a clownish trick. The other part of the army, in the meantime, shall draw towards Onys, Xaintonge,

---

[1] Menuail, Spadassin, Merdaille.

Angomois, and Gascony. Then march to Perigot, Medoc, and Elanes, taking wherever you come, without resistance, towns, castles, and forts; afterwards to Bayonne, St. John de Luc, to Fontarabia, where you shall seize upon all the ships, and coasting along Galicia and Portugal, shall pillage all the maritime places, even unto Lisbon, where you shall be supplied with all necessaries befitting a conqueror. By copsody, Spain will yield, for they are but a race of loobies. Then are you to pass by the Straits of Gibraltar, where you shall erect two pillars more stately than those of Hercules, to the perpetual memory of your name, and the narrow entrance there shall be called the Picrocholinal sea.

Having passed the Picrocholinal sea, behold, Barbarossa yields himself your slave. I will, said Picrochole, give him fair quarter and spare his life. Yea, said they, so that he be content to be christened. And you shall conquer the kingdoms of Tunis, of Hippo, Argier, Bomine [Bona], Corone, yea, all Barbary. Furthermore, you shall take into your hands Majorca, Minorca, Sardinia, Corsica, with the other islands of the Ligustic and Balearian seas. Going alongst on the left hand, you shall rule all Gallia Narbonensis, Provence, the Allobrogians, Genoa, Florence, Lucca, and then God b' w' ye, Rome. [Our poor Monsieur the Pope dies now for fear.] By my faith, said Picrochole, I will not then kiss his pantoufle.

Italy being thus taken, behold Naples, Calabria, Apulia, and Sicily, all ransacked, and Malta too. I wish the pleasant Knights of the Rhodes heretofore would but come to resist you, that we might see their urine. I would, said Picrochole, very willingly go to Loretto. No, no, said they, that shall be at our return. From thence we will sail eastwards, and take Candia, Cyprus, Rhodes, and the Cyclade Islands, and set upon [the] Morea. It is ours, by St. Trenian. The Lord preserve Jerusalem; for the great Soldan is not comparable to you in power. I will then, said he, cause Solomon's temple to be built. No, said they, not yet, have a little patience, stay awhile, be never too sudden in your enterprises. Can you tell what Octavian Augustus said? *Festina lentè*. It is requisite that you first have the Lesser Asia, Caria, Lycia, Pamphilia, Cilicia, Lydia, Phrygia, Mysia, Bithynia, Carazia, Satalia, Samagaria, Castamena, Luga, Savasta, even unto Euphrates. Shall we see, said Picrochole, Babylon and Mount Sinai? There is no need, said they, at this time. Have we not hurried up and down, travelled and toiled enough, in having transfretted and passed over the Hircanian sea, marched alongst the two Armenias and the three Arabias? Ay, by my faith, said he, we have played the fools, and are undone. Ha, poor souls! What's the matter? said they. What shall we have, said he, to drink in these deserts? For Julian Augustus with his whole army died there for thirst, as they say. We have already, said they, given order for that. In the Syriac sea you have nine thousand and fourteen great ships laden with the best wines in the world. They arrived at Port Joppa. There they found two-and-twenty thousand camels and sixteen hundred elephants, which you shall have taken at one hunting about Sigelmes, when you entered into Lybia; and, besides this, you had all the Mecca caravan. Did not they furnish you sufficiently with wine? Yes, but, said he, we did not drink it fresh. By the virtue, said they, not of a fish, a valiant man, a conqueror, who pretends and aspires to the monarchy of the world, cannot always have his ease. God be thanked that you and your men are come safe and sound unto the banks of the river Tigris. But, said he, what doth that part of our army in the meantime which overthrows that unworthy swillpot Grangousier? They are not idle, said they. We shall meet with them by-and-by. They shall have won you Brittany, Normandy, Flanders, Hainault, Brabant, Artois, Holland, Zealand; they have passed the Rhine over the bellies of the Switzers and lansquenets, and a party of these hath subdued Luxemburg, Lorraine, Champagne, and Savoy, even to Lyons, in which place they have met with your forces returning from the naval conquests of the Mediterranean sea; and have rallied again in Bohemia, after they had plundered and sacked Suevia, Wittemberg, Bavaria, Austria, Moravia, and Styria. Then they set fiercely together upon Lubeck, Norway, Swedeland, Rie, Denmark, Gitland, Greenland, the Sterlins, even unto the frozen sea. This done, they conquered the Isles of Orkney and subdued Scotland, England, and Ireland. From thence sailing through the sandy sea and by the Sarmates, they have vanquished and overcome Prussia, Poland, Lithuania, Russia, Wallachia, Transylvania, Hungary, Bulgaria, Turkeyland, and are now at Constantinople. Come, said Picrochole, let us go join with them quickly, for I will be Emperor of Trebizond also. Shall we not kill all these dogs, Turks and Mahometans? What a devil should we do else? said they. And you shall give their goods and lands to such as shall have served you honestly. Reason, said he, will have it so, that is but just. I give unto you the Caramania, Suria, and all the Palestine. Ha, sir, said they, it is out of your goodness; gramercy, we thank you. God grant you may always prosper. There was there present at that time an old gentleman well experienced in the wars, a stern soldier, and who had been in many great hazards, named Echephron, who, hearing this discourse, said, I do greatly doubt that all this enterprise will be like the tale or interlude of the pitcher full of milk wherewith a shoemaker made himself rich in conceit; but, when the pitcher was broken, he had not whereupon to dine. What do you pretend by these large conquests? What shall be the end of so many labours and crosses? Thus it shall be, said Picrochole, that when we are returned we shall sit down, rest, and be merry. But, said Echephron, if by chance you should never come back, for the voyage is long and dangerous, were it not better for us to take our rest now, than unnecessarily to expose ourselves to so many dangers? Oh, said Swashbuckler, by G—, here is a good dotard; come, let us go hide ourselves in the corner of a chimney, and there spend the whole time of our life amongst ladies, in threading of pearls, or spinning, like Sardanapalus. He that nothing ventures hath neither horse nor mule, says Solomon. He who adventureth too much, said Echephron, loseth both horse and mule, answered Malchon. Enough, said Picrochole, go forward. I fear nothing but that these devilish legions of Grangousier, whilst we are in Mesopotamia, will come on our backs and charge up our rear. What course shall we then take? What shall be our remedy? A very good one, said Dirt-tail; a pretty little commission, which you must send unto the Muscovites, shall bring you into the field in an instant four hundred and fifty thousand choice men of war. Oh that you would but make me your lieutenant-general, I should for the lightest faults of any inflict great punishments. I fret, I charge, I strike, I take, I kill, I slay, I play the devil. On, on, said Picrochole, make haste, my lads, and let him that loves me follow me.

CHAP. XXXIV.

How Gargantua left the city of Paris to succour his country, and how Gymnast encountered with the enemy.

N this same very hour Gargantua, who was gone out of Paris as soon as he had read his father's letters, coming upon his great mare, had already passed the Nunnery-bridge, himself, Ponocrates, Gymnast, and Eudemon, who all three, the better to enable them to go along with him, took post-horses. The rest of his train came after him by even journeys at a slower pace, bringing with them all his books and philosophical instruments. As soon as he had alighted at Parillé, he was informed by a farmer of Gouguet how Picrochole had fortified himself within the rock Clermond, and had sent Captain Tripet with a great army to set upon the wood of Véde and Vaugaudry, and that they had already plundered the whole country, not leaving cock nor hen, even as far as to the winepress of Billard. These strange and almost incredible news of the enormous abuses thus committed over all the land, so affrighted Gargantua that he knew not what to say nor do. But Ponocrates counselled him to go unto the Lord of Vauguyon, who at all times had been their friend and confederate, and that by him they should be better advised in their business. Which they did incontinently, and found him very willing and fully resolved to assist them, and therefore was of opinion that they should send some one of his company to scout along and discover the country, to learn in what condition and posture the enemy was, that they might take counsel, and proceed according to the present occasion. Gymnast offered himself to go. Whereupon it was concluded, that for his safety and the better expedition, he should have with him someone that knew the ways, avenues, turnings, windings, and rivers thereabout. Then away went he and Prelingot, the equerry or gentleman of Vauguyon's horse, who scouted and espied as narrowly as they could upon all quarters without any fear. In the meantime Gargantua took a little refreshment, ate somewhat himself, the like did those who were with him, and caused to give to his

mare a picotine of oats, that is, three score and fourteen quarters and three bushels. Gymnast and his comrade rode so long, that at last they met with the enemy's forces, all scattered and out of order, plundering, stealing, robbing, and pillaging all they could lay their hands on. And, as far off as they could perceive him, they ran thronging upon the back of one another in all haste towards him, to unload him of his money, and untruss his portmantles. Then cried he out unto them, My masters, I am a poor devil, I desire you to spare me. I have yet one crown left. Come, we must drink it, for it is *aurum potabile*, and this horse here shall be sold to pay my welcome. Afterwards take me for one of your own, for never yet was there any man that knew better how to take, lard, roast, and dress, yea, by G—, to tear asunder and devour a hen, than I that am here: and for my *proficiat* I drink to all good fellows. With that he unscrewed his borracho (which was a great Dutch leathern bottle), and without putting in his nose drank very honestly. The maroufle rogues looked upon him, opening their throats a foot wide, and putting out their tongues like greyhounds, in hopes to drink after him; but Captain Tripet, in the very nick of that their expectation, came running to him to see who it was. To him Gymnast offered his bottle, saying, Hold, captain, drink boldly and spare not; I have been thy taster, it is wine of La Faye Monjau. What! said Tripet, this fellow gibes and flouts us? Who art thou? said Tripet. I am, said Gymnast, a poor devil (*pauvre diable*). Ha, said Tripet, seeing thou art a poor devil, it is reason that thou shouldst be permitted to go whithersoever thou wilt, for all poor devils pass everywhere without toll or tax. But it is not the custom of poor devils to be so well mounted; therefore, sir devil, come down, and let me have your horse, and if he do not carry me well, you, master devil, must do it: for I love a life that such a devil as you should carry me away.

CHAP. XXXV.

How Gymnast very souplely and cunningly killed Captain Tripet and others of Picrochole's men.

HEN they heard these words, some amongst them began to be afraid, and blessed themselves with both hands, thinking indeed that he had been a devil disguised, insomuch that one of them, named Good John, captain of the trained bands of the country bumpkins, took his psalter out of his codpiece, and cried out aloud, *Hagios ho theos*. If thou be of God, speak; if thou be of the other spirit, avoid hence, and get thee going. Yet he went not away. Which words being heard by all the soldiers that were there, divers of them being a little inwardly terrified, departed from the place. All this did Gymnast very well remark and consider, and therefore making as if he would have alighted from off his horse, as he was poising himself on the mounting side, he most nimbly, with his short sword by his thigh, shifting his foot in the stirrup, performed the stirrup-leather feat, whereby, after the inclining of his body downwards, he forthwith launched himself aloft in the air, and placed both his feet together on the saddle, standing upright with his back turned towards the horse's head. Now, said he, my case goes backward. Then suddenly in the same very posture wherein he was, he fetched a gambol upon one foot, and, turning to the left hand, failed not to carry his body perfectly round, just into its former stance, without missing one jot. Ha, said Tripet, I will not do that at this time, and not without cause. Well, said Gymnast, I have failed, I will undo this leap. Then with a marvellous strength and agility, turning towards the right hand, he fetched another frisking gambol as before, which done, he set his right-hand thumb upon the hind-bow of the saddle, raised himself up, and sprung in the air, poising and upholding his whole body upon the muscle and nerve of the said thumb, and so turned and whirled himself about three times. At the fourth, reversing his body, and overturning it upside down, and foreside back, without touching anything, he brought himself betwixt the horse's two ears, springing with all his body into the air, upon the thumb of his left

hand, and in that posture, turning like a windmill, did most actively do that trick which is called the miller's pass. After this, clapping his right hand flat upon the middle of the saddle, he gave himself such a jerking swing that he thereby seated himself upon the crupper, after the manner of gentlewomen sitting on horseback. This done, he easily passed his right leg over the saddle, and placed himself like one that rides in croup. But, said he, it were better for me to get into the saddle; then putting the thumbs of both hands upon the crupper before him, and thereupon leaning himself, as upon the only supporters of his body, he incontinently turned heels over head in the air, and straight found himself betwixt the bow of the saddle in a good settlement. Then with a somersault springing into the air again, he fell to stand with both his feet close together upon the saddle, and there made above a hundred frisks, turns, and demi-pommads, with his arms held out across, and in so doing cried out aloud, I rage, I rage, devils, I am stark mad, devils, I am mad, hold me, devils, hold me, hold, devils, hold, hold!

Whilst he was thus vaulting, the rogues in great astonishment said to one another, By cock's death, he is a goblin or a devil thus disguised, *Ab hoste maligno libera nos, Domine*, and ran away in a full flight, as if they had been routed, looking now and then behind them, like a dog that carrieth away a goose-wing in his mouth. Then Gymnast, spying his advantage, alighted from his horse, drew his sword, and laid on great blows upon the thickest and highest crested among them, and overthrew them in great heaps, hurt, wounded, and bruised, being resisted by nobody, they thinking he had been a starved devil, as well in regard of his wonderful feats in vaulting, which they had seen, as for the talk Tripet had with him, calling him poor devil. Only Tripet would have traitorously cleft his head with his horseman's sword, or lance-knight falchion; but he was well armed, and felt nothing of the blow but the weight of the stroke. Whereupon, turning suddenly about, he gave Tripet a home-thrust, and upon the back of that, whilst he was about to ward his head from a slash, he ran him in at the breast with a hit, which at once cut his stomach, the fifth gut called the colon, and the half of his liver, wherewith he fell to the ground, and in falling gushed forth above four pottles of pottage, and his soul mingled with the pottage.

This done, Gymnast withdrew himself, very wisely considering that a case of great adventure and hazard should not be pursued unto its utmost period, and that it becomes all cavaliers modestly to use their good fortune, without troubling or stretching it too far. Wherefore, getting to horse, he gave him the spur, taking the right way unto Vauguyon, and Prelinguand with him.

CHAP. XXXVI.

How Gargantua demolished the castle at the ford of Vede, and how they passed the ford.

AS soon as he came, he related the estate and condition wherein they had found the enemy, and the stratagem which he alone had used against all their multitude, affirming that they were but rascally rogues, plunderers, thieves, and robbers, ignorant of all military discipline, and that they might boldly set forward unto the field; it being an easy matter to fell and strike them down like beasts. Then Gargantua mounted his great mare, accompanied as we have said before, and finding in his way a high and great tree, which commonly was called by the name of St. Martin's tree, because heretofore St. Martin planted a pilgrim's staff there, which in tract of time grew to that height and greatness, said, This is that which I lacked; this tree shall serve me both for a staff and lance. With that he pulled it up easily, plucked off the boughs, and trimmed it at his pleasure. In the meantime his mare pissed to ease her belly, but it was in such abundance that it did overflow the country seven leagues, and all the piss of that urinal flood ran glib away towards the ford of Vede, wherewith the water was so swollen that all the forces the enemy had there were with great horror drowned, except some who had taken the way on the left hand towards the hills. Gargantua, being come to the place of the wood of Vede, was informed by Eudemon that there was some remainder of the enemy within the castle, which to know, Gargantua cried out as loud as he was able, Are you there, or are you not there? If you be there, be there no more; and if you are not there, I have no more to say. But a ruffian gunner, whose charge was to attend the portcullis over the gate, let fly a cannon-ball at him, and hit him with that shot most furiously on the right

temple of his head, yet did him no more hurt than if he had but cast a prune or kernel of a wine-grape at him. What is this? said Gargantua; do you throw at us grape-kernels here? The vintage shall cost you dear; thinking indeed that the bullet had been the kernel of a grape, or raisin-kernel.

Those who were within the castle, being till then busy at the pillage, when they heard this noise ran to the towers and fortresses, from whence they shot at him above nine thousand and five-and-twenty falconshot and arquebusades, aiming all at his head, and so thick did they shoot at him that he cried out, Ponocrates, my friend, these flies here are like to put out mine eyes; give me a branch of those willow-trees to drive them away, thinking that the bullets and stones shot out of the great ordnance had been but dunflies. Ponocrates looked and saw that there were no other flies but great shot which they had shot from the castle. Then was it that he rushed with his great tree against the castle, and with mighty blows overthrew both towers and fortresses, and laid all level with the ground, by which means all that were within were slain and broken in pieces. Going from thence, they came to the bridge at the mill, where they found all the ford covered with dead bodies, so thick that they had choked up the mill and stopped the current of its water, and these were those that were destroyed in the urinal deluge of the mare. There they were at a stand, consulting how they might pass without hindrance by these dead carcasses. But Gymnast said, If the devils have passed there, I will pass well enough. The devils have passed there, said Eudemon, to carry away the damned souls. By St. Treignan! said Ponocrates, then by necessary consequence he shall pass there. Yes, yes, said Gymnastes, or I shall stick in the way. Then setting spurs to his horse, he passed through freely, his horse not fearing nor being anything affrighted at the sight of the dead bodies; for he had accustomed him, according to the doctrine of Ælian, not to fear armour, nor the carcasses of dead men; and that not by killing men as Diomedes did the Thracians, or as Ulysses did in throwing the corpses of his enemies at his horse's feet, as Homer saith, but by putting a Jack-a-lent amongst his hay, and making him go over it ordinarily when he gave him his oats. The other three followed him very close, except Eudemon only, whose horse's foreright or far forefoot sank up to the knee in the paunch of a great fat chuff who lay there upon his back drowned, and could not get it out. There was he pestered, until Gargantua, with the end of his staff, thrust down the rest of the villain's tripes into the water whilst the horse pulled out his foot; and, which is a wonderful thing in hippiatry, the said horse was thoroughly cured of a ringbone which he had in that foot by this touch of the burst guts of that great looby.

CHAP. XXXVII.

How Gargantua, in combing his head, made the great cannon-balls fall out of his hair.

BEING come out of the river of Vede, they came very shortly after to Grangousier's castle, who waited for them with great longing. At their coming they were entertained with many congees, and cherished with embraces. Never was seen a more joyful company, for *Supplementum Supplementi Chronicorum* saith that Gargamelle died there with joy; for my part, truly I cannot tell, neither do I care very much for her, nor for anybody else. The truth was, that Gargantua, in shifting his clothes, and combing his head with a comb, which was nine hundred foot long of the Jewish cane measure, and whereof the teeth were great tusks of elephants, whole and entire, he made fall at every rake above seven balls of bullets, at a dozen the ball, that stuck in his hair at the razing of the castle of the wood of Vede. Which his father Grangousier seeing, thought they had been lice, and said unto him, What, my dear son, hast thou brought us this far some short-winged hawks of the college of Montague? I did not mean that thou shouldst reside there. Then answered Ponocrates, My sovereign lord, think not that I have placed him in that lousy college which they call Montague; I had rather have put him amongst the grave-diggers of Sanct Innocent, so enormous is the cruelty and villainy that I have known there: for the galley-slaves are far better used amongst the Moors and Tartars, the murderers in the criminal dungeons, yea, the very dogs in your house, than are the poor wretched students in the aforesaid college. And if I were King of Paris, the devil take me if I would not set it on fire, and burn both principal and regents, for suffering this inhumanity to be exercised before their eyes. Then, taking up one of these bullets, he said, These are cannon-shot, which your son Gargantua hath lately received by the treachery of your enemies, as he was passing before the wood of Vede.

But they have been so rewarded, that they are all destroyed in the ruin of the castle, as were the Philistines by the policy of Samson, and those whom the tower of Silohim slew, as it is written in the thirteenth of Luke. My opinion is, that we pursue them whilst the luck is on our side; for occasion hath all her hair on her forehead; when she is passed, you may not recall her,—she hath no tuft whereby you can lay hold on her, for she is bald in the hind-part of her head, and never returneth again. Truly, said Grangousier, it shall not be at this time; for I will make you a feast this night, and bid you welcome.

This said, they made ready supper, and, of extraordinary besides his daily fare, were roasted sixteen oxen, three heifers, two and thirty calves, three score and three fat kids, four score and fifteen wethers, three hundred farrow pigs or sheats soused in sweet wine or must, eleven score partridges, seven hundred snipes and woodcocks, four hundred Loudun and Cornwall capons, six thousand pullets, and as many pigeons, six hundred crammed hens, fourteen hundred leverets, or young hares and rabbits, three hundred and three buzzards, and one thousand and seven hundred cockerels. For venison, they could not so suddenly come by it, only eleven wild boars, which the Abbot of Turpenay sent, and eighteen fallow deer which the Lord of Gramount bestowed; together with seven score pheasants, which were sent by the Lord of Essars; and some dozens of queests, coushats, ringdoves, and woodculvers; river-fowl, teals and awteals, bitterns, courtes, plovers, francolins, briganders, tyrasons, young lapwings, tame ducks, shovellers, woodlanders, herons, moorhens, criels, storks, canepetiers, oranges, flamans, which are phænicopters, or crimson-winged sea-fowls, terrigoles, turkeys, arbens, coots, solan-geese, curlews, termagants, and water-wagtails, with a great deal of cream, curds, and fresh cheese, and store of soup, pottages, and brewis with great variety. Without doubt there was meat enough, and it was handsomely dressed by Snapsauce, Hotchpot, and Brayver-juice, Grangousier's cooks. Jenkin Trudgeapace and Cleanglass were very careful to fill them drink.

CHAP. XXXVIII.

How Gargantua did eat up six pilgrims in a salad.

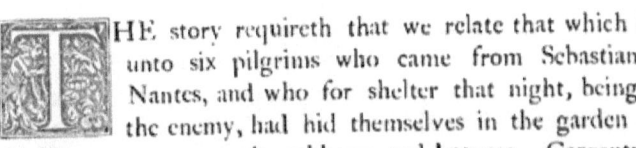HE story requireth that we relate that which happened unto six pilgrims who came from Sebastian near to Nantes, and who for shelter that night, being afraid of the enemy, had hid themselves in the garden upon the chichling peas, among the cabbages and lettuces. Gargantua finding himself somewhat dry, asked whether they could get any lettuce to make him a salad; and hearing that there were the greatest and fairest in the country, for they were as great as plum-trees or as walnut-trees, he would go thither himself, and brought thence in his hand what he thought good, and withal carried away the six pilgrims, who were in so great fear that they did not dare to speak nor cough.

Washing them, therefore, first at the fountain, the pilgrims said one to another softly, What shall we do? We are almost drowned here amongst these lettuce, shall we speak? But if we speak, he will kill us for spies. And, as they were thus deliberating what to do, Gargantua put them with the lettuce into a platter of the house, as large as the huge tun of the White Friars of the Cistercian order; which done, with oil, vinegar, and salt, he ate them up, to refresh himself a little before supper, and had already swallowed up five of the pilgrims, the sixth being in the platter, totally hid under a lettuce, except his bourdon or staff that appeared, and nothing else. Which Grangousier seeing, said to Gargantua, I think that is the horn of a shell-snail, do not eat it. Why not, said Gargantua, they are good all this month: which he no sooner said, but, drawing up the staff, and therewith taking up the pilgrim, he ate him very well, then drank a terrible draught of excellent white wine. The pilgrims, thus devoured, made shift to save themselves as well as they could, by withdrawing their bodies out of the reach of the grinders of his teeth, but could not escape from thinking they had been put in the lowest dungeon of a prison. And when Gargantua whiffed the great draught, they thought to have been drowned in his mouth, and the flood of wine had almost carried them away into the gulf of his stomach. Nevertheless, skipping with their bourdons, as St. Michael's palmers use to do, they sheltered themselves from the danger of that inundation under the banks of his teeth. But one of them by chance, groping or sounding the country with his staff, to try whether they were in safety or no, struck hard against the cleft of a hollow tooth, and hit the mandibulary sinew or nerve of the jaw, which put Gargantua to very great pain, so that he began to cry for the rage that he felt. To ease himself therefore of his smarting ache, he called for his toothpicker, and rubbing towards a young walnut-tree, where they lay skulking, unnestled you my gentlemen pilgrims.

For he caught one by the legs, another by the scrip, another by the pocket, another by the scarf, another by the band of the breeches, and the poor fellow that had hurt him with the bourdon, him he hooked to him by the codpiece, which snatch nevertheless did him a great deal of good, for it pierced unto him a pocky botch he had in the groin, which grievously tormented him ever since they were past Ancenis. The pilgrims, thus dislodged, ran away athwart the plain a pretty fast pace, and the pain ceased, even just at the time when by Eudemon he was called to supper, for all was ready. I will go then, said he, and piss away my misfortune; which he did do in such a copious measure, that the urine taking away the feet from the pilgrims, they were carried along with the stream unto the bank of a tuft of trees. Upon which, as soon as they had taken footing, and that for their self-preservation they had run a little out of the road, they on a sudden fell all six, except Fourniller, into a trap that had been made to take wolves by a train, out of which, nevertheless, they escaped by the industry of the said Fourniller, who broke all the snares and ropes. Being gone from thence, they lay all the rest of that night in a lodge near unto Coudray, where they were comforted in their miseries by the gracious words of one of their company, called Sweer-to-go, who showed them that this adventure had been foretold by the prophet David, *Psalm. Quum exsurgerent homines in nos, forte vivos deglutissent nos*; when we were eaten in the salad, with salt, oil, and vinegar. *Quum irasceretur furor eorum in nos, forsitan aqua absorbuisset nos*; when he drank the great draught. *Torrentem pertransivit anima nostra*; when the stream of his water carried us to the thicket. *Forsitan pertransisset anima nostra aquam intolerabilem;* that is, the water of his urine, the flood whereof, cutting our way, took our feet from us. *Benedictus Dominus qui non dedit nos in captionem dentibus eorum. Anima nostra sicut passer erepta est de laqueo venantium;* when we fell in the trap. *Laqueus contritus est,* by Fourniller, *et nos liberati sumus. Adjutorium nostrum,* &c.

CHAP. XXXIX.

How the Monk was feasted by Gargantua, and of the jovial discourse they had at supper.

WHEN Gargantua was set down at table, after all of them had somewhat stayed their stomachs by a snatch or two of the first bits eaten heartily, Grangousier began to relate the source and cause of the war raised between him and Picrochole; and came to tell how Friar John of the Funnels had triumphed at the defence of the close of the abbey, and extolled him for his valour above Camillus, Scipio, Pompey, Cæsar, and Themistocles. Then Gargantua desired that he might be presently sent for, to the end that with him they might consult of what was to be done. Whereupon, by a joint consent, his steward went for him, and brought him along merrily, with his staff of the cross, upon Grangousier's mule. When he was come, a thousand huggings, a thousand embracements, a thousand good days were given. Ha, Friar John, my friend Friar John, my brave cousin Friar John from the devil! Let me clip thee, my heart, about the neck; to me an armful. I must grip thee, my ballock, till thy back crack with it. Come, my cod, let me coll thee till I kill thee. And Friar John, the gladdest man in the world, never was man made welcomer, never was any more courteously and graciously received than Friar John. Come, come, said Gargantua, a stool here close by me at this end. I am content, said the monk, seeing you will have it so. Some water, page; fill, my boy, fill; it is to refresh my liver. Give me some, child, to gargle my throat withal. *Depositâ cappâ,* said Gymnast, let us pull off this frock. Ho, by G—, gentlemen, said the monk, there is a chapter *in Statutis Ordinis* which opposeth my

laying of it down. Pish! said Gymnast, a fig for your chapter! This frock breaks both your shoulders, put it off. My friend, said the monk, let me alone with it; for, by G—, I'll drink the better that it is on. It makes all my body jocund. If I should lay it aside, the waggish pages would cut to themselves garters out of it, as I was once served at Coulaines. And, which is worse, I shall lose my appetite. But if in this habit I sit down at table, I will drink, by G—, both to thee and to thy horse, and so courage, frolic, God save the company! I have already supped, yet will I eat never a whit the less for that; for I have a paved stomach, as hollow as a butt of malvoisie or St. Benedictus' boot [butt], and always open like a lawyer's pouch. Of all fishes but the tench take the wing of a partridge or the thigh of a nun. Doth not he die like a good fellow that dies with a stiff catso? Our prior loves exceedingly the white of a capon. In that, said Gymnast, he doth not resemble the foxes; for of the capons, hens, and pullets which they carry away they never eat the white. Why? said the monk. Because, said Gymnast, they have no cooks to dress them; and, if they be not competently made ready, they remain red and not white; the redness of meats being a token that they have not got enough of the fire, whether by boiling, roasting, or otherwise, except the shrimps, lobsters, crabs, and crayfishes, which are cardinalized with boiling. By God's feast-gazers, said the monk, the porter of our abbey then hath not his head well boiled, for his eyes are as red as a mazer made of an alder-tree. The thigh of this leveret is good for those that have the gout. To the purpose of the *truel*,—what is the reason that the thighs of a gentlewoman are always fresh and cool? This problem, said Gargantua, is neither in Aristotle, in Alexander Aphrodiscus, nor in Plutarch. There are three causes, said the monk, by which that place is naturally refreshed. Primo, because the water runs all along by it. Secundo, because it is a shady place, obscure and dark, upon which the sun never shines. And thirdly, because it is continually flabbelled, blown upon, and aired by the north winds of the hole arstick, the fan of the smock, and flipflap of the cod-piece. And lusty, my lads. Some bousing liquor, page! So! crack, crack, crack. O how good is God, that gives us of this excellent juice! I call him to witness, if I had been in the time of Jesus Christ, I would have kept him from being taken by the Jews in the garden of Olivet. And the devil fail me, if I should have failed to cut off the hams of these gentlemen apostles who ran away so basely after they had well supped, and left their good master in the lurch. I hate that man worse than poison that offers to run away when he should fight and lay stoutly about him. Oh that I were but King of France for fourscore or a hundred years! By G—, I should whip like curtail-dogs these runaways of Pavia. A plague take them; why did they not choose rather to die there than to leave their good prince in that pinch and necessity? Is it not better and more honourable to perish in fighting valiantly than to live in disgrace by a cowardly running away? We are like to eat no great store of goslings this year; therefore, friend, reach me some of that roasted pig there.

Diavolo, is there no more must? No more sweet wine? *Germinavit radix Jesse. Je renie ma vie, je meurs de soif*; I renounce my life, I rage for thirst. This wine is none of the worst. What wine drink you at Paris? I give myself to the devil, if I did not once keep open house at Paris for all comers six months together. Do you know Friar Claude of the high kilderkins? Oh the good fellow that he is! But I do not know what fly hath stung him of late, he is become so hard a student. For my part, I study not at all. In our abbey we never study for fear of the mumps, which disease in horses is called the mourning in the chine. Our late abbot was wont to say that it is a monstrous thing to see a learned monk. By G--, master, my friend, *Magis magnos clericos non sunt magis magnos sapientes*. You never saw so many hares as there are this year. I could not anywhere come by a goshawk nor tassel of falcon. My Lord Belloniere promised me a lanner, but he wrote to me not long ago that he was become pursy. The partridges will so multiply henceforth, that they will go near to eat up our ears. I take no delight in the stalking-horse, for I catch such cold that I am like to founder myself at that sport. If I do not run, toil, travel, and trot about, I am not well at ease. True it is that in leaping over the hedges and bushes my frock leaves always some of its wool behind it. I have recovered a dainty greyhound; I give him to the devil, if he suffer a hare to escape him. A groom was leading him to my Lord Huntlittle, and I robbed him of him. Did I ill? No, Friar John, said Gymnast, no, by all the devils that are, no! So, said the monk, do I attest these same devils so long as they last, or rather, virtue [of] G—, what could that gouty limpard have done with so fine a dog? By the body of G—, he is better pleased when one presents him with a good yoke of oxen. How now, said Ponocrates, you swear, Friar John. It is only, said the monk, but to grace and adorn my speech. They are colours of a Ciceronian rhetoric.

CHAP. XL.

Why monks are the outcasts of the world; and wherefore some have bigger noses than others.

BY the faith of a Christian, said Eudemon, I do wonderfully dote and enter in a great ecstasy when I consider the honesty and good fellowship of this monk, for he makes us here all merry. How is it, then, that they exclude the monks from all good companies, calling them feast-troublers, marrers of mirth, and disturbers of all civil conversation, as the bees drive away the drones from their hives? *Ignavum fucos pecus*, said Maro, *à præsepibus arcent*. Hereunto, answered Gargantua, there is nothing so true as that the frock and cowl draw unto itself the opprobries, injuries, and maledictions of the world, just as the wind called Cecias attracts the clouds. The peremptory reason is, because they eat the ordure and excrements of the world, that is to say, the sins of the people, and, like dung-chewers and excrementitious eaters, they are cast into the privies and secessive places, that is, the convents and abbeys, separated from political conversation, as the jakes and retreats of a house are. But if you conceive how an ape in a family is always mocked and provokingly incensed, you shall easily apprehend how monks are shunned of all men, both young and old. The ape keeps not the house as a dog doth, he draws not in the plough as the ox, he yields neither milk or wool as the sheep, he carrieth no burden as a horse doth. That which he doth, is only to conskite, spoil, and defile all, which is the cause wherefore he hath of all men mocks, frumperies, and bastinadoes.

After the same manner a monk—I mean those lither, idle, lazy monks—doth not labour and work, as do the peasant and artificer; doth not ward and defend the country, as doth the man of war; cureth not the sick and diseased, as the physician doth; doth neither preach nor teach, as do the evangelical doctors and schoolmasters; doth not import commodities and things necessary for the commonwealth, as the merchant doth. Therefore is it that by and of all men they are hooted at, hated, and abhorred. Yea, but, said Grangousier, they pray to God for us. Nothing less, answered Gargantua. True it is, that with a tingle tangle jangling of bells they trouble and disquiet all their neighbours about them. Right, said the monk; a mass, a matin, a vesper well rung, are half said. They mumble out great store of legends and psalms, by them not at all understood; they say many paternosters interlarded with Ave-Maries, without thinking upon or apprehending the meaning of what it is they say, which truly I call mocking of God, and not prayers. But so help them God, as they pray for us, and not for being afraid to lose their victuals, their manchots, and good fat pottage. All true Christians, of all estates and conditions, in all places and at all times, send up their prayers to God, and the Mediator prayeth and intercedeth for them, and God is gracious to them. Now such a one is our good Friar John; therefore every man desireth to have him in his company. He is no bigot or hypocrite; he is not torn and divided betwixt reality and appearance; no wretch of a rugged and peevish disposition, but honest, jovial, resolute, and a good fellow. He travels, he labours, he defends the oppressed, comforts the afflicted, helps the needy, and keeps the close of the abbey. Nay, said the monk, I do a great deal more than that; for whilst we are in despatching our matins and anniversaries in the choir, I make withal some crossbow-strings, polish glass bottles and bolts, I twist lines and weave purse nets wherein to catch coneys. I am never idle. But now, hither come, some drink, some drink here! Bring the fruit. These chestnuts are of the wood of Estrox, and with good new wine are able to make you a fine cracker and composer of bum-sonnets. You are not as yet, it seems, well moistened in this house with the sweet wine and must. By G—, I drink to all men freely, and at all fords, like a proctor or promoter's horse. Friar John, said Gymnast, take away the snot that hangs at your nose. Ha, ha, said the monk, am not I in danger of drowning, seeing I am in water even to the nose? No, no, *Quare?* *Quia*, though some water come out from thence, there never goes in any; for it is well antidoted with pot-proof armour and syrup of the vine-leaf.

Oh, my friend, he that hath winter-boots made of such leather may boldly fish for oysters, for they will never take water. What is the cause, said Gargantua, that Friar John hath such a fair nose? Because, said Grangousier, that God would have it so, who frameth us in such form and for such end as is most agreeable with his divine will, even as a potter fashioneth his vessels. Because, said Ponocrates, he came with the first to the fair of noses, and therefore made choice of the fairest and the greatest. Pish, said the monk, that is not the reason of it, but, according to the true monastical philosophy, it is because my nurse had soft teats, by virtue whereof, whilst she gave me suck, my nose did sink in as in so much butter. The hard breasts of nurses make children short-nosed. But hey, gay, *Ad formam nasi cognoscitur ad te levavi*. I never eat any confections, page, whilst I am at the bibbery. Item, bring me rather some toasts.

CHAP. XLI.

How the Monk made Gargantua sleep, and of his hours and breviaries.

SUPPER being ended, they consulted of the business in hand, and concluded that about midnight they should fall unawares upon the enemy, to know what manner of watch and ward they kept, and that in the meanwhile they should take a little rest the better to refresh themselves. But Gargantua could not sleep by any means, on which side soever he turned himself. Whereupon the monk said to him, I never sleep soundly but when I am at sermon or prayers. Let us therefore begin, you and I, the seven penitential psalms, to try whether you shall not quickly fall asleep. The conceit pleased Gargantua very well, and, beginning the first of these psalms, as soon as they came to the words *Beati quorum* they fell asleep, both the one and the other. But the monk, for his being formerly accustomed to the hour of claustral matins, failed not to awake a little before midnight, and, being up himself, awaked all the rest, in singing aloud, and with a full clear voice, the song:

Awake, O Reinian, ho, awake!
Awake, O Reinian, ho!
Get up, you no more sleep must take;
Get up, for we must go.

When they were all roused and up, he said, My masters, it is a usual saying, that we begin matins with coughing and supper with drinking. Let us now, in doing clean contrarily, begin our matins with drinking, and at night before supper we shall cough as hard as we can. What, said Gargantua, to drink so soon after sleep? This is not to live according to the diet and prescript rule of the physicians, for you ought first to scour and cleanse your stomach of all its superfluities and excrements. Oh, well physicked, said the monk; a hundred devils leap into my body, if there be not more old drunkards than old physicians! I have made this paction and covenant with my appetite, that it always lieth down and goes to bed with myself, for to that I every day give very good order; then the next morning it also riseth with me and gets up when I am awake. Mind you your charges, gentlemen, or tend your cures as much as you will. I will get me to my drawer; in terms of falconry, my tiring. What drawer or tiring do you mean? said Gargantua. My breviary, said the monk, for just as the falconers, before they feed their hawks, do make them draw at a hen's leg to purge their brains of phlegm and sharpen them to a good appetite, so, by taking this merry little breviary in the morning, I scour all my lungs and am presently ready to drink.

After what manner, said Gargantua, do you say these fair hours and prayers of yours? After the manner of Whipfield,[1] said the monk, by three psalms and three lessons, or nothing at all, he that will. I never tie myself to hours, prayers, and sacraments; for they are made for the man and not the man for them. Therefore is it that I make my prayers in fashion of stirrup-leathers; I shorten or lengthen them when I think good. *Brevis oratio penetrat cælos et longa potatio evacuat scyphos.* Where is that written? By my faith, said Ponocrates, I cannot tell, my pillicock, but thou art more worth than gold. Therein, said the monk, I am like you; but, *venite, apotemus.* Then made they ready store of carbonadoes, or rashers

---

[1] Fussecamp, and corruptly Fecan.

on the coals, and good fat soups, or brewis with sippets; and the monk drank what he pleased. Some kept him company, and the rest did forbear, for their stomachs were not as yet opened. Afterwards every man began to arm and befit himself for the field. And they armed the monk against his will; for he desired no other armour for back and breast but his frock, nor any other weapon in his hand but the staff of the cross. Yet at their pleasure was he completely armed cap-a-pie, and mounted upon one of the best horses in the kingdom, with a good slashing shable by his side, together with Gargantua, Ponocrates, Gymnast, Eudemon, and five-and-twenty more of the most resolute and adventurous of Grangousier's house, all armed at proof with their lances in their hands, mounted like St. George, and everyone of them having an arquebusier behind him.

CHAP. XLII.

How the Monk encouraged his fellow-champions, and how he hanged upon a tree.

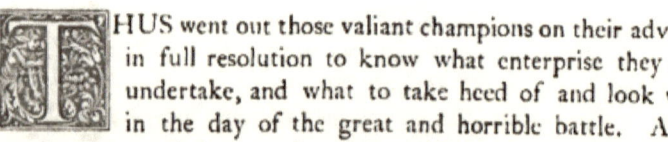

THUS went out those valiant champions on their adventure, in full resolution to know what enterprise they should undertake, and what to take heed of and look well to in the day of the great and horrible battle. And the monk encouraged them, saying, My children, do not fear nor doubt, I will conduct you safely. God and Sanct Benedict be with us! If I had strength answerable to my courage, by's death, I would plume them for you like ducks. I fear nothing but the great ordnance; yet I know of a charm by way of prayer, which the sub-sexton of our abbey taught me, that will preserve a man from the violence of guns and all manner of fire-weapons and engines; but it will do me no good, because I do not believe it. Nevertheless, I hope my staff of the cross shall this day play devilish pranks amongst them. By G—, whoever of our party shall offer to play the duck, and shrink when blows are a-dealing, I give myself to the devil, if I do not make a monk of him in my stead, and hamper him within my frock, which is a sovereign cure against cowardice. Did you never hear of my Lord Meurles his greyhound, which was not worth a straw in the fields? He put a frock about his neck: by the body of G—, there was neither hare nor fox that could escape him, and, which is more, he lined all the bitches in the country, though before that he was feeble-reined and *ex frigidis et maleficiatis*.

The monk uttering these words in choler, as he passed under a walnut-tree, in his way towards the causey, he broached the vizor of his helmet on the stump of a great branch of the said tree. Nevertheless, he set his spurs so fiercely to the horse, who was full of mettle and quick on the spur, that he bounded forwards, and the monk going about to ungrapple his vizor, let go his hold of the bridle, and so hanged by his hand upon the bough, whilst his horse stole away from under him. By this means was the monk left hanging on the walnut-tree, and crying for help, murder, murder, swearing also that he was betrayed. Eudemon perceived him first, and calling Gargantua said, Sir, come and see Absalom hanging. Gargantua, being come, considered the countenance of the monk, and in what posture he hanged; wherefore he said to Eudemon, You were mistaken in comparing him to Absalom; for Absalom hung by his hair, but this shaveling monk hangeth by the ears. Help me, said the monk, in the devil's name; is this a time for you to prate? You seem to me to be like the decretalist preachers, who say that whosoever shall see his neighbour in the danger of death, ought, upon pain of trisulk excommunication, rather choose to admonish him to make his confession to a priest, and put his conscience in the state of peace, than otherwise to help and relieve him.

And therefore when I shall see them fallen into a river, and ready to be drowned, I shall make them a fair long sermon *de contemptu mundi, et fuga seculi*; and when they are stark dead, shall then go to their aid and succour in fishing after them. Be quiet, said Gymnast, and stir not, my minion. I am now coming to unhang thee and to set thee at freedom, for thou art a pretty little gentle monachus. *Monachus in claustro non valet ova duo; sed quando est extra, bene valet triginta.* I have seen above five hundred hanged, but I never saw any have a better countenance in his dangling and pendilatory swagging. Truly, if I had so good a one, I would willingly hang thus all my lifetime. What, said the monk, have you almost done preaching? Help me, in the name of God, seeing you will not in the name of the other spirit, or, by the habit which I wear, you shall repent it, *tempore et loco prælibatis*.

Then Gymnast alighted from his horse, and, climbing up the walnut-tree, lifted up the monk with one hand by the gussets of his armour under the armpits, and with the other undid his vizor from the stump of the broken branch; which done, he let him fall to the ground and himself after. As soon as the monk was down, he put off all his armour, and threw away one piece after another about the field, and, taking to him again his staff of the cross, remounted up to his horse, which Eudemon had caught in his running away. Then went they on merrily, riding along on the highway.

CHAP. XLIII.

How the scouts and fore-party of Picrochole were met with by Gargantua, and how the Monk slew Captain Drawforth,[1] and then was taken prisoner by his enemies.

PICROCHOLE, at the relation of those who had escaped out of the broil and defeat wherein Tripet was untriped, grew very angry that the devils should have so run upon his men, and held all that night a counsel of war, at which Rashcalf and Touchfaucet[2] concluded his power to be such that he was able to defeat all the devils of hell if they should come to jostle with his forces. This Picrochole did not fully believe, though he doubted not much of it. Therefore sent he under the command and conduct of the Count Drawforth, for discovering of the country, the number of sixteen hundred horsemen, all well mounted upon light horses for skirmish and thoroughly besprinkled with holy water; and everyone for their field-mark or cognizance had the sign of a star in his scarf, to serve at all adventures in case they should happen to encounter with devils, that by the virtue, as well of that Gregorian water as of the stars which they wore, they might make them disappear and evanish.

In this equipage they made an excursion upon the country till

---

[1] Tirevant.   [2] Hastiveau, Touquedillon.

they came near to the Vauguyon, which is the valley of Guyon, and to the spital, but could never find anybody to speak unto; whereupon they returned a little back, and took occasion to pass above the aforesaid hospital to try what intelligence they could come by in those parts. In which resolution riding on, and by chance in a pastoral lodge or shepherd's cottage near to Coudray hitting upon the five pilgrims, they carried them way-bound and manacled, as if they had been spies, for all the exclamations, adjurations, and requests that they could make. Being come down from thence towards Sevillé, they were heard by Gargantua, who said then unto those that were with him, Comrades and fellow-soldiers, we have here met with an encounter, and they are ten times in number more than we. Shall we charge them or no? What a devil, said the monk, shall we do else? Do you esteem men by their number rather than by their valour and prowess? With this he cried out, Charge, devils, charge! Which when the enemies heard, they thought certainly that they had been very devils, and therefore even then began all of them to run away as hard as they could drive, Drawforth only excepted, who immediately settled his lance on its rest, and therewith hit the monk with all his force on the very middle of his breast, but, coming against his horrific frock, the point of the iron being with the blow either broke off or blunted, it was in matter of execution as if you had struck against an anvil with a little waxcandle.

Then did the monk with his staff of the cross give him such a sturdy thump and whirret betwixt his neck and shoulders, upon the acromion bone, that he made him lose both sense and motion and fall down stone dead at his horse's feet; and, seeing the sign of the star which he wore scarfwise, he said unto Gargantua, These men are but priests, which is but the beginning of a monk; by St. John, I am a perfect monk, I will kill them to you like flies. Then ran he after them at a swift and full gallop till he overtook the rear, and felled them down like tree-leaves, striking athwart and alongst and every way. Gymnast presently asked Gargantua if they should pursue them. To whom Gargantua answered, By no means; for, according to right military discipline, you must never drive your enemy unto despair, for that such a strait doth multiply his force and increase his courage, which was before broken and cast down; neither is there any better help or outgate of relief for men that are amazed, out of heart, toiled, and spent, than to hope for no favour at all. How many victories have been taken out of the hands of the victors by the vanquished, when they would not rest satisfied with reason, but attempt to put all to the sword, and totally to destroy their enemies, without leaving so much as one to carry home news of the defeat of his fellows. Open, therefore, unto your enemies all the gates and ways, and make to them a bridge of silver rather than fail, that you may be rid of them. Yea, but, said Gymnast, they have the monk. Have they the monk? said Gargantua. Upon mine honour, then, it will prove to their cost. But to prevent all dangers, let us not yet retreat, but halt here quietly as in an ambush; for I think I do already understand the policy and judgment of our enemies. They are truly more directed by chance and mere fortune than by good advice and counsel. In the meanwhile, whilst these made a stop under the walnut-trees, the monk pursued on the chase, charging all he overtook, and giving quarter to none, until he met with a trooper who carried behind him one of the poor pilgrims, and there would have rifled him. The pilgrim, in hope of relief at the sight of the monk, cried out, Ha, my lord prior, my good friend, my lord prior, save me, I beseech you, save me! Which words being heard by those that rode in the van, they instantly faced about, and seeing there was nobody but the monk that made this great havoc and slaughter among them, they loaded him with blows as thick as they use to do an ass with wood. But of all this he felt nothing, especially when they struck upon his frock, his skin was so hard. Then they committed him to two of the marshal's men to keep, and, looking about, saw nobody coming against them, whereupon they thought that Gargantua and his party were fled. Then was it that they rode as hard as they could towards the walnut-trees to meet with them, and left the monk there all alone, with his two foresaid men to guard him. Gangantua heard the noise and neighing of the horses, and said to his men, Comrades, I hear the track and beating of the enemy's horse-feet, and withal perceive that some of them come in a troop and full body against us. Let us rally and close here, then set forward in order, and by this means we shall be able to receive their charge to their loss and our honour.

CHAP. XLIV.

How the Monk rid himself of his keepers, and how Picrochole's forlorn hope was defeated.

HE monk, seeing them break off thus without order, conjectured that they were to set upon Gargantua and those that were with him, and was wonderfully grieved that he could not succour them. Then considered he the countenance of the two keepers in whose custody he was, who would have willingly run after the troops to get some booty and plunder, and were always looking towards the valley unto which they were going. Farther, he syllogized, saying, These men are but badly skilled in matters of war, for they have not required my parole, neither have they taken my sword from me. Suddenly hereafter he drew his brackmard or horseman's sword, wherewith he gave the keeper which held him on the right side such a sound slash that he cut clean through the jugulary veins and the sphagitid or transparent arteries of the neck, with the fore-part of the throat called the gargareon, even unto the two adenes, which are throat kernels; and, redoubling the blow, he opened the spinal marrow betwixt the second and third vertebræ. There fell down that keeper stark dead to the ground. Then the monk, reining his horse to the left, ran upon the other, who, seeing his fellow dead, and the monk to have the advantage of him, cried with a loud voice, Ha, my lord prior, quarter; I yield, my lord prior, quarter; quarter, my good friend, my lord prior. And the monk cried likewise, My lord posterior, my friend, my lord posterior, you shall have it upon your posteriorums. Ha, said the keeper, my lord prior, my minion, my gentle lord prior, I pray God make you an abbot. By the habit, said the monk, which I wear, I will here make you a cardinal. What! do you use to pay ransoms to religious men? You shall therefore have by-and-by a red hat of my giving. And the fellow cried, Ha, my lord prior, my lord prior, my lord abbot that shall be, my lord cardinal, my lord all! Ha, ha, hes, no, my lord prior, my good little lord the prior, I yield, render

and deliver myself up to you. And I deliver thee, said the monk, to all the devils in hell. Then at one stroke he cut off his head, cutting his scalp upon the temple-bones, and lifting up in the upper part of the skull the two triangulary bones called sincipital, or the two bones bregmatis, together with the sagittal commissure or dartlike seam which distinguisheth the right side of the head from the left, as also a great part of the coronal or forehead bone, by which terrible blow likewise he cut the two meninges or films which enwrap the brain, and made a deep wound in the brain's two posterior ventricles, and the cranium or skull abode hanging upon his shoulders by the skin of the pericranium behind, in form of a doctor's bonnet, black without and red within. Thus fell he down also to the ground stark dead.

And presently the monk gave his horse the spur, and kept the way that the enemy held, who had met with Gargantua and his companions in the broad highway, and were so diminished of their number for the enormous slaughter that Gargantua had made with his great tree amongst them, as also Gymnast, Ponocrates, Eudemon, and the rest, that they began to retreat disorderly and in great haste, as men altogether affrighted and troubled in both sense and understanding, and as if they had seen the very proper species and form of death before their eyes; or rather, as when you see an ass with a brizze or gadbee under his tail, or fly that stings him, run hither and thither without keeping any path or way, throwing down his load to the ground, breaking his bridle and reins, and taking no breath nor rest, and no man can tell what ails him, for they see not anything touch him. So fled these people destitute of wit, without knowing any cause of flying, only pursued by a panic terror which in their minds they had conceived. The monk, perceiving that their whole intent was to betake themselves to their heels, alighted from his horse and got upon a big large rock which was in the way, and with his great brackmard sword laid such load upon those runaways, and with main strength fetching a compass with his arm without feigning or sparing, slew and overthrew so many that his sword broke in two pieces. Then thought he within himself that he had slain and killed sufficiently, and that the rest should escape to carry news. Therefore he took up a battle-axe of those that lay there dead, and got upon the rock again, passing his time to see the enemy thus flying and to tumble himself amongst the dead bodies, only that he suffered none to carry pike, sword, lance, nor gun with him, and those who carried the pilgrims bound he made to alight, and gave their horses unto the said pilgrims, keeping them there with him under the hedge, and also Touchfaucet, who was then his prisoner.

CHAP. XLV.

How the Monk carried along with him the Pilgrims, and of the good words that Grangousier gave them.

HIS skirmish being ended, Gargantua retreated with his men, excepting the monk, and about the dawning of the day they came unto Grangousier, who in his bed was praying unto God for their safety and victory. And seeing them all safe and sound, he embraced them lovingly, and asked what was become of the monk. Gargantua answered him that without doubt the enemies had the monk. Then have they mischief and ill luck, said Grangousier; which was very true. Therefore is it a common proverb to this day, to give a man the monk, or, as in French, *lui bailler le moine,* when they would express the doing unto one a mischief. Then commanded he a good breakfast to be provided for their refreshment. When all was ready, they called Gargantua, but he was so aggrieved that the monk was not to be heard of that he would neither eat nor drink. In the meanwhile the monk comes, and from the gate of the outer court cries out aloud, Fresh wine, fresh wine, Gymnast my friend! Gymnast went out and saw that it was Friar John, who brought along with him five pilgrims and Touchfaucet prisoners; whereupon Gargantua likewise went forth to meet him, and all of them made him the best welcome that possibly they could, and brought him before Grangousier, who asked him of all his adventures. The monk told him all, both how he was taken, how he rid himself of his keepers, of the slaughter he had made by the way, and how he had rescued the pilgrims and brought along with him Captain Touchfaucet. Then did they altogether fall to banqueting most merrily. In the meantime Grangousier asked the pilgrims what countrymen they were, whence they came, and whither they went. Sweer-to-go

in the name of the rest answered, My sovereign lord, I am of Saint Genou in Berry, this man is of Palvau, this other is of Onzay, this of Argy, this of St. Nazarand, and this man of Villebrenin. We come from Saint Sebastian near Nantes, and are now returning, as we best may, by easy journeys. Yea, but, said Grangousier, what went you to do at Saint Sebastian? We went, said Sweer-to-go, to offer up unto that sanct our vows against the plague. Ah, poor men! said Grangousier, do you think that the plague comes from Saint Sebastian? Yes, truly, answered Sweer-to-go, our preachers tell us so indeed. But is it so, said Grangousier, do the false prophets teach you such abuses? Do they thus blaspheme the sancts and holy men of God, as to make them like unto the devils, who do nothing but hurt unto mankind,—as Homer writeth, that the plague was sent into the camp of the Greeks by Apollo, and as the poets feign a great rabble of Vejoves and mischievous gods. So did a certain cafard or dissembling religionary preach at Sinay, that Saint Anthony sent the fire into men's legs, that Saint Eutropius made men hydropic, Saint Clidas, fools, and that Saint Genou made them goutish. But I punished him so exemplarily, though he called me heretic for it, that since that time no such hypocritical rogue durst set his foot within my territories. And truly I wonder that your king should suffer them in their sermons to publish such scandalous doctrine in his dominions; for they deserve to be chastised with greater severity than those who, by magical art, or any other device, have brought the pestilence into a country. The pest killeth but the bodies, but such abominable impostors empoison our very souls. As he spake these words, in came the monk very resolute, and asked them, Whence are you, you poor wretches? Of Saint Genou, said they. And how, said the monk, does the Abbot Gulligut, the good drinker,—and the monks, what cheer make they? By G— body, they'll have a fling at your wives, and breast them to some purpose, whilst you are upon your roaming rant and gadding pilgrimage. Hin, hen, said Sweer-to-go, I am not afraid of mine, for he that shall see her by day will never break his neck to come to her in the night-time. Yea, marry, said the monk, now you have hit it. Let her be as ugly as ever was Proserpina, she will once, by the Lord G—, be overturned, and get her skin-coat shaken, if there dwell any monks near to her; for a good carpenter will make use of any kind of timber. Let me be peppered with the pox, if you find not all your wives with child at your return; for the very shadow of the steeple of an abbey is fruitful. It is, said Gargantua, like the water of Nilus in Egypt, if you believe Strabo and Pliny, *Lib.* 7, *cap.* 3. What virtue will there be then, said the monk, in their bullets of concupiscence, their habits and their bodies?

Then, said Grangousier, go your ways, poor men, in the name of God the Creator, to whom I pray to guide you perpetually, and henceforward be not so ready to undertake these idle and unprofitable journeys. Look to your families, labour every man in his vocation, instruct your children, and live as the good apostle St. Paul directeth you; in doing whereof, God, his angels and sancts, will guard and protect you, and no evil or plague at any time shall befall you. Then Gargantua led them into the hall to take their refection; but the pilgrims did nothing but sigh, and said to Gargantua, O how happy is that land which hath such a man for their lord! We have been more edified and instructed by the talk which he had with us, than by all the sermons that ever were preached in our town. This is, said Gargantua, that which Plato saith, *Lib.* 5 *de Republ.*, that those commonwealths are happy, whose rulers philosophate, and whose philosophers rule. Then caused he their wallets to be filled with victuals and their bottles with wine, and gave unto each of them a horse to ease them upon the way, together with some pence to live by.

CHAP. XLVI.

How Grangousier did very kindly entertain Touchfaucet his prisoner.

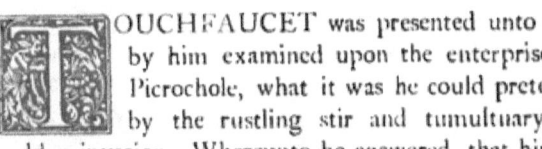OUCHFAUCET was presented unto Grangousier, and by him examined upon the enterprise and attempt of Picrochole, what it was he could pretend to, or aim at, by the rustling stir and tumultuary coil of this his sudden invasion. Whereunto he answered, that his end and purpose was to conquer all the country, if he could, for the injury done to his cake-bakers. It is too great an undertaking, said Grangousier; and, as the proverb is, He that grips too much, holds fast but little. The time is not now as formerly, to conquer the kingdoms

of our neighbour princes, and to build up our own greatness upon the loss of our nearest Christian brother. This imitation of the ancient Herculeses, Alexanders, Hannibals, Scipios, Cæsars, and other such heroes, is quite contrary to the profession of the gospel of Christ, by which we are commanded to preserve, keep, rule, and govern every man his own country and lands, and not in a hostile manner to invade others; and that which heretofore the Barbars and Saracens called prowess and valour, we do now call robbing, thievery, and wickedness. It would have been more commendable in him to have contained himself within the bounds of his own territories, royally governing them, than to insult and domineer in mine, pillaging and plundering everywhere like a most unmerciful enemy; for, by ruling his own with discretion, he might have increased his greatness, but by robbing me he cannot escape destruction. Go your ways in the name of God, prosecute good enterprises, show your king what is amiss, and never counsel him with regard unto your own particular profit, for the public loss will swallow up the private benefit. As for your ransom, I do freely remit it to you, and will that your arms and horse be restored to you; so should good neighbours do, and ancient friends, seeing this our difference is not properly war. As Plato, *Lib.* 5 *de Repub.*, would not have it called war, but sedition, when the Greeks took up arms against one another, and that therefore, when such combustions should arise amongst them, his advice was to behave themselves in the managing of them with all discretion and modesty. Although you call it war, it is but superficial; it entereth not into the closet and inmost cabinet of our hearts. For neither of us hath been wronged in his honour, nor is there any question betwixt us in the main, but only how to redress, by the bye, some petty faults committed by our men,—I mean, both yours and ours, which, although you knew, you ought to let pass; for these quarrelsome persons deserve rather to be contemned than mentioned, especially seeing I offered them satisfaction according to the wrong. God shall be the just judge of our variances, whom I beseech by death rather to take me out of this life, and to permit my goods to perish and be destroyed before mine eyes, than that by me or mine he should in any sort be wronged. These words uttered, he called the monk, and before them all thus spoke unto him, Friar John, my good friend, it is you that took prisoner the Captain Touchfaucet here present? Sir, said the monk, seeing himself is here, and that he is of the years of discretion, I had rather you should know it by his confession than by any words of mine. Then said Touchfaucet, My sovereign lord, it is he indeed that took me, and I do therefore most freely yield myself his prisoner. Have you put him to any ransom? said Grangousier to the monk. No, said the monk, of that I take no care. How much would you have for having taken him? Nothing, nothing, said the monk; I am not swayed by that, nor do I regard it. Then Grangousier commanded that, in presence of Touchfaucet, should be delivered to the monk for taking him the sum of three score and two thousand saluts (in English money, fifteen thousand and five hundred pounds), which was done, whilst they made a collation or little banquet to the said Touchfaucet, of whom Grangousier asked if he would stay with him, or if he loved rather to return to his king. Touchfaucet answered that he was content to take whatever course he would advise him to. Then, said Grangousier, return unto your king, and God be with you.

Then he gave him an excellent sword of a Vienne blade, with a golden scabbard wrought with vine-branch-like flourishes, of fair goldsmith's work, and a collar or neck-chain of gold, weighing seven hundred and two thousand marks (at eight ounces each), garnished with precious stones of the finest sort, esteemed at a hundred and sixty thousand ducats, and ten thousand crowns more, as an honourable donative, by way of present.

After this talk Touchfaucet got to his horse, and Gargantua for his safety allowed him the guard of thirty men-at-arms and six score archers to attend him, under the conduct of Gymnast, to bring him even unto the gate of the rock Clermond, if there were need. As soon as he was gone, the monk restored unto Grangousier the three score and two thousand saluts which he had received, saying, Sir, it is not as yet the time for you to give such gifts; stay till this war be at an end, for none can tell what accidents may occur, and war begun without good provision of money beforehand for going through with it, is but as a breathing of strength, and blast that will quickly pass away. Coin is the sinews of war. Well then, said Grangousier, at the end I will content you by some honest recompense, as also all those who shall do me good service.

CHAP. XLVII.

How Grangousier sent for his legions, and how Touchfaucet slew Rashcalf, and was afterwards executed by the command of Picrochole.

BOUT this same time those of Besse, of the Old Market, of St. James' Bourg, of the Draggage, of Parillé, of the Rivers, of the rocks St. Pol, of the Vaubreton, of Pautillé, of the Brehemont, of Clainbridge, of Cravant, of Grammont, of the town at the Badgerholes, of Huymes, of Segré, of Husse, of St. Lovant, of Panzoust, of the Coldraux, of Verron, of Coulaines, of Chose, of Varenes, of Bourgueil, of the Bouchard Island, of the Croullay, of Narsay, of Cande, of Montsoreau, and other bordering places, sent ambassadors unto Grangousier, to tell him that they were advised of the great wrongs which Picrochole had done him, and, in regard of their ancient confederacy, offered him what assistance they could afford, both in men, money, victuals, and ammunition, and other necessaries for war. The money which by the joint agreement of them all was sent unto him, amounted to six score and fourteen millions, two crowns and a half of pure gold. The forces wherewith they did assist him did consist in fifteen thousand cuirassiers, two-and-thirty thousand light horsemen, four score and nine thousand dragoons, and a hundred-and-forty thousand volunteer adventurers. These had with them eleven thousand and two hundred cannons, double cannons, long pieces of artillery called basilisks, and smaller sized ones known by the name of spirols, besides the mortar-pieces and grenadoes. Of pioneers they had seven-and-forty thousand, all victualled and paid for six months and four days of advance. Which offer Gargantua did not altogether refuse, nor wholly accept of; but, giving them hearty thanks, said that he would compose and order the war by such a device, that there should not be found great need to put so many honest men to trouble in the managing of it; and therefore was content at that time to give order only for bringing along the legions which he maintained in his ordinary garrison towns of the Deviniere, of Chavigny,

of Gravot, and of the Quinquenais, amounting to the number of two thousand cuirassiers, three score and six thousand foot-soldiers, six-and-twenty thousand dragoons, attended by two hundred pieces of great ordnance, two-and-twenty thousand pioneers, and six thousand light horsemen, all drawn up in troops, so well befitted and accommodated with their commissaries, sutlers, farriers, harness-makers, and other such like necessary members in a military camp, so fully instructed in the art of warfare, so perfectly knowing and following their colours, so ready to hear and obey their captains, so nimble to run, so strong at their charging, so prudent in their adventures, and every day so well disciplined, that they seemed rather to be a concert of organ-pipes, or mutual concord of the wheels of a clock, than an infantry and cavalry, or army of soldiers.

Touchfaucet immediately after his return presented himself before Picrochole, and related unto him at large all that he had done and seen, and at last endeavoured to persuade him with strong and forcible arguments to capitulate and make an agreement with Grangousier, whom he found to be the honestest man in the world; saying further, that it was neither right nor reason thus to trouble his neighbours, of whom they had never received anything but good. And in regard of the main point, that they should never be able to go through stitch with that war, but to their great damage and mischief; for the forces of Picrochole were not so considerable but that Grangousier could easily overthrow them.

He had not well done speaking when Rashcalf said out aloud, Unhappy is that prince which is by such men served, who are so easily corrupted, as I know Touchfaucet is. For I see his courage so changed that he had willingly joined with our enemies to fight against us and betray us, if they would have received him; but as virtue is of all, both friends and foes, praised and esteemed, so is wickedness soon known and suspected, and although it happen the enemies to make use thereof for their profit, yet have they always the wicked and the traitors in abomination.

Touchfaucet being at these words very impatient, drew out his sword, and therewith ran Rashcalf through the body, a little under the nipple of his left side, whereof he died presently, and pulling back his sword out of his body said boldly, So let him perish that shall a faithful servant blame. Picrochole incontinently grew furious, and seeing Touchfaucet's new sword and his scabbard so richly diapered with flourishes of most excellent workmanship, said, Did they give thee this weapon so feloniously therewith to kill before my face my so good friend Rashcalf? Then immediately commanded he his guard to hew him in pieces, which was instantly done, and that so cruelly that the chamber was all dyed with blood. Afterwards he appointed the corpse of Rashcalf to be honourably buried, and that of Touchfaucet to be cast over the walls into the ditch.

The news of these excessive violences were quickly spread through all the army; whereupon many began to murmur against Picrochole, in so far that Pinchpenny said to him, My sovereign lord, I know not what the issue of this enterprise will be. I see your men much dejected, and not well resolved in their minds, by considering that we are here very ill provided of victual, and that our number is already much diminished by three or four sallies. Furthermore, great supplies and recruits come daily in to your enemies; but we so moulder away that, if we be once besieged, I do not see how we can escape a total destruction. Tush, pish, said Picrochole, you are like the Melun eels, you cry before they come to you. Let them come, let them come, if they dare.

CHAP. XLVIII.

How Gargantua set upon Picrochole within the rock Clermond, and utterly defeated the army of the said Picrochole.

GARGANTUA had the charge of the whole army, and his father Grangousier stayed in his castle, who, encouraging them with good words, promised great rewards unto those that should do any notable service. Having thus set forward, as soon as they had gained the pass at the ford of Véde, with boats and bridges speedily made they passed over in a trice. Then considering the situation of the town, which was on a high and advantageous place, Gargantua thought fit to call his council, and pass that night in deliberation upon what was to be done. But Gymnast said unto him, My sovereign lord, such is the nature and complexion of the French, that they are worth nothing

but at the first push. Then are they more fierce than devils. But
if they linger a little and be wearied with delays, they'll prove more
faint and remiss than women. My opinion is, therefore, that now
presently, after your men have taken breath and some small refection,
you give order for a resolute assault, and that we storm them
instantly. His advice was found very good, and for effectuating
thereof he brought forth his army into the plain field, and placed the
reserves on the skirt or rising of a little hill. The monk took
along with him six companies of foot and two hundred horsemen
well armed, and with great diligence crossed the marsh, and valiantly
got upon the top of the green hillock even unto the highway which
leads to Loudun. Whilst the assault was thus begun, Picrochole's
men could not tell well what was best, to issue out and receive the
assailants, or keep within the town and not to stir. Himself in
the mean time, without deliberation, sallied forth in a rage with the
cavalry of his guard, who were forthwith received and royally entertained with great cannon-shot that fell upon them like hail from the
high grounds on which the artillery was planted. Whereupon
the Gargantuists betook themselves unto the valleys, to give the
ordnance leave to play and range with the larger scope.

Those of the town defended themselves as well as they could,
but their shot passed over us without doing us any hurt at all. Some
of Picrochole's men that had escaped our artillery set most fiercely
upon our soldiers, but prevailed little; for they were all let in betwixt the files, and there knocked down to the ground, which their
fellow-soldiers seeing, they would have retreated, but the monk
having seized upon the pass by the which they were to return, they
ran away and fled in all the disorder and confusion that could be
imagined.

Some would have pursued after them and followed the chase, but
the monk withheld them, apprehending that in their pursuit the
pursuers might lose their ranks, and so give occasion to the besieged
to sally out of the town upon them. Then staying there some space
and none coming against him, he sent the Duke Phrontist to advise
Gargantua to advance towards the hill upon the left hand, to hinder
Picrochole's retreat at that gate; which Gargantua did with all
expedition, and sent thither four brigades under the conduct of
Sebast, which had no sooner reached the top of the hill, but they
met Picrochole in the teeth, and those that were with him scattered.

Then charged they upon them stoutly, yet were they much endamaged by those that were upon the walls, who galled them with all manner of shot, both from the great ordnance, small guns, and bows. Which Gargantua perceiving, he went with a strong party to their relief, and with his artillery began to thunder so terribly upon that canton of the wall, and so long, that all the strength within the town, to maintain and fill up the breach, was drawn thither. The monk seeing that quarter which he kept besieged void of men and competent guards, and in a manner altogether naked and abandoned, did most magnanimously on a sudden lead up his men towards the fort, and never left it till he had got up upon it, knowing that such as come to the reserve in a conflict bring with them always more fear and terror than those that deal about them with their hands in the fight.

Nevertheless, he gave no alarm till all his soldiers had got within the wall, except the two hundred horsemen, whom he left without to secure his entry. Then did he give a most horrible shout, so did all those who were with him, and immediately thereafter, without resistance, putting to the edge of the sword the guard that was at that gate, they opened it to the horsemen, with whom most furiously they altogether ran towards the east gate, where all the hurlyburly was, and coming close upon them in the rear overthrew all their forces.

The besieged, seeing that the Gargantuists had won the town upon them, and that they were like to be secure in no corner of it, submitted themselves unto the mercy of the monk, and asked for quarter, which the monk very nobly granted to them, yet made them lay down their arms; then, shutting them up within churches, gave order to seize upon all the staves of the crosses, and placed men at the doors to keep them from coming forth. Then opening that east gate, he issued out to succour and assist Gargantua. But Picrochole, thinking it had been some relief coming to him from the town, adventured more forwardly than before, and was upon the giving of a most desperate home-charge, when Gargantua cried out, Ha, Friar John, my friend Friar John, you are come in a good hour. Which unexpected accident so affrighted Picrochole and his men, that, giving all for lost, they betook themselves to their heels, and fled on all hands. Gargantua chased them till they came near to Vaugaudry, killing and slaying all the way, and then sounded the retreat.

CHAP. XLIX.

How Picrochole in his flight fell into great misfortunes, and what Gargantua did after the battle.

ICROCHOLE thus in despair fled towards the Bouchard Island, and in the way to Riviere his horse stumbled and fell down, whereat he on a sudden was so incensed, that he with his sword without more ado killed him in his choler; then, not finding any that would remount him, he was about to have taken an ass at the mill that was thereby; but the miller's men did so baste his bones and so soundly bethwack him that they made him both black and blue with strokes; then stripping him of all his clothes, gave him a scurvy old canvas jacket wherewith to cover his nakedness. Thus went along this poor choleric wretch, who, passing the water at Port-Huaulx, and relating his misadventurous disasters, was foretold by an old Lourpidon hag that his kingdom should be restored to him at the coming of the Cocklicranes, which she called Coquecigrues. What is become of him since we cannot certainly tell, yet was I told that he is now a porter at Lyons, as testy and pettish in humour as ever he was before, and would be always with great lamentation inquiring at all strangers of the coming of the Cocklicranes, expecting assuredly, according to the old woman's prophecy, that at their coming he shall be re-established in his kingdom. The first thing Gargantua did after his return into the town was to call the muster-roll of his men, which when he had done, he found that there were very few either killed or wounded, only some few foot of Captain Tolmere's company, and Ponocrates, who was shot with a musket-ball through the doublet. Then he caused them all at and in their several posts and divisions to take a little refreshment, which was very plenteously provided for them in the best drink and victuals that could be had for money, and gave order to the treasurers and commissaries of the army to pay for and defray that repast, and that there should be no outrage at all nor abuse committed in the town, seeing it was his own. And furthermore commanded, that imme-

diately after the soldiers had done with eating and drinking for that time sufficiently and to their own hearts' desire, a gathering should be beaten for bringing them altogether, to be drawn up on the piazza before the castle, there to receive six months' pay completely. All which was done. After this, by his direction, were brought before him in the said place all those that remained of Picrochole's party, unto whom, in the presence of the princes, nobles, and officers of his court and army, he spoke as followeth.

CHAP. L.

Gargantua's speech to the vanquished.

UR forefathers and ancestors of all times have been of this nature and disposition, that, upon the winning of a battle, they have chosen rather, for a sign and memorial of their triumphs and victories, to erect trophies and monuments in the hearts of the vanquished by clemency than by architecture in the lands which they had conquered. For they did hold in greater estimation the lively remembrance of men purchased by liberality than the dumb inscription of arches, pillars, and pyramids, subject to the injury of storms and tempests, and to the envy of everyone. You may very well remember of the courtesy which by them was used towards the Bretons in the battle of St. Aubin of Cormier and at the demolishing of Partenay. You have heard, and hearing admire, their gentle comportment towards those at the barriers [the barbarians] of Spaniola, who had plundered, wasted, and ransacked the maritime borders of Olone and Thalmondois. All this hemisphere of the world was filled with the praises and congratulations which yourselves and your fathers made, when Alpharbal, King of Canarre, not satisfied with his own fortunes, did most furiously invade the land of Onyx, and with cruel piracies molest all the Armoric Islands and confine regions of Britany. Yet was he in a set naval fight justly taken and vanquished by my father, whom God preserve and protect. But what? Whereas other kings and emperors, yea, those who entitle themselves Catholics, would have dealt roughly with him, kept him a close prisoner, and put him to an extreme high ransom, he entreated him very courteously, lodged him

kindly with himself in his own palace, and out of his incredible mildness and gentle disposition sent him back with a safe conduct, laden with gifts, laden with favours, laden with all offices of friendship. What fell out upon it? Being returned into his country, he called a parliament, where all the princes and states of his kingdom being assembled, he showed them the humanity which he had found in us, and therefore wished them to take such course by way of compensation therein as that the whole world might be edified by the example, as well of their honest graciousness to us as of our gracious honesty towards them. The result hereof was, that it was voted and decreed by an unanimous consent, that they should offer up entirely their lands, dominions, and kingdoms, to be disposed of by us according to our pleasure.

Alpharbal in his own person presently returned with nine thousand and thirty-eight great ships of burden, bringing with him the treasures, not only of his house and royal lineage, but almost of all the country besides. For he embarking himself, to set sail with a west-north-east wind, everyone in heaps did cast into the ship gold, silver, rings, jewels, spices, drugs, and aromatical perfumes, parrots, pelicans, monkeys, civet-cats, black-spotted weasels, porcupines, &c. He was accounted no good mother's son that did not cast in all the rare and precious things he had.

Being safely arrived, he came to my said father, and would have kissed his feet. That action was found too submissively low, and therefore was not permitted, but in exchange he was most cordially embraced. He offered his presents; they were not received, because they were too excessive: he yielded himself voluntarily a servant and vassal, and was content his whole posterity should be liable to the same bondage; this was not accepted of, because it seemed not equitable: he surrendered, by virtue of the decree of his great parliamentary council, his whole countries and kingdoms to him, offering the deed and conveyance, signed, sealed, and ratified by all those that were concerned in it; this was altogether refused, and the parchments cast into the fire. In end, this free goodwill and simple meaning of the Canarians wrought such tenderness in my father's heart that he could not abstain from shedding tears, and wept most profusely; then, by choice words very congruously adapted, strove in what he could to diminish the estimation of the good offices which he had done them, saying, that any courtesy he had conferred upon them was not worth a rush, and what favour soever he had showed them he was bound to do it. But so much the more did Alpharbal augment the repute thereof. What was the issue? Whereas for his ransom, in the greatest extremity of rigour and most tyrannical dealing, could not have been exacted above twenty times a hundred thousand crowns, and his eldest sons detained as hostages till that sum had been paid, they made themselves perpetual tributaries, and obliged to give us every year two millions of gold at four and twenty carats fine. The first year we received the whole sum of two millions; the second year of their own accord they paid freely to us three and twenty hundred thousand crowns; the third year, six and twenty hundred thousand; the fourth year, three millions, and do so increase it always out of their own goodwill that we shall be constrained to forbid them to bring us any more. This is the nature of gratitude and true thankfulness. For time, which gnaws and diminisheth all things else, augments and increaseth benefits; because a noble action of liberality, done to a man of reason, doth grow continually by his generous thinking of it and remembering it.

Being unwilling therefore any way to degenerate from the hereditary mildness and clemency of my parents, I do now forgive you, deliver you from all fines and imprisonments, fully release you, set you at liberty, and every way make you as frank and free as ever you were before. Moreover, at your going out of the gate, you shall have every one of you three months' pay to bring you home into your houses and families, and shall have a safe convoy of six hundred cuirassiers and eight thousand foot under the conduct of Alexander, esquire of my body, that the clubmen of the country may not do you any injury. God be with you! I am sorry from my heart that Picrochole is not here; for I would have given him to understand that this war was undertaken against my will and without any hope to increase either my goods or renown. But seeing he is lost, and that no man can tell where nor how he went away, it is my will that his kingdom remain entire to his son; who, because he is too young, he not being yet full five years old, shall be brought up and instructed by the ancient princes and learned men of the kingdom. And because a realm thus desolate may easily come to ruin, if the covetousness and avarice of those who by their places are obliged to administer justice in it be not curbed and restrained, I ordain and will have it so, that Ponocrates be overseer and superintendent above all his governors, with whatever power and authority is requisite thereto, and that he be continually with the child until he find him able and capable to rule and govern by himself.

Now I must tell you, that you are to understand how a too feeble and dissolute facility in pardoning evildoers giveth them occasion to commit wickedness afterwards more readily, upon this pernicious confidence of receiving favour. I consider that Moses, the meekest man that was in his time upon the earth, did severely punish the mutinous and seditious people of Israel. I consider likewise that Julius Cæsar, who was so gracious an emperor that Cicero said of him that his fortune had nothing more excellent than that he could, and his virtue nothing better than that he would always save and pardon every man—he, notwithstanding all this, did in certain places most rigorously punish the authors of rebellion. After the example of these good men, it is my will and pleasure that you deliver over unto me before you depart hence, first, that fine fellow Marquet, who was the prime cause, origin, and groundwork of this war by his vain presumption and overweening; secondly, his fellow cake-bakers, who were neglective in checking and reprehending his idle hairbrained humour in the instant time; and lastly, all the councillors, captains, officers, and domestics of Picrochole, who had been incendiaries or fomenters of the war by provoking, praising, or counselling him to come out of his limits thus to trouble us.

CHAP. LI.

How the victorious Gargantuists were recompensed after the battle.

WHEN Gargantua had finished his speech, the seditious men whom he required were delivered up unto him, except Swashbuckler, Dirt-tail, and Smalltrash, who ran away six hours before the battle—one of them as far as to Lainiel-neck at one course, another to the valley of Vire, and the third even unto Logroine, without looking back or taking breath by the way—and two of the cake-bakers who were slain in the fight. Gargantua did them no other hurt but that he appointed them to

pull at the presses of his printing-house which he had newly set up. Then those who died there he caused to be honourably buried in Black-soile valley and Burn-hag field, and gave order that the wounded should be dressed and had care of in his great hospital or nosocome. After this, considering the great prejudice done to the town and its inhabitants, he reimbursed their charges and repaired all the losses that by their confession upon oath could appear they had sustained; and, for their better defence and security in times coming against all sudden uproars and invasions, commanded a strong citadel to be built there with a competent garrison to maintain it. At his departure he did very graciously thank all the soldiers of the brigades that had been at this overthrow, and sent them back to their winter-quarters in their several stations and garrisons; the decumane legion only excepted, whom in the field on that day he saw do some great exploit, and their captains also, whom he brought along with himself unto Grangousier.

At the sight and coming of them, the good man was so joyful, that it is not possible fully to describe it. He made them a feast the most magnificent, plentiful, and delicious that ever was seen since the time of the king Ahasuerus. At the taking up of the table he distributed amongst them his whole cupboard of plate, which weighed eight hundred thousand and fourteen bezants[1] of gold, in great antique vessels, huge pots, large basins, big tasses, cups, goblets, candlesticks, comfit-boxes, and other such plate, all of pure massy gold, besides the precious stones, enamelling, and workmanship, which by all men's estimation was more worth than the matter of the gold. Then unto every one of them out of his coffers caused he to be given the sum of twelve hundred thousand crowns ready money. And, further, he gave to each of them for ever and in perpetuity, unless he should happen to decease without heirs, such castles and neighbouring lands of his as were most commodious for them. To Ponocrates he gave the rock Clermond; to Gymnast, the Coudray; to Eudemon, Montpensier; Rivau, to Tolmere; to Ithibolle, Montsoreau; to Acamas, Cande; Varenes, to Chironacte; Gravot, to Sebast; Quinquenais, to Alexander; Legre, to Sophrone, and so of his other places.

[1] Each bezant is worth five pounds English money.

CHAP. LII.

How Gargantua caused to be built for the Monk the Abbey of Theleme.

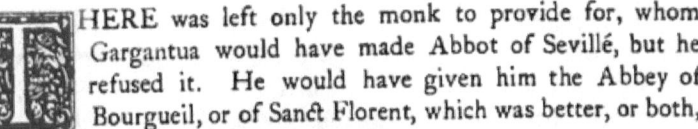HERE was left only the monk to provide for, whom Gargantua would have made Abbot of Sevillé, but he refused it. He would have given him the Abbey of Bourgueil, or of Sanét Florent, which was better, or both, if it pleased him; but the monk gave him a very peremptory answer, that he would never take upon him the charge nor government of monks. For how shall I be able, said he, to rule over others, that have not full power and command of myself? If you think I have done you, or may hereafter do any acceptable service, give me leave to found an abbey after my own mind and fancy. The motion pleased Gargantua very well, who thereupon offered him all the country of Theleme by the river of Loire till within two leagues of the great forest of Port-Huaulx. The monk then requested Gargantua to institute his religious order contrary to all others. First, then, said Gargantua, you must not build a wall about your convent, for all other abbeys are strongly walled and mured about. See, said the monk, and not without cause (seeing wall and mur signify but one and the same thing); where there is mur before and mur behind, there is store of murmur, envy, and mutual conspiracy. Moreover, seeing there are certain convents in the world whereof the custom is, if any woman come in, I mean chaste and honest women, they immediately sweep the ground which they have trod upon; therefore was it ordained, that if any man or woman entered into religious orders should by chance come within this new abbey, all the rooms should be thoroughly washed and cleansed through which they had passed. And because in all other monasteries and nunneries all is compassed, limited, and regulated by hours, it was decreed that in this new structure there should be neither clock nor dial, but that according to the opportunities and incident occasions all their hours should be disposed of; for, said Gargantua, the greatest loss of time that I know is to count the hours. What good comes of it? Nor can there be any greater dotage in the world than for one to guide

and direct his courses by the sound of a bell, and not by his own judgment and discretion.

Item, Because at that time they put no women into nunneries but such as were either purblind, blinkards, lame, crooked, ill-favoured, misshapen, fools, senseless, spoiled, or corrupt; nor encloistered any men but those that were either sickly, subject to defluxions, ill-bred louts, simple sots, or peevish trouble-houses. But to the purpose, said the monk. A woman that is neither fair nor good, to what use serves she? To make a nun of, said Gargantua. Yea, said the monk, and to make shirts and smocks. Therefore was it ordained that into this religious order should be admitted no women that were not fair, well-featured, and of a sweet disposition; nor men that were not comely, personable, and well conditioned.

Item, Because in the convents of women men come not but underhand, privily, and by stealth, it was therefore enacted that in this house there shall be no women in case there be not men, nor men in case there be not women.

Item, Because both men and women that are received into religious orders after the expiring of their noviciate or probation year were constrained and forced perpetually to stay there all the days of their life, it was therefore ordered that all whatever, men or women, admitted within this abbey, should have full leave to depart with peace and contentment whensoever it should seem good to them so to do.

Item, for that the religious men and women did ordinarily make three vows, to wit, those of chastity, poverty, and obedience, it was therefore constituted and appointed that in this convent they might be honourably married, that they might be rich, and live at liberty. In regard of the legitimate time of the persons to be initiated, and years under and above which they were not capable of reception, the women were to be admitted from ten till fifteen, and the men from twelve till eighteen.

CHAP. LIII.

How the abbey of the Thelemites was built and endowed.

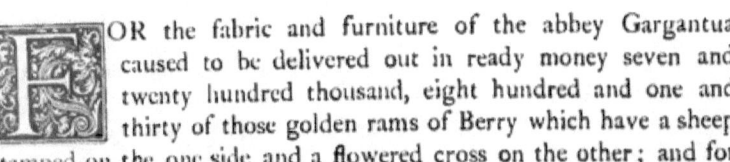OR the fabric and furniture of the abbey Gargantua caused to be delivered out in ready money seven and twenty hundred thousand, eight hundred and one and thirty of those golden rams of Berry which have a sheep stamped on the one side and a flowered cross on the other; and for every year, until the whole work were completed, he allotted threescore nine thousand crowns of the sun, and as many of the seven stars, to be charged all upon the receipt of the custom. For the foundation and maintenance thereof for ever, he settled a perpetual fee-farm-rent of three and twenty hundred, three score and nine thousand, five hundred and fourteen rose nobles, exempted from all homage, fealty, service, or burden whatsoever, and payable every year at the gate of the abbey; and of this by letters patent passed a very good grant. The architecture was in a figure hexagonal, and in such a fashion that in every one of the six corners there was built a great round tower of threescore foot in diameter, and were all of a like form and bigness. Upon the north side ran along the river of Loire, on the bank whereof was situated the tower called Arctic. Going towards the east, there was another called Calaer,—the next following Anatole,—the next Mesembrine,—the next Hesperia, and the last Criere. Every tower was distant from other the space of three hundred and twelve paces. The whole edifice was everywhere six storeys high, reckoning the cellars underground for one. The second was arched after the fashion of a basket-handle; the rest were ceiled with pure wainscot, flourished with Flanders fretwork, in the form of the foot of a lamp, and covered above with fine slates, with an endorsement of lead, carrying the antique figures of little puppets and animals of all sorts, notably well suited to one another, and gilt, together with the gutters, which, jutting without the walls from betwixt the crossbars in a diagonal figure, painted with gold and azure, reached to the very ground, where they ended into great conduit-pipes, which carried all away unto the river from under the house.

This same building was a hundred times more sumptuous and magnificent than ever was Bonnivet, Chambourg, or Chantilly; for there were in it nine thousand, three hundred and two and thirty chambers, every one whereof had a withdrawing-room, a handsome closet, a wardrobe, an oratory, and neat passage, leading into a great and spacious hall. Between every tower in the midst of the said body of building there was a pair of winding, such as we now call lantern stairs, whereof the steps were part of porphyry, which is a dark red marble spotted with white, part of Numidian stone, which is a kind of yellowishly-streaked marble upon various colours, and part of serpentine marble, with light spots on a dark green ground, each of those steps being two and twenty foot in length and three fingers thick, and the just number of twelve betwixt every rest, or, as we now term it, landing-place. In every resting-place were two fair antique arches where the light came in: and by those they went into a cabinet, made even with and of the breadth of the said winding, and the reascending above the roofs of the house ended conically in a pavilion. By that vise or winding they entered on every side into a great hall, and from the halls into the chambers. From the Arctic tower unto the Criere were the fair great libraries in Greek, Latin, Hebrew, French, Italian, and Spanish, respectively distributed in their several cantons, according to the diversity of these languages. In the midst there was a wonderful scalier or winding-stair, the entry whereof was without the house, in a vault or arch six fathom broad. It was made in such symmetry and largeness that six men-at-arms with their lances in their rests might together in a breast ride all up to the very top of all the palace. From the tower Anatole to the Mesembrine were fair spacious galleries, all coloured over and painted with the ancient prowesses, histories, and descriptions of the world. In the midst thereof there was likewise such another ascent and gate as we said there was on the river-side. Upon that gate was written in great antique letters that which followeth.

CHAP. LIV.

The inscription set upon the great gate of Theleme.

ERE enter not vile bigots, hypocrites,
    Externally devoted apes, base snites,
    Puffed-up, wry-necked beasts, worse than the Huns,
    Or Ostrogoths, forerunners of baboons:
Cursed snakes, dissembled varlets, seeming sancts,
Slipshod caffards, beggars pretending wants,
Fat chuffcats, smell-feast knockers, doltish gulls,
Out-strouting cluster-fists, contentious bulls,
Fomenters of divisions and debates,
Elsewhere, not here, make sale of your deceits.

      Your filthy trumperies
      Stuffed with pernicious lies
        (Not worth a bubble),
      Would do but trouble
      Our earthly paradise,
      Your filthy trumperies.

HERE enter not attorneys, barristers,
    Nor bridle-champing law-practitioners:
Clerks, commissaries, scribes, nor pharisees,
Wilful disturbers of the people's ease:
Judges, destroyers, with an unjust breath,
Of honest men, like dogs, even unto death.
Your salary is at the gibbet-foot:
Go drink there! for we do not here fly out
On those excessive courses, which may draw
A waiting on your courts by suits in law.

      Lawsuits, debates, and wrangling
      Hence are exiled, and jangling.
        Here we are very
        Frolic and merry,

And free from all entangling,
Lawsuits, debates, and wrangling.

HERE enter not base pinching usurers,
Pelf-lickers, everlasting gatherers,
Gold-graspers, coin-gripers, gulpers of mists,
Niggish deformed sots, who, though your chests
Vast sums of money should to you afford,
Would ne'ertheless add more unto that hoard,
And yet not be content,—you clunchfist dastards,
Insatiable fiends, and Pluto's bastards,
Greedy devourers, chichy sneakbill rogues,
Hell-mastiffs gnaw your bones, you ravenous dogs.

You beastly-looking fellows,
Reason doth plainly tell us
That we should not
To you allot
Room here, but at the gallows,
You beastly-looking fellows.

HERE enter not fond makers of demurs
In love adventures, peevish, jealous curs,
Sad pensive dotards, raisers of garboils,
Hags, goblins, ghosts, firebrands of household broils,
Nor drunkards, liars, cowards, cheaters, clowns,
Thieves, cannibals, faces o'ercast with frowns,
Nor lazy slugs, envious, covetous,
Nor blockish, cruel, nor too credulous,—
Here mangy, pocky folks shall have no place,
No ugly lusks, nor persons of disgrace.

Grace, honour, praise, delight,
Here sojourn day and night.
Sound bodies lined
With a good mind,
Do here pursue with might
Grace, honour, praise, delight.

HERE enter you, and welcome from our hearts,
    All noble sparks, endowed with gallant parts.
This is the glorious place, which bravely shall
Afford wherewith to entertain you all.
Were you a thousand, here you shall not want
For anything ; for what you'll ask we'll grant.
Stay here, you lively, jovial, handsome, brisk,
Gay, witty, frolic, cheerful, merry, frisk,
Spruce, jocund, courteous, furtherers of trades,
And, in a word, all worthy gentle blades.

      Blades of heroic breasts
      Shall taste here of the feasts,
         Both privily
         And civilly
      Of the celestial guests,
      Blades of heroic breasts.

HERE enter you, pure, honest, faithful, true
    Expounders of the Scriptures old and new.
Whose glosses do not blind our reason, but
Make it to see the clearer, and who shut
Its passages from hatred, avarice,
Pride, factions, covenants, and all sort of vice.
Come, settle here a charitable faith,
Which neighbourly affection nourisheth.
And whose light chaseth all corrupters hence,
Of the blest word, from the aforesaid sense.

      The holy sacred Word,
      May it always afford
        T" us all in common,
        Both man and woman,
      A spiritual shield and sword,
      The holy sacred Word.

HERE enter you all ladies of high birth,
    Delicious, stately, charming, full of mirth,
Ingenious, lovely, miniard, proper, fair,
Magnetic, graceful, splendid, pleasant, rare,

Obliging, sprightly, virtuous, young, solacious,
Kind, neat, quick, feat, bright, compt, ripe, choice, dear, precious.
Alluring, courtly, comely, fine, complete,
Wise, personable, ravishing, and sweet,
Come joys enjoy. The Lord celestial
Hath given enough wherewith to please us all.

> Gold give us, God forgive us,
> And from all woes relieve us;
>   That we the treasure
>   May reap of pleasure,
> And shun whate'er is grievous,
> Gold give us, God forgive us.

CHAP. LV.

What manner of dwelling the Thelemites had.

IN the middle of the lower court there was a stately fountain of fair alabaster. Upon the top thereof stood the three Graces, with their cornucopias, or horns of abundance, and did jet out the water at their breasts, mouth, ears, eyes, and other open passages of the body. The inside of the buildings in this lower court stood upon great pillars of chalcedony stone and porphyry marble made archways after a goodly antique fashion. Within those were spacious galleries, long and large, adorned with curious pictures, the horns of bucks and unicorns: with rhinoceroses, water-horses called hippopotames, the teeth and tusks of elephants, and other things well worth the beholding. The lodging of the ladies, for so we may call those gallant women, took up all from the tower Arctic unto the gate Mesembrine. The men possessed the rest. Before the said lodging of the ladies, that they might have their recreation, between the two first towers, on the outside, were placed the tiltyard, the barriers or lists for tournaments, the hippodrome or riding-court, the theatre or public playhouse, and natatory or place to swim in, with most

admirable baths in three stages, situated above one another, well furnished with all necessary accommodation, and store of myrtle-water. By the river-side was the fair garden of pleasure, and in the midst of that the glorious labyrinth. Between the two other towers were the courts for the tennis and the balloon. Towards the tower Criere stood the orchard full of all fruit-trees, set and ranged in a quincuncial order. At the end of that was the great park, abounding with all sort of venison. Betwixt the third couple of towers were the butts and marks for shooting with a snapwork gun, an ordinary bow for common archery, or with a crossbow. The office-houses were without the tower Hesperia, of one storey high. The stables were beyond the offices, and before them stood the falconry, managed by ostrich-keepers and falconers very expert in the art, and it was yearly supplied and furnished by the Candians, Venetians, Sarmates, now called Muscoviters, with all sorts of most excellent hawks, eagles, gerfalcons, goshawks, sacres, lanners, falcons, sparrowhawks, marlins, and other kinds of them, so gentle and perfectly well manned, that, flying of themselves sometimes from the castle for their own disport, they would not fail to catch whatever they encountered. The venery, where the beagles and hounds were kept, was a little farther off, drawing towards the park.

All the halls, chambers, and closets or cabinets were richly hung with tapestry and hangings of divers sorts, according to the variety of the seasons of the year. All the pavements and floors were covered with green cloth. The beds were all embroidered. In every back-chamber or withdrawing-room there was a looking-glass of pure crystal set in a frame of fine gold, garnished all about with pearls, and was of such greatness that it would represent to the full the whole lineaments and proportion of the person that stood before it. At the going out of the halls which belong to the ladies' lodgings were the perfumers and trimmers through whose hands the gallants passed when they were to visit the ladies. Those sweet artificers did every morning furnish the ladies' chambers with the spirit of roses, orange-flower-water, and angelica; and to each of them gave a little precious casket vapouring forth the most odoriferous exhalations of the choicest aromatical scents.

CHAP. LVI.

How the men and women of the religious order of Theleme were apparelled.

HE ladies at the foundation of this order were apparelled after their own pleasure and liking ; but, since that of their own accord and free will they have reformed themselves, their accoutrement is in manner as followeth. They wore stockings of scarlet crimson, or ingrained purple dye, which reached just three inches above the knee, having a list beautified with exquisite embroideries and rare incisions of the cutter's art. Their garters were of the colour of their bracelets, and circled the knee a little both over and under. Their shoes, pumps, and slippers were either of red, violet, or crimson-velvet, pinked and jagged like lobster waddles.

Next to their smock they put on the pretty kirtle or vasquin of pure silk camlet: above that went the taffety or tabby farthingale, of white, red, tawny, grey, or of any other colour. Above this taffety petticoat they had another of cloth of tissue or brocade, embroidered with fine gold and interlaced with needlework, or as they thought good, and according to the temperature and disposition of the weather had their upper coats of satin, damask, or velvet, and those either orange, tawny, green, ash-coloured, blue, yellow, bright red, crimson, or white, and so forth ; or had them of cloth of gold cloth of silver, or some other choice stuff, enriched with purl, or embroidered according to the dignity of the festival days and times wherein they wore them.

Their gowns, being still correspondent to the season, were either of cloth of gold frizzled with a silver-raised work ; of red satin covered with gold purl ; of tabby, or taffety, white, blue, black, tawny, &c., of silk serge, silk camlet, velvet, cloth of silver, silver tissue, cloth of gold, gold wire, figured velvet, or figured satin tinselled and overcast with golden threads, in divers variously purfled draughts.

In the summer some days instead of gowns they wore light handsome mantles, made either of the stuff of the aforesaid attire, or like

Moresco rugs, of violet velvet frizzled, with a raised work of gold upon silver purl, or with a knotted cord-work of gold embroidery, everywhere garnished with little Indian pearls. They always carried a fair panache, or plume of feathers, of the colour of their muff, bravely adorned and tricked out with glistering spangles of gold. In the winter time they had their taffety gowns of all colours, as above-named, and those lined with the rich furrings of hind-wolves, or speckled lynxes, black-spotted weasels, martlet skins of Calabria, sables, and other costly furs of an inestimable value. Their beads, rings, bracelets, collars, carcanets, and neck-chains were all of precious stones, such as carbuncles, rubies, baleus, diamonds, sapphires, emeralds, turquoises, garnets, agates, beryls, and excellent margarites. Their head-dressing also varied with the season of the year, according to which they decked themselves. In winter it was of the French fashion; in the spring, of the Spanish; in summer, of the fashion of Tuscany, except only upon the holy days and Sundays, at which times they were accoutred in the French mode, because they accounted it more honourable and better befitting the garb of a matronal pudicity.

The men were apparelled after their fashion. Their stockings were of tamine or of cloth serge, of white, black, scarlet, or some other ingrained colour. Their breeches were of velvet, of the same colour with their stockings, or very near, embroidered and cut according to their fancy. Their doublet was of cloth of gold, of cloth of silver, of velvet, satin, damask, taffeties, &c., of the same colours, cut, embroidered, and suitably trimmed up in perfection. The points were of silk of the same colours; the tags were of gold well enamelled. Their coats and jerkins were of cloth of gold, cloth of silver, gold, tissue or velvet embroidered, as they thought fit. Their gowns were every whit as costly as those of the ladies. Their girdles were of silk, of the colour of their doublets. Every one had a gallant sword by his side, the hilt and handle whereof were gilt, and the scabbard of velvet, of the colour of his breeches, with a chape of gold, and pure goldsmith's work. The dagger was of the same. Their caps or bonnets were of black velvet, adorned with jewels and buttons of gold. Upon that they wore a white plume, most prettily and minion-like parted by so many rows of gold spangles, at the end whereof hung dangling in a more sparkling resplendency fair rubies, emeralds, diamonds, &c., but there was such a sympathy betwixt the gallants and the ladies, that every day they were apparelled in the same livery.

And that they might not miss, there were certain gentlemen appointed to tell the youths every morning what vestments the ladies would on that day wear: for all was done according to the pleasure of the ladies. In these so handsome clothes, and habiliments so rich, think not that either one or other of either sex did waste any time at all; for the masters of the wardrobes had all their raiments and apparel so ready for every morning, and the chamber-ladies so well skilled, that in a trice they would be dressed and completely in their clothes from head to foot. And to have those accoutrements with the more conveniency, there was about the wood of Theleme a row of houses of the extent of half a league, very neat and cleanly, wherein dwelt the goldsmiths, lapidaries, jewellers, embroiderers, tailors, gold-drawers, velvet-weavers, tapestry-makers and upholsterers, who wrought there every one in his own trade, and all for the aforesaid jolly friars and nuns of the new stamp. They were furnished with matter and stuff from the hands of the Lord Nausiclete, who every year brought them seven ships from the Perlas and Cannibal Islands, laden with ingots of gold, with raw silk, with pearls and precious stones. And if any margarites, called unions, began to grow old and lose somewhat of their natural whiteness and lustre, those with their art they did renew by tendering them to eat to some pretty cocks, as they use to give casting unto hawks.

CHAP. LVII.

How the Thelemites were governed, and of their manner of living.

ALL their life was spent not in laws, statutes, or rules, but according to their own free will and pleasure. They rose out of their beds when they thought good; they did eat, drink, labour, sleep, when they had a mind to it and were disposed for it. None did awake them, none did offer to constrain them to eat, drink, nor to do any other thing; for so had Gargantua established it. In all their rule and strictest tie of their order there was but this one clause to be observed,

DO WHAT THOU WILT;

because men that are free, well-born, well-bred, and conversant in honest companies, have naturally an instinct and spur that prompteth them unto virtuous actions, and withdraws them from vice, which is called honour. Those same men, when by base subjection and constraint they are brought under and kept down, turn aside from that noble disposition by which they formerly were inclined to virtue, to shake off and break that bond of servitude wherein they are so tyrannously enslaved; for it is agreeable with the nature of man to long after things forbidden and to desire what is denied us.

By this liberty they entered into a very laudable emulation to do all of them what they saw did please one. If any of the gallants or ladies should say, Let us drink, they would all drink. If any one of them said, Let us play, they all played. If one said, Let us go a-walking into the fields, they went all. If it were to go a-hawking or a-hunting, the ladies mounted upon dainty well-paced nags, seated in a stately palfrey saddle, carried on their lovely fists, miniardly begloved every one of them, either a sparrowhawk or a laneret or a marlin, and the young gallants carried the other kinds of hawks. So nobly were they taught, that there was neither he nor she amongst them but could read, write, sing, play upon several musical instruments, speak five or six several languages, and compose in them all very quaintly, both in verse and prose. Never were seen so valiant knights, so noble and worthy, so dexterous and skilful both on foot and a-horseback, more brisk and lively, more nimble and quick, or better handling all manner of weapons than were there. Never were seen ladies so proper and handsome, so miniard and dainty, less froward, or more ready with their hand and with their needle in every honest and free action belonging to that sex, than were there. For this reason, when the time came that any man of the said abbey, either at the request of his parents, or for some other cause, had a mind to go out of it, he carried along with him one of the ladies, namely, her whom he had before that chosen for his mistress, and [they] were married together. And if they had formerly in Theleme lived in good devotion and amity, they did continue therein and increase it to a greater height in their state of matrimony; and did entertain that mutual love till the very last day of their life, in no less vigour and fervency than at the very day of their wedding. Here must not I forget to set down unto you a riddle which was found under the ground as they were laying the foundation of the abbey, engraven in a copper plate, and it was thus as followeth.

CHAP. LVIII.

A prophetical Riddle.

POOR mortals, who wait for a happy day,
Cheer up your hearts, and hear what I shall say:
If it be lawful firmly to believe
That the celestial bodies can us give
Wisdom to judge of things that are not yet;
Or if from heaven such wisdom we may get
As may with confidence make us discourse
Of years to come, their destiny and course;
I to my hearers give to understand
That this next winter, though it be at hand,
Yea and before, there shall appear a race
Of men who, loth to sit still in one place,
Shall boldly go before all people's eyes,
Suborning men of divers qualities
To draw them unto covenants and sides,
In such a manner that, whate'er betides,
They'll move you, if you give them ear, no doubt,
With both your friends and kindred to fall out.
They'll make a vassal to gain-stand his lord,
And children their own parents; in a word,
All reverence shall then be banished,
No true respect to other shall be had.
They'll say that every man should have his turn,
Both in his going forth and his return;
And hereupon there shall arise such woes,
Such jarrings, and confused to's and fro's,
That never were in history such coils
Set down as yet, such tumults and garboils.
Then shall you many gallant men see by
Valour stirr'd up, and youthful fervency,
Who, trusting too much in their hopeful time,
Live but a while, and perish in their prime.

Neither shall any, who this course shall run,
Leave off the race which he hath once begun,
Till they the heavens with noise by their contention
Have fill'd, and with their steps the earth's dimension.
Then those shall have no less authority,
That have no faith, than those that will not lie;
For all shall be governed by a rude,
Base, ignorant, and foolish multitude;
The veriest lout of all shall be their judge,
O horrible and dangerous deluge!
Deluge I call it, and that for good reason,
For this shall be omitted in no season;
Nor shall the earth of this foul stir be free,
Till suddenly you in great store shall see
The waters issue out, with whose streams the
Most moderate of all shall moistened be,
And justly too; because they did not spare
The flocks of beasts that innocentest are,
But did their sinews and their bowels take,
Not to the gods a sacrifice to make,
But usually to serve themselves for sport:
And now consider, I do you exhort,
In such commotions so continual,
What rest can take the globe terrestrial?
Most happy then are they, that can it hold,
And use it carefully as precious gold,
By keeping it in gaol, whence it shall have
No help but him who being to it gave.
And to increase his mournful accident,
The sun, before it set in th' occident,
Shall cease to dart upon it any light,
More than in an eclipse, or in the night,—
So that at once its favour shall be gone,
And liberty with it be left alone.
And yet, before it come to ruin thus,
Its quaking shall be as impetuous
As Ætna's was when Titan's sons lay under,
And yield, when lost, a fearful sound like thunder.
Inarime did not more quickly move,

When Typheus did the vast huge hills remove,
And for despite into the sea them threw.
  Thus shall it then be lost by ways not few,
And changed suddenly, when those that have it
To other men that after come shall leave it.
Then shall it be high time to cease from this
So long, so great, so tedious exercise;
For the great waters told you now by me,
Will make each think where his retreat shall be;
And yet, before that they be clean disperst,
You may behold in th' air, where nought was erst,
The burning heat of a great flame to rise,
Lick up the water, and the enterprise.
  It resteth after those things to declare,
That those shall sit content who chosen are,
With all good things, and with celestial man[ne,]
And richly recompensed every man:
The others at the last all stripp'd shall be,
That after this great work all men may see,
How each shall have his due. This is their lot;
O he is worthy praise that shrinketh not!

  No sooner was this enigmatical monument read over, but Gargantua, fetching a very deep sigh, said unto those that stood by, It is not now only, I perceive, that people called to the faith of the gospel, and convinced with the certainty of evangelical truths, are persecuted. But happy is that man that shall not be scandalized, but shall always continue to the end in aiming at that mark which God by his dear Son hath set before us, without being distracted or diverted by his carnal affections and depraved nature.

  The monk then said, What do you think in your conscience is meant and signified by this riddle? What? said Gargantua,—the progress and carrying on of the divine truth. By St. Goderan, said the monk, that is not my exposition. It is the style of the prophet Merlin. Make upon it as many grave allegories and glosses as you will, and dote upon it you and the rest of the world as long as you please; for my part, I can conceive no other meaning in it but a description of a set at tennis in dark and obscure terms. The suborners of men are the makers of matches, which are commonly friends. After the two chases are made, he that was in the upper end of the tennis-court goeth out, and the other cometh in. They believe the first that saith the ball was over or under the line. The waters are the heats that the players take till they sweat again. The cords of the rackets are made of the guts of sheep or goats. The globe terrestrial is the tennis-ball. After playing, when the game is done, they refresh themselves before a clear fire, and change their shirts; and very willingly they make all good cheer, but most merrily those that have gained. And so, farewell!

The Second BOOK
Of the WORKS of
Mr. FRANCIS RABELAIS,
DOCTOR IN
Phyſick:
Treating of the Heroick Deeds and
Sayings of the good
PANTAGRUEL.
Written Originally in the
FRENCH TONGUE,
And now faithfully Tranſlated into
ENGLISH.

By *S. T. U. C.*

Ἐυνοεῖ ἐυλογεῖ καὶ ἐυπράτ]ε.
Mean, ſpeak, and do well.

LONDON,
Printed for *Richard Baddeley*, within the middle
Temple-gate.   1653.

For the Reader.

HE Reader here may be pleased to take notice that the copy of verses by the title of Rablophila, premised to the first book of this translation, being but a kind of mock poem, in imitation of somewhat lately published (as to any indifferent observer will easily appear, by the false quantities in the Latin, the abusive strain of the English, and extravagant subscription to both), and as such, by a friend of the translator's, at the desire of some frolic gentlemen of his acquaintance, more for a trial of skill than prejudicacy to any, composed in his jollity to please their fancies, was only ordained to be prefixed to a dozen of books, and no more, thereby to save the labour of transcribing so many as were requisite for satisfying the curiosity of a company of just that number; and that, therefore, the charging of the whole impression with it is merely to be imputed to the negligence of the pressmen, who, receiving it about the latter end of the night, were so eager before the next morning to afford complete books, that, as they began, they went on, without animadverting what was recommended to their discretion. This is hoped will suffice to assure the ingenuous Reader that in no treatise of the translator's, whether original or translatitious, shall willingly be offered the meanest rub to the reputation of any worthy gentleman, and that, however providence dispose of him, no misfortune shall be able to induce his mind to any complacency in the disparagement of another.

Again.

The Pentateuch of Rabelais mentioned in the title-page of the first book of this translation being written originally in the French tongue (as it comprehendeth some of its brusquest dialects), with so much ingeniosity and wit, that more impressions have been sold thereof in that language than of any other book that hath been set forth at any time within these fifteen hundred years; so difficult nevertheless to be turned into any other speech that many prime spirits in most of the nations of Europe, since the year 1573, which was fourscore years ago, after having attempted it, were constrained with no small regret to give it over as a thing impossible to be done, is now in its translation thus far advanced, and the remainder faithfully undertaken with the same hand to be rendered into English by a person of quality, who (though his lands be sequestered, his house garrisoned, his other goods sold, and himself detained a prisoner of war at London, for his having been at Worcester fight) hath, at the most earnest entreaty of some of his especial friends well acquainted with his inclination to the performance of conducible singularities, promised, besides his version of these two already published, very speedily to offer up unto this Isle of Britain the virginity of the translation of the other three most admirable books of the aforesaid author; provided that by the plurality of judicious and understanding men it be not declared he hath already proceeded too far, or that the continuation of the rigour whereby he is dispossessed of all his both real and personal estate, by pressing too hard upon him, be not an impediment thereto, and to other more eminent undertakings of his, as hath been oftentimes very fully mentioned by the said translator in several original treatises of his own penning, lately by him so numerously dispersed that there is scarce any, who being skilful in the English idiom, or curious of any new ingenious invention, hath not either read them or heard of them.

Mr. Hugh Salel to
Rabelais.

F profit mixed with pleasure may suffice
T' extol an author's worth above the skies,
Thou certainly for both must praised be:
I know it; for thy judgment hath in the
Contexture of this book set down such high
Contentments, mingled with utility,
That (as I think) I see Democritus
Laughing at men as things ridiculous.
Insist in thy design; for, though we prove
Ungrate on earth, thy merit is above.

The Author's Prologue.

OST illustrious and thrice valorous champions, gentlemen and others, who willingly apply your minds to the entertainment of pretty conceits and honest harmless knacks of wit; you have not long ago seen, read, and understood the great and inestimable Chronicle of the huge and mighty giant Gargantua, and, like upright faithfullists, have firmly believed all to be true that is contained in them, and have very often passed your time with them amongst honourable ladies and gentlewomen, telling them fair long stories, when you were out of all other talk, for which you are worthy of great praise and sempiternal memory. And I do heartily wish that every man would lay aside his own business, meddle no more with his profession nor trade, and throw all affairs concerning himself behind his back, to attend this wholly, without distracting or troubling his mind with anything else, until he have learned them without book; that if by chance the art of printing should cease, or in case that in time to come all books should perish, every man might truly teach them unto his children, and deliver them over to his successors and survivors from hand to hand as a religious cabal; for there is in it more profit than a rabble of great pocky loggerheads are able to discern, who surely understand far less in these little merriments than the fool Raclet did in the Institutions of Justinian.

I have known great and mighty lords, and of those not a few, who, going a-deer-hunting, or a-hawking after wild ducks, when the chase had not encountered with the blinks that were cast in her way to retard her course, or that the hawk did but plain and smoothly fly without moving her wings, perceiving the prey by force of flight to have gained bounds of her, have been much chafed and vexed, as you understand well enough; but the comfort unto which they had refuge, and that they might not take cold, was to relate the inestimable deeds of the said Gargantua. There are others in the world—these are no flimflam stories, nor tales of a tub—who, being much troubled with the toothache, after they had spent their goods upon physicians without receiving at all any ease of their pain, have found no more ready remedy than to put the said Chronicles betwixt two pieces of linen cloth made somewhat hot, and so apply them to the place that smarteth, sinapizing them with a little powder of projection, otherwise called doribus.

But what shall I say of those poor men that are plagued with the pox and the gout? O how often have we seen them, even immediately after they were anointed and thoroughly greased, till their faces did glister like the keyhole of a powdering tub, their teeth dance like the jacks of a pair of little organs or virginals when they are played upon, and that they foamed from their very throats like a boar which the mongrel mastiff-hounds have driven in and overthrown amongst the toils,—what did they then? All their consolation was to have some page of the said jolly book read unto them. And we have seen those who have given themselves to a hundred puncheons of old devils, in case that they did not feel a manifest ease and assuagement of pain at the hearing of the said book read, even when they were kept in a purgatory of torment; no more nor less than women in travail use to find their sorrow abated when the life of St. Margaret is read unto them. Is this nothing? Find me a book in any language, in any faculty or science whatsoever, that hath such virtues, properties, and prerogatives, and I will be content to pay you a quart of tripes. No, my masters, no; it is peerless, incomparable, and not to be matched; and this am I resolved for ever to maintain even unto the fire *exclusive*. And those that will pertinaciously hold the contrary opinion, let them be accounted abusers, predestinators, impostors, and seducers of the people. It is very true that there are found in some gallant and stately books, worthy of high estimation, certain occult and hid properties; in the number of which are reckoned Whippot, Orlando Furioso, Robert the Devil, Fierabras, William without Fear, Huon of Bordeaux, Monteville, and Matabrune: but they are not comparable to that which we speak of, and the world hath well known by infallible experience the great emolument and utility which it hath received by this Gargantuine Chronicle; for the printers have sold more of them in two months' time than there will be bought of Bibles in nine years.

I therefore, your humble slave, being very willing to increase your solace and recreation yet a little more, do offer you for a present another book of the same stamp, only that it is a little more reasonable and worthy of credit than the other was. For think not, unless you wilfully will err against your knowledge, that I speak of it as the Jews do of the Law. I was not born under such a planet, neither did it ever befall me to lie, or affirm a thing for true that was not. I speak of it like a lusty frolic onocrotary,[1] I should say crotenotary[2] of the martyrized lovers, and croquenotary of love. *Quod vidimus, testamur.* It is of the horrible and dreadful feats and prowesses of Pantagruel, whose menial servant I have been ever since I was a page, till this hour that by his leave I am permitted to visit my cow-country, and to know if any of my kindred there be alive.

And therefore, to make an end of this Prologue, even as I give myself to a hundred panniersful of fair devils, body and soul, tripes and guts, in case that I lie so much as one single word in this whole history; after the like manner, St. Anthony's fire burn you, Mahoom's disease whirl you, the squinance with a stitch in your side and the wolf in your stomach truss you, the bloody flux seize upon you, the cursed sharp inflammations of wild-fire, as slender and thin as cow's hair strengthened with quicksilver, enter into your fundament, and, like those of Sodom and Gomorrah, may you fall into sulphur, fire, and bottomless pits, in case you do not firmly believe all that I shall relate unto you in this present Chronicle.

[1] Onocratal is a bird not much unlike a swan, which sings like an ass's braying.
[2] Crotenotaire or notaire crotté, croquenotaire or notaire croqué are but allusions in derision of protonotaire, which signifieth a pregnotary.

The Second Book of

Rabelais,

treating of the heroic Deeds and Sayings of the good

Pantagruel.

CHAP. I.

Of the original and antiquity of the great Pantagruel.

IT will not be an idle nor unprofitable thing, seeing we are at leisure, to put you in mind of the fountain and original source whence is derived unto us the good Pantagruel. For I see that all good historiographers have thus handled their chronicles, not only the Arabians, Barbarians, and Latins, but also the gentle Greeks, who were eternal drinkers. You must therefore remark that at the beginning of the world—I speak of a long time; it is above forty quarantains, or forty times forty nights, according to the supputation of the ancient Druids—a little after that Abel was killed by his brother Cain, the earth, imbrued with the blood of the just, was one year so exceeding fertile in all those fruits which it usually produceth to us, and especially in medlars, that ever since throughout all ages it hath been called the year of the great medlars; for three of them did fill a bushel. In it the kalends were found by the Grecian almanacks. There was that year nothing of the month of March in the time of Lent, and the middle

of August was in May. In the month of October, as I take it, or at least September, that I may not err, for I will carefully take heed of that, was the week so famous in the annals, which they call the week of the three Thursdays; for it had three of them by means of their irregular leap-years, called Bissextiles, occasioned by the sun's having tripped and stumbled a little towards the left hand, like a debtor afraid of sergeants, coming right upon him to arrest him: and the moon varied from her course above five fathom, and there was manifestly seen the motion of trepidation in the firmament of the fixed stars, called Aplanes, so that the middle Pleiade, leaving her fellows, declined towards the equinoctial, and the star named Spica left the constellation of the Virgin to withdraw herself towards the Balance, known by the name of Libra, which are cases very terrible, and matters so hard and difficult that astrologians cannot set their teeth in them; and indeed their teeth had been pretty long if they could have reached thither.

However, account you it for a truth that everybody then did most heartily eat of these medlars, for they were fair to the eye and in taste delicious. But even as Noah, that holy man, to whom we are so much beholding, bound, and obliged, for that he planted to us the vine, from whence we have that nectarian, delicious, precious, heavenly, joyful, and deific liquor which they call the piot or tiplage, was deceived in the drinking of it, for he was ignorant of the great virtue and power thereof; so likewise the men and women of that time did delight much in the eating of that fair great fruit, but divers and very different accidents did ensue thereupon; for there fell upon them all in their bodies a most terrible swelling, but not upon all in the same place, for some were swollen in the belly, and their belly strouted out big like a great tun, of whom it is written, *Ventrem omnipotentem*, who were all very honest men, and merry blades. And of this race came St. Fatgulch and Shrove Tuesday.[1] Others did swell at the shoulders, who in that place were so crump and knobby that they were therefore called Montifers, which is as much to say as Hill-carriers, of whom you see some yet in the world, of divers sexes and degrees. Of this race came Æsop, some of whose excellent words and deeds you have in writing. Some other puffs did swell in length by the member which they call the labourer of

---

[1] Pansart, Mardigras.

nature, in such sort that it grew marvellous long, fat, great, lusty, stirring, and crest-risen, in the antique fashion, so that they made use of it as of a girdle, winding it five or six times about their waist: but if it happened the foresaid member to be in good case, spooming with a full sail bunt fair before the wind, then to have seen those strouting champions, you would have taken them for men that had their lances settled on their rest to run at the ring or tilting whintam [quintain]. Of these, believe me, the race is utterly lost and quite extinct, as the women say; for they do lament continually that there are none extant now of those great, &c. You know the rest of the song. Others did grow in matter of ballocks so enormously that three of them would well fill a sack able to contain five quarters of wheat. From them are descended the ballocks of Lorraine, which never dwell in codpieces, but fall down to the bottom of the breeches. Others grew in the legs, and to see them you would have said they had been cranes, or the reddish-long-billed-storklike-scrank-legged sea-fowls called flamans, or else men walking upon stilts or scatches. The little grammar-school boys, known by the name of Grimos, called those leg-grown slangams Jambus, in allusion to the French word jambe, which signifieth a leg. In others, their nose did grow so, that it seemed to be the beak of a limbeck, in every part thereof most variously diapered with the twinkling sparkles of crimson blisters budding forth, and purpled with pimples all enamelled with thickset wheals of a sanguine colour, bordered with gules; and such have you seen the Canon or Prebend Panzoult, and Woodenfoot, the physician of Angiers. Of which race there were few that liked the ptisane, but all of them were perfect lovers of the pure Septembral juice. Naso and Ovid had their extraction from thence, and all those of whom it is written, *Ne reminiscaris*. Others grew in ears, which they had so big that out of one would have been stuff enough got to make a doublet, a pair of breeches, and a jacket, whilst with the other they might have covered themselves as with a Spanish cloak: and they say that in Bourbonnois this race remaineth yet. Others grew in length of body, and of those came the Giants, and of them Pantagruel.

And the first was Chalbroth,
Who begat Sarabroth,
Who begat Faribroth,

Who begat Hurtali, that was a brave eater of pottage, and reigned in the time of the flood ;
Who begat Nembroth,
Who begat Atlas, that with his shoulders kept the sky from falling ;
Who begat Goliah,
Who begat Erix, that invented the hocus pocus plays of legerdemain ;
Who begat Titius,
Who begat Eryon,
Who begat Polyphemus,
Who begat Cacus,
Who begat Etion, the first man that ever had the pox, for not drinking fresh in summer, as Bartachin witnesseth ;
Who begat Enceladus,
Who begat Ceus,
Who begat Tiphæus,
Who begat Alæus,
Who begat Othus,
Who begat Ægeon,
Who begat Briareus, that had a hundred hands ;
Who begat Porphyrio,
Who begat Adamastor,
Who begat Anteus,
Who begat Agatho,
Who begat Porus, against whom fought Alexander the Great ;
Who begat Aranthas,
Who begat Gabbara, that was the first inventor of the drinking of healths;
Who begat Goliah of Secondille,
Who begat Offot, that was terribly well nosed for drinking at the barrel-head ;
Who begat Artachæus,
Who begat Oromedon,
Who begat Gemmagog, the first inventor of Poulan shoes, which are open on the foot and tied over the instep with a latchet ;
Who begat Sisyphus,
Who begat the Titans, of whom Hercules was born ;
Who begat Enay, the most skilful man that ever was in matter of taking the little worms (called cirons) out of the hands ;

Who begat Fierabras, that was vanquished by Oliver, peer of France and Roland's comrade;

Who begat Morgan, the first in the world that played at dice with spectacles;

Who begat Fracassus, of whom Merlin Coccaius hath written, and of him was born Ferragus,

Who begat Hapmouche, the first that ever invented the drying of neat's tongues in the chimney; for, before that, people salted them as they do now gammons of bacon;

Who begat Bolivorax,

Who begat Longis,

Who begat Gayoffo, whose ballocks were of poplar, and his pr... of the service or sorb-apple-tree;

Who begat Maschefain,

Who begat Bruslefer,

Who begat Angoulevent,

Who begat Galehaut, the inventor of flagons;

Who begat Mirelangaut,

Who begat Gallaffre,

Who begat Falourdin,

Who begat Roboast,

Who begat Sortibrant of Conimbres,

Who begat Brushant of Mommiere,

Who begat Bruyer that was overcome by Ogier the Dane, peer of France;

Who begat Mabrun,

Who begat Foutasnon,

Who begat Haquelebac,

Who begat Vitdegrain,

Who begat Grangousier,

Who begat Gargantua,

Who begat the noble Pantagruel, my master.

I know that, reading this passage, you will make a doubt within yourselves, and that grounded upon very good reason, which is this—how it is possible that this relation can be true, seeing at the time of the flood all the world was destroyed, except Noah and seven persons more with him in the ark, into whose number Hurtali is not admitted. Doubtless the demand is well made and very apparent, but the answer shall satisfy you, or my wit is not rightly caulked. And because I was not at that time to tell you anything of my own fancy, I will bring unto you the authority of the Massorets, good honest fellows, true hallockeering blades and exact Hebraical bagpipers, who affirm that verily the said Hurtali was not within the ark of Noah, neither could he get in, for he was too big, but he sat astride upon it, with one leg on the one side and another on the other, as little children use to do upon their wooden horses; or as the great bull of Berne, which was killed at Marinian, did ride for his hackney the great murdering piece called the canon-pevier, a pretty beast of a fair and pleasant amble without all question.

In that posture, he, after God, saved the said ark from danger, for with his legs he gave it the brangle that was needful, and with his foot turned it whither he pleased, as a ship answereth her rudder. Those that were within sent him up victuals in abundance by a chimney, as people very thankfully acknowledging the good that he did them. And sometimes they did talk together as Icaromenippus did to Jupiter, according to the report of Lucian. Have you understood all this well? Drink then one good draught without water, for if you believe it not,—no truly do I not, quoth she.

CHAP. II.

Of the nativity of the most dread and redoubted Pantagruel.

GARGANTUA at the age of four hundred fourscore forty and four years begat his son Pantagruel, upon his wife named Badebec, daughter to the king of the Amaurots in Utopia, who died in childbirth ; for he was so wonderfully great and lumpish that he could not possibly come forth into the light of the world without thus suffocating his mother. But that we may fully understand the cause and reason of the name of Pantagruel which at his baptism was given him, you are to remark that in that year there was so great drought over all the country of Africa that there passed thirty and six months, three weeks, four days, thirteen hours and a little more without rain, but with a heat so vehement that the whole earth was parched and withered by it. Neither was

it more scorched and dried up with heat in the days of Elijah than it was at that time; for there was not a tree to be seen that had either leaf or bloom upon it. The grass was without verdure or greenness, the rivers were drained, the fountains dried up, the poor fishes, abandoned and forsaken by their proper element, wandering and crying upon the ground most horribly. The birds did fall down from the air for want of moisture and dew wherewith to refresh them. The wolves, foxes, harts, wild boars, fallow deer, hares, coneys, weasels, brocks, badgers, and other such beasts, were found dead in the fields with their mouths open. In respect of men, there was the pity, you should have seen them lay out their tongues like hares that have been run six hours. Many did throw themselves into the wells. Others entered within a cow's belly to be in the shade; those Homer calls Alibants. All the country was idle, and could do no virtue. It was a most lamentable case to have seen the labour of mortals in defending themselves from the vehemency of this horrific drought; for they had work enough to do to save the holy water in the churches from being wasted; but there was such order taken by the counsel of my lords the cardinals and of our holy Father, that none did dare to take above one lick. Yet when anyone came into the church, you should have seen above twenty poor thirsty fellows hang upon him that was the distributor of the water, and that with a wide open throat, gaping for some little drop, like the rich glutton in Luke, that might fall by, lest anything should be lost. O how happy was he in that year who had a cool cellar under ground, well plenished with fresh wine!

The philosopher reports, in moving the question, Wherefore it is that the sea-water is salt, that at the time when Phœbus gave the government of his resplendent chariot to his son Phaeton, the said Phaeton, unskilful in the art, and not knowing how to keep the ecliptic line betwixt the two tropics of the latitude of the sun's course, strayed out of his way, and came so near the earth that he dried up all the countries that were under it, burning a great part of the heavens which the philosophers call Via lactea, and the huffsnuffs St. James's way; although the most coped, lofty, and high-crested poets affirm that to be the place where Juno's milk fell when she gave suck to Hercules. The earth at that time was so excessively heated that it fell into an enormous sweat, yea, such a one as made it sweat out the sea, which is therefore salt, because all sweat is salt;

and this you cannot but confess to be true if you will taste of your own, or of those that have the pox, when they are put into sweating, it is all one to me.

Just such another case fell out this same year: for on a certain Friday, when the whole people were bent upon their devotions, and had made goodly processions, with store of litanies, and fair preachings, and beseechings of God Almighty to look down with his eye of mercy upon their miserable and disconsolate condition, there was even then visibly seen issue out of the ground great drops of water, such as fall from a puff-bagged man in a top sweat, and the poor hoidens began to rejoice as if it had been a thing very profitable unto them; for some said that there was not one drop of moisture in the air whence they might have any rain, and that the earth did supply the default of that. Other learned men said that it was a shower of the antipodes, as Seneca saith in his fourth book *Quæstionum naturalium*, speaking of the source and spring of Nilus. But they were deceived, for, the procession being ended, when everyone went about to gather of this dew, and to drink of it with full bowls, they found that it was nothing but pickle and the very brine of salt, more brackish in taste than the saltest water of the sea. And because in that very day Pantagruel was born, his father gave him that name; for *Panta* in Greek is as much to say as all, and *Gruel* in the Hagarene language doth signify thirsty, inferring hereby that at his birth the whole world was a-dry and thirsty, as likewise foreseeing that he would be some day supreme lord and sovereign of the thirsty Ethrappels, which was shown to him at that very same hour by a more evident sign. For when his mother Badebec was in the bringing of him forth, and that the midwives did wait to receive him, there came first out of her belly three score and eight tregeneers, that is, salt-sellers, every one of them leading in a halter a mule heavy laden with salt; after whom issued forth nine dromedaries, with great loads of gammons of bacon and dried neat's tongues on their backs. Then followed seven camels loaded with links and chitterlings, hogs' puddings, and sausages. After them came out five great wains, full of leeks, garlic, onions, and chibots, drawn with five-and-thirty strong cart-horses, which was six for every one, besides the thiller. At the sight hereof the said midwives were much amazed, yet some of them said, Lo, here is good provision, and indeed we need it; for we drink but lazily, as if our tongues walked on crutches, and not lustily like Lansman Dutches. Truly this is a good sign; there is nothing here but what is fit for us; these are the spurs of wine, that set it a-going. As they were tattling thus together after their own manner of chat, behold! out comes Pantagruel all hairy like a bear, whereupon one of them, inspired with a prophetical spirit, said, This will be a terrible fellow; he is born with all his hair; he is undoubtedly to do wonderful things, and if he live he shall have age.

CHAP. III.

Of the grief wherewith Gargantua was moved at the decease of his wife Badebec.

WHEN Pantagruel was born, there was none more astonished and perplexed than was his father Gargantua; for of the one side seeing his wife Badebec dead, and on the other side his son Pantagruel born, so fair and so great, he knew not what to say nor what to do. And the doubt that troubled his brain was to know whether he should cry for the death of his wife or laugh for the joy of his son. He was *hinc indè* choked with sophistical arguments, for he framed them very well *in modo et figura*, but he could not resolve them, remaining pestered and entangled by this means, like a mouse caught in a trap or kite snared in a gin. Shall I weep? said he. Yes, for why? My so good wife is dead, who was the most this, the most that, that ever was in the world. Never shall I see her, never shall I recover such another; it is unto me an inestimable loss! O my good God, what had I done that thou shouldest thus punish me? Why didst thou not take me away before her, seeing for me to live without her is but to languish? Ah, Badebec, Badebec, my minion, my dear heart, my sugar, my sweeting, my honey, my little c— (yet it had in circumference full six acres, three rods, five poles, four yards, two foot, one inch and a half of good woodland measure), my tender peggy, my codpiece darling, my bob and hit, my slipshoe-lovey, never shall I see thee! Ah, poor Pantagruel, thou hast lost thy good mother, thy sweet nurse, thy well-beloved lady! O false death, how injurious and despiteful hast thou been to me! How malicious and outrageous have I found thee

in taking her from me, my well-beloved wife, to whom immortality did of right belong!

With these words he did cry like a cow, but on a sudden fell a-laughing like a calf, when Pantagruel came into his mind. Ha, my little son, said he, my childilolly, fedlifondy, dandlichucky, my ballocky, my pretty rogue! O how jolly thou art, and how much am I bound to my gracious God, that hath been pleased to bestow on me a son so fair, so spriteful, so lively, so smiling, so pleasant, and so gentle! Ho, ho, ho, ho, how glad I am! Let us drink, ho, and put away melancholy! Bring of the best, rinse the glasses, lay the cloth, drive out these dogs, blow this fire, light candles, shut that door there, cut this bread in sippets for brewis, send away these poor folks in giving them what they ask, hold my gown. I will strip myself into my doublet (*en cuerpo*), to make the gossips merry, and keep them company.

As he spake this, he heard the litanies and the mementos of the priests that carried his wife to be buried, upon which he left the good purpose he was in, and was suddenly ravished another way, saying, Lord God! must I again contrist myself? This grieves me. I am no longer young, I grow old, the weather is dangerous; I may perhaps take an ague, then shall I be foiled, if not quite undone. By the faith of a gentleman, it were better to cry less, and drink more. My wife is dead, well, by G—! (*da jurandi*) I shall not raise her again by my crying: she is well, she is in paradise at least, if she be no higher: she prayeth to God for us, she is happy, she is above the sense of our miseries, nor can our calamities reach her. What though she be dead, must not we also die? The same debt which she hath paid hangs over our heads; nature will require it of us, and we must all of us some day taste of the same sauce. Let her pass then, and the Lord preserve the survivors; for I must now cast about how to get another wife. But I will tell you what you shall do, said he to the midwives, in France called wise women (where be they, good folks? I cannot see them): Go you to my wife's interment, and I will the while rock my son; for I find myself somewhat altered and distempered, and should otherwise be in danger of falling sick; but drink one good draught first, you will be the better for it. And believe me, upon mine honour, they at his request went to her burial and funeral obsequies. In the meanwhile, poor Gargantua staying at home, and willing to have somewhat in remembrance of her to be engraven upon her tomb, made this epitaph in the manner as followeth.

>Dead is the noble Badebec,
>Who had a face like a rebeck;
>A Spanish body, and a belly
>Of Switzerland; she died, I tell ye,
>In childbirth. Pray to God, that her
>He pardon wherein she did err.
>Here lies her body, which did live
>Free from all vice, as I believe,
>>And did decease at my bedside,
>>The year and day in which she died.

CHAP. IV.

Of the infancy of Pantagruel.

I FIND by the ancient historiographers and poets that divers have been born in this world after very strange manners, which would be too long to repeat; read therefore the seventh chapter of Pliny, if you have so much leisure. Yet have you never heard of any so wonderful as that of Pantagruel; for it is a very difficult matter to believe, how in the little time he was in his mother's belly he grew both in body and strength. That which Hercules did was nothing, when in his cradle he slew two serpents, for those serpents were but little and weak, but Pantagruel, being yet in the cradle, did far more admirable things, and more to be amazed at. I pass by here the relation of how at every one of his meals he supped up the milk of four thousand and six hundred cows, and how, to make him a skillet to boil his milk in, there were set a-work all the braziers of Somure in Anjou, of Villedieu in Normandy, and of Bramont in Lorraine. And they served in this whitepot-meat to him in a huge great bell, which is yet to be seen in the city of Bourges in Berry, near the palace, but his teeth were already so well grown, and so strengthened with vigour, that of the said bell he bit off a great morsel, as very plainly doth appear till this hour.

One day in the morning, when they would have made him suck one of his cows—for he never had any other nurse, as the history tells us—he got one of his arms loose from the swaddling bands wherewith he was kept fast in the cradle, laid hold on the said cow under the left foreham, and grasping her to him ate up her udder and half of her paunch, with the liver and the kidneys, and had devoured all up if she had not cried out most horribly, as if the wolves had held her by the legs, at which noise company came in and took away the said cow from Pantagruel. Yet could they not so well do it but that the quarter whereby he caught her was left in his hand, of which quarter he gulped up the flesh in a trice, even with as much ease as you would eat a sausage, and that so greedily with desire of more, that, when they would have taken away the bone from him, he swallowed it down whole, as a cormorant would do a little fish; and afterwards began fumblingly to say, Good, good, good—for he could not yet speak plain—giving them to understand thereby that he had found it very good, and that he did lack but so much more. Which when they saw that attended him, they bound him with great cable-ropes, like those that are made at Tain for the carriage of salt to Lyons, or such as those are whereby the great French ship rides at anchor in the road of Newhaven in Normandy. But, on a certain time, a great bear, which his father had bred, got loose, came towards him, began to lick his face, for his nurses had not thoroughly wiped his chaps, at which unexpected approach being on a sudden offended, he as lightly rid himself of those great cables as Samson did of the hawser ropes wherewith the Philistines had tied him, and, by your leave, takes me up my lord the bear, and tears him to you in pieces like a pullet, which served him for a gorgeful or good warm bit for that meal.

Whereupon Gargantua, fearing lest the child should hurt himself, caused four great chains of iron to be made to bind him, and so many strong wooden arches unto his cradle, most firmly stocked and morticed in huge frames. Of those chains you have one at Rochelle, which they draw up at night betwixt the two great towers of the haven. Another is at Lyons,—a third at Angiers,—and the fourth was carried away by the devils to bind Lucifer, who broke his chains in those days by reason of a colic that did extraordinarily torment him, taken with eating a sergeant's soul fried for his breakfast. And therefore you may believe that which Nicholas de

Lyra saith upon that place of the Psalter where it is written, *Et Og Regem Basan*, that the said Og, being yet little, was so strong and robustious, that they were fain to bind him with chains of iron in his cradle. Thus continued Pantagruel for a while very calm and quiet, for he was not able so easily to break those chains, especially having no room in the cradle to give a swing with his arms. But see what happened once upon a great holiday that his father Gargantua made a sumptuous banquet to all the princes of his court. I am apt to believe that the menial officers of the house were so embusied in waiting each on his proper service at the feast, that nobody took care of poor Pantagruel, who was left *a reculorum*, behindhand, all alone, and as forsaken. What did he? Hark what he did, good people. He strove and essayed to break the chains of the cradle with his arms, but could not, for they were too strong for him. Then did he keep with his feet such a stamping stir, and so long, that at last he beat out the lower end of his cradle, which notwithstanding was made of a great post five foot in square; and as soon as he had gotten out his feet, he slid down as well as he could till he had got his soles to the ground, and then with a mighty force he rose up, carrying his cradle upon his back, bound to him like a tortoise that crawls up against a wall; and to have seen him, you would have thought it had been a great carrick of five hundred tons upon one end. In this manner he entered into the great hall where they were banqueting, and that very boldly, which did much affright the company; yet, because his arms were tied in, he could not reach anything to eat, but with great pain stooped now and then a little to take with the whole flat of his tongue some lick, good bit, or morsel. Which when his father saw, he knew well enough that they had left him without giving him anything to eat, and therefore commanded that he should be loosed from the said chains, by the counsel of the princes and lords there present. Besides that also the physicians of Gargantua said that, if they did thus keep him in the cradle, he would be all his lifetime subject to the stone. When he was unchained, they made him to sit down, where, after he had fed very well, he took his cradle and broke it into more than five hundred thousand pieces with one blow of his fist that he struck in the midst of it, swearing that he would never come into it again.

CHAP. V.

Of the acts of the noble Pantagruel in his youthful age.

THUS grew Pantagruel from day to day, and to everyone's eye waxed more and more in all his dimensions, which made his father to rejoice by a natural affection. Therefore caused he to be made for him, whilst he was yet little, a pretty crossbow wherewith to shoot at small birds, which now they call the great crossbow at Chantelle. Then he sent him to the school to learn, and to spend his youth in virtue. In the prosecution of which design he came first to Poictiers, where, as he studied and profited very much, he saw that the scholars were oftentimes at leisure and knew not how to bestow their time, which moved him to take such compassion on them, that one day he took from a long ledge of rocks, called there Passelourdin, a huge great stone, of about twelve fathom square and fourteen handfuls thick, and with great ease set it upon four pillars in the midst of a field, to no other end but that the said scholars, when they had nothing else to do, might pass their time in getting up on that stone, and feast it with store of gammons, pasties, and flagons, and carve their names upon it with a knife, in token of which deed till this hour the stone is called the lifted stone. And in remembrance hereof there is none entered into the register and matricular book of the said university, or accounted capable of taking any degree therein, till he have first drunk in the caballine fountain of Croustelles, passed at Passelourdin, and got up upon the lifted stone.

Afterwards, reading the delectable chronicles of his ancestors, he found that Geoffrey of Lusignan, called Geoffrey with the great tooth, grandfather to the cousin-in-law of the eldest sister of the aunt of the son-in-law of the uncle of the good daughter of his stepmother, was interred at Maillezais; therefore one day he took campos (which is a little vacation from study to play a while), that he might give him a visit as unto an honest man. And going from Poictiers with some of his companions, they passed by the Gugé [Legugé], visiting the noble Abbot Ardillon; then by Lusignan, by Sansay, by

Celles, by Coolonges, by Fontenay-le-Comte, saluting the learned Tiraqueau, and from thence arrived at Maillezais, where he went to see the sepulchre of the said Geoffrey with the great tooth; which made him somewhat afraid, looking upon the picture, whose lively draughts did set him forth in the representation of a man in an extreme fury, drawing his great Malchus falchion half way out of his scabbard. When the reason hereof was demanded, the canons of the said place told him that there was no other cause of it but that *Pictoribus atque Poetis, &c.*, that is to say, that painters and poets have liberty to paint and devise what they list after their own fancy. But he was not satisfied with their answer, and said, He is not thus painted without a cause, and I suspect that at his death there was some wrong done him, whereof he requireth his kindred to take revenge. I will inquire further into it, and then do what shall be reasonable. Then he returned not to Poictiers, but would take a view of the other universities of France. Therefore, going to Rochelle, he took shipping and arrived at Bordeaux, where he found no great exercise, only now and then he would see some mariners and lightermen a-wrestling on the quay or strand by the river-side. From thence he came to Toulouse, where he learned to dance very well, and to play with the two-handed sword, as the fashion of the scholars of the said university is to bestir themselves in games whereof they may have their hands full; but he stayed not long there when he saw that they did cause burn their regents alive like red herring, saying, Now God forbid that I should die this death! for I am by nature sufficiently dry already, without heating myself any further.

He went then to Montpellier, where he met with the good wives of Mirevaux, and good jovial company withal, and thought to have set himself to the study of physic; but he considered that that calling was too troublesome and melancholic, and that physicians did smell of glisters like old devils. Therefore he resolved he would study the laws; but seeing that there were but three scald- and one bald-pated legist in that place, he departed from thence, and in his way made the bridge of Guard and the amphitheatre of Nîmes in less than three hours, which, nevertheless, seems to be a more divine than human work. After that he came to Avignon, where he was not above three days before he fell in love; for the women there take great delight in playing at the close-buttock game, because it is papal ground. Which his tutor and pedagogue Epistemon perceiving, he drew him out of that place, and brought him to Valence in the Dauphiny, where he saw no great matter of recreation, only that the lubbers of the town did beat the scholars, which so incensed him with anger, that when, upon a certain very fair Sunday, the people being at their public dancing in the streets, and one of the scholars offering to put himself into the ring to partake of that sport, the foresaid lubberly fellows would not permit him the admittance into their society, he, taking the scholar's part, so belaboured them with blows, and laid such load upon them, that he drove them all before him, even to the brink of the river Rhone, and would have there drowned them, but that they did squat to the ground, and there lay close a full half-league under the river. The hole is to be seen there yet.

After that he departed from thence, and in three strides and one leap came to Angiers, where he found himself very well, and would have continued there some space, but that the plague drove them away. So from thence he came to Bourges, where he studied a good long time, and profited very much in the faculty of the laws, and would sometimes say that the books of the civil law were like unto a wonderfully precious, royal, and triumphant robe of cloth of gold edged with dirt; for in the world are no goodlier books to be seen, more ornate, nor more eloquent than the texts of the Pandects, but the bordering of them, that is to say, the gloss of Accursius, is so scurvy, vile, base, and unsavoury, that it is nothing but filthiness and villainy.

Going from Bourges, he came to Orleans, where he found store of swaggering scholars that made him great entertainment at his coming, and with whom he learned to play at tennis so well that he was a master at that game. For the students of the said place make a prime exercise of it; and sometimes they carried him unto Cupid's houses of commerce (in that city termed islands, because of their being most ordinarily environed with other houses, and not contiguous to any), there to recreate his person at the sport of poussavant, which the wenches of London call the ferkers in and in. As for breaking his head with over-much study, he had an especial care not to do it in any case, for fear of spoiling his eyes. Which he the rather observed, for that it was told him by one of his teachers, there called regents, that the pain of the eyes was the most hurtful thing of any to the sight. For this cause, when he one day was made a licentiate, or graduate in law, one of the scholars of his acquaintance, who of learning had not much more than his burden, though instead of that he could dance very well and play at tennis, made the blazon and device of the licentiates in the said university, saying,

> So you have in your hand a racket,
> A tennis-ball in your cod-placket,
> A Pandect law in your cap's tippet,
> And that you have the skill to trip it
> In a low dance, you will b' allowed
> The grant of the licentiate's hood.

CHAP. VI.

How Pantagruel met with a Limousin, who too affectedly did counterfeit the French language.

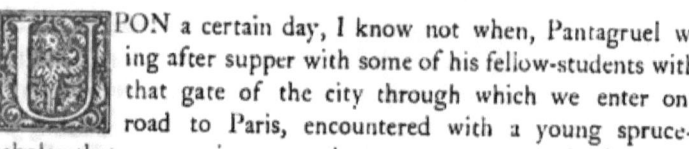

UPON a certain day, I know not when, Pantagruel walking after supper with some of his fellow-students without that gate of the city through which we enter on the road to Paris, encountered with a young spruce-like scholar that was coming upon the same very way, and, after they had saluted one another, asked him thus, My friend, from whence comest thou now? The scholar answered him, From the alme, inclyte, and celebrate academy, which is vocitated Lutetia. What is the meaning of this? said Pantagruel to one of his men. It is, answered he, from Paris. Thou comest from Paris then, said Pantagruel; and how do you spend your time there, you my masters the students of Paris? The scholar answered, We transfretate the Sequan at the dilucul and crepuscul; we deambulate by the compites and quadrives of the urb; we despumate the Latial verbocination; and, like verisimilary amorabons, we captat the benevolence of the omnijugal, omniform, and omnigenal feminine sex. Upon certain diecules we invisat the lupanares, and in a venerian ecstasy inculcate our veretres into the penitissime recesses of the pudends of these amicabilissim meretricules. Then do we cauponisate in the meritory taberns of the Pineapple, the Castle, the Magdalene, and the Mule, goodly vervecine spatules perforaminated with petrocile. And if by fortune there be rarity or penury of pecune in our marsupies, and that they be exhausted of ferruginean metal, for the shot we dimit our codices and oppignerat our vestments, whilst we prestolate the coming of the tabellaries from the Penates and patriotic Lares. To which Pantagruel answered, What devilish language is this? By the Lord, I think thou art some kind of heretick. My lord, no, said the scholar; for libentissimally, as soon as it illucesceth any minutule slice of the day, I demigrate into one of these so well architected minsters, and there, irrorating myself with fair lustral water, I mumble off little parcels of some missic precation of our sacrificuls, and, submurmurating my horary precules, I elevate and absterge my anime from its nocturnal inquinations. I revere the Olympicols. I latrially venere the supernal Astripotent. I dilige and redame my proxims. I observe the decalogical precepts, and, according to the facultatule of my vires, I do not discede from them one late unguicule. Nevertheless, it is veriform, that because Mammona doth not supergurgitate anything in my loculs, that I am somewhat rare and lent to supererogate the elemosynes to those egents that hostially queritate their stipe.

Prut, tut, said Pantagruel, what doth this fool mean to say? I think he is upon the forging of some diabolical tongue, and that enchanter-like he would charm us. To whom one of his men said, Without doubt, sir, this fellow would counterfeit the language of the Parisians, but he doth only flay the Latin, imagining by so doing that he doth highly Pindarize it in most eloquent terms, and strongly conceiteth himself to be therefore a great orator in the French, because he disdaineth the common manner of speaking. To which Pantagruel said, Is it true? The scholar answered, My worshipful lord, my genie is not apt nate to that which this flagitious nebulon saith, to excoriate the cut[ic]ule of our vernacular Gallic, but viceversally I gnave opere, and by veles and rames enite to locupletate it with the Latinicome redundance. By G—, said Pantagruel, I will teach you to speak. But first come hither, and tell me whence thou art. To this the scholar answered, The primeval origin of my aves and ataves was indigenary of the Lemovic regions, where requiesceth the corpor of the hagiotat St. Martial. I understand thee very well, said Pantagruel. When all comes to all, thou art a Limousin, and thou wilt here by thy affected speech counterfeit the Parisians. Well now, come hither, I must show thee a new trick, and handsomely give thee the combfeat. With this he took him by the throat, saying to him, Thou flayest the Latin; by St. John, I will make thee flay the fox, for I will now flay thee alive. Then began the poor Limousin to cry, Haw, gwid maaster! haw, Laord, my halp, and St. Marshaw! haw, I'm worried. Haw, my thropple, the bean of my cragg is bruck! Haw, for gauad's seck lawt my lean, mawster; waw, waw, waw. Now, said Pantagruel, thou speakest naturally, and so let him go, for the poor Limousin had totally bewrayed and thoroughly conshit his breeches, which were not deep and large enough, but round straight cannioned gregs, having in the seat a piece like a keeling's tail, and therefore in French called, *de chausses à queüe de merlus*. Then, said Pantagruel, St. Alipantin, what civet? Fie! to the devil with this turnip-eater, as he stinks! and so let him go. But this hug of Pantagruel's was such a terror to him all the days of his life, and took such deep impression in his fancy, that very often, distracted with sudden affrightments, he would startle and say that Pantagruel held him by the neck. Besides that, it procured him a continual drought and desire to drink, so that after some few years he died of the death Roland, in plain English called thirst, a work of divine vengeance, showing us that which saith the philosopher and Aulus Gellius, that it becometh us to speak according to the common language; and that we should, as said Octavian Augustus, strive to shun all strange and unknown terms with as much heedfulness and circumspection as pilots of ships use to avoid the rocks and banks in the sea.

.

CHAP. VII.

How Pantagruel came to Paris, and of the choice books of the Library of St. Victor.

FTER that Pantagruel had studied very well at Orleans, he resolved to see the great University at Paris; but, before his departure, he was informed that there was a huge big bell at St. Anian in the said town of Orleans, under the ground, which had been there above two hundred and fourteen years, for it was so great that they could not by any device get it so much as above the ground, although they used all the means that are

found in Vitruvius *de Architectura*, Albertus *de Re Ædificatoria*, Euclid, Theon, Archimedes, and Hero *de Ingeniis*; for all that was to no purpose. Wherefore, condescending heartily to the humble request of the citizens and inhabitants of the said town, he determined to remove it to the tower that was erected for it. With that he came to the place where it was, and lifted it out of the ground with his little finger as easily as you would have done a hawk's bell or bellwether's tingle-tangle; but, before he would carry it to the foresaid tower or steeple appointed for it, he would needs make some music with it about the town, and ring it alongst all the streets as he carried it in his hand, wherewith all the people were very glad. But there happened one great inconveniency, for with carrying it so, and ringing it about the streets, all the good Orleans wine turned instantly, waxed flat and was spoiled, which nobody there did perceive till the night following; for every man found himself so altered and a-dry with drinking these flat wines, that they did nothing but spit, and that as white as Malta cotton, saying, We have of the Pantagruel, and our very throats are salted. This done, he came to Paris with his retinue. And at his entry everyone came out to see him—as you know well enough that the people of Paris is sottish by nature, by B flat and B sharp—and beheld him with great astonishment, mixed with no less fear that he would carry away the palace into some other country, *a remotis*, and far from them, as his father formerly had done the great peal of bells at Our Lady's Church to tie about his mare's neck. Now after he had stayed there a pretty space, and studied very well in all the seven liberal arts, he said it was a good town to live in, but not to die; for that the grave-digging rogues of St. Innocent used in frosty nights to warm their bums with dead men's bones. In his abode there he found the library of St. Victor a very stately and magnific one, especially in some books which were there, of which followeth the Repertory and Catalogue, *Et primò*,

The for Godsake of Salvation.
The Codpiece of the Law.
The Slipshoe of the Decretals.
The Pomegranate of Vice.
The Clew-bottom of Theology.
The Duster or Foxtail-flap of Preachers, composed by Turlupin.
The Churning Ballock of the Valiant.

The Henbane of the Bishops.
Marmotretus de baboonis et apis, cum Commento Dorbellis.
Decretum Universitatis Parisiensis super gorgiasitate muliercularum ad placitum.
The Apparition of Sancte Geltrude to a Nun of Poissy, being in travail at the bringing forth of a child.
Ars honeste fartandi in societate, per Marcum Corvinum [Ortuinum].
The Mustard-pot of Penance.
The Gamashes, alias the Boots of Patience.
Formicarium artium.
De brodiorum usu, et honestate quartandi, per Sylvestrem Prioratem Jacobinum.
The Cosened or Gulled in Court.
The Frail of the Scriveners.
The Marriage-packet.
The Cruizy or Crucible of Contemplation.
The Flimflams of the Law.
The Prickle of Wine.
The Spur of Cheese.
Ruboffatorium [Decrotatorium] scholarium.
Tartaretus de modo cacandi.
The Bravades of Rome.
Bricot de Differentiis Browsarum.
The Tailpiece-Cushion, or Close-breech of Discipline.
The Cobbled Shoe of Humility.
The Trivet of good Thoughts.
The Kettle of Magnanimity.
The Cavilling Entanglements of Confessors.
The Snatchfare of the Curates.
Reverendi patris fratris Lubini, provincialis Bavardiæ, de gulpendis lardslicionibus libri tres.
Pasquilli Doctoris Marmorei, de capreolis cum artichoketa comedendis, tempore Papali ab Ecclesia interdicto.
The Invention of the Holy Cross, personated by six wily Priests.
The Spectacles of Pilgrims bound for Rome.
Majoris de modo faciendi puddinos.
The Bagpipe of the Prelates.
Beda de optimitate triparum.

The Complaint of the Barristers upon the Reformation of Comfits.
The Furred Cat of the Solicitors and Attorneys.
Of Peas and Bacon, *cum Commento*.
The Small Vales or Drinking Money of the Indulgences.
Præclarissimi juris utriusque Doctoris Maistre Pilloti, &c., Scrap-farthingi de botchandis glossæ Accursianæ Triflis repetitio enucidi-luculidissima.
Stratagemata Francharchiæri de Baniolet.
Carlbumpkinus de Re Militari cum Figuris Tevoti.
De usu et utilitate flayandi equos et equas, authore Magistro nostro de Quebecu.
The Sauciness of Country-Stewards.
M. N. Rostocostojambedanesse de mustarda post prandium servienda, libri quatuordecim, apostillati per M. Vaurillonis.
The Covillage or Wench-tribute of Promoters.
[Jabolenus de Cosmographia Purgatorii.]
Quæstio subtilissima, utrum Chimæra in vacuo bombinans possit comedere secundas intentiones ; et fuit debatuta per decem hebdomadas in Consilio Constantiensi.
The Bridle-champer of the Advocates.
Smutchudlamenta Scoti.
The Rasping and Hard-scraping of the Cardinals.
De calcaribus removendis, Decades undecim, per M. Albericum de Rosata.
Ejusdem de castramentandis criminibus libri tres.
The Entrance of Anthony de Leve into the Territories of Brazil.
[Marforii, bacalarii cubantis Romæ] de peelandis aut unskinnandis blurrandisque Cardinalium mulis.
The said Author's Apology against those who allege that the Pope's mule doth eat but at set times.
Prognosticatio quæ incipit, Silvii Triquebille, balata per M. N., the deep-dreaming gull Sion.
Boudarini Episcopi de emulgentiarum profectibus Æneades novem, cum privilegio Papali ad triennium et postea non.
The Shitabranna of the Maids.
The Bald Arse or Peeled Breech of the Widows.
The Cowl or Capouch of the Monks.
The Mumbling Devotion of the Celestine Friars.
The Passage-toll of Beggarliness.

The Teeth-chatter or Gum-didder of Lubberly Lusks.
The Paring-shovel of the Theologues.
The Drench-horn of the Masters of Arts.
The Scullions of Olcam, the uninitiated Clerk.
Magistri N. Lickdishetis, de garbellisiftationibus horarum canonicarum, libri quadriginta.
Arsiversitatorium confratriarum, incerto authore.
The Gulsgoatony or Rasher of Cormorants and Ravenous Feeders.
The Rammishness of the Spaniards supergivuregondigaded by Friar Inigo.
The Muttering of Pitiful Wretches.
Dastardismus rerum Italicarum, authore Magistro Burnegad.
R. Lullius de Batisfolagiis Principum.
Calibistratorium caffardiæ, authore M. Jacobo Hocstraten hereticometra.
Codtickler de Magistro nostrandorum Magistro nostratorumque beuvetis, libri octo galantissimi.
The Crackarades of Balists or stone-throwing Engines, Contrepate Clerks, Scriveners, Brief-writers, Rapporters, and Papal Bull-despatchers lately compiled by Regis.
A perpetual Almanack for those that have the gout and the pox.
Manera sweepandi fornacellos per Mag. Eccium.
The Shable or Scimetar of Merchants.
The Pleasures of the Monachal Life.
The Hotchpot of Hypocrites.
The History of the Hobgoblins.
The Ragamuffinism of the pensionary maimed Soldiers.
The Gulling Fibs and Counterfeit Shows of Commissaries.
The Litter of Treasurers.
The Juglingatorium of Sophisters.
Antipericatametanaparbeugedamphicribrationes Toordicantium.
The Periwinkle of Ballad-makers.
The Push-forward of the Alchemists.
The Niddy-noddy of the Satchel-loaded Seekers, by Friar Bindfastatis.
The Shackles of Religion.
The Racket of Swag-waggers.
The Leaning-stock of old Age.
The Muzzle of Nobility.

The Ape's Paternoster.
The Crickets and Hawk's-bells of Devotion.
The Pot of the Ember-weeks.
The Mortar of the Politic Life.
The Flap of the Hermits.
The Riding-hood or Monterg of the Penitentiaries.
The Trictrac of the Knocking Friars.
Blockheadodus, de vita et honestate bragadochiorum.
Lyrippii Sorbonici Moralisationes, per M. Lupoldum.
The Carrier-horse-bells of Travellers.
The Bibbings of the tippling Bishops.
Dolloporediones Doctorum Coloniensium adversus Reuclin.
The Cymbals of Ladies.
The Dunger's Martingale.
Whirlingfriskorum Chasemarkerorum per Fratrem Crackwoodloguetis.
The Clouted Patches of a Stout Heart.
The Mummery of the Racket-keeping Robin-goodfellows.
Gerson, de auferibilitate Papæ ab Ecclesia.
The Catalogue of the Nominated and Graduated Persons.
Jo. Dytebrodii, de terribilitate excommunicationis libellus acephalos.
Ingeniositas invocandi diabolos et diabolas, per M. Guingolphum.
The Hotchpotch or Gallimaufry of the perpetually begging Friars.
The Morris-dance of the Heretics.
The Whinings of Cajetan.
Muddisnout Doctoris Cherubici, de origine Roughfootedarum, et Wryneckedorum ritibus, libri septem.
Sixty-nine fat Breviaries.
The Nightmare of the five Orders of Beggars.
The Skinnery of the new Start-ups extracted out of the fallow-butt, incornifistibulated and plodded upon in the angelic sum.
The Raver and idle Talker in cases of Conscience.
The Fat Belly of the Presidents.
The Baffling Flouter of the Abbots.
Sutoris adversus eum qui vocaverat eum Slabsauceatorem, et quod Slabsauceatores non sunt damnati ab Ecclesia.
Cacatorium medicorum.
The Chimney-sweeper of Astrology.
Campi clysteriorum per paragraph C.

The Bumsquibcracker of Apothecaries.
The Kissbreech of Chirurgery.
Justinianus de Whiteleperotis tollendis.
Antidotarium animæ.
Merlinus Coccaius, de patria diabolorum.
The Practice of Iniquity, by Cleuraunes Sadden.
The Mirror of Baseness, by Radnecu Waldenses.
The Engrained Rogue, by Dwarsencas Eldenu.
The Merciless Cormorant, by Hoxinidno the Jew.

Of which library some books are already printed, and the rest are now at the press in this noble city of Tubingen.

CHAP. VIII.

How Pantagruel, being at Paris, received letters from his father Gargantua, and the copy of them.

PANTAGRUEL studied very hard, as you may well conceive, and profited accordingly; for he had an excellent understanding and notable wit, together with a capacity in memory equal to the measure of twelve oil budgets or butts of olives. And, as he was there abiding one day, he received a letter from his father in manner as followeth.

Most dear Son,—Amongst the gifts, graces, and prerogatives, with which the sovereign plasmator God Almighty hath endowed and adorned human nature at the beginning, that seems to me most singular and excellent by which we may in a mortal state attain to a kind of immortality, and in the course of this transitory life perpetuate our name and seed, which is done by a progeny issued from us in the lawful bonds of matrimony. Whereby that in some measure is restored unto us which was taken from us by the sin of our first parents, to whom it was said that, because they had not obeyed the commandment of God their Creator, they should die, and by death should be brought to nought that so stately frame and plasmature wherein the man at first had been created.

But by this means of seminal propagation there[1] continueth in

---

[1] "Which continueth" in the old copy.

the children what was lost in the parents, and in the grandchildren that which perished in their fathers, and so successively until the day of the last judgment, when Jesus Christ shall have rendered up to God the Father his kingdom in a peaceable condition, out of all danger and contamination of sin; for then shall cease all generations and corruptions, and the elements leave off their continual transmutations, seeing the so much desired peace shall be attained unto and enjoyed, and that all things shall be brought to their end and period. And, therefore, not without just and reasonable cause do I give thanks to God my Saviour and Preserver, for that he hath enabled me to see my bald old age reflourish in thy youth; for when, at his good pleasure, who rules and governs all things, my soul shall leave this mortal habitation, I shall not account myself wholly to die, but to pass from one place unto another, considering that, in and by that, I continue in my visible image living in the world, visiting and conversing with people of honour, and other my good friends, as I was wont to do. Which conversation of mine, although it was not without sin, because we are all of us trespassers, and therefore ought continually to beseech his divine majesty to blot our transgressions out of his memory, yet was it, by the help and grace of God, without all manner of reproach before men.

Wherefore, if those qualities of the mind but shine in thee wherewith I am endowed, as in thee remaineth the perfect image of my body, thou wilt be esteemed by all men to be the perfect guardian and treasure of the immortality of our name. But, if otherwise, I shall truly take but small pleasure to see it, considering that the lesser part of me, which is the body, would abide in thee, and the best, to wit, that which is the soul, and by which our name continues blessed amongst men, would be degenerate and abastardized. This I do not speak out of any distrust that I have of thy virtue, which I have heretofore already tried, but to encourage thee yet more earnestly to proceed from good to better. And that which I now write unto thee is not so much that thou shouldst live in this virtuous course, as that thou shouldst rejoice in so living and having lived, and cheer up thyself with the like resolution in time to come; to the prosecution and accomplishment of which enterprise and generous undertaking thou mayst easily remember how that I have spared nothing, but have so helped thee, as if I had had no other treasure in this world but to see thee once in my life completely well-bred and accomplished, as well in virtue, honesty, and valour, as in all liberal knowledge and civility, and so to leave thee after my death as a mirror representing the person of me thy father, and if not so excellent, and such in deed as I do wish thee, yet such in my desire.

But although my deceased father of happy memory, Grangousier, had bent his best endeavours to make me profit in all perfection and political knowledge, and that my labour and study was fully correspondent to, yea, went beyond his desire, nevertheless, as thou mayst well understand, the time then was not so proper and fit for learning as it is at present, neither had I plenty of such good masters as thou hast had. For that time was darksome, obscured with clouds of ignorance, and savouring a little of the infelicity and calamity of the Goths, who had, wherever they set footing, destroyed all good literature, which in my age hath by the divine goodness been restored unto its former light and dignity, and that with such amendment and increase of the knowledge, that now hardly should I be admitted unto the first form of the little grammar-schoolboys—I say, I, who in my youthful days was, and that justly, reputed the most learned of that age. Which I do not speak in vain boasting, although I might lawfully do it in writing unto thee—in verification whereof thou hast the authority of Marcus Tullius in his book of old age, and the sentence of Plutarch in the book entitled How a man may praise himself without envy—but to give thee an emulous encouragement to strive yet further.

Now is it that the minds of men are qualified with all manner of discipline, and the old sciences revived which for many ages were extinct. Now it is that the learned languages are to their pristine purity restored, viz., Greek, without which a man may be ashamed to account himself a scholar, Hebrew, Arabic, Chaldæan, and Latin. Printing likewise is now in use, so elegant and so correct that better cannot be imagined, although it was found out but in my time by divine inspiration, as by a diabolical suggestion on the other side was the invention of ordnance. All the world is full of knowing men, of most learned schoolmasters, and vast libraries; and it appears to me as a truth, that neither in Plato's time, nor Cicero's, nor Papinian's, there was ever such conveniency for studying as we see at this day there is. Nor must any adventure henceforward to come in public, or present himself in company, that hath not been pretty well polished in the shop of Minerva. I see robbers, hangmen, freebooters, tapsters, ostlers, and such like, of the very rubbish of the people, more learned now than the doctors and preachers were in my time.

What shall I say? The very women and children have aspired to this praise and celestial manner of good learning. Yet so it is that, in the age I am now of, I have been constrained to learn the Greek tongue—which I contemned not like Cato, but had not the leisure in my younger years to attend the study of it—and take much delight in the reading of Plutarch's Morals, the pleasant Dialogues of Plato, the Monuments of Pausanias, and the Antiquities of Athenæus, in waiting on the hour wherein God my Creator shall call me and command me to depart from this earth and transitory pilgrimage. Wherefore, my son, I admonish thee to employ thy youth to profit as well as thou canst, both in thy studies and in virtue. Thou art at Paris, where the laudable examples of many brave men may stir up thy mind to gallant actions, and hast likewise for thy tutor and pedagogue the learned Epistemon, who by his lively and vocal documents may instruct thee in the arts and sciences.

I intend, and will have it so, that thou learn the languages perfectly; first of all the Greek, as Quintilian will have it; secondly, the Latin; and then the Hebrew, for the Holy Scripture sake; and then the Chaldee and Arabic likewise, and that thou frame thy style in Greek in imitation of Plato, and for the Latin after Cicero. Let there be no history which thou shalt not have ready in thy memory; unto the prosecuting of which design, books of cosmography will be very conducible and help thee much. Of the liberal arts of geometry, arithmetic, and music, I gave thee some taste when thou wert yet little, and not above five or six years old. Proceed further in them, and learn the remainder if thou canst. As for astronomy, study all the rules thereof. Let pass, nevertheless, the divining and judicial astrology, and the art of Lullius, as being nothing else but plain abuses and vanities. As for the civil law, of that I would have thee to know the texts by heart, and then to confer them with philosophy.

Now, in matter of the knowledge of the works of nature, I would have thee to study that exactly, and that so there be no sea, river, nor fountain, of which thou dost not know the fishes; all the fowls of the air; all the several kinds of shrubs and trees, whether in forests or orchards; all the sorts of herbs and flowers that grow upon the ground; all the various metals that are hid within the bowels of the earth; together with all the diversity of precious stones that are to be seen in the orient and south parts of the world. Let nothing of all these be hidden from thee. Then fail not most carefully to peruse the books of the Greek, Arabian, and Latin physicians, not despising the Talmudists and Cabalists; and by frequent anatomies get thee the perfect knowledge of the other world, called the microcosm, which is man. And at some hours of the day apply thy mind to the study of the Holy Scriptures; first in Greek, the New Testament, with the Epistles of the Apostles; and then the Old Testament in Hebrew. In brief, let me see thee an abyss and bottomless pit of knowledge; for from henceforward, as thou growest great and becomest a man, thou must part from this tranquillity and rest of study, thou must learn chivalry, warfare, and the exercises of the field, the better thereby to defend my house and our friends, and to succour and protect them at all their needs against the invasion and assaults of evildoers.

Furthermore, I will that very shortly thou try how much thou hast profited, which thou canst not better do than by maintaining publicly theses and conclusions in all arts against all persons whatsoever, and by haunting the company of learned men, both at Paris and otherwhere. But because, as the wise man Solomon saith, Wisdom entereth not into a malicious mind, and that knowledge without conscience is but the ruin of the soul, it behoveth thee to serve, to love, to fear God, and on him to cast all thy thoughts and all thy hope, and by faith formed in charity to cleave unto him, so that thou mayst never be separated from him by thy sins. Suspect the abuses of the world. Set not thy heart upon vanity, for this life is transitory, but the Word of the Lord endureth for ever. Be serviceable to all thy neighbours, and love them as thyself. Reverence thy preceptors: shun the conversation of those whom thou desirest not to resemble, and receive not in vain the graces which God hath bestowed upon thee. And, when thou shalt see that thou hast attained to all the knowledge that is to be acquired in that part, return unto me, that I may see thee and give thee my blessing before I die. My son, the peace and grace of our Lord be with thee. Amen.

Thy father Gargantua.

From Utopia the 17th day of the
    month of March.

These letters being received and read, Pantagruel plucked up his heart, took a fresh courage to him, and was inflamed with a desire to profit in his studies more than ever, so that if you had seen him, how he took pains, and how he advanced in learning, you would have said that the vivacity of his spirit amidst the books was like a great fire amongst dry wood, so active it was, vigorous and indefatigable.

CHAP. IX.

How Pantagruel found Panurge, whom he loved all his lifetime.

ONE day, as Pantagruel was taking a walk without the city, towards St. Anthony's abbey, discoursing and philosophating with his own servants and some other scholars, [he] met with a young man of very comely stature and surpassing handsome in all the lineaments of his body, but in several parts thereof most pitifully wounded; in such bad equipage in matter of his apparel, which was but tatters and rags, and every way so far out of order that he seemed to have been a-fighting with mastiff-dogs, from whose fury he had made an escape; or, to say better, he looked, in the condition wherein he then was, like an apple-gatherer of the country of Perche.

As far off as Pantagruel saw him, he said to those that stood by, Do you see that man there, who is a-coming hither upon the road from Charenton bridge? By my faith, he is only poor in fortune; for I may assure you that by his physiognomy it appeareth that nature hath extracted him from some rich and noble race, and that too much curiosity hath thrown him upon adventures which possibly have reduced him to this indigence, want, and penury. Now as he was just amongst them, Pantagruel said unto him, Let me entreat you, friend, that you may be pleased to stop here a little and answer me to that which I shall ask you, and I am confident you will not think your time ill bestowed; for I have an extreme desire, according to my ability, to give you some supply in this distress wherein I see you are; because I do very much commiserate your case, which truly moves me to great pity. Therefore, my friend, tell me who you are; whence you come; whither you go; what you desire;

and what your name is. The companion answered him in the German[1] tongue, thus

"Junker, Gott geb euch glück und heil. Furwahr, lieber Junker, ich lasz euch wissen, das da ihr mich von fragt, ist ein arm und erbärmlich Ding, und wer viel darvon zu sagen, welches euch verdrüssig zu hören, und mir zu erzelen wer, wiewol die Poeten und Oratorn vorzeiten haben gesagt in ihren Sprüchen und Sentenzen, dasz die gedechtniss des Elends und Armuth vorlängst erlitten ist eine grosse Lust." My friend, said Pantagruel, I have no skill in that gibberish of yours; therefore, if you would have us to understand you, speak to us in some other language. Then did the droll answer him thus:

"Albarildim gotfano dechmin brin alabo dordio falbroth ringuam albaras. Nin portzadikin almucatin milko prin alelmin en thoth dalheben ensouim: kuthim al dum alkatim nim broth dechoth porth min michais im endoth, pruch dalmaisoulum hol moth danfrihim lupaldas in voldemoth. Nin hur diavosth mnarbotim dalgousch palfrapin duch im scoth pruch galeth dal chinon, min foulchrich al conin brutathen doth dal prin." Do you understand none of this? said Pantagruel to the company. I believe, said Epistemon, that this is the language of the Antipodes, and such a hard one that the devil himself knows not what to make of it. Then said Pantagruel, Gossip, I know not if the walls do comprehend the meaning of your words, but none of us here doth so much as understand one syllable of them. Then said my blade again:

"Signor mio, voi vedete per essempio, che la cornamusa non suona mai, s'ella non ha il ventre pieno. Cosi io parimente non vi saprei contare le mie fortune, se prima il tribulato ventre non ha la solita refettione. Al quale è adviso che le mani et li denti habbiano perso il loro ordine naturale et del tutto annichilati." To which Epistemon answered, As much of the one as of the other, and nothing of either. Then said Panurge:

"Lord, if you be so virtuous of intelligence as you be naturally relieved to the body, you should have pity of me. For nature hath made us equal, but fortune hath some exalted and others deprived; nevertheless is virtue often deprived and the virtuous men despised; for before the last end none is good."[2] Yet less, said Pantagruel. Then said my jolly Panurge:

[1] The first edition reads "Dutch."
[2] The following is the passage as it stands in the first edition. Urquhart seems

"Jona andie guaussa goussy etan beharda er remedio beharde versela ysser landa. Anbat es otoy y es nausu ey nessassust gourray proposian ordine den. Non yssena bayta facheria egabe gen herassy badia sadassu noura assia. Aran hondavan gualde cydassu naydassuna. Estou oussye eg vinan soury hien er darstura eguy harm. Genicoa plasar vadu." Are you there, said Eudemon, Genicoa? To this said Carpalim, St. Trinian's rammer unstitch your bum, for I had almost understood it. Then answered Panurge:

"Prust frest frinst sorgdmand strochdi drhds pag brlelang Gravot Chavigny Pomardiere rusth pkaldracg Deviniere pres Nays. Couille kalmuch monach drupp del meupplist rincq drlnd dodelb up drent loch mine stz rinq jald de vins ders cordelis bur jocst stzampenards." Do you speak Christian, said Epistemon, or the buffoon language, otherwise called Patelinois? Nay, it is the puzlatory tongue, said another, which some call Lanternois. Then said Panurge:

"Heere, ik en spreeke anders geen taele dan kersten taele: my dunkt noghtans, al en seg ik u niet een wordt, mynen noot verklaert genoegh wat ik begeere: geeft my uyt bermhertigheit yets waar van ik gevoet magh zyn." To which answered Pantagruel, As much of that. Then said Panurge:

"Sennor, de tanto hablar yo soy cansado, porque yo suplico a vuestra reverentia que mire a los preceptos evangelicos, para que ellos movan vuestra reverentia a lo que es de conscientia; y si ellos non bastaren, para mouer vuestra reverentia a piedad, yo suplico que mire a la piedad natural, la qual yo creo que le movera como es de razon: y con esso non digo mas." Truly, my friend, [said Pantagruel,] I doubt not but you can speak divers languages; but tell us that which you would have us to do for you in some tongue which you conceive we may understand. Then said the companion:

"Min Herre, endog ieg med ingen tunge talede, ligesom bærn, oc uskellige creatuure: Mine klædebon oc mit legoms magerhed uduiser alligeuel klarlig huad ting mig best behof gioris, som er sandelig mad oc

to have rendered Rabelais' indifferent English into worse Scotch, and this, with probably the use of contractions in his MS., or "the oddness" of handwriting which he owns to in his Logopandecteision (p. 419, Mait. Club. Edit.), has led to a chaotic jumble, which it is nearly impossible to reduce to order.—Instead of any attempt to do so, it is here given *verbatim*: "Lard gestholb besua virtuisbe intelligence: ass yi body scalbisbe natural reloth cholb suld osme pety have; for natur hass visse equaly maide bot fortune sum exaiti hesse andoyis deprevit: non yeless iviss mou virtiuss deprevit, and virtuiss men decreviss for anen ye ladeniss non quid." Here is a morsel for critical ingenuity to fix its teeth in.—M.

dricke: Huorfor forbarme dig ofuer mig, oc befal at giue mig noguet, af huilcket ieg kand slyre min giæendis mage, ligeruiis som mand *Cerbero* en suppe forsetter: Saa skalt du lefue længe oc lycksalig." I think really, said Eusthenes, that the Goths spoke thus of old, and that, if it pleased God, we would all of us speak so with our tails. Then again said Panurge:

"Adon, scalom lecha: im ischar harob hal hebdeca bimcherah thithen li kikar lehem: chanchat ub laah al Adonai cho nen ral." To which answered Epistemon, At this time have I understood him very well; for it is the Hebrew tongue most rhetorically pronounced. Then again said the gallant:

"Despota tinyn panagathe, diati sy mi ouk artodotis? horas gar limo analiscomenon eme athlion, ke en to metaxy me ouk eleis oudamos, zetis de par emou ha ou chre. Ke homos philologi pantes homologousi tote logous te ke remata peritta hyparchin, hopote pragma afto pasi delon esti. Entha gar anankei monon logi isin, hina pragmata (hon peri amphisbetoumen), me prosphoros epiphenete." What? said Carpalim, Pantagruel's footman, It is Greek, I have understood him. And how? hast thou dwelt any while in Greece? Then said the droll again:

"Agonou dont oussys vous desdagnez algorou: nou den farou zamist vous mariston ulbrou, fousques voubrol tant bredaguez moupreton dengoulhoust, daguez daguez non cropys fost pardonnoflist nougrou. Agou paston tol nalprissys hourtou los echatonous, prou dhouquys brol pany gou den bascrou noudous caguons goulfren goul oustaroppassou."[1] Methinks I understand him, said Pantagruel; for either it is the language of my country of Utopia, or sounds very like it. And, as he was about to have begun some purpose, the companion said:

"Jam toties vos per sacra, perque deos deasque omnes obtestatus sum, ut si quæ vos pietas permovet, egestatem meam solaremini, nec hilum proficio clamans et ejulans. Sinite, quæso, sinite, viri impii, quo me fata vocant abire; nec ultra vanis vestris interpellationibus obtundatis, memores veteris illius adagii, quo venter famelicus auriculis carere dicitur." Well, my friend, said Pantagruel, but cannot you speak French? That I can do, sir, very well, said the companion,

---

[1] In this and the preceding speeches of Panurge, the Paris Variorum Edition of 1823 has been followed in correcting Urquhart's text, which is full of inaccuracies.—M.

God be thanked. It is my natural language and mother tongue, for I was born and bred in my younger years in the garden of France, to wit, Touraine. Then, said Pantagruel, tell us what is your name, and from whence you are come; for, by my faith, I have already stamped in my mind such a deep impression of love towards you, that, if you will condescend unto my will, you shall not depart out of my company, and you and I shall make up another couple of friends such as Æneas and Achates were. Sir, said the companion, my true and proper Christian name is Panurge, and now I come out of Turkey, to which country I was carried away prisoner at that time when they went to Metelin with a mischief. And willingly would I relate unto you my fortunes, which are more wonderful than those of Ulysses were; but, seeing that it pleaseth you to retain me with you, I most heartily accept of the offer, protesting never to leave you should you go to all the devils in hell. We shall have therefore more leisure at another time, and a fitter opportunity wherein to report them; for at this present I am in a very urgent necessity to feed; my teeth are sharp, my belly empty, my throat dry, and my stomach fierce and burning, all is ready. If you will but set me to work, it will be as good as a balsamum for sore eyes to see me gulch and raven it. For God's sake, give order for it. Then Pantagruel commanded that they should carry him home and provide him good store of victuals; which being done, he ate very well that evening, and, capon-like, went early to bed; then slept until dinner-time the next day, so that he made but three steps and one leap from the bed to the board.

CHAP. X.

How Pantagruel judged so equitably of a controversy, which was wonderfully obscure and difficult, that, by reason of his just decree therein, he was reputed to have a most admirable judgment.

ANTAGRUEL, very well remembering his father's letter and admonitions, would one day make trial of his knowledge. Thereupon, in all the carrefours, that is, throughout all the four quarters, streets, and corners of the city, he set up conclusions to the number of nine thousand seven hundred

sixty and four, in all manner of learning, touching in them the hardest doubts that are in any science. And first of all, in the Fodder Street he held dispute against all the regents or fellows of colleges, artists or masters of arts, and orators, and did so gallantly that he overthrew them and set them all upon their tails. He went afterwards to the Sorbonne, where he maintained argument against all the theologians or divines, for the space of six weeks, from four o'clock in the morning until six in the evening, except an interval of two hours to refresh themselves and take their repast. And at this were present the greatest part of the lords of the court, the masters of requests, presidents, counsellors, those of the accompts, secretaries, advocates, and others; as also the sheriffs of the said town, with the physicians and professors of the canon law. Amongst which, it is to be remarked, that the greatest part were stubborn jades, and in their opinions obstinate; but he took such course with them that, for all their ergoes and fallacies, he put their backs to the wall, gravelled them in the deepest questions, and made it visibly appear to the world that, compared to him, they were but monkeys and a knot of muffled calves. Whereupon everybody began to keep a bustling noise and talk of his so marvellous knowledge, through all degrees of persons in both sexes, even to the very laundresses, brokers, roast-meat sellers, penknife makers, and others, who, when he passed along in the street, would say, This is he! in which he took delight, as Demosthenes, the prince of Greek orators, did, when an old crouching wife, pointing at him with her fingers, said, That is the man.

Now at this same very time there was a process or suit in law depending in court between two great lords, of which one was called my Lord Kissbreech, plaintiff of one side, and the other my Lord Suckfist, defendant of the other; whose controversy was so high and difficult in law that the court of parliament could make nothing of it. And therefore, by the commandment of the king, there were assembled four of the greatest and most learned of all the parliaments of France, together with the great council, and all the principal regents of the universities, not only of France, but of England also and Italy, such as Jason, Philippus Decius, Petrus de Petronibus, and a rabble of other old Rabbinists. Who being thus met together, after they had thereupon consulted for the space of six-and-forty weeks, finding that they could not fasten their teeth in it, nor with such clearness understand the case as that they might in any manner of way be able to right it, or take up the difference betwixt the two aforesaid parties, it did so grievously vex them that they most villainously conshit themselves for shame. In this great extremity one amongst them, named Du Douhet, the learnedest of all, and more expert and prudent than any of the rest, whilst one day they were thus at their wits' end, all-to-be-dunced and philogrobolized in their brains, said unto them, We have been here, my masters, a good long space, without doing anything else than trifle away both our time and money, and can nevertheless find neither brim nor bottom in this matter, for the more we study about it the less we understand therein, which is a great shame and disgrace to us, and a heavy burden to our consciences; yea, such that in my opinion we shall not rid ourselves of it without dishonour, unless we take some other course ; for we do nothing but dote in our consultations.

See, therefore, what I have thought upon. You have heard much talking of that worthy personage named Master Pantagruel, who hath been found to be learned above the capacity of this present age, by the proofs he gave in those great disputations which he held publicly against all men. My opinion is, that we send for him to confer with him about this business ; for never any man will encompass the bringing of it to an end if he do it not.

Hereunto all the counsellors and doctors willingly agreed, and according to that their result having instantly sent for him, they entreated him to be pleased to canvass the process and sift it thoroughly, that, after a deep search and narrow examination of all the points thereof, he might forthwith make the report unto them such as he shall think good in true and legal knowledge. To this effect they delivered into his hands the bags wherein were the writs and pancarts concerning that suit, which for bulk and weight were almost enough to lade four great couillard or stoned asses. But Pantagruel said unto them, Are the two lords between whom this debate and process is yet living ? It was answered him, Yes. To what a devil, then, said he, serve so many paltry heaps and bundles of papers and copies which you give me ? Is it not better to hear their controversy from their own mouths whilst they are face to face before us, than to read these vile fopperies, which are nothing but trumperies, deceits, diabolical cozenages of Cepola, pernicious slights and subversions of equity ? For I am sure that you, and all those through whose hands this process hath passed, have by your devices added what you could to it *pro et contra* in such sort that, although their difference perhaps was clear and easy enough to determine at first, you have obscured it and made it more intricate by the frivolous, sottish, unreasonable, and foolish reasons and opinions of Accursius, Baldus, Bartolus, de Castro, de Imola, Hippolytus, Panormo, Bertachin, Alexander, Curtius, and those other old mastiffs, who never understood the least law of the Pandects, they being but mere blockheads and great tithe calves, ignorant of all that which was needful for the understanding of the laws; for, as it is most certain, they had not the knowledge either of the Greek or Latin tongue, but only of the Gothic and barbarian. The laws, nevertheless, were first taken from the Greeks, according to the testimony of Ulpian, *L. poster. de origine juris*, which we likewise may perceive by that all the laws are full of Greek words and sentences. And then we find that they are reduced into a Latin style the most elegant and ornate that whole language is able to afford, without excepting that of any that ever wrote therein, nay, not of Sallust, Varro, Cicero, Seneca, Titus Livius, nor Quintilian. How then could these old dotards be able to understand aright the text of the laws who never in their time had looked upon a good Latin book, as doth evidently enough appear by the rudeness of their style, which is fitter for a chimney-sweeper, or for a cook or a scullion, than for a jurisconsult and doctor in the laws?

Furthermore, seeing the laws are excerpted out of the middle of moral and natural philosophy, how should these fools have understood it, that have, by G—, studied less in philosophy than my mule? In respect of human learning and the knowledge of antiquities and history they were truly laden with those faculties as a toad is with feathers. And yet of all this the laws are so full that without it they cannot be understood, as I intend more fully to show unto you in a peculiar treatise which on that purpose I am about to publish. Therefore, if you will that I take any meddling in this process, first cause all these papers to be burnt; secondly, make the two gentlemen come personally before me, and afterwards, when I shall have heard them, I will tell you my opinion freely without any feignedness or dissimulation whatsoever.

Some amongst them did contradict this motion, as you know that in all companies there are more fools than wise men, and that the greater part always surmounts the better, as saith Titus Livius in speaking of the Carthaginians. But the foresaid Du Douhet held the contrary opinion, maintaining that Pantagruel had said well, and what was right, in affirming that these records, bills of inquest, replies, rejoinders, exceptions, depositions, and other such diableries of truth-entangling writs, were but engines wherewith to overthrow justice and unnecessarily to prolong such suits as did depend before them; and that, therefore, the devil would carry them all away to hell if they did not take another course and proceeded not in times coming according to the prescripts of evangelical and philosophical equity. In fine, all the papers were burnt, and the two gentlemen summoned and personally convented. At whose appearance before the court Pantagruel said unto them, Are you they that have this great difference betwixt you? Yes, my lord, said they. Which of you, said Pantagruel, is the plaintiff? It is I, said my Lord Kissbreech. Go to, then, my friend, said he, and relate your matter unto me from point to point, according to the real truth, or else, by cock's body, if I find you to lie so much as in one word, I will make you shorter by the head, and take it from off your shoulders to show others by your example that in justice and judgment men ought to speak nothing but the truth. Therefore take heed you do not add nor impair anything in the narration of your case. Begin.

CHAP. XI.

How the Lords of Kissbreech and Suckfist did plead before Pantagruel without an attorney.

THEN began Kissbreech in manner as followeth. My lord, it is true that a good woman of my house carried eggs to the market to sell. Be covered, Kissbreech, said Pantagruel. Thanks to you, my lord, said the Lord Kissbreech; but to the purpose. There passed betwixt the two tropics the sum of threepence towards the zenith and a halfpenny, forasmuch as the Riphæan mountains had been that year oppressed with a great sterility of counterfeit gudgeons and shows without substance, by means of the babbling tattle and fond fibs seditiously raised between

the gibblegabblers and Accursian gibberish-mongers for the rebellion of the Switzers, who had assembled themselves to the full number of the bumbees and myrmidons to go a-handsel-getting on the first day of the new year, at that very time when they give brewis to the oxen and deliver the key of the coals to the country-girls for serving in of the oats to the dogs. All the night long they did nothing else, keeping their hands still upon the pot, but despatch, both on foot and horseback, leaden-sealed writs or letters, to wit, papal commissions commonly called bulls, to stop the boats; for the tailors and seamsters would have made of the stolen shreds and clippings a goodly sagbut to cover the face of the ocean, which then was great with child of a potful of cabbage, according to the opinion of the hay-bundle-makers. But the physicians said that by the urine they could discern no manifest sign of the bustard's pace, nor how to eat double-tongued mattocks with mustard, unless the lords and gentlemen of the court should be pleased to give by B.mol express command to the pox not to run about any longer in gleaning up of coppersmiths and tinkers; for the jobbernolls had already a pretty good beginning in their dance of the British jig called the *estrindore*, to a perfect diapason, with one foot in the fire, and their head in the middle, as goodman Ragot was wont to say.

Ha, my masters, God moderates all things, and disposeth of them at his pleasure, so that against unlucky fortune a carter broke his frisking whip, which was all the wind-instrument he had. This was done at his return from the little paltry town, even then when Master Antitus of Cressplots was licentiated, and had passed his degrees in all dullery and blockishness, according to this sentence of the canonists, *Beati Dunces, quoniam ipsi stumblaverunt.* But that which makes Lent to be so high, by St. Fiacre of Bry, is for nothing else but that the Pentecost never comes but to my cost; yet, on afore there, ho! a little rain stills a great wind, and we must think so, seeing that the sergeant hath propounded the matter so far above my reach, that the clerks and secondaries could not with the benefit thereof lick their fingers, feathered with ganders, so orbicularly as they were wont in other things to do. And we do manifestly see that everyone acknowledgeth himself to be in the error wherewith another hath been charged, reserving only those cases whereby we are obliged to take an ocular inspection in a perspective glass of these things towards the place in the chimney where hangeth the sign of the wine of forty girths, which have been always accounted very necessary for the number of twenty pannels and pack-saddles of the bankrupt protectionaries of five years' respite. Howsoever, at least, he that would not let fly the fowl before the cheesecakes ought in law to have discovered his reason why not, for the memory is often lost with a wayward shoeing. Well, God keep Theobald Mitain from all danger! Then said Pantagruel, Hold there! Ho, my friend, soft and fair, speak at leisure and soberly without putting yourself in choler. I understand the case,—go on. Now then, my lord, said Kissbreech, the foresaid good woman saying her *gaudez* and *audi nos*, could not cover herself with a treacherous backblow, ascending by the wounds and passions of the privileges of the universities, unless by the virtue of a warming-pan she had angelically fomented every part of her body in covering them with a hedge of garden-beds; then giving in a swift unavoidable thirst [thrust] very near to the place where they sell the old rags whereof the painters of Flanders make great use when they are about neatly to clap on shoes on grasshoppers, locusts, cigals, and such like fly-fowls, so strange to us that I am wonderfully astonished why the world doth not lay, seeing it is so good to hatch.

Here the Lord of Suckfist would have interrupted him and spoken somewhat, whereupon Pantagruel said unto him, St! by St. Anthony's belly, doth it become thee to speak without command? I sweat here with the extremity of labour and exceeding toil I take to understand the proceeding of your mutual difference, and yet thou comest to trouble and disquiet me. Peace, in the devil's name, peace. Thou shalt be permitted to speak thy bellyful when this man hath done, and no sooner. Go on, said he to Kissbreech; speak calmly, and do not overheat yourself with too much haste.

I perceiving, then, said Kissbreech, that the Pragmatical Sanction did make no mention of it, and that the holy Pope to everyone gave liberty to fart at his own ease, if that the blankets had no streaks wherein the liars were to be crossed with a ruffian-like crew, and, the rainbow being newly sharpened at Milan to bring forth larks, gave his full consent that the good woman should tread down the heel of the hipgut-pangs, by virtue of a solemn protestation put in by the little testiculated or codsted fishes, which, to tell the truth, were at that time very necessary for understanding the syntax and construction of old boots. Therefore John Calf, her cousin gervais once removed with a log from the woodstack, very seriously advised her not to put herself into the hazard of quagswagging in the lee, to be scoured with a buck of linen clothes till first she had kindled the paper. This counsel she laid hold on, because he desired her to take nothing and throw out, for *Non de pontevadit, qui cum sapientia cadit.* Matters thus standing, seeing the masters of the chamber of accompts or members of that committee did not fully agree amongst themselves in casting up the number of the Almany whistles, whereof were framed those spectacles for princes which have been lately printed at Antwerp, I must needs think that it makes a bad return of the writ, and that the adverse party is not to be believed, *in sacer verbo dotis.* For that, having a great desire to obey the pleasure of the king, I armed myself from toe to top with belly furniture, of the soles of good venison-pasties, to go see how my grape-gatherers and vintagers had pinked and cut full of small holes their high-coped caps, to lecher it the better, and play at in and in. And indeed the time was very dangerous in coming from the fair, in so far that many trained bowmen were cast at the muster and quite rejected, although the chimneytops were high enough, according to the proportion of the windgalls in the legs of horses, or of the malanders, which in the esteem of expert farriers is no better disease, or else the story of Ronypatifam or Lamibaudichon, interpreted by some to be the tale of a tub or of a roasted horse, savours of apocrypha, and is not an authentic history. And by this means there was that year great abundance, throughout all the country of Artois, of tawny buzzing beetles, to the no small profit of the gentlemen-great-stick-faggot-carriers, when they did eat without disdaining the cocklicranes, till their belly was like to crack with it again. As for my own part, such is my Christian charity towards my neighbours, that I could wish from my heart everyone had as good a voice; it would make us play the better at the tennis and the balloon. And truly, my lord, to express the real truth without dissimulation, I cannot but say that those petty subtle devices which are found out in the etymologizing of pattens would descend more easily into the river of Seine, to serve for ever at the millers' bridge upon the said water, as it was heretofore decreed by the king of the Canarians, according to the sentence or judgment given thereupon, which is to be seen in the registry and records within the clerk's office of this house.

And therefore, my lord, I do most humbly require, that by

your lordship there may be said and declared upon the case what is reasonable, with costs, damages, and interests. Then said Pantagruel, My friend, is this all you have to say? Kissbreech answered, Yes, my lord, for I have told all the *tu autem*, and have not varied at all upon mine honour in so much as one single word. You then, said Pantagruel, my Lord of Suckfist, say what you will, and be brief, without omitting, nevertheless, anything that may serve to the purpose.

CHAP. XII.

How the Lord of Suckfist pleaded before Pantagruel.

HEN began the Lord Suckfist in manner as followeth. My lord, and you my masters, if the iniquity of men were as easily seen in categorical judgment as we can discern flies in a milkpot, the world's four oxen had not been so eaten up with rats, nor had so many ears upon the earth been nibbled away so scurvily. For although all that my adversary hath spoken be of a very soft and downy truth, in so much as concerns the letter and history of the factum, yet nevertheless the crafty slights, cunning subtleties, sly cozenages, and little troubling entanglements are hid under the rosepot, the common cloak and cover of all fraudulent deceits.

Should I endure that, when I am eating my pottage equal with the best, and that without either thinking or speaking any manner of ill, they rudely come to vex, trouble, and perplex my brains with that antique proverb which saith,

> Who in his pottage-eating drinks will not,
> When he is dead and buried, see one jot.

And, good lady, how many great captains have we seen in the day of battle, when in open field the sacrament was distributed in luncheons of the sanctified bread of the confraternity, the more honestly to nod their heads, play on the lute, and crack with their tails, to make pretty little platform leaps in keeping level by the ground? But now the world is unshackled from the corners of the packs of Leicester.

One flies out lewdly and becomes debauched; another, likewise, five, four, and two, and that at such random that, if the court take not some course therein, it will make as bad a season in matter of gleaning this year as ever it made, or it will make goblets. If any poor creature go to the stoves to illuminate his muzzle with a cowsherd or to buy winter-boots, and that the sergeants passing by, or those of the watch, happen to receive the decoction of a clyster or the fecal matter of a close-stool upon their rustling-wrangling-clutter-keeping masterships, should any because of that make bold to clip the shillings and testers and fry the wooden dishes? Sometimes, when we think one thing, God does another; and when the sun is wholly set all beasts are in the shade. Let me never be believed again, if I do not gallantly prove it by several people that have seen the light of the day.

In the year thirty and six, buying a Dutch curtail, which was a middle-sized horse, both high and short, of a wool good enough and dyed in grain, as the goldsmiths assured me, although the notary put an &c. in it, I told really that I was not a clerk of so much learning as to snatch at the moon with my teeth; but, as for the butter-firkin where Vulcanian deeds and evidences were sealed, the rumour was, and the report thereof went current, that salt-beef will make one find the way to the wine without a candle, though it were hid in the bottom of a collier's sack, and that with his drawers on he were mounted on a barbed horse furnished with a fronstal, and such arms, thighs, and leg-pieces as are requisite for the well frying and broiling of a swaggering sauciness. Here is a sheep's head, and it is well they make a proverb of this, that it is good to see black cows in burnt wood when one attains to the enjoyment of his love. I had a consultation upon this point with my masters the clerks, who for resolution concluded in frisesomorum that there is nothing like to mowing in the summer, and sweeping clean away in water, well garnished with paper, ink, pens, and penknives, of Lyons upon the river of Rhône, dolopym dolopof, tarabin tarabas, tut, prut, pish; for, incontinently after that armour begins to smell of garlic, the rust will go near to eat the liver, not of him that wears it, and then do they nothing else but withstand others' courses, and wryneckedly set up their bristles 'gainst one another, in lightly passing over their afternoon's sleep, and this is that which maketh salt so dear. My lords, believe not when the said good woman had with birdlime caught the shoveler fowl, the better before a sergeant's witness to deliver the younger son's portion to him, that the sheep's pluck or hog's haslet did dodge and shrink back in the usurers' purses, or that there could be anything better to preserve one from the cannibals than to take a rope of onions, knit with three hundred turnips, and a little of a calf's chaldern of the best allay that the alchemists have provided, [and] that they daub and do over with clay, as also calcinate and burn to dust these pantoufles, muff in muff out, mouflin mouflard, with the fine sauce of the juice of the rabble rout, whilst they hide themselves in some petty mouldwarphole, saving always the little slices of bacon. Now, if the dice will not favour you with any other throw but ambes-ace and the chance of three at the great end, mark well the ace, then take me your dame, settle her in a corner of the bed, and whisk me her up drilletrille, there, there, toureloura la la; which when you have done, take a hearty draught of the best, *despicando grenovillibus*, in despite of the frogs, whose fair coarse bebuskined stockings shall be set apart for the little green geese or mewed goslings, which, fattened in a coop, take delight to sport themselves at the wagtail game, waiting for the beating of the metal and heating of the wax by the slavering drivellers of consolation.

Very true it is, that the four oxen which are in debate, and whereof mention was made, were somewhat short in memory. Nevertheless, to understand the game aright, they feared neither the cormorant nor mallard of Savoy, which put the good people of my country in great hope that their children some time should become very skilful in algorism. Therefore is it, that by a law rubric and special sentence thereof, that we cannot fail to take the wolf if we make our hedges higher than the windmill, whereof somewhat was spoken by the plaintiff. But the great devil did envy it, and by that means put the High Dutches far behind, who played the devils in swilling down and tippling at the good liquor, trink, mein herr, trink, trink, by two of my table-men in the corner-point I have gained the lurch. For it is not probable, nor is there any appearance of truth in this saying, that at Paris upon a little bridge the hen is proportionable, and were they as copped and high-crested as marsh whoops, if veritably they did not sacrifice the printer's pumpet-balls at Moreb, with a new edge set upon them by text letters or those of a swift-writing hand, it is all one to me, so that the headband of the book breed not moths or worms in it. And put the case that, at the coupling together of the buckhounds, the little puppies should have waxed proud before the notary could have given an account of the serving of his writ by the cabalistic art, it will necessarily follow, under correction of the better judgment of the court, that six acres of meadow ground of the greatest breadth will make three butts of fine ink, without paying ready money; considering that, at the funeral of King Charles, we might have had the fathom in open market for one and two, that is, deuce ace. This I may affirm with a safe conscience, upon my oath of wool.

And I see ordinarily in all good bagpipes, that, when they go to the counterfeiting of the chirping of small birds, by swinging a broom three times about a chimney, and putting his name upon record, they do nothing but bend a crossbow backwards, and wind a horn, if perhaps it be too hot, and that, by making it fast to a rope he was to draw, immediately after the sight of the letters, the cows were restored to him. Such another sentence after the homeliest manner was pronounced in the seventeenth year, because of the bad government of Louzefougarouse, whereunto it may please the court to have regard. I desire to be rightly understood; for truly, I say not but that in all equity, and with an upright conscience, those may very well be dispossessed who drink holy water as one would do a weaver's shuttle, whereof suppositories are made to those that will not resign, but on the terms of ell and tell and giving of one thing for another. *Tunc*, my lords, *quid juris pro minoribus?* For the common custom of the Salic law is such, that the first incendiary or firebrand of sedition that flays the cow and wipes his nose in a full concert of music without blowing in the cobbler's stitches, should in the time of the nightmare sublimate the penury of his member by moss gathered when people are like to founder themselves at the mess at midnight, to give the estrapade to these white wines of Anjou that do the fear of the leg in lifting it by horsemen called the gambetta, and that neck to neck after the fashion of Brittany, concluding as before with costs, damages, and interests.

After that the Lord of Suckfist had ended, Pantagruel said to the Lord of Kissbreech, My friend, have you a mind to make any reply to what is said? No, my lord, answered Kissbreech; for I have spoke all I intended, and nothing but the truth. Therefore, put an end for God's sake to our difference, for we are here at great charge.

CHAP. XIII.

How Pantagruel gave judgment upon the difference of the two lords.

THEN Pantagruel, rising up, assembled all the presidents, counsellors, and doctors that were there, and said unto them, Come now, my masters, you have heard *vivæ vocis oraculo*, the controversy that is in question; what do you think of it? They answered him, We have indeed heard it, but have not understood the devil so much as one circumstance of the case; and therefore we beseech you, *una voce*, and in courtesy request you that you would give sentence as you think good, and, *ex nunc prout ex tunc*, we are satisfied with it, and do ratify it with our full consents. Well, my masters, said Pantagruel, seeing you are so pleased, I will do it; but I do not truly find the case so difficult as you make it. Your paragraph *Caton*, the law *Frater*, the law *Gallus*, the law *Quinque pedum*, the law *Vinum*, the law *Si Dominus*, the law *Mater*, the law *Mulier bona*, the law *Si quis*, the law *Pomponius*, the law *Fundi*, the law *Emptor*, the law *Prætor*, the law *Venditor*, and a great many others, are far more intricate in my opinion. After he had spoke this, he walked a turn or two about the hall, plodding very profoundly, as one may think; for he did groan like an ass whilst they girth him too hard, with the very intensiveness of considering how he was bound in conscience to do right to both parties, without varying or accepting of persons. Then he returned, sat down, and began to pronounce sentence as followeth.

Having seen, heard, calculated, and well considered of the difference between the Lords of Kissbreech and Suckfist, the court saith unto them, that in regard of the sudden quaking, shivering, and hoariness of the flickermouse, bravely declining from the estival solstice, to attempt by private means the surprisal of toyish trifles in those who are a little unwell for having taken a draught too much, through the lewd demeanour and vexation of the beetles that inhabit the diarodal [diarhomal] climate of an hypocritical ape on horseback, bending a crossbow backwards, the plaintiff truly had just cause to calfet, or with oakum to stop the chinks of the galleon which the good woman blew up with wind, having one foot shod and the other bare, reimbursing and restoring to him, low and stiff in his conscience, as many bladder-nuts and wild pistaches as there is of hair in eighteen cows, with as much for the embroiderer, and so much for that. He is likewise declared innocent of the case privileged from the knapdardies, into the danger whereof it was thought he had incurred; because he could not jocundly and with fulness of freedom untruss and dung, by the decision of a pair of gloves perfumed with the scent of bum-gunshot at the walnut-tree taper, as is usual in his country of Mirebalais. Slacking, therefore, the topsail, and letting go the bowline with the brazen bullets, wherewith the mariners did by way of protestation bake in pastemeat great store of pulse interquilted with the dormouse, whose hawk's-bells were made with a puntinaria, after the manner of Hungary or Flanders lace, and which his brother-in-law carried in a pannier, lying near to three chevrons or bordered gules, whilst he was clean out of heart, drooping and crestfallen by the too narrow sifting, canvassing, and curious examining of the matter in the angularly doghole of nasty scoundrels, from whence we shoot at the vermiformal popinjay with the flap made of a foxtail.

But in that he chargeth the defendant that he was a botcher, cheese-eater, and trimmer of man's flesh embalmed, which in the arsiversy swagfall tumble was not found true, as by the defendant was very well discussed.

The court, therefore, doth condemn and amerce him in three porringers of curds, well cemented and closed together, shining like pearls, and codpieced after the fashion of the country, to be paid unto the said defendant about the middle of August in May. But, on the other part, the defendant shall be bound to furnish him with hay and stubble for stopping the caltrops of his throat, troubled and impulregafized, with gabardines garbled shufflingly, and friends as before, without costs and for cause.

Which sentence being pronounced, the two parties departed both contented with the decree, which was a thing almost incredible. For it never came to pass since the great rain, nor shall the like occur in thirteen jubilees hereafter, that two parties contradictorily contending in judgment be equally satisfied and well pleased with the definitive sentence. As for the counsellors and other doctors in the law that were there present, they were all so ravished with admiration at the more than human wisdom of Pantagruel, which they did most clearly perceive to be in him by his so accurate decision of this so difficult and thorny cause, that their spirits with the extremity of the rapture being elevated above the pitch of actuating the organs of the body, they fell into a trance and sudden ecstasy, wherein they stayed for the space of three long hours, and had been so as yet in that condition had not some good people fetched store of vinegar and rose-water to bring them again unto their former sense and understanding, for the which God be praised everywhere. And so be it.

CHAP. XIV.

How Panurge related the manner how he escaped out of the hands of the Turks.

THE great wit and judgment of Pantagruel was immediately after this made known unto all the world by setting forth his praises in print, and putting upon record this late wonderful proof he hath given thereof amongst the rolls of the crown and registers of the palace, in such sort that everybody began to say that Solomon, who by a probable guess only, without any further certainty, caused the child to be delivered to its own mother, showed never in his time such a masterpiece of wisdom as the good Pantagruel hath done. Happy are we, therefore, that have him in our country. And indeed they would have made him thereupon master of the requests and president in the court; but he refused all, very graciously thanking them for their offer. For, said he, there is too much slavery in these offices, and very hardly can they be saved that do exercise them, considering the great corruption that is amongst men. Which makes me believe, if the empty seats of angels be not filled with other kind of people than those, we shall not have the final judgment these seven thousand, sixty and seven jubilees yet to come, and so Cusanus will be deceived in his conjecture. Remember that I have told you of it, and given you fair advertisement in time and place convenient.

But if you have any hogsheads of good wine, I willingly will accept of a present of that. Which they very heartily did do, in sending him of the best that was in the city, and he drank reasonably well, but poor Panurge bibbed and boused of it most villainously, for he was as dry as a red-herring, as lean as a rake, and, like a poor, lank, slender cat, walked gingerly as if he had trod upon eggs. So that by someone being admonished, in the midst of his draught of a large deep bowl full of excellent claret with these words—Fair and softly, gossip, you suck up as if you were mad—I give thee to the devil, said he; thou hast not found here thy little tippling sippers of Paris, that drink no more than the little bird called a spink or chaffinch, and never take in their beakful of liquor till they be bobbed on the tails after the manner of the sparrows. O companion! if I could mount up as well as I can get down, I had been long ere this above the sphere of the moon with Empedocles. But I cannot tell what a devil this means. This wine is so good and delicious, that the more I drink thereof the more I am athirst. I believe that the shadow of my master Pantagruel engendereth the altered and thirsty men, as the moon doth the catarrhs and defluxions. At which word the company began to laugh, which Pantagruel perceiving, said, Panurge, what is that which moves you to laugh so? Sir, said he, I was telling them that these devilish Turks are very unhappy in that they never drink one drop of wine, and that though there were no other harm in all Mahomet's Alcoran, yet for this one base point of abstinence from wine which therein is commanded, I would not submit myself unto their law. But now tell me, said Pantagruel, how you escaped out of their hands. By G—, sir, said Panurge, I will not lie to you in one word.

The rascally Turks had broached me upon a spit all larded like a rabbit, for I was so dry and meagre that otherwise of my flesh they would have made but very bad meat, and in this manner began to roast me alive. As they were thus roasting me, I recommended myself unto the divine grace, having in my mind the good St. Lawrence, and always hoped in God that he would deliver me out of this torment. Which came to pass, and that very strangely. For as I did commit myself with all my heart unto God, crying, Lord God, help me! Lord God, save me! Lord God, take me out of this pain and hellish torture, wherein these traitorous dogs detain me for my sincerity in the maintenance of thy law! the roaster or turnspit fell asleep by the divine will, or else by the virtue of some good Mercury, who cunningly brought Argus into a sleep for all his hundred eyes. When I saw that he did no longer turn me in roasting, I looked upon him, and perceived that he was fast asleep. Then took I up in my teeth a firebrand by the end where it was not burnt, and cast it into the lap of my roaster, and another did I throw as well as I could under a field-couch that was placed near to the chimney, wherein was the straw-bed of my master turnspit. Presently the fire took hold in the straw, and from the straw to the bed, and from the bed to the loft, which was planked and ceiled with fir, after the fashion of the foot of a lamp. But the best was, that the fire which I had cast into the lap of my paltry roaster burnt all his groin, and was beginning to cease [seize] upon his cullions, when he became sensible of the danger, for his smelling was not so bad but that he felt it sooner than he could have seen daylight. Then suddenly getting up, and in a great amazement running to the window, he cried out to the streets as high as he could, Dal baroth, dal baroth, dal baroth, which is as much to say as Fire, fire, fire. Incontinently turning about, he came straight towards me to throw me quite into the fire, and to that effect had already cut the ropes wherewith my hands were tied, and was undoing the cords from off my feet, when the master of the house hearing him cry Fire, and smelling the smoke from the very street where he was walking with some other Bashaws and Mustaphas, ran with all the speed he had to save what he could, and to carry away his jewels. Yet such was his rage, before he could well resolve how to go about it, that he caught the broach whereon I was spitted and therewith killed my roaster stark dead, of which wound he died there for want of government or otherwise; for he ran him in with the spit a little above the navel, towards the right flank, till he pierced the third lappet of his liver, and the blow slanting upwards from the midriff or diaphragm, through which it had made penetration, the spit passed athwart the pericardium or capsule of his heart, and came out above at his shoulders, betwixt the spondyls or turning joints of the chine of the back and the left homoplat, which we call the shoulder-blade.

True it is, for I will not lie, that, in drawing the spit out of my body I fell to the ground near unto the andirons, and so by the fall took some hurt, which indeed had been greater, but that the lardons, or little slices of bacon wherewith I was stuck, kept off the blow. My Bashaw then seeing the case to be desperate, his house burnt without remission, and all his goods lost, gave himself over unto all the devils in hell, calling upon some of them by their names, Grilgoth, Astaroth, Rappalus, and Gribouillis, nine several times. Which when I saw, I had above sixpence' worth of fear, dreading that the devils would come even then to carry away this fool, and, seeing me so near him, would perhaps snatch me up too. I am already, thought I, half roasted, and my lardons will be the cause of my mischief; for these devils are very liquorous of lardons, according to the authority which you have of the philosopher Jamblicus, and Murmault, in the Apology of Bossutis, adulterated *pro magistros nostros*. But for my better security I made the sign of the cross, crying, *Hageos, athanatos, ho theos*, and none came. At which my rogue Bashaw being very much aggrieved would, in transpiercing his heart with my spit, have killed himself, and to that purpose had set it against his breast, but it could not enter, because it was not sharp enough. Whereupon I perceiving that he was not like to work upon his body the effect which he intended, although he did not spare all the force he had to thrust it forward, came up to him and said, Master Bugrino, thou dost here but trifle away thy time, or rashly lose it, for thou wilt never kill thyself thus as thou doest. Well, thou mayst hurt or bruise somewhat within thee, so as to make thee languish all thy lifetime most pitifully amongst the hands of the chirurgeons; but if thou wilt be counselled by me, I will kill thee clear outright, so that thou shalt not so much as feel it, and trust me, for I have killed a great many others, who have found themselves very well after it. Ha, my friend, said he, I prithee do so, and for thy pains I will give thee my codpiece [budget]; take, here it is, there are six hundred seraphs in it, and some fine diamonds and most excellent rubies. And where are they? said Epistemon. By St. John, said Panurge, they are a good way hence, if they always keep going. But where is the last year's snow? This was the greatest care that Villon the Parisian poet took. Make an end, said Pantagruel, that we may know how thou didst dress thy Bashaw. By the faith of an honest man, said Panurge, I do not lie in one word. I swaddled him in a scurvy swathel-binding which I found lying there half burnt, and with my cords tied him roister-like both hand and foot, in such sort that he was not able to wince; then passed my spit through his throat, and hanged him thereon, fastening the end thereof at two great hooks or crampirons, upon which they did hang their halberds; and then, kindling a fair fire under him, did flame you up my Milourt, as they use to do dry herrings in a chimney. With this, taking his budget and a little javelin that was upon the foresaid hooks, I ran away a fair gallop-rake, and God he knows how I did smell my shoulder of mutton.

When I was come down into the street, I found everybody come to put out the fire with store of water, and seeing me so half-roasted, they did naturally pity my case, and threw all their water upon me, which, by a most joyful refreshing of me, did me very much good. Then did they present me with some victuals, but I could not eat much, because they gave me nothing to drink but water after their fashion. Other hurt they did me none, only one little villainous Turkey knobbreasted rogue came thiefteously to snatch away some of my lardons, but I gave him such a sturdy thump and sound rap on the fingers with all the weight of my javelin, that he came no more the second time. Shortly after this there came towards me a pretty young Corinthian wench, who brought me a boxful of conserves, of round Mirabolan plums, called emblicks, and looked upon my poor robin with an eye of great compassion, as it was flea-bitten and pinked with the sparkles of the fire from whence it came, for it reached no farther in length, believe me, than my knees. But note that this roasting cured me entirely of a sciatica, whereunto I had been subject above seven years before, upon that side which my roaster by falling asleep suffered to be burnt.

Now, whilst they were thus busy about me, the fire triumphed, never ask how? For it took hold on above two thousand houses, which one of them espying cried out, saying, By Mahoom's belly, all the city is on fire, and we do nevertheless stand gazing here, without offering to make any relief. Upon this everyone ran to save his own; for my part, I took my way towards the gate. When I was got upon the knap of a little hillock not far off, I turned me about as did Lot's wife, and, looking back, saw all the city burning in a fair fire, whereat I was so glad that I had almost beshit myself for joy. But God punished me well for it. How? said Pantagruel. Thus, said Panurge; for when with pleasure I beheld this jolly fire, jesting with myself, and saying—Ha! poor flies, ha! poor mice, you will have a bad winter of it this year; the fire is in your reeks, it is in your bed-straw—out come more than six, yea, more than thirteen hundred and eleven dogs, great and small, altogether out of the town, flying away from the fire. At the first approach they ran all upon me, being carried on by the scent of my lecherous half-roasted flesh, and had even then devoured me in a trice, if my good angel had not well inspired me with the instruction of a remedy very sovereign against the toothache. And wherefore, said Pantagruel, wert thou afraid of the toothache or pain of the teeth? Wert thou not cured of thy rheums? By Palm Sunday, said Panurge, is there any greater pain of the teeth than when the dogs have you by the legs? But on a sudden, as my good angel directed me, I thought upon my lardons, and threw them into the midst of the field amongst them. Then did the dogs run, and fight with one another at fair teeth which should have the lardons. By this means they left me, and I left them also bustling with and hairing one another. Thus did I escape frolic and lively, gramercy roastmeat and cookery.

CHAP. XV.

How Panurge shewed a very new way to build the walls of Paris.

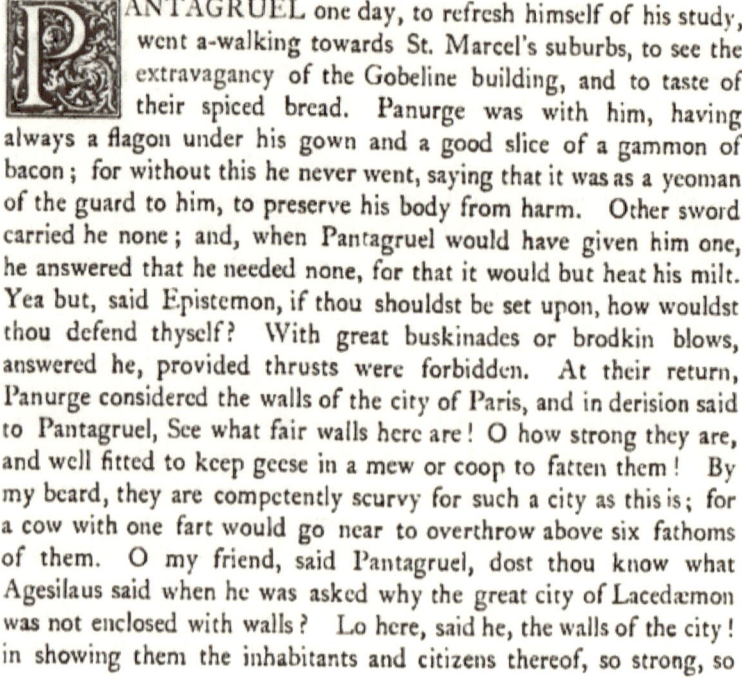

PANTAGRUEL one day, to refresh himself of his study, went a-walking towards St. Marcel's suburbs, to see the extravagancy of the Gobeline building, and to taste of their spiced bread. Panurge was with him, having always a flagon under his gown and a good slice of a gammon of bacon; for without this he never went, saying that it was as a yeoman of the guard to him, to preserve his body from harm. Other sword carried he none; and, when Pantagruel would have given him one, he answered that he needed none, for that it would but heat his milt. Yea but, said Epistemon, if thou shouldst be set upon, how wouldst thou defend thyself? With great buskinades or brodkin blows, answered he, provided thrusts were forbidden. At their return, Panurge considered the walls of the city of Paris, and in derision said to Pantagruel, See what fair walls here are! O how strong they are, and well fitted to keep geese in a mew or coop to fatten them! By my beard, they are competently scurvy for such a city as this is; for a cow with one fart would go near to overthrow above six fathoms of them. O my friend, said Pantagruel, dost thou know what Agesilaus said when he was asked why the great city of Lacedæmon was not enclosed with walls? Lo here, said he, the walls of the city! in showing them the inhabitants and citizens thereof, so strong, so well armed, and so expert in military discipline; signifying thereby that there is no wall but of bones, and that towns and cities cannot have a surer wall nor better fortification than the prowess and virtue of the citizens and inhabitants. So is this city so strong, by the great number of warlike people that are in it, that they care not for making any other walls. Besides, whosoever would go about to wall it, as Strasburg, Orleans, or Ferrara, would find it almost impossible, the cost and charges would be so excessive. Yea but, said Panurge, it is good, nevertheless, to have an outside of stone when we are invaded by our enemies, were it but to ask, Who is below there? As for the enormous expense which you say would be needful for undertaking the great work of walling this city about, if the gentlemen of the town will be pleased to give me a good rough cup of wine, I will show them a pretty, strange, and new way, how they may build them good cheap. How? said Pantagruel. Do not speak of it then, answered Panurge, and I will tell it you. I see that the sine quo nons, kallibistris, or contrapunctums of the women of this country are better cheap than stones. Of them should the walls be built, ranging them in good symmetry by the rules of architecture, and placing the largest in the first ranks, then sloping downwards ridgewise, like the back of an ass. The middle-sized ones must be ranked next, and last of all the least and smallest. This done, there must be a fine little interlacing of them, like points of diamonds, as is to be seen in the great tower of Bourges, with a like number of the nudinnudos, nilnisistandos, and stiff bracmards, that dwell in amongst the claustral codpieces. What devil were able to overthrow such walls? There is no metal like it to resist blows, in so far that, if culverin-shot should come to graze upon it, you would incontinently see distil from thence the blessed fruit of the great pox as small as rain. Beware, in the name of the devils, and hold off. Furthermore, no thunderbolt or lightning would fall upon it. For why? They are all either blest or consecrated. I see but one inconveniency in it. Ho, ho, ha, ha, ha! said Pantagruel, and what is that? It is, that the flies would be so liquorish of them that you would wonder, and would quickly gather there together, and there leave their ordure and excretions, and so all the work would be spoiled. But see how that might be remedied: they must be wiped and made rid of the flies with fair foxtails, or great good viedazes, which are ass-pizzles, of Provence. And to this purpose I will tell you, as we go to supper, a brave example set down by *Frater Lubinus, Libro de compotationibus mendicantium.*

In the time that the beasts did speak, which is not yet three days since, a poor lion, walking through the forest of Bieure, and saying his own little private devotions, passed under a tree where there was a roguish collier gotten up to cut down wood, who, seeing the lion, cast his hatchet at him and wounded him enormously in one of his legs; whereupon the lion halting, he so long toiled and turmoiled himself in roaming up and down the forest to find help, that at last he met with a carpenter, who willingly looked upon his wound, cleansed it as well as he could, and filled it with moss, telling him that he must wipe his wound well that the flies might not do their excrements in it, whilst he should go search for some yarrow or millefoil, commonly called the carpenter's herb. The lion, being thus healed, walked along in the forest at what time a sempiternous crone and old hag was picking up and gathering some sticks in the said forest, who, seeing the lion coming towards her, for fear fell down backwards, in such sort that the wind blew up her gown, coats, and smock, even as far as above her shoulders; which the lion perceiving, for pity ran to see whether she had taken any hurt by the fall, and thereupon considering her how do you call it, said, O poor woman, who hath thus wounded thee? Which words when he had spoken, he espied a fox, whom he called to come to him, saying, Gossip Reynard, hau, hither, hither, and for cause! When the fox was come, he said unto him, My gossip and friend, they have hurt this good woman here between the legs most villainously, and there is a manifest solution of continuity. See how great a wound it is, even from the tail up to the navel, in measure four, nay full five handfuls and a half. This is the blow of a hatchet, I doubt me; it is an old wound, and therefore, that the flies may not get into it, wipe it lustily well and hard, I prithee, both within and without; thou hast a good tail, and long. Wipe, my friend, wipe, I beseech thee, and in the meanwhile I will go get some moss to put into it; for thus ought we to succour and help one another. Wipe it hard, thus, my friend; wipe it well, for this wound must be often wiped, otherwise the party cannot be at ease. Go to, wipe well, my little gossip, wipe; God hath furnished thee with a tail; thou hast a long one, and of a bigness proportionable; wipe hard, and be not weary. A good wiper, who, in wiping continually, wipeth with his wipard, by wasps shall never be wounded. Wipe, my pretty minion; wipe, my little bully; I will not stay long. Then went he to get store of moss; and when he was a little way off, he cried out in speaking to the fox thus, Wipe well still, gossip, wipe, and let it never grieve thee to wipe well, my little gossip; I will put thee into service to be wiper to Don Pedro de Castile; wipe, only wipe, and no more. The poor fox wiped as hard as he could, here and there, within and without; but the false old trot did so fizzle and fist that she stunk like a hundred devils, which put the poor fox to a great deal of ill ease, for he knew not to what side to turn himself to escape the unsavoury perfume of this old woman's postern blasts. And whilst to that effect he was shifting hither and thither, without knowing how to shun the annoyance of those unwholesome gusts, he saw that behind there was yet another hole, not so great as that which he did wipe, out of which came this filthy and infectious air. The lion at last returned, bringing with him of moss more than eighteen packs would hold, and began to put into the wound with a staff which he had provided for that purpose, and had already put in full sixteen packs and a half, at which he was amazed. What a devil! said he, this wound is very deep; it would hold above two cartloads of moss. The fox, perceiving this, said unto the lion, O gossip lion, my friend, I pray thee do not put in all thy moss there; keep somewhat, for there is yet here another little hole, that stinks like five hundred devils; I am almost choked with the smell thereof, it is so pestiferous and empoisoning.

Thus must these walls be kept from the flies, and wages allowed to some for wiping of them. Then said Pantagruel, How dost thou know that the privy parts of women are at such a cheap rate? For in this city there are many virtuous, honest, and chaste women besides the maids. *Et ubi prenus?* said Panurge. I will give you my opinion of it, and that upon certain and assured knowledge. I do not brag that I have bumbasted four hundred and seventeen since I came into this city, though it be but nine days ago; but this very morning I met with a good fellow, who, in a wallet such as Æsop's was, carried two little girls of two or three years old at the most, one before and the other behind. He demanded alms of me, but I made him answer that I had more cods than pence. Afterwards I asked him, Good man, these two girls, are they maids? Brother, said he, I have carried them thus these two years, and in regard of her that is before, whom I see continually, in my opinion she is a virgin, nevertheless I will not put my finger in the fire for it; as for her that is behind, doubtless I can say nothing.

Indeed, said Pantagruel, thou art a gentle companion; I will have thee to be apparelled in my livery. And therefore caused him to be clothed most gallantly according to the fashion that then was, only that Panurge would have the codpiece of his breeches three foot long, and in shape square, not round; which was done, and was well worth the seeing. Oftentimes was he wont to say, that the world had not yet known the emolument and utility that is in wearing great codpieces; but time would one day teach it them, as all things have been invented in time. God keep from hurt, said he, the good fellow whose long codpiece or braguet hath saved his life! God keep from hurt him whose long braguet hath been worth to him in one day one hundred threescore thousand and nine crowns! God keep from hurt him who by his long braguet hath saved a whole city from dying by famine! And, by G——, I will make a book of the commodity of long braguets when I shall have more leisure. And indeed he composed a fair great book with figures, but it is not printed as yet that I know of.

CHAP. XVI.

Of the qualities and conditions of Panurge.

PANURGE was of a middle stature, not too high nor too low, and had somewhat an aquiline nose, made like the handle of a razor. He was at that time five and thirty years old or thereabouts, fine to gild like a leaden dagger —for he was a notable cheater and coneycatcher—he was a very gallant and proper man of his person, only that he was a little lecherous, and naturally subject to a kind of disease which at that time they called lack of money—it is an incomparable grief, yet, notwithstanding, he had three score and three tricks to come by it at his need, of which the most honourable and most ordinary was in manner of thieving, secret purloining and filching, for he was a wicked lewd rogue, a cozener, drinker, roister, rover, and a very dissolute and debauched fellow, if there were any in Paris; otherwise, and in all matters else, the best and most virtuous man in the world; and he was still contriving some plot, and devising mischief against the sergeants and the watch.

At one time he assembled three or four especial good hacksters and roaring boys, made them in the evening drink like Templars, afterwards led them till they came under St. Geneviève, or about the college of Navarre, and, at the hour that the watch was coming up that way—which he knew by putting his sword upon the pavement, and his ear by it, and, when he heard his sword shake, it was an infallible sign that the watch was near at that instant—then he and his companions took a tumbrel or dung-cart, and gave it the brangle, hurling it with all their force down the hill, and so overthrew all the poor watchmen like pigs, and then ran away upon the other side; for in less than two days he knew all the streets, lanes, and turnings in Paris as well as his *Deus det*.

At another time he made in some fair place, where the said watch was to pass, a train of gunpowder, and, at the very instant that they went along, set fire to it, and then made himself sport to see what good grace they had in running away, thinking that St. Anthony's fire had caught them by the legs. As for the poor masters of arts, he did persecute them above all others. When he encountered with any of them upon the street, he would not never fail to put some trick or other upon them, sometimes putting the bit of a fried turd in their graduate hoods, at other times pinning on little foxtails or hares'-ears behind them, or some such other roguish prank. One day that they were appointed all to meet in the Fodder Street [Sorbonne], he made a Borbonesa tart, or filthy and slovenly compound, made of store of garlic, of assafœtida, of castoreum, of dogs' turds very warm, which he steeped, tempered, and liquefied in the corrupt matter of pocky boils and pestiferous botches; and, very early in the morning therewith anointed all the pavement, in such sort that the devil could not have endured it, which made all these good people there to lay up their gorges, and vomit what was upon their stomachs before all the world, as if they had flayed the fox; and ten or twelve of them died of the plague, fourteen became lepers, eighteen grew lousy, and above seven and twenty had the pox, but he did not care a button for it. He commonly carried a whip under his gown, wherewith he whipped without remission the pages whom he found carrying wine to their masters, to make them mend their pace. In his coat he had above six and twenty little fobs and pockets always full; one with some lead-water, and a little knife as sharp as a glover's needle, wherewith he used to cut purses; another with some kind of bitter stuff, which he threw into the eyes of those he met; another with clotburrs, penned with little geese' or capon's feathers, which he cast upon the gowns and caps of honest people, and often made them fair horns, which they wore about all the city, sometimes all their life. Very often, also, upon the women's French hoods would he stick in the hind part somewhat made in the shape of a man's member. In another, he had a great many little horns full of fleas and lice, which he borrowed from the beggars of St. Innocent, and cast them with small canes or quills to write with into the necks of the daintiest gentlewomen that he could find, yea, even in the church, for he never seated himself above in the choir, but always sat in the body of the church amongst the women, both at mass, at vespers, and at sermon. In another, he used to have good store of hooks and buckles, wherewith he would couple men and women together that sat in company close to one another, but especially those that wore gowns of crimson taffeties, that, when they were about to go away, they might rend all their gowns. In another, he had a squib furnished with tinder, matches, stones to strike fire, and all other tackling necessary for it. In another, two or three burning glasses, wherewith he made both men and women sometimes mad, and in the church put them quite out of countenance ; for he said that there was but an antistrophe, or little more difference than of a literal inversion, between a woman *folle à la messe* and *molle à la fesse*, that is, foolish at the mass and of a pliant buttock.

In another, he had a good deal of needles and thread, wherewith he did a thousand little devilish pranks. One time, at the entry of the palace unto the great hall, where a certain grey friar or cordelier was to say mass to the counsellors, he did help to apparel him and put on his vestments, but in the accoutring of him he sewed on his alb, surplice, or stole, to his gown and shirt, and then withdrew himself when the said lords of the court or counsellors came to hear the said mass; but when it came to the *Ite, missa est*, that the poor frater would have laid by his stole or surplice, as the fashion then was, he plucked off withal both his frock and shirt, which were well sewed together, and thereby stripping himself up to the very shoulders showed his *bel vedere* to all the world, together with his Don Cypriano, which was no small one, as you may imagine. And the friar still kept haling, but so much the more did he discover himself and lay open his back parts, till one of the lords of the court said, How now! what's the matter? Will this fair father make us here an offering of his tail to kiss it? Nay, St. Anthony's fire kiss it for us! From thenceforth it was ordained that the poor fathers should never disrobe themselves any more before the world, but in their vestry-room, or sextry, as they call it; especially in the presence of women, lest it should tempt them to the sin of longing and disordinate desire. The people then asked why it was the friars had so long and large genitories? The said Panurge resolved the problem very neatly, saying, That which makes asses to have such great ears is that their dams did put no biggins on their heads, as Alliaco mentioneth in his Suppositions. By the like reason, that which makes the genitories or generation-tools of those so fair fraters so long is, for that they wear no bottomed breeches, and therefore their jolly member, having no impediment, hangeth dangling at liberty as far as it can reach, with a wiggle-waggle down to their knees, as women carry their paternoster beads. And the cause wherefore they have it so correspondently great is, that in this constant wig-wagging the humours of the body descend into the said member. For, according to the Legists, agitation and continual motion is cause of attraction.

Item, he had another pocket full of itching powder, called stonealum, whereof he would cast some into the backs of those women whom he judged to be most beautiful and stately, which did so ticklishly gall them, that some would strip themselves in the open view of the world, and others dance like a cock upon hot embers, or a drumstick on a tabor. Others, again, ran about the streets, and he would run after them. To such as were in the stripping vein he would very civilly come to offer his attendance, and cover them with his cloak, like a courteous and very gracious man.

Item, in another he had a little leather bottle full of old oil, wherewith, when he saw any man or woman in a rich new handsome suit, he would grease, smutch, and spoil all the best parts of it under colour and pretence of touching them, saying, This is good cloth; this is good satin; good taffeties! Madam, God give you all that your noble heart desireth! You have a new suit, pretty sir;—and you a new gown, sweet mistress;—God give you joy of it, and maintain you in all prosperity! And with this would lay his hand upon their shoulder, at which touch such a villainous spot was left behind, so enormously engraven to perpetuity in the very soul, body, and reputation, that the devil himself could never have taken it away. Then, upon his departing, he would say, Madam, take heed you do not fall, for there is a filthy great hole before you, whereinto if you put your foot, you will quite spoil yourself.

Another he had all full of euphorbium, very finely pulverized. In that powder did he lay a fair handkerchief curiously wrought, which he had stolen from a pretty seamstress of the palace, in taking away a louse from off her bosom which he had put there himself, and, when he came into the company of some good ladies, he would trifle them into a discourse of some fine workmanship of bone-lace, then immediately put his hand into their bosom, asking them, And this work, is it of Flanders, or of Hainault? and then drew out his handkerchief, and said, Hold, hold, look what work here is, it is of Foutignan or of Fontarabia, and, shaking it hard at their nose, made them sneeze for four hours without ceasing. In the meanwhile he would fart like a horse, and the women would laugh and say, How now, do you fart, Panurge? No, no, madam, said he, I do but tune my tail to the plain song of the music which you make with your nose. In another he had a picklock, a pelican, a crampiron, a crook, and some other iron tools, wherewith there was no door nor coffer which he would not pick open. He had another full of little cups, wherewith he played very artificially, for he had his fingers made to his hand, like those of Minerva or Arachne, and had heretofore cried treacle. And when he changed a teston, cardecu, or any other piece of money, the changer had been more subtle than a fox if Panurge had not at every time made five or six sols (that is, some six or seven pence,) vanish away invisibly, openly, and manifestly, without making any hurt or lesion, whereof the changer should have felt nothing but the wind.

CHAP. XVII.

𝕳𝖔𝖜 𝕻𝖆𝖓𝖚𝖗𝖌𝖊 𝖌𝖆𝖎𝖓𝖊𝖉 𝖙𝖍𝖊 𝖕𝖆𝖗𝖉𝖔𝖓𝖘, 𝖆𝖓𝖉 𝖒𝖆𝖗𝖗𝖎𝖊𝖉 𝖙𝖍𝖊 𝖔𝖑𝖉 𝖜𝖔𝖒𝖊𝖓, 𝖆𝖓𝖉 𝖔𝖋 𝖙𝖍𝖊 𝖘𝖚𝖎𝖙 𝖎𝖓 𝖑𝖆𝖜 𝖜𝖍𝖎𝖈𝖍 𝖍𝖊 𝖍𝖆𝖉 𝖆𝖙 𝕻𝖆𝖗𝖎𝖘.

NE day I found Panurge very much out of countenance, melancholic, and silent, which made me suspect that he had no money; whereupon I said unto him, Panurge, you are sick, as I do very well perceive by your physiognomy, and I know the disease. You have a flux in your purse; but take no care. I have yet sevenpence halfpenny that never saw father nor mother, which shall not be wanting, no more than the pox, in your necessity. Whereunto he answered me, Well, well; for money one day I shall have but too much, for I have a philosopher's stone which attracts money out of men's purses as the adamant doth iron. But will you go with me to gain the pardons? said he. By my faith, said I, I am no great pardon-taker in this world—if I shall be any such in the other, I cannot tell; yet let us go, in God's name; it is but one farthing more or less. But, said he, lend me then a farthing upon interest. No, no, said I; I will give it you freely, and from my heart. *Grates vobis dominos,* said he.

So we went along, beginning at St. Gervase, and I got the pardons at the first box only, for in those matters very little contenteth me. Then did I say my small suffrages and the prayers of St. Brigid; but he gained them at all the boxes, and always gave money to everyone of the pardoners. From thence we went to Our Lady's Church, to St. John's, to St. Anthony's, and so to the other churches, where there was a banquet [bank] of pardons. For my part, I gained no more of them, but he at all the boxes kissed the relics, and gave at everyone. To be brief, when we were returned, he brought me to drink at the castle-tavern, and there showed me ten or twelve of his little bags full of money, at which I blessed myself, and made the sign of the cross, saying, Where have you recovered so much money in so little time? Unto which he answered me that he had taken it out of the basins of the pardons. For in giving them the first farthing, said he, I put it in with such sleight of hand and so dexterously that it appeared to be a threepence; thus with one hand I took threepence, ninepence, or sixpence at the least, and with the other as much, and so through all the churches where we have been. Yea but, said I, you damn yourself like a snake, and are withal a thief and sacrilegious person. True, said he, in your opinion, but I am not of that mind; for the pardoners do give me it, when they say unto me in presenting the relics to kiss, *Centuplum accipies*, that is, that for one penny I should take a hundred; for *accipies* is spoken according to the manner of the Hebrews, who use the future tense instead of the imperative, as you have in the law, *Diliges Dominum*, that is, *Dilige*. Even so, when the pardon-bearer says to me, *Centuplum accipies*, his meaning is, *Centuplum accipe*; and so doth Rabbi Kimy and Rabbi Aben Ezra expound it, and all the Massorets, *et ibi Bartholus*. Moreover, Pope Sixtus gave me fifteen hundred francs of yearly pension, which in English money is a hundred and fifty pounds, upon his ecclesiastical revenues and treasure, for having cured him of a cankerous botch, which did so torment him that he thought to have been a cripple by it all his life. Thus I do pay myself at my own hand, for otherwise I get nothing upon the said ecclesiastical treasure. Ho, my friend! said he, if thou didst know what advantage I made, and how well I feathered my nest, by the Pope's bull of the crusade, thou wouldst wonder exceedingly. It was worth to me above six thousand florins, in English coin six hundred pounds. And what a devil is become of them? said I; for of that money thou hast not one halfpenny. They returned from whence they came, said he; they did no more but change their master.

But I employed at least three thousand of them, that is, three hundred pounds English, in marrying—not young virgins, for they find but too many husbands—but great old sempiternous trots which had not so much as one tooth in their heads; and that out of the consideration I had that these good old women had very well spent the time of their youth in playing at the close-buttock game to all comers, serving the foremost first, till no man would have any more dealing with them. And, by G—, I will have their skin-coat shaken once yet before they die. By this means, to one I gave a hundred florins, to another six score, to another three hundred, according to that they were infamous, detestable, and abominable. For, by how much the more horrible and execrable they were, so much the more must I needs have given them, otherwise the devil would not have jummed them. Presently I went to some great and fat wood-porter, or such like, and did myself make the match. But, before I did show him the old hags, I made a fair muster to him of the crowns, saying, Good fellow, see what I will give thee if thou wilt but condescend to duffle, dinfredaille, or lecher it one good time. Then began the poor rogues to gape like old mules, and I caused to be provided for them a banquet, with drink of the best, and store of spiceries, to put the old women in rut and heat of lust. To be short, they occupied all, like good souls; only, to those that were horribly ugly and ill-favoured, I caused their head to be put within a bag, to hide their face.

Besides all this, I have lost a great deal in suits of law. And what lawsuits couldst thou have? said I; thou hast neither house nor lands. My friend, said he, the gentlewomen of this city had found out, by the instigation of the devil of hell, a manner of high-mounted bands and neckerchiefs for women, which did so closely cover their bosoms that men could no more put their hands under. For they had put the slit behind, and those neckcloths were wholly shut before, whereat the poor sad contemplative lovers were much discontented. Upon a fair Tuesday I presented a petition to the court, making myself a party against the said gentlewomen, and showing the great interest that I pretended therein, protesting that by the same reason I would cause the codpiece of my breeches to be sewed behind, if the court would not take order for it. In sum, the gentlewomen put in their defences, showed the grounds they went upon, and constituted their attorney for the prosecuting of the cause. But I pursued them so vigorously, that by a sentence of the court it was decreed those high neckcloths should be no longer worn if they were not a little cleft and open before; but it cost me a good sum of money. I had another very filthy and beastly process against the dung-farmer called Master Fifi and his deputies, that they should no more read privily the pipe, puncheon, nor quart of sentences, but in fair full day, and that in the Fodder schools, in face of the Arrian [Artitian] sophisters, where I was ordained to pay the charges, by reason of some clause mistaken in the relation of the sergeant. Another time I framed a complaint to the court against the mules of the presidents, counsellors, and others, tending to this purpose, that, when in the lower court of the palace they left them to champ on their bridles, some bibs were made for them [by the counsellors' wives], that with their drivelling they might not spoil the pavement; to the end that the pages of the palace might play upon it with their dice, or at the game of coxbody, at their own ease, without spoiling their breeches at the knees. And for this I had a fair decree, but it cost me dear. Now reckon up what expense I was at in little banquets which from day to day I made to the pages of the palace. And to what end? said I. My friend, said he, thou hast no pastime at all in this world. I have more than the king, and if thou wilt join thyself with me, we will do the devil together. No, no, said I; by St. Adauras, that will I not, for thou wilt be hanged one time or another. And thou, said he, wilt be interred some time or other. Now which is most honourable, the air or the earth? Ho, grosse pecore!

Whilst the pages are at their banqueting, I keep their mules, and to someone I cut the stirrup-leather of the mounting side till it hang but by a thin strap or thread, that when the great puffguts of the counsellor or some other hath taken his swing to get up, he may fall flat on his side like a pork, and so furnish the spectators with more than a hundred francs' worth of laughter. But I laugh yet further to think how at his home-coming the master-page is to be whipped like green rye, which makes me not to repent what I have bestowed in feasting them. In brief, he had, as I said before, three score and three ways to acquire money, but he had two hundred and fourteen to spend it, besides his drinking.

CHAP. XVIII.

How a great scholar of England would have argued against Pantagruel, and was overcome by Panurge.

N that same time a certain learned man named Thaumast, hearing the fame and renown of Pantagruel's incomparable knowledge, came out of his own country of England with an intent only to see him, to try thereby and prove whether his knowledge in effect was so great as it was reported to be. In this resolution being arrived at Paris, he went forthwith unto the house of the said Pantagruel, who was lodged in the palace of St. Denis, and was then walking in the garden thereof with Panurge,

philosophizing after the fashion of the Peripatetics. At his first entrance he startled, and was almost out of his wits for fear, seeing him so great and so tall. Then did he salute him courteously as the manner is, and said unto him, Very true it is, saith Plato the prince of philosophers, that if the image and knowledge of wisdom were corporeal and visible to the eyes of mortals, it would stir up all the world to admire her. Which we may the rather believe that the very bare report thereof, scattered in the air, if it happen to be received into the ears of men, who, for being studious and lovers of virtuous things are called philosophers, doth not suffer them to sleep nor rest in quiet, but so pricketh them up and sets them on fire to run unto the place where the person is, in whom the said knowledge is said to have built her temple and uttered her oracles. As it was manifestly shown unto us in the Queen of Sheba, who came from the utmost borders of the East and Persian Sea, to see the order of Solomon's house and to hear his wisdom; in Anacharsis, who came out of Scythia, even unto Athens, to see Solon; in Pythagoras, who travelled far to visit the memphitical vaticinators; in Plato, who went a great way off to see the magicians of Egypt, and Architus of Tarentum; in Apollonius Tyaneus, who went as far as unto Mount Caucasus, passed along the Scythians, the Massagetes, the Indians, and sailed over the great river Phison, even to the Brachmans to see Hiarchas; as likewise unto Babylon, Chaldea, Media, Assyria, Parthia, Syria, Phœnicia, Arabia, Palestina, and Alexandria, even unto Æthiopia, to see the Gymnosophists. The like example have we of Titus Livius, whom to see and hear divers studious persons came to Rome from the confines of France and Spain. I dare not reckon myself in the number of those so excellent persons, but well would be called studious, and a lover, not only of learning, but of learned men also. And indeed, having heard the report of your so inestimable knowledge, I have left my country, my friends, my kindred, and my house, and am come thus far, valuing at nothing the length of the way, the tediousness of the sea, nor strangeness of the land, and that only to see you and to confer with you about some passages in philosophy, of geomancy, and of the cabalistic art, whereof I am doubtful and cannot satisfy my mind; which if you can resolve, I yield myself unto you for a slave henceforward, together with all my posterity, for other gift have I none that I can esteem a recompense sufficient for so great a favour. I will reduce them into writing, and to-morrow publish them to all the learned men in the city, that we may dispute publicly before them.

But see in what manner I mean that we shall dispute. I will not argue *pro et contra*, as do the sottish sophisters of this town and other places. Likewise I will not dispute after the manner of the Academics by declamation; nor yet by numbers, as Pythagoras was wont to do, and as Picus de la Mirandula did of late at Rome. But I will dispute by signs only without speaking, for the matters are so abstruse, hard, and arduous, that words proceeding from the mouth of man will never be sufficient for unfolding of them to my liking. May it, therefore, please your magnificence to be there; it shall be at the great hall of Navarre at seven o'clock in the morning. When he had spoke these words, Pantagruel very honourably said unto him: Sir, of the graces that God hath bestowed upon me, I would not deny to communicate unto any man to my power. For whatever comes from him is good, and his pleasure is that it should be increased when we come amongst men worthy and fit to receive this celestial manna of honest literature. In which number, because that in this time, as I do already very plainly perceive, thou holdest the first rank, I give thee notice that at all hours thou shalt find me ready to condescend to every one of thy requests according to my poor ability; although I ought rather to learn of thee than thou of me. But, as thou hast protested, we will confer of these doubts together, and will seek out the resolution, even unto the bottom of that undrainable well where Heraclitus says the truth lies hidden. And I do highly commend the manner of arguing which thou hast proposed, to wit, by signs without speaking; for by this means thou and I shall understand one another well enough, and yet shall be free from this clapping of hands which these blockish sophisters make when any of the arguers hath gotten the better of the argument. Now to-morrow I will not fail to meet thee at the place and hour that thou hast appointed, but let me entreat thee that there be not any strife or uproar between us, and that we seek not the honour and applause of men, but the truth only. To which Thaumast answered: The Lord God maintain you in his favour and grace, and, instead of my thankfulness to you, pour down his blessings upon you, for that your highness and magnificent greatness hath not disdained to descend to the grant of the request of my poor baseness. So farewell till to-morrow! Farewell, said Pantagruel.

Gentlemen, you that read this present discourse, think not that ever men were more elevated and transported in their thoughts than all this night were both Thaumast and Pantagruel; for the said Thaumast said to the keeper of the house of Cluny, where he was lodged, that in all his life he had never known himself so dry as he was that night. I think, said he, that Pantagruel held me by the throat. Give order, I pray you, that we may have some drink, and see that some fresh water be brought to us, to gargle my palate. On the other side, Pantagruel stretched his wits as high as he could, entering into very deep and serious meditations, and did nothing all that night but dote upon and turn over the book of Beda, *De numeris et signis*; Plotin's book, *De inenarrabilibus*; the book of Proclus, *De magia*; the book of Artemidorus, περὶ Ὀνειροκριτικῶν; of Anaxagoras, περὶ Σημείων; Dinarius, περὶ Ἀφάτων; the books of Philistion; Hipponax, περὶ Ἀνεκφωνητῶν, and a rabble of others, so long, that Panurge said unto him:

My lord, leave all these thoughts and go to bed; for I perceive your spirits to be so troubled by a too intensive bending of them, that you may easily fall into some quotidian fever with this so excessive thinking and plodding. But, having first drunk five and twenty or thirty good draughts, retire yourself and sleep your fill, for in the morning I will argue against and answer my master the Englishman, and if I drive him not *ad metam non loqui*, then call me knave. Yea but, said he, my friend Panurge, he is marvellously learned; how wilt thou be able to answer him? Very well, answered Panurge; I pray you talk no more of it, but let me alone. Is any man so learned as the devils are? No, indeed, said Pantagruel, without God's especial grace. Yet for all that, said Panurge, I have argued against them, gravelled and blanked them in disputation, and laid them so squat upon their tails that I have made them look like monkeys. Therefore be assured that to-morrow I will make this vain-glorious Englishman to skite vinegar before all the world. So Panurge spent the night with tippling amongst the pages, and played away all the points of his breeches at *primus secundus* and at peck point, in French called *La Vergette*. Yet, when the condescended on time was come, he failed not to conduct his master Pantagruel to the appointed place, unto which, believe me, there was neither great nor small in Paris but came, thinking with themselves that this devilish Pantagruel, who had overthrown and vanquished in dispute all these doting fresh-water sophisters, would now get full payment and be tickled to some purpose. For this Englishman is a terrible bustler and horrible coil-keeper. We will see who will be conqueror, for he never met with his match before.

Thus all being assembled, Thaumast stayed for them, and then, when Pantagruel and Panurge came into the hall, all the schoolboys, professors of arts, senior sophisters, and bachelors began to clap their hands, as their scurvy custom is. But Pantagruel cried out with a loud voice, as if it had been the sound of a double cannon, saying, Peace, with a devil to you, peace! By G—, you rogues, if you trouble me here, I will cut off the heads of everyone of you. At which words they remained all daunted and astonished like so many ducks, and durst not do so much as cough, although they had swallowed fifteen pounds of feathers. Withal they grew so dry with this only voice, that they laid out their tongues a full half foot beyond their mouths, as if Pantagruel had salted all their throats. Then began Panurge to speak, saying to the Englishman, Sir, are you come hither to dispute contentiously in those propositions you have set down, or, otherwise, but to learn and know the truth? To which answered Thaumast, Sir, no other thing brought me hither but the great desire I had to learn and to know that of which I have doubted all my life long, and have neither found book nor man able to content me in the resolution of those doubts which I have proposed. And, as for disputing contentiously, I will not do it, for it is too base a thing, and therefore leave it to those sottish sophisters who in their disputes do not search for the truth, but for contradiction only and debate. Then said Panurge, If I, who am but a mean and inconsiderable disciple of my master my lord Pantagruel, content and satisfy you in all and everything, it were a thing below my said master wherewith to trouble him. Therefore is it fitter that he be chairman, and sit as a judge and moderator of our discourse and purpose, and give you satisfaction in many things wherein perhaps I shall be wanting to your expectation. Truly, said Thaumast, it is very well said; begin then. Now you must note that Panurge had set at the end of his long codpiece a pretty tuft of red silk, as also of white, green, and blue, and within it had put a fair orange.

CHAP. XIX.

How Panurge put to a nonplus the Englishman that argued by signs.

EVERYBODY then taking heed, and hearkening with great silence, the Englishman lift up on high into the air his two hands severally, clunching in all the tops of his fingers together, after the manner which, *à la Chinonnese*, they call the hen's arse, and struck the one hand on the other by the nails four several times. Then he, opening them, struck the one with the flat of the other till it yielded a clashing noise, and that only once. Again, in joining them as before, he struck twice, and afterwards four times in opening them. Then did he lay them joined, and extended the one towards the other, as if he had been devoutly to send up his prayers unto God. Panurge suddenly lifted up in the air his right hand, and put the thumb thereof into the nostril of the same side, holding his four fingers straight out, and closed orderly in a parallel line to the point of his nose, shutting the left eye wholly, and making the other wink with a profound depression of the eyebrows and eyelids. Then lifted he up his left hand, with hard wringing and stretching forth his four fingers and elevating his thumb, which he held in a line directly correspondent to the situation of his right hand, with the distance of a cubit and a half between them. This done, in the same form he abased towards the ground both the one and the other hand. Lastly, he held them in the midst, as aiming right at the Englishman's nose. And if Mercury,—said the Englishman. There Panurge interrupted him, and said, You have spoken, Mask.

Then made the Englishman this sign. His left hand all open he lifted up into the air, then instantly shut into his fist the four fingers thereof, and his thumb extended at length he placed upon the gristle of his nose. Presently after, he lifted up his right hand all open, and all open abased and bent it downwards, putting the thumb thereof in the very place where the little finger of the left hand did close in the fist, and the four right-hand fingers he softly moved in the air. Then contrarily he did with the right hand what he had done with the left, and with the left what he had done with the right.

Panurge, being not a whit amazed at this, drew out into the air his trismegist codpiece with the left hand, and with his right drew forth a truncheon of a white ox-rib, and two pieces of wood of a like form, one of black ebony and the other of incarnation brasil, and put them betwixt the fingers of that hand in good symmetry; then, knocking them together, made such a noise as the lepers of Brittany use to do with their clappering clickets, yet better resounding and far more harmonious, and with his tongue contracted in his mouth did very merrily warble it, always looking fixedly upon the Englishman. The divines, physicians, and chirurgeons that were there thought that by this sign he would have inferred that the Englishman was a leper. The counsellors, lawyers, and decretalists conceived that by doing this he would have concluded some kind of mortal felicity to consist in leprosy, as the Lord maintained heretofore.

The Englishman for all this was nothing daunted, but holding up his two hands in the air, kept them in such form that he closed the three master-fingers in his fist, and passing his thumbs through his indical or foremost and middle fingers, his auricular or little fingers remained extended and stretched out, and so presented he them to Panurge. Then joined he them so that the right thumb touched the left, and the left little finger touched the right. Hereat Panurge, without speaking one word, lift up his hands and made this sign.

He put the nail of the forefinger of his left hand to the nail of the thumb of the same, making in the middle of the distance as it were a buckle, and of his right hand shut up all the fingers into his fist, except the forefinger, which he often thrust in and out through the said two others of the left hand. Then stretched he out the forefinger and middle finger or medical of his right hand, holding them asunder as much as he could, and thrusting them towards Thaumast. Then did he put the thumb of his left hand upon the corner of his left eye, stretching out all his hand like the wing of a bird or the fin of a fish, and moving it very daintily this way and that way, he did as much with his right hand upon the corner of his right eye. Thaumast began then to wax somewhat pale, and to tremble, and made him this sign.

With the middle finger of his right hand he struck against the muscle of the palm or pulp which is under the thumb. Then put he the forefinger of the right hand in the like buckle of the left, but he put it under, and not over, as Panurge did. Then Panurge knocked one hand against another, and blowed in his palm, and put again the forefinger of his right hand into the overture or mouth of the left, pulling it often in and out. Then held he out his chin, most intentively looking upon Thaumast. The people there, which understood nothing in the other signs, knew very well that therein he demanded, without speaking a word to Thaumast, What do you mean by that? In effect, Thaumast then began to sweat great drops, and seemed to all the spectators a man strangely ravished in high contemplation. Then he bethought himself, and put all the nails of his left hand against those of his right, opening his fingers as if they had been semicircles, and with this sign lift up his hands as high as he could. Whereupon Panurge presently put the thumb of his right hand under his jaws, and the little finger thereof in the mouth of the left hand, and in this posture made his teeth to sound very melodiously, the upper against the lower. With this Thaumast, with great toil and vexation of spirit, rose up, but in rising let a great baker's fart, for the bran came after, and pissing withal very strong vinegar, stunk like all the devils in hell. The company began to stop their noses; for he had conskited himself with mere anguish and perplexity. Then lifted he up his right hand, clunching it in such sort that he brought the ends of all his fingers to meet together, and his left hand he laid flat upon his breast. Whereat Panurge drew out his long codpiece with his tuff, and stretched it forth a cubit and a half, holding it in the air with his right hand, and with his left took out his orange, and, casting it up into the air seven times, at the eighth he hid it in the fist of his right hand, holding it steadily up on high, and then began to shake his fair codpiece, showing it to Thaumast.

After that, Thaumast began to puff up his two cheeks like a player on a bagpipe, and blew as if he had been to puff up a pig's bladder. Whereupon Panurge put one finger of his left hand in his nockandrow, by some called St. Patrick's hole, and with his mouth sucked in the air, in such a manner as when one eats oysters in the shell, or when we sup up our broth. This done, he opened his mouth somewhat, and struck his right hand flat upon it, making therewith a great and a deep sound, as if it came from the superficies of the midriff through the trachiartery or pipe of the lungs, and this he did for sixteen times; but Thaumast did always keep blowing like a goose. Then Panurge put the forefinger of his right hand into his mouth, pressing it very hard to the muscles thereof; then he drew it out, and withal made a great noise, as when little boys shoot pellets out of the pot-cannons made of the hollow sticks of the branch of an alder-tree, and he did it nine times.

Then Thaumast cried out, Ha, my masters, a great secret! With this he put in his hand up to the elbow, then drew out a dagger that he had, holding it by the point downwards. Whereat Panurge took his long codpiece, and shook it as hard as he could against his thighs; then put his two hands entwined in manner of a comb upon his head, laying out his tongue as far as he was able, and turning his eyes in his head like a goat that is ready to die. Ha, I understand, said Thaumast, but what? making such a sign that he put the haft of his dagger against his breast, and upon the point thereof the flat of his hand, turning in a little the ends of his fingers. Whereat Panurge held down his head on the left side, and put his middle finger into his right ear, holding up his thumb bolt upright. Then he crossed his two arms upon his breast and coughed five times, and at the fifth time he struck his right foot against the ground. Then he lift up his left arm, and closing all his fingers into his fist, held his thumb against his forehead, striking with his right hand six times against his breast. But Thaumast, as not content therewith, put the thumb of his left hand upon the top of his nose, shutting the rest of his said hand, whereupon Panurge set his two master-fingers upon each side of his mouth, drawing it as much as he was able, and widening it so that he showed all his teeth, and with his two thumbs plucked down his two eyelids very low, making therewith a very ill-favoured countenance, as it seemed to the company.

CHAP. XX.

How Thaumast relateth the virtues and knowledge of Panurge.

THEN Thaumast rose up, and, putting off his cap, did very kindly thank the said Panurge, and with a loud voice said unto all the people that were there: My lords, gentlemen, and others, at this time may I to some good purpose speak that evangelical word, *Et ecce plus quàm Salomon hic!* You have here in your presence an incomparable treasure, that is, my lord

Pantagruel, whose great renown hath brought me hither, out of the very heart of England, to confer with him about the insoluble problems, both in magic, alchemy, the cabal, geomancy, astrology, and philosophy, which I had in my mind. But at present I am angry even with fame itself, which I think was envious to him, for that it did not declare the thousandth part of the worth that indeed is in him. You have seen how his disciple only hath satisfied me, and hath told me more than I asked of him. Besides, he hath opened unto me, and resolved other inestimable doubts, wherein I can assure you he hath to me discovered the very true well, fountain, and abyss of the encyclopædia of learning; yea, in such a sort that I did not think I should ever have found a man that could have made his skill appear in so much as the first elements of that concerning which we disputed by signs, without speaking either word or half word. But, in fine, I will reduce into writing that which we have said and concluded, that the world may not take them to be fooleries, and will thereafter cause them to be printed, that everyone may learn as I have done. Judge, then, what the master had been able to say, seeing the disciple hath done so valiantly; for, *Non est discipulus super magistrum*. Howsoever, God be praised! and I do very humbly thank you for the honour that you have done us at this act. God reward you for it eternally! The like thanks gave Pantagruel to all the company, and, going from thence, he carried Thaumast to dinner with him, and believe that they drank as much as their skins could hold, or, as the phrase is, with unbuttoned bellies (for in that age they made fast their bellies with buttons, as we do now the collars of our doublets or jerkins), even till they neither knew where they were nor whence they came. Blessed Lady, how they did carouse it, and pluck, as we say, at the kid's leather! And flagons to trot, and they to toot, Draw; give, page, some wine here; reach hither; fill with a devil, so! There was not one but did drink five and twenty or thirty pipes. Can you tell how? Even *sicut terra sine aqua*; for the weather was hot, and, besides that, they were very dry. In matter of the exposition of the propositions set down by Thaumast, and the signification of the signs which they used in their disputation, I would have set them down for you according to their own relation, but I have been told that Thaumast made a great book of it, imprinted at London, wherein he hath set down all, without omitting anything, and therefore at this time I do pass by it.

CHAP. XXI.

How Panurge was in love with a lady of Paris.

ANURGE began to be in great reputation in the city of Paris by means of this disputation wherein he prevailed against the Englishman, and from thenceforth made his codpiece to be very useful to him. To which effect he had it pinked with pretty little embroideries after the Romanesca fashion. And the world did praise him publicly, in so far that there was a song made of him, which little children did use to sing when they were to fetch mustard. He was withal made welcome in all companies of ladies and gentlewomen, so that at last he became presumptuous, and went about to bring to his lure one of the greatest ladies in the city. And, indeed, leaving a rabble of long prologues and protestations, which ordinarily these dolent contemplative lent-lovers make who never meddle with the flesh, one day he said unto her, Madam, it would be a very great benefit to the commonwealth, delightful to you, honourable to your progeny, and necessary for me, that I cover you for the propagating of my race, and believe it, for experience will teach it you. The lady at this word thrust him back above a hundred leagues, saying, You mischievous fool, is it for you to talk thus unto me? Whom do you think you have in hand? Begone, never to come in my sight again; for, if one thing were not, I would have your legs and arms cut off. Well, said he, that were all one to me, to want both legs and arms, provided you and I had but one merry bout together at the brangle-buttock game; for herewithin is—in showing her his long codpiece—Master John Thursday, who will play you such an antic that you shall feel the sweetness thereof even to the very marrow of your bones. He is a gallant, and doth so well know how to find out all the corners, creeks, and ingrained inmates in your carnal trap, that after him there needs no broom, he'll sweep so well before, and leave nothing to his followers to work upon. Whereunto the lady answered, Go, villain, go. If you speak to me one such word more, I will cry out and make you to be knocked down with blows. Ha, said he, you are not so bad as you say—no, or else I am deceived in your physiognomy. For

sooner shall the earth mount up unto the heavens, and the highest heavens descend unto the hells, and all the course of nature be quite perverted, than that in so great beauty and neatness as in you is there should be one drop of gall or malice. They say, indeed, that hardly shall a man ever see a fair woman that is not also stubborn. Yet that is spoke only of those vulgar beauties; but yours is so excellent, so singular, and so heavenly, that I believe nature hath given it you as a paragon and masterpiece of her art, to make us know what she can do when she will employ all her skill and all her power. There is nothing in you but honey, but sugar, but a sweet and celestial manna. To you it was to whom Paris ought to have adjudged the golden apple, not to Venus, no, nor to Juno, nor to Minerva, for never was there so much magnificence in Juno, so much wisdom in Minerva, nor so much comeliness in Venus as there is in you. O heavenly gods and goddesses! How happy shall that man be to whom you will grant the favour to embrace her, to kiss her, and to rub his bacon with hers! By G—, that shall be I, I know it well; for she loves me already her bellyful, I am sure of it, and so was I predestinated to it by the fairies. And therefore, that we lose no time, put on, thrust out your gammons!—and would have embraced her, but she made as if she would put out her head at the window to call her neighbours for help. Then Panurge on a sudden ran out, and in his running away said, Madam, stay here till I come again; I will go call them myself; do not you take so much pains. Thus went he away, not much caring for the repulse he had got, nor made he any whit the worse cheer for it. The next day he came to the church at the time she went to mass. At the door he gave her some of the holy water, bowing himself very low before her. Afterwards he kneeled down by her very familiarly and said unto her, Madam, know that I am so amorous of you that I can neither piss nor dung for love. I do not know, lady, what you mean, but if I should take any hurt by it, how much you would be to blame! Go, said she, go! I do not care; let me alone to say my prayers. Ay but, said he, equivocate upon this: *à beau mont le viconte*, or, to fair mount the prick-cunts. I cannot, said she. It is, said he, *à beau con le vit monte*, or to a fair c . . . the pr . . . mounts. And upon this, pray to God to give you that which your noble heart desireth, and I pray you give me these paternosters. Take them, said she, and trouble me no longer. This done, she would have taken off her paternosters, which were made of a kind of yellow stone called cestrin, and adorned with great spots of gold, but Panurge nimbly drew out one of his knives, wherewith he cut them off very handsomely, and whilst he was going away to carry them to the brokers, he said to her, Will you have my knife? No, no, said she. But, said he, to the purpose. I am at your commandment, body and goods, tripes and bowels.

In the meantime the lady was not very well content with the want of her paternosters, for they were one of her implements to keep her countenance by in the church; then thought with herself, This bold flouting roister is some giddy, fantastical, light-headed fool of a strange country. I shall never recover my paternosters again. What will my husband say? He will no doubt be angry with me. But I will tell him that a thief hath cut them off from my hands in the church, which he will easily believe, seeing the end of the ribbon left at my girdle. After dinner Panurge went to see her, carrying in his sleeve a great purse full of palace-crowns, called counters, and began to say unto her, Which of us two loveth other best, you me, or I you? Whereunto she answered, As for me, I do not hate you; for, as God commands, I love all the world. But to the purpose, said he; are not you in love with me? I have, said she, told you so many times already that you should talk so no more to me, and if you speak of it again I will teach you that I am not one to be talked unto dishonestly. Get you hence packing, and deliver me my paternosters, that my husband may not ask me for them.

How now, madam, said he, your paternosters? Nay, by mine oath, I will not do so, but I will give you others. Had you rather have them of gold well enamelled in great round knobs, or after the manner of love-knots, or, otherwise, all massive, like great ingots, or if you had rather have them of ebony, of jacinth, or of grained gold, with the marks of fine turquoises, or of fair topazes, marked with fine sapphires, or of baleu rubies, with great marks of diamonds of eight and twenty squares? No, no, all this is too little. I know a fair bracelet of fine emeralds, marked with spotted ambergris, and at the buckle a Persian pearl as big as an orange. It will not cost above five and twenty thousand ducats. I will make you a present of it, for I have ready coin enough,—and withal he made a noise with his counters as if they had been French crowns.

Will you have a piece of velvet, either of the violet colour or of crimson dyed in grain, or a piece of broached or crimson satin? Will you have chains, gold, tablets, rings? You need no more but say, Yes; so far as fifty thousand ducats may reach, it is but as nothing to me. By the virtue of which words he made the water come in her mouth; but she said unto him, No, I thank you, I will have nothing of you. By G—, said he, but I will have somewhat of you; yet shall it be that which shall cost you nothing, neither shall you have a jot the less when you have given it. Hold!—showing his long codpiece—this is Master John Goodfellow, that asks for lodging!—and with that would have embraced her; but she began to cry out, yet not very loud. Then Panurge put off his counterfeit garb, changed his false visage, and said unto her, You will not then otherwise let me do a little? A turd for you! You do not deserve so much good, nor so much honour; but, by G—, I will make the dogs ride you;—and with this he ran away as fast as he could, for fear of blows, whereof he was naturally fearful.

CHAP. XXII.

How Panurge served a Parisian lady a trick that pleased her not very well.

NOW you must note that the next day was the great festival of Corpus Christi, called the Sacre, wherein all women put on their best apparel, and on that day the said lady was clothed in a rich gown of crimson satin, under which she wore a very costly white velvet petticoat.

The day of the eve, called the vigil, Panurge searched so long of one side and another that he found a hot or salt bitch, which, when he had tied her with his girdle, he led to his chamber and fed her very well all that day and night. In the morning thereafter he killed her, and took that part of her which the Greek geomancers know, and cut it into several small pieces as small as he could. Then, carrying it away as close as might be, he went to the place where the lady was to come along to follow the procession, as the custom is upon the said holy day; and when she came in Panurge sprinkled some holy water on her, saluting her very courteously. Then, a little while after she had said her petty devotions, he sat down close by her upon the same bench, and gave her this roundelay in writing, in manner as followeth.

A ROUNDELAY.

For this one time, that I to you my love
Discovered, you did too cruel prove,
To send me packing, hopeless, and so soon,
Who never any wrong to you had done,
In any kind of action, word, or thought:
So that, if my suit liked you not, you ought
T' have spoke more civilly, and to this sense,
My friend, be pleased to depart from hence,
          For this one time.

What hurt do I, to wish you to remark,
With favour and compassion, how a spark
Of your great beauty hath inflamed my heart
With deep affection, and that, for my part,
I only ask that you with me would dance
The brangle gay in feats of dalliance,
          For this one time?

And, as she was opening this paper to see what it was, Panurge very promptly and lightly scattered the drug that he had upon her in divers places, but especially in the plaits of her sleeves and of her gown. Then said he unto her, Madam, the poor lovers are not always at ease. As for me, I hope that those heavy nights, those pains and troubles, which I suffer for love of you, shall be a deduction to me of so much pain in purgatory; yet, at the least, pray to God to give me patience in my misery. Panurge had no sooner spoke this but all the dogs that were in the church came running to this lady with the smell of the drugs that he had strewed upon her, both small and great, big and little, all came, laying out their member, smelling to her, and pissing everywhere upon her—it was the greatest villainy in the world. Panurge made the fashion of driving them away; then took his leave of her and withdrew himself into some chapel or oratory of the said church to see the sport; for these villainous dogs did compiss all her habiliments, and left none of her attire unbesprinkled with their staling; insomuch that a tall greyhound pissed upon her head, others in her sleeves, others on her crupper-piece, and the little ones pissed upon her pataines; so that all the women that were round about her had much ado to save her. Whereat Panurge very heartily laughing, he said to one of the lords of the city, I believe that same lady is hot, or else that some greyhound hath covered her lately. And when he saw that all the dogs were flocking about her, yarring at the retardment of their access to her, and every way keeping such a coil with her as they are wont to do about a proud or salt bitch, he forthwith departed from thence, and went to call Pantagruel, not forgetting in his way alongst the streets through which he went, where he found any dogs to give them a bang with his foot, saying, Will you not go with your fellows to the wedding? Away, hence, avant, avant, with a devil avant! And being come home, he said to Pantagruel, Master, I pray you come and see all the dogs of the country, how they are assembled about a lady, the fairest in the city, and would duffle and line her. Whereunto Pantagruel willingly condescended, and saw the mystery, which he found very pretty and strange. But the best was at the procession, in which were seen above six hundred thousand and fourteen dogs about her, which did very much trouble and molest her, and whithersoever she passed, those dogs that came afresh, tracing her footsteps, followed her at the heels, and pissed in the way where her gown had touched. All the world stood gazing at this spectacle, considering the countenance of those dogs, who, leaping up, got about her neck and spoiled all her gorgeous accoutrements, for the which she could find no remedy but to retire unto her house, which was a palace. Thither she went, and the dogs after her; she ran to hide herself, but the chambermaids could not abstain from laughing. When she was entered into the house and had shut the door upon herself, all the dogs came running of half a league round, and did so well bepiss the gate of her house that there they made a stream with their urine wherein a duck might have very well swimmed, and it is the same current that now runs at St. Victor, in which Gobelin dyeth scarlet, for the specifical virtue of these piss-dogs, as our master Doribus did heretofore preach publicly. So may God help you, a mill would have ground corn with it. Yet not so much as those of Basacle at Toulouse.

CHAP. XXIII.

How Pantagruel departed from Paris, hearing news that the Dipsodes had invaded the land of the Amaurots; and the cause wherefore the leagues are so short in France.

A LITTLE while after Pantagruel heard news that his father Gargantua had been translated into the land of the fairies by Morgue, as heretofore were Ogier and Arthur; as also,[1] that the report of his translation being spread abroad, the Dipsodes had issued out beyond their borders, with inroads had wasted a great part of Utopia, and at that very time had besieged the great city of the Amaurots. Whereupon departing from Paris without bidding any man farewell, for the business required diligence, he came to Rouen.

Now Pantagruel in his journey seeing that the leagues of that little territory about Paris called France were very short in regard of those of other countries, demanded the cause and reason of it from Panurge, who told him a story which Marotus of the Lac, monachus, set down in the Acts of the Kings of Canarre, saying that in old times countries were not distinguished into leagues, miles, furlongs, nor parasangs, until that King Pharamond divided them, which was done in manner as followeth. The said king chose at Paris a hundred fair, gallant, lusty, brisk young men, all resolute and bold adventurers in Cupid's duels, together with a hundred comely, pretty, handsome, lovely and well-complexioned wenches of Picardy, all which he caused to be well entertained and highly fed for the space of eight days. Then having called for them, he delivered to every one of the young men his wench, with store of money to defray their charges, and this injunction besides, to go unto diver places here and there. And wheresoever they should biscot and thrum their wenches, that, they setting a stone there, it should be accounted for a league. Thus went away those brave fellows and sprightly blades most merrily, and because they were fresh and had been at rest, they very often jummed and fanfreluched almost at every field's end, and

---

[1] In the original edition it stands "together, and that."—M.

this is the cause why the leagues about Paris are so short. But when they had gone a great way, and were now as weary as poor devils, all the oil in their lamps being almost spent, they did not chink and duffle so often, but contented themselves (I mean for the men's part) with one scurvy paltry bout in a day, and this is that which makes the leagues in Brittany, Delanes, Germany, and other more remote countries so long. Other men give other reasons for it, but this seems to me of all other the best. To which Pantagruel willingly adhered. Parting from Rouen, they arrived at Honfleur, where they took shipping, Pantagruel, Panurge, Epistemon, Eusthenes, and Carpalin.

In which place, waiting for a favourable wind, and caulking their ship, he received from a lady of Paris, which I [he] had formerly kept and entertained a good long time, a letter directed on the outside thus,—To the best beloved of the fair women, and least loyal of the valiant men—P.N.T.G.R.L.

CHAP. XXIV.

A letter which a messenger brought to Pantagruel from a lady of Paris, together with the exposition of a posy written in a gold ring.

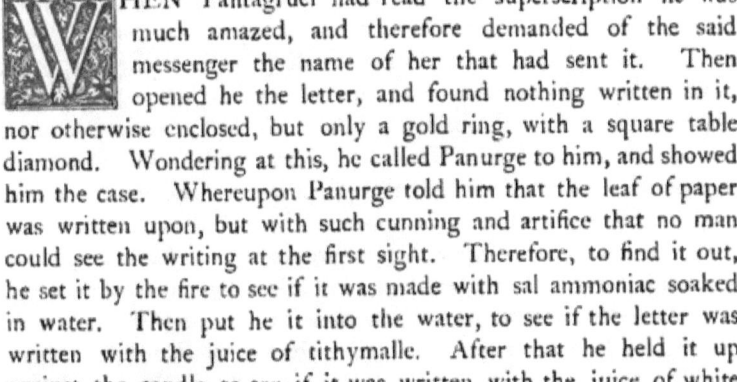

WHEN Pantagruel had read the superscription he was much amazed, and therefore demanded of the said messenger the name of her that had sent it. Then opened he the letter, and found nothing written in it, nor otherwise enclosed, but only a gold ring, with a square table diamond. Wondering at this, he called Panurge to him, and showed him the case. Whereupon Panurge told him that the leaf of paper was written upon, but with such cunning and artifice that no man could see the writing at the first sight. Therefore, to find it out, he set it by the fire to see if it was made with sal ammoniac soaked in water. Then put he it into the water, to see if the letter was written with the juice of tithymalle. After that he held it up against the candle, to see if it was written with the juice of white onions.

Then he rubbed one part of it with oil of nuts, to see if it were not written with the lee of a fig-tree, and another part of it with the milk of a woman giving suck to her eldest daughter, to see if it was written with the blood of red toads or green earth-frogs. Afterwards he rubbed one corner with the ashes of a swallow's nest, to see if it were not written with the dew that is found within the herb alcakengy, called the winter-cherry. He rubbed, after that, one end with ear-wax, to see if it were not written with the gall of a raven. Then did he dip it into vinegar, to try if it was not written with the juice of the garden spurge. After that he greased it with the fat of a bat or flittermouse, to see if it was not written with the sperm of a whale, which some call ambergris. Then put it very fairly into a basinful of fresh water, and forthwith took it out, to see whether it were written with stone-alum. But after all experiments, when he perceived that he could find out nothing, he called the messenger and asked him, Good fellow, the lady that sent thee hither, did she not give thee a staff to bring with thee? thinking that it had been according to the conceit whereof Aulus Gellius maketh mention. And the messenger answered him, No, sir. Then Panurge would have caused his head to be shaven, to see whether the lady had written upon his bald pate, with the hard lye whereof soap is made, that which she meant; but, perceiving that his hair was very long, he forbore, considering that it could not have grown to so great a length in so short a time.

Then he said to Pantagruel, Master, by the virtue of G—, I cannot tell what to do nor say in it. For, to know whether there be anything written upon this or no, I have made use of a good part of that which Master Francisco di Nianto, the Tuscan, sets down, who hath written the manner of reading letters that do not appear; that which Zoroastes published, *Peri grammaton acriton*; and Calphurnius Bassus, *De literis illegibilibus*. But I can see nothing, nor do I believe that there is anything else in it than the ring. Let us, therefore, look upon it. Which when they had done, they found this in Hebrew written within, *Lamach saba[ch]thani*; whereupon they called Epistemon, and asked him what that meant. To which he answered that they were Hebrew words, signifying, Wherefore hast thou forsaken me? Upon that Panurge suddenly replied, I know the mystery. Do you see this diamond? It is a false one. This, then, is the exposition of that which the lady means, *Diamant faux*, that is, false lover, why hast thou forsaken me? Which interpretation Pantagruel presently understood, and withal remembering that at his departure he had not bid the lady farewell, he was very sorry, and would fain have returned to Paris to make his peace with her. But Epistemon put him in mind of Æneas's departure from Dido, and the saying of Heraclitus of Tarentum, That the ship being at anchor, when need requireth we must cut the cable rather than lose time about untying of it,—and that he should lay aside all other thoughts to succour the city of his nativity, which was then in danger. And, indeed, within an hour after that the wind arose at the north-north-west, wherewith they hoist sail, and put out, even into the main sea, so that within few days, passing by Porto Sancto and by the Madeiras, they went ashore in the Canary Islands. Parting from thence, they passed by Capobianco, by Senege, by Capoverde, by Gambre, by Sagres, by Melli, by the Cap di Buona Speranza, and set ashore again in the kingdom of Melinda. Parting from thence, they sailed away with a tramontane or northerly wind, passing by Meden, by Uti, by Uden, by Gelasim, by the Isles of the Fairies, and alongst the kingdom of Achorie, till at last they arrived at the port of Utopia, distant from the city of the Amaurots three leagues and somewhat more.

When they were ashore, and pretty well refreshed, Pantagruel said, Gentlemen, the city is not far from hence; therefore, were it not amiss, before we set forward, to advise well what is to be done, that we be not like the Athenians, who never took counsel until after the fact? Are you resolved to live and die with me? Yes, sir, said they all, and be as confident of us as of your own fingers. Well, said he, there is but one thing that keeps my mind in great doubt and suspense, which is this, that I know not in what order nor of what number the enemy is that layeth siege to the city; for, if I were certain of that, I should go forward and set on with the better assurance. Let us therefore consult together, and bethink ourselves by what means we may come to this intelligence. Whereunto they all said, Let us go thither and see, and stay you here for us; for this very day, without further respite, do we make account to bring you a certain report thereof.

Myself, said Panurge, will undertake to enter into their camp, within the very midst of their guards, unespied by their watch, and merrily feast and lecher it at their cost, without being known of any, to see the artillery and the tents of all the captains, and thrust myself in with a grave and magnific carriage amongst all their troops and companies, without being discovered. The devil would not be able to peck me out with all his circumventions, for I am of the race of Zopyrus.

And I, said Epistemon, know all the plots and stratagems of the valiant captains and warlike champions of former ages, together with all the tricks and subtleties of the art of war. I will go, and, though I be detected and revealed, I will escape by making them believe of you whatever I please, for I am of the race of Sinon.

I, said Eusthenes, will enter and set upon them in their trenches, in spite of their sentries and all their guards; for I will tread upon their bellies and break their legs and arms, yea, though they were every whit as strong as the devil himself, for I am of the race of Hercules.

And I, said Carpalin, will get in there if the birds can enter, for I am so nimble of body, and light withal, that I shall have leaped over their trenches, and ran clean through all their camp, before that they perceive me; neither do I fear shot, nor arrow, nor horse, how swift soever, were he the Pegasus of Perseus or Pacolet, being assured that I shall be able to make a safe and sound escape before them all without any hurt. I will undertake to walk upon the ears of corn or grass in the meadows, without making either of them do so much as bow under me, for I am of the race of Camilla the Amazon.

CHAP. XXV.

How Panurge, Carpalin, Eusthenes, and Epistemon, the gentlemen attendants of Pantagruel, vanquished and discomfited six hundred and threescore horsemen very cunningly.

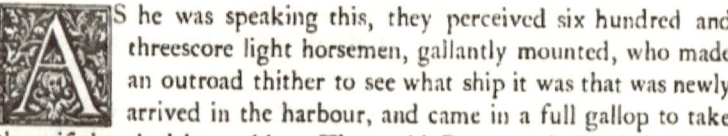

S he was speaking this, they perceived six hundred and threescore light horsemen, gallantly mounted, who made an outroad thither to see what ship it was that was newly arrived in the harbour, and came in a full gallop to take them if they had been able. Then said Pantagruel, My lads, retire yourselves unto the ship; here are some of our enemies coming apace, but I will kill them here before you like beasts, although they were ten times so many; in the meantime, withdraw yourselves, and take your sport at it. Then answered Panurge, No, sir; there is no reason that you should do so, but, on the contrary, retire you unto the ship, both you and the rest, for I alone will here discomfit them; but we must not linger; come, set forward. Whereunto the others said, It is well advised, sir; withdraw yourself, and we will help Panurge here; so shall you know what we are able to do. Then said Pantagruel, Well, I am content; but, if that you be too weak, I will not fail to come to your assistance. With this Panurge took two great cables of the ship and tied them to the kemstock or capstan which was on the deck towards the hatches, and fastened them in the ground, making a long circuit, the one further off, the other within that. Then said he to Epistemon, Go aboard the ship, and, when I give you a call, turn about the capstan upon the orlop diligently, drawing unto you the two cable-ropes; and said to Eusthenes and to Carpalin, My bullies, stay you here, and offer yourselves freely to your enemies. Do as they bid you, and make as if you would yield unto them, but take heed you come not within the compass of the ropes—be sure to keep yourselves free of them. And presently he went aboard the ship, and took a bundle of straw and a barrel of gunpowder, strewed it round about the compass of the cords, and stood by with a brand of fire or match lighted in his hand. Presently came the horsemen with great fury, and the foremost ran almost home to the ship, and, by reason of the slipperiness of the bank, they fell, they and their horses, to the number of four and forty; which the rest seeing, came on, thinking that resistance had been made them at their arrival. But Panurge said unto them, My masters, I believe that you have hurt yourselves; I pray you pardon us, for it is not our fault, but the slipperiness of the sea-water that is always flowing; we submit ourselves to your good pleasure. So said likewise his two other fellows, and Epistemon that was upon the deck. In the meantime Panurge withdrew himself, and seeing that they were all within the compass of the cables, and that his two companions were retired, making room for all those horses which came in a crowd, thronging upon the neck of one another to see the ship and such as were in it, cried out on a sudden to Epistemon, Draw, draw! Then began Epistemon to wind about the capstan, by doing whereof the two cables so entangled and empestered the legs of the horses, that they were all of them thrown down to the ground easily, together with their riders. But they, seeing that, drew their swords, and would have cut them; whereupon Panurge set fire to the train, and there burnt them up all like damned souls, both men and horses, not one escaping save one alone, who being mounted on a fleet Turkey courser, by mere speed in flight got himself out of the circle of the ropes. But when Carpalin perceived him, he ran after him with such nimbleness and celerity that he overtook him in less than a hundred paces; then, leaping close behind him upon the crupper of his horse, clasped him in his arms, and brought him back to the ship.

This exploit being ended, Pantagruel was very jovial, and wondrously commended the industry of these gentlemen, whom he called his fellow-soldiers, and made them refresh themselves and feed well and merrily upon the seashore, and drink heartily with their bellies upon the ground, and their prisoner with them, whom they admitted to that familiarity; only that the poor devil was somewhat afraid that Pantagruel would have eaten him up whole, which, considering the wideness of his mouth and capacity of his throat was no great matter for him to have done; for he could have done it as easily as you would eat a small comfit, he showing no more in his throat than would a grain of millet-seed in the mouth of an ass.

CHAP. XXVI.

How Pantagruel and his company were weary in eating still salt meats; and how Carpalin went a-hunting to have some venison.

THUS as they talked and chatted together, Carpalin said, And, by the belly of St. Quenet, shall we never eat any venison? This salt meat makes me horribly dry. I will go fetch you a quarter of one of those horses which we have burnt; it is well roasted already. As he was rising up to go about it, he perceived under the side of a wood a fair great roebuck, which was come out of his fort, as I conceive, at the sight of Panurge's fire. Him did he pursue and run after with as much vigour and swiftness as if it had been a bolt out of a crossbow, and caught him in a moment; and whilst he was in his course he with his hands

took in the air four great bustards, seven bitterns, six and twenty grey partridges, two and thirty red-legged ones, sixteen pheasants, nine woodcocks, nineteen herons, two and thirty cushats and ringdoves; and with his feet killed ten or twelve hares and rabbits, which were then at relief and pretty big withal, eighteen rails in a knot together, with fifteen young wild-boars, two little beavers, and three great foxes. So, striking the kid with his falchion athwart the head, he killed him, and, bearing him on his back, he in his return took up his hares, rails, and young wild-boars, and, as far off as he could be heard, cried out and said, Panurge, my friend, vinegar, vinegar! Then the good Pantagruel, thinking he had fainted, commanded them to provide him some vinegar; but Panurge knew well that there was some good prey in hands, and forthwith showed unto noble Pantagruel how he was bearing upon his back a fair roebuck, and all his girdle bordered with hares. Then immediately did Epistemon make, in the name of the nine Muses, nine antique wooden spits. Eusthenes did help to flay, and Panurge placed two great cuirassier saddles in such sort that they served for andirons, and making their prisoner to be their cook, they roasted their venison by the fire wherein the horsemen were burnt; and making great cheer with a good deal of vinegar, the devil a one of them did forbear from his victuals—it was a triumphant and incomparable spectacle to see how they ravened and devoured. Then said Pantagruel, Would to God every one of you had two pairs of little anthem or sacring bells hanging at your chin, and that I had at mine the great clocks of Rennes, of Poictiers, of Tours, and of Cambray, to see what a peal they would ring with the wagging of our chaps. But, said Panurge, it were better we thought a little upon our business, and by what means we might get the upper hand of our enemies. That is well remembered, said Pantagruel. Therefore spoke he thus to the prisoner, My friend, tell us here the truth, and do not lie to us at all, if thou wouldst not be flayed alive, for it is I that eat the little children. Relate unto us at full the order, the number, and the strength of the army. To which the prisoner answered, Sir, know for a truth that in the army there are three hundred giants, all armed with armour of proof, and wonderful great. Nevertheless, not fully so great as you, except one that is their head, named Loupgarou, who is armed from head to foot with cyclopical anvils. Furthermore, one hundred three score and three thousand foot, all armed with the skins of hobgoblins, strong and valiant men;

eleven thousand four hundred men-at-arms or cuirassiers; three thousand six hundred double cannons, and arquebusiers without number; four score and fourteen thousand pioneers; one hundred and fifty thousand whores, fair like goddesses—(That is for me, said Panurge)—whereof some are Amazons, some Lionnoises, others Parisiennes, Taurangelles, Angevines, Poictevines, Normandes, and High Dutch—there are of them of all countries and all languages.

Yea but, said Pantagruel, is the king there? Yes, sir, said the prisoner; he is there in person, and we call him Anarchus, king of the Dipsodes, which is as much to say as thirsty people, for you never saw men more thirsty, nor more willing to drink, and his tent is guarded by the giants. It is enough, said Pantagruel. Come, brave boys, are you resolved to go with me? To which Panurge answered, God confound him that leaves you! I have already bethought myself how I will kill them all like pigs, and so the devil one leg of them shall escape. But I am somewhat troubled about one thing. And what is that? said Pantagruel. It is, said Panurge, how I shall be able to set forward to the justling and bragmardizing of all the whores that be there this afternoon, in such sort that there escape not one unbumped by me, breasted and jummed after the ordinary fashion of man and women in the Venetian conflict. Ha, ha, ha, ha, said Pantagruel.

And Carpalin said: The devil take these sink-holes, if, by G—, I do not bumbaste some one of them. Then said Eusthenes: What! shall not I have any, whose paces, since we came from Rouen, were never so well winded up as that my needle could mount to ten or eleven o'clock, till now that I have it hard, stiff, and strong, like a hundred devils? Truly, said Panurge, thou shalt have of the fattest, and of those that are most plump and in the best case.

How now! said Epistemon; everyone shall ride, and I must lead the ass? The devil take him that will do so. We will make use of the right of war, *Qui potest capere, capiat.* No, no, said Panurge, but tie thine ass to a crook, and ride as the world doth. And the good Pantagruel laughed at all this, and said unto them, You reckon without your host. I am much afraid that, before it be night, I shall see you in such taking that you will have no great stomach to ride, but more like to be rode upon with sound blows of pike and lance. Baste, said Epistemon, enough of that! I will not fail to bring them to you, either to roast or boil, to fry or put in paste.

They are not so many in number as were in the army of Xerxes, for he had thirty hundred thousand fighting-men, if you will believe Herodotus and Trogus Pompeius, and yet Themistocles with a few men overthrew them all. For God's sake, take you no care for that. Cobsminny, cobsminny, said Panurge; my codpiece alone shall suffice to overthrow all the men; and my St. Sweephole, that dwells within it, shall lay all the women squat upon their backs. Up then, my lads, said Pantagruel, and let us march along.

CHAP. XXVII.

How Pantagruel set up one trophy in memorial of their valour, and Panurge another in remembrance of the hares. How Pantagruel likewise with his farts begat little men, and with his fisgs little women; and how Panurge broke a great staff over two glasses.

EFORE we depart hence, said Pantagruel, in remembrance of the exploit that you have now performed I will in this place erect a fair trophy. Then every man amongst them, with great joy and fine little country songs, set up a huge big post, whereunto they hanged a great cuirassier saddle, the fronstal of a barbed horse, bridle-bosses, pulley-pieces for the knees, stirrup-leathers, spurs, stirrups, a coat of mail, a corslet tempered with steel, a battle-axe, a strong, short, and sharp horseman's sword, a gauntlet, a horseman's mace, gushet-armour for the armpits, leg-harness, and a gorget, with all other furniture needful for the decorement of a triumphant arch, in sign of a trophy. And then Pantagruel, for an eternal memorial, wrote this victorial ditton, as followeth :—

> Here was the prowess made apparent of
> Four brave and valiant champions of proof,
> Who, without any arms but wit, at once,
> Like Fabius, or the two Scipions,
> Burnt in a fire six hundred and threescore
> Crablice, strong rogues ne'er vanquished before.

By this each king may learn, rook, pawn, and knight,
That sleight is much more prevalent than might.

> For victory,
> As all men see,
> Hangs on the ditty
> Of that committee
> Where the great God
> Hath his abode.

Nor doth he it to strong and great men give,
But to his elect, as we must believe;
Therefore shall he obtain wealth and esteem,
Who thorough faith doth put his trust in him.

Whilst Pantagruel was writing these foresaid verses, Panurge halved and fixed upon a great stake the horns of a roebuck, together with the skin and the right forefoot thereof, the ears of three leverets, the chine of a coney, the jaws of a hare, the wings of two bustards, the feet of four queest-doves, a bottle or borracho full of vinegar, a horn wherein to put salt, a wooden spit, a larding stick, a scurvy kettle full of holes, a dripping-pan to make sauce in, an earthen salt-cellar, and a goblet of Beauvais. Then, in imitation of Pantagruel's verses and trophy, wrote that which followeth:—

> Here was it that four jovial blades sat down
> To a profound carousing, and to crown
> Their banquet with those wines which please best great
> Bacchus, the monarch of their drinking state.
> Then were the reins and furch of a young hare,
> With salt and vinegar, displayed there,
> Of which to snatch a bit or two at once
> They all fell on like hungry scorpions.

> For th' Inventories
> Of Defensories
> Say that in heat
> We must drink neat
> All out, and of
> The choicest stuff.

> But it is bad to eat of young hare's flesh,
> Unless with vinegar we it refresh.
> Receive this tenet, then, without control,
> That vinegar of that meat is the soul.

Then said Pantagruel, Come, my lads, let us begone! we have stayed here too long about our victuals; for very seldom doth it fall out that the greatest eaters do the most martial exploits. There is no shadow like that of flying colours, no smoke like that of horses, no clattering like that of armour. At this Epistemon began to smile, and said, There is no shadow like that of the kitchen, no smoke like that of pasties, and no clattering like that of goblets. Unto which answered Panurge, There is no shadow like that of curtains, no smoke like that of women's breasts, and no clattering like that of ballocks. Then forthwith rising up he gave a fart, a leap, and a whistle, and most joyfully cried out aloud, Ever live Pantagruel! When Pantagruel saw that, he would have done as much; but with the fart that he let the earth trembled nine leagues about, wherewith and with the corrupted air he begot above three and fifty thousand little men, ill-favoured dwarfs, and with one fisg that he let he made as many little women, crouching down, as you shall see in divers places, which never grow but like cow's tails, downwards, or, like the Limosin radishes, round. How now! said Panurge, are your farts so fertile and fruitful? By G—, here be brave farted men and fisgued women; let them be married together; they will beget fine hornets and dorflies. So did Pantagruel, and called them pigmies. Those he sent to live in an island thereby, where since that time they are increased mightily. But the cranes make war with them continually, against which they do most courageously defend themselves; for these little ends of men and dandiprats (whom in Scotland they call whiphandles and knots of a tar-barrel) are commonly very testy and choleric; the physical reason whereof is, because their heart is near their spleen.

At this same time Panurge took two drinking glasses that were there, both of one bigness, and filled them with water up to the brim, and set one of them upon one stool and the other upon another, placing them about five foot from one another. Then he took the staff of a javelin, about five foot and a half long, and put it upon the two glasses, so that the two ends of the staff did come just to the brims of the glasses. This done, he took a great stake or billet of wood, and said to Pantagruel and to the rest, My masters, behold how easily we shall have the victory over our enemies; for just as I shall break this staff here upon these glasses, without either breaking or crazing of them, nay, which is more, without spilling one drop of the water that is within them, even so shall we break the heads of our Dipsodes without receiving any of us any wound or loss in our person or goods. But, that you may not think there is any witchcraft in this, hold! said he to Eusthenes, strike upon the midst as hard as thou canst with this log. Eusthenes did so, and the staff broke in two pieces, and not one drop of the water fell out of the glasses. Then said he, I know a great many such other tricks; let us now therefore march boldly and with assurance.

CHAP. XXVIII.

How Pantagruel got the victory very strangely over the Dipsodes and the Giants.

AFTER all this talk, Pantagruel took the prisoner to him and sent him away, saying, Go thou unto thy king in his camp, and tell him tidings of what thou hast seen, and let him resolve to feast me to-morrow about noon; for, as soon as my galleys shall come, which will be to-morrow at furthest, I will prove unto him by eighteen hundred thousand fighting-men and seven thousand giants, all of them greater than I am, that he hath done foolishly and against reason thus to invade my country. Wherein Pantagruel feigned that he had an army at sea. But the prisoner answered that he would yield himself to be his slave, and that he was content never to return to his own people, but rather with Pantagruel to fight against them, and for God's sake besought him that he might be permitted so to do. Whereunto Pantagruel would not give consent, but commanded him to depart thence speedily and begone as he had told him, and to that effect gave him a boxful of euphorbium, together with some grains of the black chameleon thistle, steeped into aqua vitæ, and made up into the condiment of a wet sucket, commanding him to carry it to his king, and to say unto

him, that if he were able to eat one ounce of that without drinking after it, he might then be able to resist him without any fear or apprehension of danger.

The prisoner then besought him with joined hands that in the hour of the battle he would have compassion upon him. Whereat Pantagruel said unto him, After that thou hast delivered all unto the king, put thy whole confidence in God, and he will not forsake thee; because, although for my part I be mighty, as thou mayst see, and have an infinite number of men in arms, I do nevertheless trust neither in my force nor in mine industry, but all my confidence is in God my protector, who doth never forsake those that in him do put their trust and confidence. This done, the prisoner requested him that he would afford him some reasonable composition for his ransom. To which Pantagruel answered, that his end was not to rob nor ransom men, but to enrich them and reduce them to total liberty. Go thy way, said he, in the peace of the living God, and never follow evil company, lest some mischief befall thee. The prisoner being gone, Pantagruel said to his men, Gentlemen, I have made this prisoner believe that we have an army at sea; as also that we will not assault them till to-morrow at noon, to the end that they, doubting of the great arrival of our men, may spend this night in providing and strengthening themselves, but in the meantime my intention is that we charge them about the hour of the first sleep.

Let us leave Pantagruel here with his apostles, and speak of King Anarchus and his army. When the prisoner was come, he went unto the king and told him how there was a great giant come, called Pantagruel, who had overthrown and made to be cruelly roasted all the six hundred and nine and fifty horsemen, and he alone escaped to bring the news. Besides that, he was charged by the said giant to tell him that the next day, about noon, he must make a dinner ready for him, for at that hour he was resolved to set upon him. Then did he give him that box wherein were those confitures. But as soon as he had swallowed down one spoonful of them, he was taken with such a heat in the throat, together with an ulceration in the flap of the top of the windpipe, that his tongue peeled with it in such sort that, for all they could do unto him, he found no ease at all but by drinking only without cessation; for as soon as ever he took the goblet from his head, his tongue was on a fire, and therefore they did nothing but still pour in wine into his throat with a funnel. Which when his captains, bashaws, and guard of his body did see, they tasted of the same drugs to try whether they were so thirst-procuring and alterative or no. But it so befell them as it had done their king, and they plied the flagon so well that the noise ran throughout all the camp, how the prisoner was returned; that the next day they were to have an assault; that the king and his captains did already prepare themselves for it, together with his guards, and that with carousing lustily and quaffing as hard as they could. Every man, therefore, in the army began to tipple, ply the pot, swill and guzzle it as fast as they could. In sum, they drunk so much, and so long, that they fell asleep like pigs, all out of order throughout the whole camp.

Let us now return to the good Pantagruel, and relate how he carried himself in this business. Departing from the place of the trophies, he took the mast of their ship in his hand like a pilgrim's staff, and put within the top of it two hundred and seven and thirty puncheons of white wine of Anjou, the rest was of Rouen, and tied up to his girdle the bark all full of salt, as easily as the lansquenets carry their little panniers, and so set onward on his way with his fellow-soldiers. When he was come near to the enemy's camp, Panurge said unto him, Sir, if you would do well, let down this white wine of Anjou from the scuttle of the mast of the ship, that we may all drink thereof, like Bretons.

Hereunto Pantagruel very willingly consented, and they drank so neat that there was not so much as one poor drop left of two hundred and seven and thirty puncheons, except one boracho or leathern bottle of Tours which Panurge filled for himself, for he called that his vademecum, and some scurvy lees of wine in the bottom, which served him instead of vinegar. After they had whittled and curried the can pretty handsomely, Panurge gave Pantagruel to eat some devilish drugs compounded of lithotripton, which is a stone-dissolving ingredient, nephrocatarticon, that purgeth the reins, the marmalade of quinces, called codiniac, a confection of cantharides, which are green flies breeding on the tops of olive-trees, and other kinds of diuretic or piss-procuring simples. This done, Pantagruel said to Carpalin, Go into the city, scrambling like a cat up against the wall, as you can well do, and tell them that now presently they come out and charge their enemies as rudely as they can, and having said so, come down, taking a lighted torch with you, wherewith you shall set on fire all the tents and pavilions in the camp; then cry as loud as you are able with your great voice, and then come away from thence. Yea but, said Carpalin, were it not good to cloy all their ordnance? No, no, said Pantagruel, only blow up all their powder. Carpalin, obeying him, departed suddenly and did as he was appointed by Pantagruel, and all the combatants came forth that were in the city, and when he had set fire in the tents and pavilions, he passed so lightly through them, and so highly and profoundly did they snort and sleep, that they never perceived him. He came to the place where their artillery was, and set their munition on fire. But here was the danger. The fire was so sudden that poor Carpalin had almost been burnt. And had it not been for his wonderful agility he had been fried like a roasting pig. But he departed away so speedily that a bolt or arrow out of a crossbow could not have had a swifter motion. When he was clear of their trenches, he shouted aloud, and cried out so dreadfully, and with such amazement to the hearers, that it seemed all the devils of hell had been let loose. At which noise the enemies awaked, but can you tell how? Even no less astonished than are monks at the ringing of the first peal to matins, which in Lusonnois is called rub-ballock.

In the meantime Pantagruel began to sow the salt that he had in his bark, and because they slept with an open gaping mouth, he filled all their throats with it, so that those poor wretches were by it made to cough like foxes. Ha, Pantagruel, how thou addest greater heat to the firebrand that is in us! Suddenly Pantagruel had will to piss, by means of the drugs which Panurge had given him, and pissed amidst the camp so well and so copiously that he drowned them all, and there was a particular deluge ten leagues round about, of such considerable depth that the history saith, if his father's great mare had been there, and pissed likewise, it would undoubtedly have been a more enormous deluge than that of Deucalion; for she did never piss but she made a river greater than is either the Rhône or the Danube. Which those that were come out of the city seeing, said, They are all cruelly slain; see how the blood runs along. But they were deceived in thinking Pantagruel's urine had been the blood of their enemies, for they could not see but by the light of the fire of the pavilions and some small light of the moon.

The enemies, after that they were awaked, seeing on one side the fire in the camp, and on the other the inundation of the urinal deluge, could not tell what to say nor what to think. Some said that it was the end of the world and the final judgment, which ought to be by fire. Others again thought that the sea-gods, Neptune, Proteus, Triton, and the rest of them, did persecute them, for that indeed they found it to be like sea-water and salt.

O who were able now condignly to relate how Pantagruel did demean himself against the three hundred giants! O my Muse, my Calliope, my Thalia, inspire me at this time, restore unto me my spirits; for this is the logical bridge of asses! Here is the pitfall, here is the difficulty, to have ability enough to express the horrible battle that was fought. Ah, would to God that I had now a bottle of the best wine that ever those drank who shall read this so veridical history!

CHAP. XXIX.

How Pantagruel discomfited the three hundred giants armed with free-stone, and Loupgarou their captain.

THE giants, seeing all their camp drowned, carried away their king Anarchus upon their backs as well as they could out of the fort, as Æneas did to his father Anchises, in the time of the conflagration of Troy. When Panurge perceived them, he said to Pantagruel, Sir, yonder are the giants coming forth against you; lay on them with your mast gallantly, like an old fencer; for now is the time that you must show yourself a brave man and an honest. And for our part we will not fail you. I myself will kill to you a good many boldly enough; for why, David killed Goliath very easily; and then this great lecher, Eusthenes, who is stronger than four oxen, will not spare himself. Be of good courage, therefore, and valiant; charge amongst them with point and edge, and by all manner of means. Well, said Pantagruel, of courage I have more than for fifty francs, but let us be wise, for Hercules first never undertook against two. That is well cacked, well scummered, said Panurge; do you compare yourself with Hercules? You have, by G—, more strength in your teeth, and more scent in your bum, than ever Hercules had in all his body and soul. So much is a man worth as he esteems himself. Whilst they spake those words, behold! Loupgarou was come with all his giants, who, seeing Pantagruel in a manner alone, was carried away with temerity and presumption, for hopes that he had to kill the good man. Whereupon he said to his companions the giants, You wenchers of the low country, by Mahoom! if any of you undertake to fight against these men here, I will put you cruelly to death. It is my will that you let me fight single. In the meantime you shall have good sport to look upon us.

Then all the other giants retired with their king to the place where the flagons stood, and Panurge and his comrades with them, who counterfeited those that have had the pox, for he wreathed about his mouth, shrunk up his fingers, and with a harsh and hoarse voice said unto them, I forsake —od, fellow-soldiers, if I would have it to be believed that we make any war at all. Give us somewhat to eat with you whilest our masters fight against one another. To this the king and giants jointly condescended, and accordingly made them to banquet with them. In the meantime Panurge told them the follies of Turpin, the examples of St. Nicholas, and the tale of a tub. Loupgarou then set forward towards Pantagruel, with a mace all of steel, and that of the best sort, weighing nine thousand seven hundred quintals and two quarterons, at the end whereof were thirteen pointed diamonds, the least whereof was as big as the greatest bell of Our Lady's Church at Paris—there might want perhaps the thickness of a nail, or at most, that I may not lie, of the back of those knives which they call cutlugs or earcutters, but for a little off or on, more or less, it is no matter—and it was enchanted in such sort that it could never break, but, contrarily, all that it did touch did break immediately. Thus, then, as he approached with great fierceness and pride of heart, Pantagruel, casting up his eyes to heaven, recommended himself to God with all his soul, making such a vow as followeth.

O thou Lord God, who hast always been my protector and my saviour! thou seest the distress wherein I am at this time. Nothing brings me hither but a natural zeal, which thou hast permitted unto mortals, to keep and defend themselves, their wives and children, country and family, in case thy own proper cause were not in question, which is the faith; for in such a business thou wilt have no coadjutors, only a catholic confession and service of thy word, and hast forbidden us all arming and defence. For thou art the Almighty, who in thine own cause, and where thine own business is taken to heart, canst defend it far beyond all that we can conceive, thou who hast thousand thousands of hundreds of millions of legions of angels, the least of which is able to kill all mortal men, and turn about the heavens and earth at his pleasure, as heretofore it very plainly appeared in the army of Sennacherib. If it may please thee, therefore, at this time to assist me, as my whole trust and confidence is in thee alone, I vow unto thee, that in all countries whatsoever wherein I shall have any power or authority, whether in this of Utopia or elsewhere, I will cause thy holy gospel to be purely, simply, and entirely preached, so that the abuses of a rabble of hypocrites and false prophets, who by human constitutions and depraved inventions have empoisoned all the world, shall be quite exterminated from about me.

This vow was no sooner made, but there was heard a voice from heaven saying, *Hoc fac et vinces;* that is to say, Do this, and thou shalt overcome. Then Pantagruel, seeing that Loupgarou with his mouth wide open was drawing near to him, went against him boldly, and cried out as loud as he was able, Thou diest, villain, thou diest! purposing by his horrible cry to make him afraid, according to the discipline of the Lacedæmonians. Withal, he immediately cast at him out of his bark, which he wore at his girdle, eighteen cags and four bushels of salt, wherewith he filled both his mouth, throat, nose, and eyes. At this Loupgarou was so highly incensed that, most fiercely setting upon him, he thought even then with a blow of his mace to have beat out his brains. But Pantagruel was very nimble, and had always a quick foot and a quick eye, and therefore with his left foot did he step back one pace, yet not so nimbly but that the blow, falling upon the bark, broke it in four thousand four score and six pieces, and threw all the rest of the salt about the ground. Pantagruel, seeing that, most gallantly displayed the vigour of his arms, and, according to the art of the axe, gave him with the great end of his mast a homethrust a little above the breast; then, bringing along the blow to the left side, with a slash struck him between the neck and shoulders. After that, advancing his right foot, he gave him a push upon the couillons with the upper end of his said mast, wherewith breaking the scuttle on the top thereof, he spilt three or four puncheons of wine that were left therein.

Upon that Loupgarou thought that he had pierced his bladder, and that the wine that came forth had been his urine. Pantagruel, being not content with this, would have doubled it by a side-blow; but Loupgarou, lifting up his mace, advanced one step upon him, and with all his force would have dashed it upon Pantagruel, wherein, to speak the truth, he so sprightfully carried himself, that, if God had not succoured the good Pantagruel, he had been cloven from the top of his head to the bottom of his milt. But the blow glanced to the right side by the brisk nimbleness of Pantagruel, and his mace sank into the ground above threescore and thirteen foot, through a huge rock, out of which the fire did issue greater than nine thousand and six tons. Pantagruel, seeing him busy about plucking out his mace, which stuck in the ground between the rocks, ran upon him, and would have clean cut off his head, if by mischance his mast had not touched a little against the stock of Loupgarou's mace, which was enchanted, as we have said before. By this means his mast broke off about three handfuls above his hand, whereat he stood amazed like a bell-founder, and cried out, Ah, Panurge, where art thou? Panurge, seeing that, said to the king and the giants, By G—, they will hurt one another if they be not parted. But the giants were as merry as if they had been at a wedding. Then Carpalin would have risen from thence to help his master; but one of the giants said unto him, By Golfarin, the nephew of Mahoom, if thou stir hence I will put thee in the bottom of my breeches instead of a suppository, which cannot choose but do me good. For in my belly I am very costive, and cannot well cagar without gnashing my teeth and making many filthy faces. Then Pantagruel, thus destitute of a staff, took up the end of his mast, striking athwart and alongst upon the giant, but he did him no more hurt than you would do with a fillip upon a smith's anvil. In the [mean] time Loupgarou was drawing his mace out of the ground, and, having already plucked it out, was ready therewith to have struck Pantagruel, who, being very quick in turning, avoided all his blows in taking only the defensive part in hand, until on a sudden he saw that Loupgarou did threaten him with these words, saying, Now, villain, will not I fail to chop thee as small as minced meat, and keep thee henceforth from ever making any more poor men athirst! For then, without any more ado, Pantagruel struck him such a blow with his foot against the belly that he made him fall backwards, his heels over his head, and dragged him thus along at flay-buttock above a flight-shot. Then Loupgarou cried out, bleeding at the throat, Mahoom, Mahoom, Mahoom! at which noise all the giants arose to succour him. But Panurge said unto them, Gentlemen, do not go, if you will believe me, for our master is mad, and strikes athwart and alongst, he cares not where; he will do you a mischief. But the giants made no account of it, seeing that Pantagruel had never a staff.

And when Pantagruel saw those giants approach very near unto him, he took Loupgarou by the two feet, and lift up his body like a pike in the air, wherewith, it being harnessed with anvils, he laid such heavy load amongst those giants armed with free-stone, that, striking them down as a mason doth little knobs of stones, there was not one of them that stood before him whom he threw not flat to the ground. And by the breaking of this stony armour there was made such a horrible rumble as put me in mind of the fall of the butter-tower of St. Stephen's at Bourges when it melted before the sun. Panurge, with Carpalin and Eusthenes, did cut in the mean time the throats of those that were struck down, in such sort that there escaped not one. Pantagruel to any man's sight was like a mower, who with his scythe, which was Loupgarou, cut down the meadow grass, to wit, the giants; but with this fencing of Pantagruel's Loupgarou lost his head, which happened when Pantagruel struck down one whose name was Riflandouille, or Pudding-plunderer, who was armed cap-a-pie with Grison stones, one chip whereof splintering abroad cut off Epistemon's neck clean and fair. For otherwise the most part of them were but lightly armed with a kind of sandy brittle stone, and the rest with slates. At last, when he saw that they were all dead, he threw the body of Loupgarou as hard as he could against the city, where falling like a frog upon his belly in the great Piazza thereof, he with the said fall killed a singed he-cat, a wet she-cat, a farting duck, and a bridled goose.

CHAP. XXX.

How Epistemon, who had his head cut off, was finely healed by Panurge, and of the news which he brought from the devils, and of the damned people in hell.

THIS gigantal victory being ended, Pantagruel withdrew himself to the place of the flagons, and called for Panurge and the rest, who came unto him safe and sound, except Eusthenes, whom one of the giants had scratched a little in the face whilst he was about the cutting of his throat, and Epistemon, who appeared not at all. Whereat Pantagruel was so aggrieved that he would have killed himself. But Panurge said unto him, Nay, sir, stay a while, and we will search for him amongst the dead, and find out the truth of all. Thus as they went seeking after him, they found him stark dead, with his head between his arms all bloody. Then Eusthenes cried out, Ah, cruel death! hast thou taken from me the perfectest amongst men? At which words Pantagruel rose up with the greatest grief that ever any man did see, and said to Panurge, Ha, my friend! the prophecy of your two glasses and the javelin staff was a great deal too deceitful. But Panurge answered, My dear bullies all, weep not one drop more, for, he being yet all hot, I will make him as sound as ever he was. In saying this, he took the head and held it warm foregainst his codpiece, that the wind might not enter into it. Eusthenes and Carpalin carried the body to the place where they had banqueted, not out of any hope that ever he would recover, but that Pantagruel might see it.

Nevertheless Panurge gave him very good comfort, saying, If I do not heal him, I will be content to lose my head, which is a fool's wager. Leave off, therefore, crying, and help me. Then cleansed he his neck very well with pure white wine, and, after that, took his head, and into it synapised some powder of diamerdis, which he always carried about him in one of his bags. Afterwards he anointed it with I know not what ointment, and set it on very just, vein against vein, sinew against sinew, and spondyle against spondyle, that he might not be wry-necked—for such people he mortally hated. This done, he gave it round about some fifteen or sixteen stitches with a needle that it might not fall off again; then, on all sides and everywhere, he put a little ointment on it, which he called resuscitative.

Suddenly Epistemon began to breathe, then opened his eyes, yawned, sneezed, and afterwards let a great household fart. Whereupon Panurge said, Now, certainly, he is healed,—and therefore gave him to drink a large full glass of strong white wine, with a sugared toast. In this fashion was Epistemon finely healed, only that he was somewhat hoarse for above three weeks together, and had a dry cough of which he could not be rid but by the force of continual drinking. And now he began to speak, and said that he had seen the devil, had spoken with Lucifer familiarly, and had been very merry in hell and in the Elysian fields, affirming very seriously before them all that the devils were boon companions and merry fellows. But, in respect of the damned, he said he was very sorry that Panurge had so soon called him back into this world again; for, said he, I took wonderful delight to see them. How so? said Pantagruel. Because they do not use them there, said Epistemon, so badly as you think they do. Their estate and condition of living is but only changed after a very strange manner; for I saw Alexander the Great there amending and patching on clouts upon old breeches and stockings, whereby he got but a very poor living.

Xerxes was a crier of mustard.
Romulus, a salter and patcher of pattens.
Numa, a nailsmith.
Tarquin, a porter.
Piso, a clownish swain.
Sylla, a ferryman.
Cyrus, a cowherd.
Themistocles, a glass-maker.
Epaminondas, a maker of mirrors or looking-glasses.
Brutus and Cassius, surveyors or measurers of land.
Demosthenes, a vine-dresser.
Cicero, a fire-kindler.
Fabius, a threader of beads.
Artaxerxes, a rope-maker.
Æneas, a miller.

Achilles was a scaldpated maker of hay-bundles.
Agamemnon, a lick-box.
Ulysses, a hay-mower.
Nestor, a deer-keeper or forester.
Darius, a gold-finder or jakes-farmer.
Ancus Martius, a ship-trimmer.
Camillus, a foot-post.
Marcellus, a sheller of beans.
Drusus, a taker of money at the doors of playhouses.
Scipio Africanus, a crier of lee in a wooden slipper.
Asdrubal, a lantern-maker.
Hannibal, a kettlemaker and seller of eggshells.
Priamus, a seller of old clouts.
Lancelot of the Lake was a flayer of dead horses.

All the Knights of the Round Table were poor day-labourers, employed to row over the rivers of Cocytus, Phlegeton, Styx, Acheron, and Lethe, when my lords the devils had a mind to recreate themselves upon the water, as in the like occasion are hired the boatmen at Lyons, the gondoliers of Venice, and oars at London. But with this difference, that these poor knights have only for their fare a bob or flirt on the nose, and in the evening a morsel of coarse mouldy bread.

Trajan was a fisher of frogs.
Antoninus, a lackey.
Commodus, a jet-maker.
Pertinax, a peeler of walnuts.
Lucullus, a maker of rattles and hawks'-bells.
Justinian, a pedlar.
Hector, a snap-sauce scullion.
Paris was a poor beggar.
Cambyses, a mule-driver.

Nero, a base blind fiddler, or player on that instrument which is called a windbroach. Fierabras was his serving-man, who did him a thousand mischievous tricks, and would make him eat of the brown bread and drink of the turned wine when himself did both eat and drink of the best.

Julius Cæsar and Pompey were boat-wrights and tighters of ships.

Valentine and Orson did serve in the stoves of hell, and were sweat-rubbers in hot houses.

Giglan and Govian [Gauvin] were poor swineherds.

Geoffrey with the great tooth was a tinder-maker and seller of matches.

Godfrey de Bouillon, a hood-maker.

Jason was a bracelet-maker.

Don Pietro de Castille, a carrier of indulgences.

Morgan, a beer-brewer.

Huon of Bordeaux, a hooper of barrels.

Pyrrhus, a kitchen-scullion.

Antiochus, a chimney-sweeper.

Octavian, a scraper of parchment.

Nerva, a mariner.

Pope Julius was a crier of pudding-pies, but he left off wearing there his great buggerly beard.

John of Paris was a greaser of boots.

Arthur of Britain, an ungreaser of caps.

Perce-Forest, a carrier of faggots.

Pope Boniface the Eighth, a scummer of pots.

Pope Nicholas the Third, a maker of paper.

Pope Alexander, a ratcatcher.

Pope Sixtus, an anointer of those that have the pox.

What, said Pantagruel, have they the pox there too? Surely, said Epistemon, I never saw so many: there are there, I think, above a hundred millions; for believe, that those who have not had the pox in this world must have it in the other.

Cotsbody, said Panurge, then I am free; for I have been as far as the hole of Gibraltar, reached unto the outmost bounds of Hercules, and gathered of the ripest.

Ogier the Dane was a furbisher of armour.

The King Tigranes, a mender of thatched houses

Galien Restored, a taker of moldwarps.

The four sons of Aymon were all toothdrawers.

Pope Calixtus was a barber of a woman's *sine qua non*.

Pope Urban, a bacon-picker.

Melusina was a kitchen drudge-wench.

Matabrune, a laundress.

Cleopatra, a crier of onions.

Helen, a broker for chambermaids.

Semiramis, the beggars' lice-killer.

Dido did sell mushrooms.
Penthesilea sold cresses.
Lucretia was an alehouse-keeper.
Hortensia, a spinstress.
Livia, a grater of verdigris.

After this manner, those that had been great lords and ladies here, got but a poor scurvy wretched living there below. And, on the contrary, the philosophers and others, who in this world had been altogether indigent and wanting, were great lords there in their turn. I saw Diogenes there strut it out most pompously, and in great magnificence, with a rich purple gown on him, and a golden sceptre in his right hand. And, which is more, he would now and then make Alexander the Great mad, so enormously would he abuse him when he had not well patched his breeches; for he used to pay his skin with sound bastinadoes. I saw Epictetus there, most gallantly apparelled after the French fashion, sitting under a pleasant arbour, with store of handsome gentlewomen, frolicking, drinking, dancing, and making good cheer, with abundance of crowns of the sun. Above the lattice were written these verses for his device:

> To leap and dance, to sport and play,
> And drink good wine both white and brown,
> Or nothing else do all the day
> But tell bags full of many a crown.

When he saw me, he invited me to drink with him very courteously, and I being willing to be entreated, we tippled and chopined together most theologically. In the meantime came Cyrus to beg one farthing of him for the honour of Mercury, therewith to buy a few onions for his supper. No, no, said Epictetus, I do not use in my almsgiving to bestow farthings. Hold, thou varlet, there's a crown for thee; be an honest man. Cyrus was exceeding glad to have met with such a booty; but the other poor rogues, the kings that are there below, as Alexander, Darius, and others, stole it away from him by night. I saw Pathelin, the treasurer of Rhadamanthus, who, in cheapening the pudding-pies that Pope Julius cried, asked him how much a dozen. Three blanks, said the Pope. Nay, said Pathelin, three blows with a cudgel. Lay them down here, you rascal, and go fetch more. The poor Pope went away weeping, who, when he came to his master the pie-maker, told him that they had taken away his pudding-pies. Whereupon his master gave him such a sound lash with an eel-skin, that his own would have been worth nothing to make bag-pipe-bags of. I saw Master John Le Maire there personate the Pope in such fashion that he made all the poor kings and popes of this world kiss his feet, and, taking great state upon him, gave them his benediction, saying, Get the pardons, rogues, get the pardons; they are good cheap. I absolve you of bread and pottage, and dispense with you to be never good for anything. Then, calling Caillet and Triboulet to him, he spoke these words, My lords the cardinals, despatch their bulls, to wit, to each of them a blow with a cudgel upon the reins. Which accordingly was forthwith performed. I heard Master Francis Villon ask Xerxes, How much the mess of mustard? A farthing, said Xerxes. To which the said Villon answered, The pox take thee for a villain! As much of square-eared wheat is not worth half that price, and now thou offerest to enhance the price of victuals. With this he pissed in his pot, as the mustard-makers of Paris used to do. I saw the trained bowman of the bathing tub, known by the name of the Francarcher de Baignolet, who, being one of the trustees of the Inquisition, when he saw Perce-Forest making water against a wall in which was painted the fire of St. Anthony, declared him heretic, and would have caused him to be burnt alive had it not been for Morgant, who, for his proficiat and other small fees, gave him nine tuns of beer.

Well, said Pantagruel, reserve all these fair stories for another time, only tell us how the usurers are there handled. I saw them, said Epistemon, all very busily employed in seeking of rusty pins and old nails in the kennels of the streets, as you see poor wretched rogues do in this world. But the quintal, or hundredweight, of this old ironware is there valued but at the price of a cantle of bread, and yet they have but a very bad despatch and riddance in the sale of it. Thus the poor misers are sometimes three whole weeks without eating one morsel or crumb of bread, and yet work both day and night, looking for the fair to come. Nevertheless, of all this labour, toil, and misery, they reckon nothing, so cursedly active they are in the prosecution of that their base calling, in hopes, at the end of the year, to earn some scurvy penny by it.

Come, said Pantagruel, let us now make ourselves merry one bout, and drink, my lads, I beseech you, for it is very good drinking all this month. Then did they uncase their flagons by heaps and dozens, and with their leaguer-provision made excellent good cheer. But the poor King Anarchus could not all this while settle himself towards any fit of mirth; whereupon Panurge said, Of what trade shall we make my lord the king here, that he may be skilful in the art when he goes thither to sojourn amongst all the devils of hell? Indeed, said Pantagruel, that was well advised of thee. Do with him what thou wilt, I give him to thee. Gramercy, said Panurge, the present is not to be refused, and I love it from you.

CHAP. XXXI.

How Pantagruel entered into the city of the Amaurots, and how Panurge married King Anarchus to an old lantern-carrying hag, and made him a crier of green sauce.

AFTER this wonderful victory, Pantagruel sent Carpalin unto the city of the Amaurots to declare and signify unto them how the King Anarchus was taken prisoner and all the enemies of the city overthrown. Which news when they heard all the inhabitants of the city came forth to meet him in good order, and with a great triumphant pomp, conducting him with a heavenly joy into the city, where innumerable bonfires were set on through all the parts thereof, and fair round tables, which were furnished with store of good victuals, set out in the middle of the streets. This was a renewing of the golden age in the time of Saturn, so good was the cheer which then they made.

But Pantagruel, having assembled the whole senate and common councilmen of the town, said, My masters, we must now strike the iron whilst it is hot. It is therefore my will that, before we frolic it any longer, we advise how to assault and take the whole kingdom of the Dipsodes. To which effect let those that will go with me provide themselves against to-morrow after drinking, for then will I begin to march. Not that I need any more men than I have to help me to conquer it, for I could make it as sure that way as if I had it already; but I see this city is so full of inhabitants that they scarce can turn in the streets. I will, therefore, carry them as a colony into

Dipsody, and will give them all that country, which is fair, wealthy, fruitful, and pleasant, above all other countries in the world, as many of you can tell who have been there heretofore. Everyone of you, therefore, that will go along, let him provide himself as I have said. This counsel and resolution being published in the city, the next morning there assembled in the piazza before the palace to the number of eighteen hundred fifty-six thousand and eleven, besides women and little children. Thus began they to march straight into Dipsody, in such good order as did the people of Israel when they departed out of Egypt to pass over the Red Sea.

But before we proceed any further in this purpose, I will tell you how Panurge handled his prisoner the King Anarchus; for, having remembered that which Epistemon had related, how the kings and rich men in this world were used in the Elysian fields, and how they got their living there by base and ignoble trades, he, therefore, one day apparelled his king in a pretty little canvas doublet, all jagged and pinked like the tippet of a light horseman's cap, together with a pair of large mariner's breeches, and stockings without shoes,—For, said he, they would but spoil his sight,—and a little peach-coloured bonnet with a great capon's feather in it—I lie, for I think he had two —and a very handsome girdle of a sky-colour and green (in French called *pers et vert*), saying that such a livery did become him well, for that he had always been perverse, and in this plight bringing him before Pantagruel, said unto him, Do you know this roister? No, indeed, said Pantagruel. It is, said Panurge, my lord the king of the three batches, or threadbare sovereign. I intend to make him an honest man. These devilish kings which we have here are but as so many calves; they know nothing and are good for nothing but to do a thousand mischiefs to their poor subjects, and to trouble all the world with war for their unjust and detestable pleasure. I will put him to a trade, and make him a crier of green sauce. Go to, begin and cry, Do you lack any green sauce? and the poor devil cried. That is too low, said Panurge; then took him by the ear, saying, Sing higher in Ge, sol, re, ut. So, so, poor devil, thou hast a good throat; thou wert never so happy as to be no longer king. And Pantagruel made himself merry with all this; for I dare boldly say that he was the best little gaffer that was to be seen between this and the end of a staff. Thus was Anarchus made a good crier of green sauce. Two days thereafter Panurge married him with an old lantern-carrying hag, and he himself made the wedding with fine sheep's heads, brave haslets with mustard, gallant salligots with garlic, of which he sent five horseloads unto Pantagruel, which he ate up all, he found them so appetizing. And for their drink they had a kind of small well-watered wine, and some sorbapple-cider. And, to make them dance, he hired a blind man that made music to them with a wind-broach.

After dinner he led them to the palace and showed them to Pantagruel, and said, pointing to the married woman, You need not fear that she will crack. Why? said Pantagruel. Because, said Panurge, she is well slit and broke up already. What do you mean by that? said Pantagruel. Do not you see, said Panurge, that the chestnuts which are roasted in the fire, if they be whole they crack as if they were mad, and, to keep them from cracking, they make an incision in them and slit them? So this new bride is in her lower parts well slit before, and therefore will not crack behind.

Pantagruel gave them a little lodge near the lower street and a mortar of stone wherein to bray and pound their sauce, and in this manner did they do their little business, he being as pretty a crier of green sauce as ever was seen in the country of Utopia. But I have been told since that his wife doth beat him like plaister, and the poor sot dare not defend himself, he is so simple.

CHAP. XXXII.

How Pantagruel with his tongue covered a whole army, and what the author saw in his mouth.

THUS, as Pantagruel with all his army had entered into the country of the Dipsodes, everyone was glad of it, and incontinently rendered themselves unto him, bringing him out of their own good wills the keys of all the cities where he went, the Almirods only excepted, who, being resolved to hold out against him, made answer to his heralds that they would not yield but upon very honourable and good conditions.

What! said Pantagruel, do they ask any better terms than the hand at the pot and the glass in their fist? Come, let us go sack

them, and put them all to the sword. Then did they put themselves in good order, as being fully determined to give an assault, but by the way, passing through a large field, they were overtaken with a great shower of rain, whereat they began to shiver and tremble, to crowd, press, and thrust close to one another. When Pantagruel saw that, he made their captains tell them that it was nothing, and that he saw well above the clouds that it would be nothing but a little dew; but, howsoever, that they should put themselves in order, and he would cover them. Then did they put themselves in a close order, and stood as near to [each] other as they could, and Pantagruel drew out his tongue only half-way and covered them all, as a hen doth her chickens. In the meantime, I, who relate to you these so veritable stories, hid myself under a burdock-leaf, which was not much less in largeness than the arch of the bridge of Montrible, but when I saw them thus covered, I went towards them to shelter myself likewise; which I could not do, for that they were so, as the saying is, *At the yard's end there is no cloth left.* Then, as well as I could, I got upon it, and went along full two leagues upon his tongue, and so long marched that at last I came into his mouth. But, O gods and goddesses! what did I see there? Jupiter confound me with his trisulc lightning if I lie! I walked there as they do in Sophia [at] Constantinople, and saw there great rocks, like the mountains in Denmark—I believe that those were his teeth. I saw also fair meadows, large forests, great and strong cities not a jot less than Lyons or Poictiers. The first man I met with there was a good honest fellow planting coleworts, whereat being very much amazed, I asked him, My friend, what dost thou make here? I plant coleworts, said he. But how, and wherewith? said I. Ha, sir, said he, everyone cannot have his ballocks as heavy as a mortar, neither can we be all rich. Thus do I get my poor living, and carry them to the market to sell in the city which is here behind. Jesus! said I, is there here a new world? Sure, said he, it is never a jot new, but it is commonly reported that, without this, there is an earth, whereof the inhabitants enjoy the light of a sun and a moon, and that it is full of and replenished with very good commodities; but yet this is more ancient than that. Yea but, said I, my friend, what is the name of that city whither thou carriest thy coleworts to sell? It is called Aspharage, said he, and all the indwellers are Christians, very honest men, and will make you good cheer. To be brief, I resolved to go thither.

Now, in my way, I met with a fellow that was lying in wait to catch pigeons, of whom I asked, My friend, from whence come these pigeons? Sir, said he, they come from the other world. Then I thought that, when Pantagruel yawned, the pigeons went into his mouth in whole flocks, thinking that it had been a pigeon-house.

Then I went into the city, which I found fair, very strong, and seated in a good air; but at my entry the guard demanded of me my pass or ticket. Whereat I was much astonished, and asked them, My masters, is there any danger of the plague here? O Lord! said they, they die hard by here so fast that the cart runs about the streets. Good God! said I, and where? Whereunto they answered that it was in Larynx and Pharynx, which are two great cities such as Rouen and Nantes, rich and of great trading. And the cause of the plague was by a stinking and infectious exhalation which lately vapoured out of the abysms, whereof there have died above two and twenty hundred and threescore thousand and sixteen persons within this sevennight. Then I considered, calculated, and found that it was a rank and unsavoury breathing which came out of Pantagruel's stomach when he did eat so much garlic, as we have aforesaid.

Parting from thence, I passed amongst the rocks, which were his teeth, and never left walking till I got up on one of them; and there I found the pleasantest places in the world, great large tennis-courts, fair galleries, sweet meadows, store of vines, and an infinite number of banqueting summer outhouses in the fields, after the Italian fashion, full of pleasure and delight, where I stayed full four months, and never made better cheer in my life as then. After that I went down by the hinder teeth to come to the chaps. But in the way I was robbed by thieves in a great forest that is in the territory towards the ears. Then, after a little further travelling, I fell upon a pretty petty village—truly I have forgot the name of it—where I was yet merrier than ever, and got some certain money to live by. Can you tell how? By sleeping. For there they hire men by the day to sleep, and they get by it sixpence a day, but they that can snort hard get at least ninepence. How I had been robbed in the valley I informed the senators, who told me that, in very truth, the people of that side were bad livers and naturally thievish, whereby I perceived well that, as we have with us the countries Cisalpine and Transalpine, that is, behither and beyond the mountains, so have they there the countries Cidentine and Tradentine, that is, behither and beyond the teeth. But it is far better living on this side, and the air is purer. There I began to think that it is very true which is commonly said, that the one half of the world knoweth not how the other half liveth; seeing none before myself had ever written of that country, wherein are above five-and-twenty kingdoms inhabited, besides deserts, and a great arm of the sea. Concerning which purpose I have composed a great book, entitled, The History of the Throttias, because they dwell in the throat of my master Pantagruel.

At last I was willing to return, and, passing by his beard, I cast myself upon his shoulders, and from thence slid down to the ground, and fell before him. As soon as I was perceived by him, he asked me, Whence comest thou, Alcofribas? I answered him, Out of your mouth, my lord. And how long hast thou been there? said he. Since the time, said I, that you went against the Almirods. That is about six months ago, said he. And wherewith didst thou live? What didst thou drink? I answered, My lord, of the same that you did, and of the daintiest morsels that passed through your throat I took toll. Yea but, said he, where didst thou shite? In your throat, my lord, said I. Ha, ha! thou art a merry fellow, said he. We have with the help of God conquered all the land of the Dipsodes; I will give thee the Chastelleine, or Lairdship of Salmigondin. Gramercy, my lord, said I, you gratify me beyond all that I have deserved of you.

CHAP. XXXIII.

How Pantagruel became sick, and the manner how he was recovered.

WHILE after this the good Pantagruel fell sick, and had such an obstruction in his stomach that he could neither eat nor drink; and, because mischief seldom comes alone, a hot piss seized on him, which tormented him more than you would believe. His physicians nevertheless helped him very well, and with store of lenitives and diuretic drugs made him piss away his pain. His urine was so hot that since that time it is not yet cold, and you have of it in divers places of France, according to the course that it took, and they are called the hot baths, as—

At Coderets.
At Limous.
At Dast.
At Ballervie [Balleruc].
At Neric.
At Bourbonansie, and elsewhere in Italy.
At Mongros.
At Appone.
At Sancto Petro de Padua.
At St. Helen.
At Casa Nuova.
At St. Bartholomew, in the county of Boulogne.
At the Porrette, and a thousand other places.

And I wonder much at a rabble of foolish philosophers and physicians, who spend their time in disputing whence the heat of the said waters cometh, whether it be by reason of borax, or sulphur, or alum, or saltpetre, that is within the mine. For they do nothing but dote, and better were it for them to rub their arse against a thistle than to waste away their time thus in disputing of that whereof they know not the original; for the resolution is easy, neither need we to inquire any further than that the said baths came by a hot piss of the good Pantagruel.

Now to tell you after what manner he was cured of his principal disease. I let pass how for a minorative or gentle potion he took four hundred pound weight of colophoniac scammony, six score and eighteen cartloads of cassia, an eleven thousand and nine hundred pound weight of rhubarb, besides other confuse jumblings of sundry drugs. You must understand that by the advice of the physicians it was ordained that what did offend his stomach should be taken away; and therefore they made seventeen great balls of copper, each whereof was bigger than that which is to be seen on the top of St. Peter's needle at Rome, and in such sort that they did open in the midst and shut with a spring. Into one of them entered one of his men carrying a lantern and a torch lighted, and so Pantagruel swallowed him down like a little pill. Into seven others went seven country-fellows, having every one of them a shovel on his neck. Into nine others entered nine wood-carriers, having each of them a basket hung at his neck, and so were they swallowed down like pills. When they were in his stomach, every one undid his spring, and came out of their cabins The first whereof was he that carried the lantern, and so they fell more than half a league into a most horrible gulf, more stinking and infectious than ever was Mephitis, or the marshes of the Camerina, or the abominably unsavoury lake of Sorbona, whereof Strabo maketh mention. And had it not been that they had very well antidoted their stomach, heart, and wine-pot, which is called the noddle, they had been altogether suffocated and choked with these detestable vapours. O what a perfume! O what an evaporation wherewith to bewray the masks or mufflers of young mangy queans. After that, with groping and smelling they came near to the fæcal matter and the corrupted humours. Finally, they found a montjoy or heap of ordure and filth. Then fell the pioneers to work to dig it up, and the rest with their shovels filled the baskets; and when all was cleansed every one retired himself into his ball.

This done, Pantagruel enforcing himself to vomit, very easily brought them out, and they made no more show in his mouth than a fart in yours. But, when they came merrily out of their pills, I thought upon the Grecians coming out of the Trojan horse. By this means was he healed and brought unto his former state and convalescence; and of these brazen pills, or rather copper balls, you have one at Orleans, upon the steeple of the Holy Cross Church.

CHAP. XXXIV.

The conclusion of this present book, and the excuse of the author.

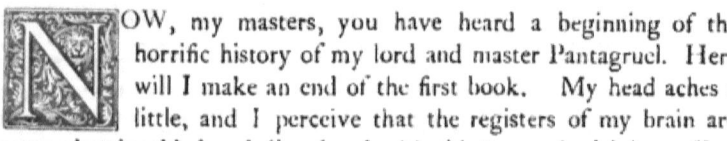OW, my masters, you have heard a beginning of the horrific history of my lord and master Pantagruel. Here will I make an end of the first book. My head aches a little, and I perceive that the registers of my brain are somewhat jumbled and disordered with this Septembral juice. You shall have the rest of the history at Frankfort mart next coming, and there shall you see how Panurge was married and made a cuckold within a month after his wedding; how Pantagruel found

out the philosopher's stone, the manner how he found it, and the way how to use it; how he passed over the Caspian mountains, and how he sailed through the Atlantic sea, defeated the Cannibals, and conquered the isles of Pearls; how he married the daughter of the King of India, called Presthan; how he fought against the devil and burnt up five chambers of hell, ransacked the great black chamber, threw Proserpina into the fire, broke five teeth to Lucifer, and the horn that was in his arse; how he visited the regions of the moon to know whether indeed the moon were not entire and whole, or if the women had three quarters of it in their heads, and a thousand other little merriments all veritable. These are brave things truly. Good night, gentlemen. *Perdonate mi*, and think not so much upon my faults that you forget your own.

If you say to me, Master, it would seem that you were not very wise in writing to us these flimflam stories and pleasant fooleries; I answer you, that you are not much wiser to spend your time in reading them. Nevertheless, if you read them to make yourselves merry, as in manner of pastime I wrote them, you and I both are far more worthy of pardon than a great rabble of squint-minded fellows, dissembling and counterfeit saints, demure lookers, hypocrites, pretended zealots, tough friars, buskin-monks, and other such sects of men, who disguise themselves like masquers to deceive the world. For, whilst they give the common people to understand that they are busied about nothing but contemplation and devotion in fastings and maceration of their sensuality—and that only to sustain and aliment the small frailty of their humanity—it is so far otherwise that, on the contrary, God knows what cheer they make; *Et Curios simulant, sed Bacchanalia vivunt*. You may read it in great letters in the colouring of their red snouts, and gulching bellies as big as a tun, unless it be when they perfume themselves with sulphur. As for their study, it is wholly taken up in reading of Pantagruelian books, not so much to pass the time merrily as to hurt someone or other mischievously, to wit, in articling, sole-articling, wry-neckifying, buttock-stirring, ballocking, and diabliculating, that is, calumniating. Wherein they are like unto the poor rogues of a village that are busy in stirring up and scraping in the ordure and filth of little children, in the season of cherries and guinds, and that only to find the kernels, that they may sell them to the druggists to make thereof pomander oil. Fly from these men, abhor and hate them as much as I do, and upon my faith you will find yourselves the better for it. And if you desire to be good Pantagruelists, that is to say, to live in peace, joy, health, making yourselves always merry, never trust those men that always peep out at one hole.

THE
THIRD BOOK
OF THE
WORKS
OF
Mr. Francis Rabelais,
Doctor in Physick.

Containing the Heroick Deeds of
Pantagruel the Son of *Gargantua*.
Now faithfully Translated into *English*,
by the unimitable Pen of
Sir *Thomas Urwhart*, K*t.* & Bar.
The Translator of the Two First
BOOKS.

Never before Printed.

LONDON:
Printed for *Richard Baldwin*, near the
Oxford Arms in *Warwick-Lane*, 1693.

Francis Rabelais

to the Soul of the Deceased Queen of Navarre.

BSTRACTED soul, ravished with ecstasies,
Gone back, and now familiar in the skies,
Thy former host, thy body, leaving quite,
Which to obey thee always took delight,—
Obsequious, ready,—now from motion free,
Senseless, and as it were in apathy,
Wouldst thou not issue forth, for a short space,
From that divine, eternal, heavenly place,
To see the third part, in this earthy cell,
Of the brave acts of good Pantagruel?

The Third Book

of the heroic Deeds and Sayings of the good

Pantagruel.

The Author's Prologue.

OOD people, most illustrious drinkers, and you, thrice precious gouty gentlemen, did you ever see Diogenes, the cynic philosopher? If you have seen him, you then had your eyes in your head, or I am very much out of my understanding and logical sense. It is a gallant thing to see the clearness of (wine, gold,) the sun. I'll be judged by the blind born so renowned in the sacred Scriptures, who, having at his choice to ask whatever he would from him who is Almighty, and whose word in an instant is effectually performed, asked nothing else but that he might see. Item, you are not young, which is a competent quality for you to philosophate more than physically in wine, not in vain, and henceforwards to be of the Bacchic Council; to the end that, opining there, you may give your opinion faithfully of the substance, colour, excellent odour, eminency, propriety, faculty, virtue, and effectual dignity of the said blessed and desired liquor.

If you have not seen him, as I am easily induced to believe that you have not, at least you have heard some talk of him. For through the air, and the whole extent of this hemisphere of the heavens, hath his report and fame, even until this present time, remained very memorable and renowned. Then all of you are derived from the Phrygian blood, if I be not deceived. If you have not so many crowns as Midas had, yet have you something, I know not what, of him, which the Persians of old esteemed more of in all their otacusts, and which was more desired by the Emperor Antonine, and gave occasion thereafter to the Basilisco at Rohan to be surnamed Goodly Ears. If you have not heard of him, I will presently tell you a story to make your wine relish. Drink then,—so, to the purpose. Hearken now whilst I give you notice, to the end that you may not, like infidels, be by your simplicity abused, that in his time he was a rare philosopher and the cheerfullest of a thousand. If he had some imperfection, so have you, so have we; for there is nothing, but God, that is perfect. Yet so it was, that by Alexander the Great, although he had Aristotle for his instructor and domestic, was he held in such estimation, that he wished, if he had not been Alexander, to have been Diogenes the Sinopian.

When Philip, King of Macedon, enterprised the siege and ruin of Corinth, the Corinthians having received certain intelligence by their spies that he with a numerous army in battle-rank was coming against them, were all of them, not without cause, most terribly afraid; and therefore were not neglective of their duty in doing their best endeavours to put themselves in a fit posture to resist his hostile approach and defend their own city.

Some from the fields brought into the fortified places their movables, bestial, corn, wine, fruit, victuals, and other necessary provision.

Others did fortify and rampire their walls, set up little fortresses, bastions, squared ravelins, digged trenches, cleansed countermines, fenced themselves with gabions, contrived platforms, emptied casemates, barricaded the false brays, erected the cavaliers, repaired the counterscarps, plastered the curtains, lengthened ravelins, stopped parapets, morticed barbacans, assured the portcullises, fastened the herses, sarasinesques, and cataracts, placed their sentries, and doubled their patrol. Everyone did watch and ward, and not one was exempted from carrying the basket. Some polished corslets, varnished backs and breasts, cleaned the headpieces, mail-coats, brigandines, salads, helmets, morions, jacks, gushets, gorgets, hoguines, brassars, and cuissars, corslets, haubergeons, shields, bucklers, targets, greaves, gauntlets, and spurs. Others made ready bows, slings, crossbows, pellets, catapults, migrains or fire-balls, firebrands, balists, scorpions, and other such warlike engines expugnatory and destructive to the Hellepolides. They sharpened and prepared spears, staves, pikes, brown bills, halberds, long hooks, lances, zagayes, quarterstaves, eel-spears, partisans, troutstaves, clubs, battle-axes, maces, darts, dartlets, glaives, javelins, javelots, and truncheons. They set edges upon scimitars, cutlasses, badelairs, backswords, tucks, rapiers, bayonets, arrow-heads, dags, daggers, mandousians, poniards, whinyards, knives, skeans, shables, chipping knives, and raillons.

Every man exercised his weapon, every man scoured off the rust from his natural hanger; nor was there a woman amongst them, though never so reserved or old, who made not her harness to be well furbished; as you know the Corinthian women of old were reputed very courageous combatants.

Diogenes seeing them all so warm at work, and himself not employed by the magistrates in any business whatsoever, he did very seriously, for many days together, without speaking one word, consider and contemplate the countenance of his fellow-citizens.

Then on a sudden, as if he had been roused up and inspired by a martial spirit, he girded his cloak scarfwise about his left arm, tucked up his sleeves to the elbow, trussed himself like a clown gathering apples, and, giving to one of his old acquaintance his wallet, books, and opistographs, away went he out of town towards a little hill or promontory of Corinth called [the] Cranie; and there on the strand, a pretty level place, did he roll his jolly tub, which served him for a house to shelter him from the injuries of the weather: there, I say, in a great vehemency of spirit, did he turn it, veer it, wheel it, whirl it, frisk it, jumble it, shuffle it, huddle it, tumble it, hurry it, jolt it, justle it, overthrow it, evert it, invert it, subvert it, overturn it, beat it, thwack it, bump it, batter it, knock it, thrust it, push it, jerk it, shock it, shake it, toss it, throw it, overthrow it, upside down, topsy-turvy, arsiturvy, tread it, trample it, stamp it, tap it, ting it, ring it, tingle it, towl it, sound it, resound it, stop it, shut it, unbung it, close it, unstopple it. And then again in a mighty bustle he bandied it, slubbered it, hacked it, whittled it, wayed it, darted it, hurled it, staggered it, reeled it, swinged it, brangled it, tottered it, lifted it, heaved it, transformed it, transfigured it, transposed it, transplaced it, reared it, raised it, hoised it, washed it, dighted it, cleansed it, rinsed it, nailed it, settled it, fastened it, shackled it, fettered it, levelled it, blocked it, tugged it, tewed it, carried it, bedashed it, bewrayed it, parched it, mounted it, broached it, nicked it, notched it, bespattered it, decked it, adorned it, trimmed it, garnished it, guaged it, furnished it, bored it, pierced it, trapped it, rumbled it, slid it down the hill, and precipitated it from the very height of the Cranie; then from the foot to the top (like another Sisyphus with his stone) bore it up again, and every way so banged it and belaboured it that it was ten thousand to one he had not struck the bottom of it out.

Which when one of his friends had seen, and asked him why he did so toil his body, perplex his spirit, and torment his tub, the philosopher's answer was that, not being employed in any other charge by the Republic, he thought it expedient to thunder and storm it so tempestuously upon his tub, that amongst a people so fervently busy and earnest at work he alone might not seem a loitering slug and lazy fellow. To the same purpose may I say of myself,

> Though I be rid from fear,
> I am not void of care.

For, perceiving no account to be made of me towards the discharge of a trust of any great concernment, and considering that through all the parts of this most noble kingdom of France, both on this and on the other side of the mountains, everyone is most diligently exercised and busied, some in the fortifying of their own native country for its defence, others in the repulsing of their enemies by an offensive war; and all this with a policy so excellent and such admirable order, so manifestly profitable for the future, whereby France shall have its frontiers most magnificently enlarged, and the French assured of a long and well-grounded peace, that very little withholds me from the opinion of good Heraclitus, which affirmeth war to be the father of all good things; and therefore do I believe that war is in Latin called *bellum*, not by antiphrasis, as some patchers of old rusty Latin would have us to think, because in war there is little beauty to be seen, but absolutely and simply; for that in war appeareth all that is good and graceful, and that by the wars is purged out all manner of wickedness and deformity. For proof whereof the wise and pacific Solomon could no better represent the unspeakable perfection of the divine wisdom, than by comparing it to the due disposure and ranking of an army in battle array, well provided and ordered.

Therefore, by reason of my weakness and inability, being reputed by my compatriots unfit for the offensive part of warfare; and on the other side, being no way employed in matter of the defensive, although it had been but to carry burthens, fill ditches, or break clods, either whereof had been to me indifferent, I held it not a little disgraceful to be only an idle spectator of so many valorous, eloquent, and warlike persons, who in the view and sight of all Europe act this notable interlude or tragi-comedy, and not make some effort towards the performance of this, nothing at all remains for me to be done.[1] In my opinion, little honour is due to such as are mere lookers-on, liberal of their eyes, and of their crowns, and hide their silver; scratching their head with one finger like grumbling puppies, gaping at the flies like tithe calves; clapping down their ears like Arcadian asses at the melody of musicians, who with their very countenances in the depth of silence express their consent to the prosopopœia. Having made this choice and election, it seemed to me that my exercise therein would be neither unprofitable nor troublesome to any, whilst I should thus set a-going my Diogenical tub, which is all that is left me safe from the shipwreck of my former misfortunes.

At this dingle dangle wagging of my tub, what would you have me to do? By the Virgin that tucks up her sleeve, I know not as yet. Stay a little, till I suck up a draught of this bottle; it is my true and only Helicon; it is my Caballine fountain; it is my sole enthusiasm. Drinking thus, I meditate, discourse, resolve, and conclude. After that the epilogue is made, I laugh, I write, I compose, and drink again. Ennius drinking wrote, and writing drank. Æschylus, if Plutarch in his Symposiacs merit any faith, drank composing, and drinking composed. Homer never wrote fasting, and Cato never wrote till after he had drunk. These passages I have brought before you to the end you may not say that I live without the example of men well praised and better prized. It is good and fresh enough, even as if you would say it is entering upon the second degree. God, the good God Sabaoth, that is to say, the God of armies, be praised for it eternally! If you after the same manner

---

[1] "And not exert myself, and contribute thereto this nothing, my all, which remained for me to do."—OZELL.

would take one great draught, or two little ones, whilst you have your gown about you, I truly find no kind of inconveniency in it, provided you send up to God for all some small scantling of thanks.

Since then my luck or destiny is such as you have heard—for it is not for everybody to go to Corinth—I am fully resolved to be so little idle and unprofitable, that I will set myself to serve the one and the other sort of people. Amongst the diggers, pioneers, and rampire-builders, I will do as did Neptune and Apollo at Troy under Laomedon, or as did Renault of Montauban in his latter days: I will serve the masons, I'll set on the pot to boil for the bricklayers; and, whilst the minced meat is making ready at the sound of my small pipe, I'll measure the muzzle of the musing dotards. Thus did Amphion with the melody of his harp found, build, and finish the great and renowned city of Thebes.

For the use of the warriors I am about to broach of new my barrel to give them a taste (which by two former volumes of mine, if by the deceitfulness and falsehood of printers they had not been jumbled, marred, and spoiled, you would have very well relished), and draw unto them, of the growth of our own trippery pastimes, a gallant third part of a gallon, and consequently a jolly cheerful quart of Pantagruelic sentences, which you may lawfully call, if you please, Diogenical: and shall have me, seeing I cannot be their fellow-soldier, for their faithful butler, refreshing and cheering, according to my little power, their return from the alarms of the enemy; as also for an indefatigable extoller of their martial exploits and glorious achievements. I shall not fail therein, par *lapathium acutum* de dieu; if Mars fail not in Lent, which the cunning lecher, I warrant you, will be loth to do.

I remember nevertheless to have read, that Ptolemy, the son of Lagus, one day, amongst the many spoils and booties which by his victories he had acquired, presenting to the Egyptians, in the open view of the people, a Bactrian camel all black, and a party-coloured slave, in such sort as that the one half of his body was black and the other white, not in partition of breadth by the diaphragma, as was that woman consecrated to the Indian Venus whom the Tyanean philosopher did see between the river Hydaspes and Mount Caucasus, but in a perpendicular dimension of altitude; which were things never before that seen in Egypt. He expected by the show of these novelties to win the love of the people. But what happened thereupon? At the production of the camel they were all affrighted, and offended at the sight of the party-coloured man—some scoffed at him as a detestable monster brought forth by the error of nature; in a word, of the hope which he had to please these Egyptians, and by such means to increase the affection which they naturally bore him, he was altogether frustrate and disappointed; understanding fully by their deportments that they took more pleasure and delight in things that were proper, handsome, and perfect, than in misshapen, monstrous, and ridiculous creatures. Since which time he had both the slave and the camel in such dislike, that very shortly thereafter, either through negligence, or for want of ordinary sustenance, they did exchange their life with death.

This example putteth me in a suspense between hope and fear, misdoubting that, for the contentment which I aim at, I will but reap what shall be most distasteful to me: my cake will be dough, and for my Venus I shall have but some deformed puppy: instead of serving them, I shall but vex them, and offend them whom I purpose to exhilarate; resembling in this dubious adventure Euclion's cook, so renowned by Plautus in his Pot, and by Ausonius in his Griphon, and by divers others; which cook, for having by his scraping discovered a treasure, had his hide well curried. Put the case I get no anger by it, though formerly such things fell out, and the like may occur again. Yet, by Hercules! it will not. So I perceive in them all one and the same specifical form, and the like individual properties, which our ancestors called Pantagruelism; by virtue whereof they will bear with anything that floweth from a good, free, and loyal heart. I have seen them ordinarily take goodwill in part of payment, and remain satisfied therewith when one was not able to do better. Having despatched this point, I return to my barrel.

Up, my lads, to this wine, spare it not! Drink, boys, and trowl it off at full bowls! If you do not think it good, let it alone. I am not like those officious and importunate sots, who by force, outrage, and violence, constrain an easy good-natured fellow to whiffle, quaff, carouse, and what is worse. All honest tipplers, all honest gouty men, all such as are a-dry, coming to this little barrel of mine, need not drink thereof if it please them not; but if they have a mind to it, and that the wine prove agreable to the tastes of their worshipful worships, let them drink, frankly, freely, and boldly, without paying anything, and welcome. This is my decree, my statute and ordinance. And let none fear there shall be any want of wine, as at the marriage of Cana in Galilee; for how much soever you shall draw forth at the faucet, so much shall I tun in at the bung. Thus shall the barrel remain inexhaustible; it hath a lively spring and perpetual current. Such was the beverage contained within the cup of Tantalus, which was figuratively represented amongst the Brachman sages. Such was in Iberia the mountain of salt so highly written of by Cato. Such was the branch of gold consecrated to the subterranean goddess, which Virgil treats of so sublimely. It is a true cornucopia of merriment and raillery. If at any time it seem to you to be emptied to the very lees, yet shall it not for all that be drawn wholly dry. Good hope remains there at the bottom, as in Pandora's bottle; and not despair, as in the puncheon of the Danaids. Remark well what I have said, and what manner of people they be whom I do invite; for, to the end that none be deceived, I, in imitation of Lucilius, who did protest that he wrote only to his own Tarentines and Consentines, have not pierced this vessel for any else but you honest men, who are drinkers of the first edition, and gouty blades of the highest degree. The great dorophages, bribe-mongers, have on their hands occupation enough, and enough on the hooks for their venison. There may they follow their prey; here is no garbage for them. You pettifoggers, garblers, and masters of chicanery, speak not to me, I beseech you, in the name of, and for the reverence you bear to the four hips that engendered you and to the quickening peg which at that time conjoined them. As for hypocrites, much less; although they were all of them unsound in body, pockified, scurvy, furnished with unquenchable thirst and insatiable eating. [And wherefore?] Because indeed they are not of good but of evil, and of that evil from which we daily pray to God to deliver us. And albeit we see them sometimes counterfeit devotion, yet never did old ape make pretty moppet. Hence, mastiffs; dogs in a doublet, get you behind; aloof, villains, out of my sunshine; curs, to the devil! Do you jog hither, wagging your tails, to pant at my wine, and bepiss my barrel? Look, here is the cudgel which Diogenes, in his last will, ordained to be set by him after his death, for beating away, crushing the reins, and breaking the backs of these bustuary hobgoblins and Cerberian hellhounds. Pack you hence, therefore, you hypocrites, to your sheep-dogs; get you gone, you dissemblers, to the devil! Hay!

What, are you there yet? I renounce my part of Papimanie, if I snatch you, Grr, Grrr, Grrrrrr. Avaunt, avaunt! Will you not be gone? May you never shit till you be soundly lashed with stirrup leather, never piss but by the strapado, nor be otherwise warmed than by the bastinado.

The Third Book of

Rabelais.

CHAPTER I.

How Pantagruel transported a colony of Utopians into Dipsody.

ANTAGRUEL, having wholly subdued the land of Dipsody, transported thereunto a colony of Utopians, to the number of 9,876,543,210 men, besides the women and little children, artificers of all trades, and professors of all sciences, to people, cultivate, and improve that country, which otherwise was ill inhabited, and in the greatest part thereof but a mere desert and wilderness; and did transport them [not] so much for the excessive multitude of men and women, which were in Utopia multiplied, for number, like grasshoppers upon the face of the land. You understand well enough, nor is it needful further to explain it to you, that the Utopian men had so rank and fruitful genitories, and that the Utopian women carried matrixes so ample, so gluttonous, so tenaciously retentive, and so architectonically cellulated, that at the end of every ninth month seven children at the least, what male what female, were brought forth by every married woman, in imitation of the people of Israel in Egypt, if Anthony [Nicholas] de Lyra be to be trusted. Nor yet was this transplantation made so much for the fertility of the soil, the wholesomeness of the air, or commodity of the country of Dipsody, as to retain that rebellious people within the bounds of their duty and obedience, by this new transport of his

ancient and most faithful subjects, who, from all time out of mind, never knew, acknowledged, owned, or served any other sovereign lord but him; and who likewise, from the very instant of their birth, as soon as they were entered into this world, had, with the milk of their mothers and nurses, sucked in the sweetness, humanity, and mildness of his government, to which they were all of them so nourished and habituated, that there was nothing surer than that they would sooner abandon their lives than swerve from this singular and primitive obedience naturally due to their prince, whithersoever they should be dispersed or removed.

And not only should they, and their children successively descending from their blood, be such, but also would keep and maintain in this same fealty and obsequious observance all the nations lately annexed to his empire; which so truly came to pass that therein he was not disappointed of his intent. For if the Utopians were before their transplantation thither dutiful and faithful subjects, the Dipsodes, after some few days conversing with them, were every whit as, if not more, loyal than they; and that by virtue of I know not what natural fervency incident to all human creatures at the beginning of any labour wherein they take delight: solemnly attesting the heavens and supreme intelligences of their being only sorry that no sooner unto their knowledge had arrived the great renown of the good Pantagruel.

Remark therefore here, honest drinkers, that the manner of preserving and retaining countries newly conquered in obedience is not, as hath been the erroneous opinion of some tyrannical spirits to their own detriment and dishonour, to pillage, plunder, force, spoil, trouble, oppress, vex, disquiet, ruin and destroy the people, ruling, governing and keeping them in awe with rods of iron; and, in a word, eating and devouring them, after the fashion that Homer calls an unjust and wicked king, Δημόβορον, that is to say, a devourer of his people.

I will not bring you to this purpose the testimony of ancient writers. It shall suffice to put you in mind of what your fathers have seen thereof, and yourselves too, if you be not very babes. Newborn, they must be given suck to, rocked in a cradle, and dandled. Trees newly planted must be supported, underpropped, strengthened and defended against all tempests, mischiefs, injuries, and calamities. And one lately saved from a long and dangerous sickness, and new upon his recovery, must be forborn, spared, and cherished, in such sort that they may harbour in their own breasts this opinion, that there is not in the world a king or a prince who does not desire fewer enemies and more friends. Thus Osiris, the great king of the Egyptians, conquered almost the whole earth, not so much by force of arms as by easing the people of their troubles, teaching them how to live well, and honestly giving them good laws, and using them with all possible affability, courtesy, gentleness, and liberality. Therefore was he by all men deservedly entitled the Great King Euergetes, that is to say, Benefactor, which style he obtained by virtue of the command of Jupiter to [one] Pamyla.

And in effect, Hesiod, in his Hierarchy, placed the good demons (call them angels if you will, or geniuses,) as intercessors and mediators betwixt the gods and men, they being of a degree inferior to the gods, but superior to men. And for that through their hands the riches and benefits we get from heaven are dealt to us, and that they are continually doing us good and still protecting us from evil, he saith that they exercise the offices of kings; because to do always good, and never ill, is an act most singularly royal.

Just such another was the emperor of the universe, Alexander the Macedonian. After this manner was Hercules sovereign possessor of the whole continent, relieving men from monstrous oppressions, exactions, and tyrannies; governing them with discretion, maintaining them in equity and justice, instructing them with seasonable policies and wholesome laws, convenient for and suitable to the soil, climate, and disposition of the country, supplying what was wanting, abating what was superfluous, and pardoning all that was past, with a sempiternal forgetfulness of all preceding offences, as was the amnesty of the Athenians, when by the prowess, valour, and industry of Thrasybulus the tyrants were exterminated; afterwards at Rome by Cicero exposed, and renewed under the Emperor Aurelian. These are the philtres, allurements, iynges, inveiglements, baits, and enticements of love, by the means whereof that may be peaceably revived which was painfully acquired. Nor can a conqueror reign more happily, whether he be a monarch, emperor, king, prince, or philosopher, than by making his justice to second his valour. His valour shows itself in victory and conquest; his justice will appear in the goodwill and affection of the people, when he maketh laws, publisheth ordinances, establisheth religion, and doth what is right to everyone, as the noble poet Virgil writes of Octavian Augustus:

Victorque volentes
Per populos dat jura.

Therefore is it that Homer in his Iliads calleth a good prince and great king Κοσμήτορα λαῶν, that is, the ornament of the people.

Such was the consideration of Numa Pompilius, the second king of the Romans, a just politician and wise philosopher, when he ordained that to god Terminus, on the day of his festival called Terminales, nothing should be sacrificed that had died; teaching us thereby that the bounds, limits, and frontiers of kingdoms should be guarded, and preserved in peace, amity, and meekness, without polluting our hands with blood and robbery. Who doth otherwise, shall not only lose what he hath gained, but also be loaded with this scandal and reproach, that he is an unjust and wicked purchaser, and his acquests perish with him; *Juxta illud, male parta, male dilabuntur*. And although during his whole lifetime he should have peaceable possession thereof, yet if what hath been so acquired moulder away in the hands of his heirs, the same opprobry, scandal, and imputation will be charged upon the defunct, and his memory remain accursed for his unjust and unwarrantable conquest; *Juxta illud, de male quæsitis vix gaudet tertius hæres*.

Remark, likewise, gentlemen, you gouty feoffees, in this main point worthy of your observation, how by these means Pantagruel of one angel made two, which was a contingency opposite to the counsel of Charlemagne, who made two devils of one when he transplanted the Saxons into Flanders and the Flemings into Saxony. For, not being able to keep in such subjection the Saxons, whose dominion he had joined to the empire, but that ever and anon they would break forth into open rebellion if he should casually be drawn into Spain or other remote kingdoms, he caused them to be brought unto his own country of Flanders, the inhabitants whereof did naturally obey him, and transported the Hainaults and Flemings, his ancient loving subjects, into Saxony, not mistrusting their loyalty now that they were transplanted into a strange land. But it happened that the Saxons persisted in their rebellion and primitive obstinacy, and the Flemings dwelling in Saxony did imbibe the stubborn manners and conditions of the Saxons.

CHAP. II.

How Panurge was made Laird of Salmigondin in Dipsody, and did waste his revenue before it came in.

WHILST Pantagruel was giving order for the government of all Dipsody, he assigned to Panurge the lairdship of Salmigondin, which was yearly worth 6,789,106,789 reals of certain rent, besides the uncertain revenue of the locusts and periwinkles, amounting, one year with another, to the value of 435,768, or 2,435,769 French crowns of Berry. Sometimes it did amount to 1,230,554,321 seraphs, when it was a good year, and that locusts and periwinkles were in request; but that was not every year.

Now his worship, the new laird, husbanded this his estate so providently well and prudently, that in less than fourteen days he wasted and dilapidated all the certain and uncertain revenue of his lairdship for three whole years. Yet did not he properly dilapidate it, as you might say, in founding of monasteries, building of churches, erecting of colleges, and setting up of hospitals, or casting his bacon-flitches to the dogs; but spent it in a thousand little banquets and jolly collations, keeping open house for all comers and goers; yea, to all good fellows, young girls, and pretty wenches; felling timber, burning great logs for the sale of the ashes, borrowing money beforehand, buying dear, selling cheap, and eating his corn, as it were, whilst it was but grass.

Pantagruel, being advertised of this his lavishness, was in good sooth no way offended at the matter, angry nor sorry; for I once told you, and again tell it you, that he was the best, little, great goodman that ever girded a sword to his side. He took all things in good part, and interpreted every action to the best sense. He never vexed nor disquieted himself with the least pretence of dislike to anything, because he knew that he must have most grossly abandoned the divine mansion of reason if he had permitted his mind to be never so little grieved, afflicted, or altered at any occasion whatsoever. For all the goods that the heaven covereth, and that the earth containeth, in all their dimensions of height, depth, breadth, and length, are not of so much worth as that we should for them disturb or disorder our affections, trouble or perplex our senses or spirits.

He drew only Panurge aside, and then, making to him a sweet remonstrance and mild admonition, very gently represented before him in strong arguments, that, if he should continue in such an unthrifty course of living, and not become a better *mesnagier*, it would prove altogether impossible for him, or at least hugely difficult, at any time to make him rich. Rich! answered Panurge; have you fixed your thoughts there? Have you undertaken the task to enrich me in this world? Set your mind to live merrily, in the name of God and good folks; let no other cark nor care be harboured within the sacrosanctified domicile of your celestial brain. May the calmness and tranquillity thereof be never incommodated with, or overshadowed by any frowning clouds of sullen imaginations and displeasing annoyance! For if you live joyful, merry, jocund, and glad, I cannot be but rich enough. Everybody cries up thrift, thrift, and good husbandry. But many speak of Robin Hood that never shot in his bow, and talk of that virtue of *mesnagery* who know not what belongs to it. It is by me that they must be advised. From me, therefore, take this advertisement and information, that what is imputed to me for a vice hath been done in imitation of the university and parliament of Paris, places in which is to be found the true spring and source of the lively idea of Pantheology and all manner of justice. Let him be counted a heretic that doubteth thereof, and doth not firmly believe it. Yet they in one day eat up their bishop, or the revenue of the bishopric—is it not all one?—for a whole year; yea, sometimes for two. This is done on the day he makes his entry, and is installed. Nor is there any place for an excuse; for he cannot avoid it, unless he would be hooted at and stoned for his parsimony.

It hath been also esteemed an act flowing from the habit of the four cardinal virtues. Of prudence in borrowing money beforehand; for none knows what may fall out. Who is able to tell if the world shall last yet three years? But although it should continue longer, is there any man so foolish as to have the confidence to promise himself three years?

> What fool so confident to say,
> That he shall live one other day?

Of commutative justice, in buying dear, I say, upon trust, and selling goods cheap, that is, for ready money. What says Cato in his Book of Husbandry to this purpose? The father of a family, says he, must be a perpetual seller; by which means it is impossible but that at last he shall become rich, if he have of vendible ware enough still ready for sale.

Of distributive justice it doth partake, in giving entertainment to good—remark, good—and gentle fellows, whom fortune had shipwrecked, like Ulysses, upon the rock of a hungry stomach without provision of sustenance; and likewise to the good—remark, the good—and young wenches. For, according to the sentence of Hippocrates, Youth is impatient of hunger, chiefly if it be vigorous, lively, frolic, brisk, stirring, and bouncing. Which wanton lasses willingly and heartily devote themselves to the pleasure of honest men; and are in so far both Platonic and Ciceronian, that they do acknowledge their being born into this world not to be for themselves alone, but that in their proper persons their acquaintance may claim one share, and their friends another.

The virtue of fortitude appears therein by the cutting down and overthrowing of the great trees, like a second Milo making havoc of the dark forest, which did serve only to furnish dens, caves, and shelter to wolves, wild boars, and foxes, and afford receptacles, withdrawing corners, and refuges to robbers, thieves, and murderers, lurking holes and skulking places for cutthroat assassinators, secret obscure shops for coiners of false money, and safe retreats for heretics, laying them even and level with the plain champaign fields and pleasant heathy ground, at the sound of the hautboys and bagpipes playing reeks with the high and stately timber, and preparing seats and benches for the eve of the dreadful day of judgment.

I gave thereby proof of my temperance in eating my corn whilst it was but grass, like a hermit feeding upon salads and roots, that, so affranchising myself from the yoke of sensual appetites to the utter disclaiming of their sovereignty, I might the better reserve somewhat in store for the relief of the lame, blind, crippled, maimed, needy, poor, and wanting wretches.

In taking this course I save the expense of the weed-grubbers, who gain money,—of the reapers in harvest-time, who drink lustily, and without water,—of gleaners, who will expect their cakes and bannocks,—of threshers, who leave no garlic, scallions, leeks, nor onions in our gardens, by the authority of Thestilis in Virgil,—and of the millers, who are generally thieves,—and of the bakers, who are little better. Is this small saving or frugality? Besides the mischief and damage of the field-mice, the decay of barns, and the destruction usually made by weasels and other vermin.

Of corn in the blade you may make good green sauce of a light concoction and easy digestion, which recreates the brain and exhilarates the animal spirits, rejoiceth the sight, openeth the appetite, delighteth the taste, comforteth the heart, tickleth the tongue, cheereth the countenance, striking a fresh and lively colour, strengthening the muscles, tempers the blood, disburdens the midriff, refresheth the liver, disobstructs the spleen, easeth the kidneys, suppleth the reins, quickens the joints of the back, cleanseth the urine-conduits, dilates the spermatic vessels, shortens the cremasters, purgeth the bladder, puffeth up the genitories, correcteth the prepuce, hardens the nut, and rectifies the member. It will make you have a current belly to trot, fart, dung, piss, sneeze, cough, spit, belch, spew, yawn, snuff, blow, breathe, snort, sweat, and set taut your Robin, with a thousand other rare advantages. I understand you very well, says Pantagruel; you would thereby infer that those of a mean spirit and shallow capacity have not the skill to spend much in a short time. You are not the first in whose conceit that heresy hath entered. Nero maintained it, and above all mortals admired most his uncle Caius Caligula, for having in a few days, by a most wonderfully pregnant invention, totally spent all the goods and patrimony which Tiberius had left him.

But, instead of observing the sumptuous supper-curbing laws of the Romans—to wit, the Orchia, the Fannia, the Didia, the Licinia, the Cornelia, the Lepidiana, the Antia, and of the Corinthians—by the which they were inhibited, under pain of great punishment, not to spend more in one year than their annual revenue did amount to, you have offered up the oblation of Protervia, which was with the Romans such a sacrifice as the paschal lamb was amongst the Jews, wherein all that was eatable was to be eaten, and the remainder to be thrown into the fire, without reserving anything for the next day. I may very justly say of you, as Cato did of Albidius, who after that he had by a most extravagant expense wasted all the means and possessions he had to one only house, he fairly set it on fire, that he might the better say, *Consummatum est.* Even just as since his time St. Thomas

Aquinas did, when he had eaten up the whole lamprey, although there was no necessity in it.

CHAP. III.

𝔥𝔬𝔴 𝔓𝔞𝔫𝔲𝔯𝔤𝔢 𝔭𝔯𝔞𝔦𝔰𝔢𝔱𝔥 𝔱𝔥𝔢 𝔡𝔢𝔟𝔱𝔬𝔯𝔰 𝔞𝔫𝔡 𝔟𝔬𝔯𝔯𝔬𝔴𝔢𝔯𝔰.

UT, quoth Pantagruel, when will you be out of debt? At the next ensuing term of the Greek kalends, answered Panurge, when all the world shall be content, and that it be your fate to become your own heir. The Lord forbid that I should be out of debt, as if, indeed, I could not be trusted. Who leaves not some leaven over night, will hardly have paste the next morning.

Be still indebted to somebody or other, that there may be somebody always to pray for you, that the giver of all good things may grant unto you a blessed, long, and prosperous life; fearing, if fortune should deal crossly with you, that it might be his chance to come short of being paid by you, he will always speak good of you in every company, ever and anon purchase new creditors unto you; to the end, that through their means you may make a shift by borrowing from Peter to pay Paul, and with other folk's earth fill up his ditch. When of old, in the region of the Gauls, by the institution of the Druids, the servants, slaves, and bondmen were burnt quick at the funerals and obsequies of their lords and masters, had not they fear enough, think you, that their lords and masters should die? For, perforce, they were to die with them for company. Did not they incessantly send up their supplications to their great god Mercury, as likewise unto Dis, the father of wealth, to lengthen out their days, and to preserve them long in health? Were not they very careful to entertain them well, punctually to look unto them, and to attend them faithfully and circumspectly? For by those means were they to live together at least until the hour of death. Believe me, your creditors with a more fervent devotion will beseech Almighty God to prolong your life, they being of nothing more afraid than that you should die; for that they are more concerned for the sleeve than the arm, and love silver better than their own lives. As it evidently appeareth by the usurers of Landerousse, who not long since hanged themselves because the price of the corn and wines was fallen by the return of a gracious season. To this Pantagruel answering nothing, Panurge went on in his discourse, saying, Truly and in good sooth, sir, when I ponder my destiny aright, and think well upon it, you put me shrewdly to my plunges, and have me at a bay in twitting me with the reproach of my debts and creditors. And yet did I, in this only respect and consideration of being a debtor, esteem myself worshipful, reverend, and formidable. For against the opinion of most philosophers, that of nothing ariseth nothing, yet, without having bottomed on so much as that which is called the First Matter, did I out of nothing become such [a] maker and creator, that I have created—what?—a gay number of fair and jolly creditors. Nay, creditors, I will maintain it, even to the very fire itself exclusively, are fair and goodly creatures. Who lendeth nothing is an ugly and wicked creature, and an accursed imp of the infernal Old Nick. And there is made—what? Debts. A thing most precious and dainty, of great use and antiquity. Debts, I say, surmounting the number of syllables which may result from the combinations of all the consonants, with each of the vowels heretofore projected, reckoned, and calculated by the noble Xenocrates. To judge of the perfection of debtors by the numerosity of their creditors is the readiest way for entering into the mysteries of practical arithmetic.

You can hardly imagine how glad I am, when every morning I perceive myself environed and surrounded with brigades of creditors —humble, fawning, and full of their reverences. And whilst I remark that, as I look more favourably upon and give a cheerfuller countenance to one than to another, the fellow thereupon buildeth a conceit that he shall be the first despatched and the foremost in the date of payment, and he valueth my smiles at the rate of ready money, it seemeth unto me that I then act and personate the god of the passion of Saumure, accompanied with his angels and cherubims.

These are my flatterers, my soothers, my clawbacks, my smoothers, my parasites, my saluters, my givers of good-morrows, and perpetual orators; which makes me verily think that the supremest height of heroic virtue described by Hesiod consisteth in being a debtor, wherein I held the first degree in my commencement. Which dignity, though all human creatures seem to aim at and aspire thereto, few nevertheless, because of the difficulties in the way and encumbrances of hard passages, are able to reach it, as is easily perceivable by the ardent desire and vehement longing harboured in the breast of everyone to be still creating more debts and new creditors.

Yet doth it not lie in the power of everyone to be a debtor. To acquire creditors is not at the disposure of each man's arbitrament. You nevertheless would deprive me of this sublime felicity. You ask me when I will be out of debt. Well, to go yet further on, and possibly worse in your conceit, may Saint Bablin, the good saint, snatch me, if I have not all my lifetime held debt to be as a union or conjunction of the heavens with the earth, and the whole cement whereby the race of mankind is kept together; yea, of such virtue and efficacy that, I say, the whole progeny of Adam would very suddenly perish without it. Therefore, perhaps, I do not think amiss, when I repute it to be the great soul of the universe, which, according to the opinion of the Academics, vivifieth all manner of things. In confirmation whereof, that you may the better believe it to be so, represent unto yourself, without any prejudicacy of spirit, in a clear and serene fancy, the idea and form of some other world than this; take, if you please, and lay hold on the thirtieth of those which the philosopher Metrodorus did enumerate, wherein it is to be supposed there is no debtor or creditor, that is to say, a world without debts.

There amongst the planets will be no regular course, all will be in disorder. Jupiter, reckoning himself to be nothing indebted unto Saturn, will go near to detrude him out of his sphere, and with the Homeric chain will be like to hang up the intelligences, gods, heavens, demons, heroes, devils, earth and sea, together with the other elements. Saturn, no doubt, combining with Mars will reduce that so disturbed world into a chaos of confusion.

Mercury then would be no more subjected to the other planets; he would scorn to be any longer their Camillus, as he was of old termed in the Etrurian tongue. For it is to be imagined that he is no way a debtor to them.

Venus will be no more venerable, because she shall have lent nothing. The moon will remain bloody and obscure. For to what end should the sun impart unto her any of his light? He owed her nothing. Nor yet will the sun shine upon the earth, nor the stars send down any good influence, because the terrestrial globe hath desisted from sending up their wonted nourishment by vapours and exhalations, wherewith Heraclitus said, the Stoics proved, Cicero maintained, they were cherished and alimented. There would likewise be in such a world no manner of symbolization, alteration, nor transmutation amongst the elements; for the one will not esteem itself obliged to the other, as having borrowed nothing at all from it. Earth then will not become water, water will not be changed into air, of air will be made no fire, and fire will afford no heat unto the earth; the earth will produce nothing but monsters, Titans, giants; no rain will descend upon it, nor light shine thereon; no wind will blow there, nor will there be in it any summer or harvest. Lucifer will break loose, and issuing forth of the depth of hell, accompanied with his furies, fiends, and horned devils, will go about to unnestle and drive out of heaven all the gods, as well of the greater as of the lesser nations. Such a world without lending will be no better than a dog-kennel, a place of contention and wrangling, more unruly and irregular than that of the rector of Paris; a devil of an hurlyburly, and more disordered confusion than that of the plagues of Douay. Men will not then salute one another; it will be but lost labour to expect aid or succour from any, or to cry fire, water, murder, for none will put to their helping hand. Why? He lent no money, there is nothing due to him. Nobody is concerned in his burning, in his shipwreck, in his ruin, or in his death; and that because he hitherto had lent nothing, and would never thereafter have lent anything. In short, Faith, Hope, and Charity would be quite banished from such a world—for men are born to relieve and assist one another; and in their stead should succeed and be introduced Defiance, Disdain, and Rancour, with the most execrable troop of all evils, all imprecations, and all miseries. Whereupon you will think, and that not amiss, that Pandora had there spilt her unlucky bottle. Men unto men will be wolves, hobthrushers, and goblins (as were Lycaon, Bellerophon, Nebuchodonosor), plunderers, highway robbers, cutthroats, rapparees, murderers, poisoners, assassinators, lewd, wicked, malevolent, pernicious haters, set against everybody, like to Ishmael, Metabus, or Timon the Athenian, who for that cause was named Misanthropos; in such sort that it would prove much more easy in nature to have fish entertained in the air and bullocks fed in the bottom of the ocean, than to support or tolerate a rascally rabble of people that will not lend. These fellows, I vow, do I hate with a perfect hatred; and if, conform to the pattern of this grievous, peevish, and perverse world which lendeth nothing, you figure and liken the little world, which is man, you will find in him a terrible justling coil and clutter. The head will not lend the sight of his eyes to guide the feet and hands; the legs will refuse to bear up the body; the hands will leave off working any more for the rest of the members; the heart will be weary of its continual motion for the beating of the pulse, and will no longer lend his assistance; the lungs will withdraw the use of their bellows; the liver will desist from convoying any more blood through the veins for the good of the whole; the bladder will not be indebted to the kidneys, so that the urine thereby will be totally stopped. The brains, in the interim, considering this unnatural course, will fall into a raving dotage, and withhold all feeling from the sinews and motion from the muscles. Briefly, in such a world without order and array, owing nothing, lending nothing, and borrowing nothing, you would see a more dangerous conspiration than that which Æsop exposed in his Apologue. Such a world will perish undoubtedly; and not only perish, but perish very quickly. Were it Æsculapius himself, his body would immediately rot, and the chafing soul, full of indignation, take its flight to all the devils of hell after my money.

CHAP. IV.

Panurge continueth his discourse in the praise of borrowers and lenders.

N the contrary, be pleased to represent unto your fancy another world, wherein everyone lendeth and everyone oweth, all are debtors and all creditors. O how great will that harmony be, which shall thereby result from the regular motions of the heavens! Methinks I hear it every whit as well as ever Plato did. What sympathy will there be amongst the elements! O how delectable then unto nature will be our own works and productions! Whilst Ceres appeareth laden with corn, Bacchus with wines, Flora with flowers, Pomona with fruits, and Juno fair in a clear air, wholesome and pleasant. I lose myself in this high contemplation.

Then will among the race of mankind peace, love, benevolence, fidelity, tranquillity, rest, banquets, feastings, joy, gladness, gold, silver, single money, chains, rings, with other ware and chaffer of that nature be found to trot from hand to hand. No suits at law, no wars, no strife, debate, nor wrangling; none will be there a usurer, none will be there a pinch-penny, a scrape-good wretch, or churlish hard-hearted refuser. Good God! Will not this be the golden age in the reign of Saturn? the true idea of the Olympic regions, wherein all [other] virtues cease, charity alone ruleth, governeth, domineereth, and triumpheth? All will be fair and goodly people there, all just and virtuous.

O happy world! O people of that world most happy! Yea, thrice and four times blessed is that people! I think in very deed that I am amongst them, and swear to you, by my good forsooth, that if this glorious aforesaid world had a pope, abounding with cardinals, that so he might have the association of a sacred college, in the space of very few years you should be sure to see the saints much thicker in the roll, more numerous, wonder-working and mirific, more services, more vows, more staves and wax-candles than are all those in the nine bishoprics of Britany, St. Yves only excepted. Consider, sir, I pray you, how the noble Patelin, having a mind to deify and extol even to the third heavens the father of William Josseaulme, said no more but this, And he did lend his goods to those who were desirous of them.

O the fine saying! Now let our microcosm be fancied conform to this model in all its members; lending, borrowing, and owing, that is to say, according to its own nature. For nature hath not to any other end created man, but to owe, borrow, and lend; no greater is the harmony amongst the heavenly spheres than that which shall be found in its well-ordered policy. The intention of the founder of this microcosm is, to have a soul therein to be entertained, which is lodged there, as a guest with its host, [that] it may live there for a while. Life consisteth in blood, blood is the seat of the soul; therefore the chiefest work of the microcosm is, to be making blood continually.

At this forge are exercised all the members of the body; none is exempted from labour, each operates apart, and doth its proper office. And such is their hierarchy, that perpetually the one borrows from the other, the one lends the other, and the one is the other's debtor. The stuff and matter convenient, which nature giveth to be turned into blood, is bread and wine. All kind of nourishing victuals is understood to be comprehended in these two, and from hence in the Gothish tongue is called *companage*. To find out this meat and drink, to prepare and boil it, the hands are put to work, the feet do walk and bear up the whole bulk of the corporal mass; the eyes guide and conduct all; the appetite in the orifice of the stomach, by means of [a] little sourish black humour, called melancholy, which is transmitted thereto from the milt, giveth warning to shut in the food. The tongue doth make the first essay, and tastes it; the teeth do chew it, and the stomach doth receive, digest, and chylify it. The mesaraic veins suck out of it what is good and fit, leaving behind the excrements, which are, through special conduits for that purpose, voided by an expulsive faculty. Thereafter it is carried to the liver, where it being changed again, it by the virtue of that new transmutation becomes blood. What joy, conjecture you, will then be found amongst those officers when they see this rivulet of gold, which is their sole restorative? No greater is the joy of alchemists, when after long travail, toil, and expense they see in their furnaces the transmutation. Then is it that every member doth prepare itself, and strive anew to purify and to refine this treasure. The kidneys through the emulgent veins draw that aquosity from thence which you call urine, and there send it away through the ureters to be slipped downwards; where, in a lower receptacle, and proper for it, to wit, the bladder, it is kept, and stayeth there until an opportunity to void it out in his due time. The spleen draweth from the blood its terrestrial part, viz., the grounds, lees, or thick substance settled in the bottom thereof, which you term melancholy. The bottle of the gall subtracts from thence all the superfluous choler; whence it is brought to another shop or work-house to be yet better purified and fined, that is, the heart, which by its agitation of diastolic and systolic motions so neatly subtilizeth and inflames it, that in the right side ventricle it is brought to perfection, and through the veins is sent to all the members. Each parcel of the body draws it then unto itself, and after its own fashion is cherished and alimented by it. Feet, hands, thighs, arms, eyes, ears, back, breast, yea, all; and then it is, that who before were lenders, now become debtors. The heart doth in its left side ventricle so thinnify the blood, that it thereby obtains the name of spiritual; which being sent through the arteries to all the members of the body, serveth to warm and winnow the other blood which runneth through the veins. The lights never cease with its lappets and bellows to cool and refresh it, in acknowledgment of which good the heart, through the arterial vein, imparts unto it the choicest of its blood. At last it is made so fine and subtle within the rete mirabile, that thereafter those animal spirits are framed and composed of it, by means whereof the imagination, discourse, judgment, resolution, deliberation, ratiocination, and memory have their rise, actings, and operations.

Cops body, I sink, I drown, I perish, I wander astray, and quite fly out of myself, when I enter into the consideration of the profound abyss of this world, thus lending, thus owing. Believe me, it is a divine thing to lend,—to owe, an heroic virtue. Yet is not this all. This little world thus lending, owing, and borrowing, is so good and charitable, that no sooner is the above-specified alimentation finished, but that it forthwith projecteth, and hath already forecast, how it shall lend to those who are not as yet born, and by that loan endeavour what it may to eternize itself, and multiply in images like the pattern, that is, children. To this end every member doth of the choicest and most precious of its nourishment pare and cut off a portion, then instantly despatcheth it downwards to that place where nature hath prepared for it very fit vessels and receptacles, through which descending to the genitories by long ambages, circuits, and flexuosities, it receiveth a competent form, and rooms apt enough both in the man and woman for the future conservation and perpetuating of human kind. All this is done by loans and debts of the one unto the other; and hence have we this word, the debt of marriage. Nature doth reckon pain to the refuser, with a most grievous vexation to his members and an outrageous fury amidst his senses. But, on the other part, to the lender a set reward, accompanied with pleasure, joy, solace, mirth, and merry glee.

CHAP. V.

How Pantagruel altogether abhorreth the debtors and borrowers.

UNDERSTAND you very well, quoth Pantagruel, and take you to be very good at topics, and thoroughly affectioned to your own cause. But preach it up, and patrocinate it, prattle on it, and defend it as much as you will, even from hence to the next Whitsuntide, if you please so to do, yet in the end will you be astonished to find how you shall have gained no ground at all upon me, nor persuaded me by your fair speeches and smooth talk to enter never so little into the thraldom of debt. You shall owe to none, saith the holy Apostle, anything save love, friendship, and a mutual benevolence.

You serve me here, I confess, with fine graphides and diatyposes, descriptions and figures, which truly please me very well. But let me tell you, if you will represent unto your fancy an impudent blustering bully and an importunate borrower, entering afresh and newly into a town already advertised of his manners, you shall find that at his ingress the citizens will be more hideously affrighted and amazed, and in a greater terror and fear, dread, and trembling, than if the pest itself should step into it in the very same garb and accoutrement wherein the Tyanean philosopher found it within the city of Ephesus. And I am fully confirmed in the opinion, that the Persians erred not when they said that the second vice was to lie, the first being that of owing money. For, in very truth, debts and lying are ordinarily joined together. I will nevertheless not from hence infer that none must owe anything or lend anything. For who so rich can be that sometimes may not owe, or who can be so poor that sometimes may not lend?

Let the occasion, notwithstanding, in that case, as Plato very wisely sayeth and ordaineth in his laws, be such that none be permitted to draw any water out of his neighbour's well until first they by continual digging and delving into their own proper ground shall have hit upon a kind of potter's earth, which is called ceramite, and there had found no source or drop of water; for that sort of earth, by reason of its substance, which is fat, strong, firm, and close, so retaineth its humidity, that it doth not easily evaporate it by any outward excursion or evaporation.

In good sooth, it is a great shame to choose rather to be still borrowing in all places from everyone, than to work and win. Then only in my judgment should one lend, when the diligent, toiling, and industrious person is no longer able by his labour to make any purchase unto himself, or otherwise, when by mischance he hath suddenly fallen into an unexpected loss of his goods.

Howsoever, let us leave this discourse, and from henceforwards do not hang upon creditors, nor tie yourself to them. I make account for the time past to rid you freely of them, and from their bondage to deliver you. The least I should in this point, quoth Panurge, is to thank you, though it be the most I can do. And if gratitude and thanksgiving be to be estimated and prized by the affection of the benefactor, that is to be done infinitely and sempiternally; for the love which you bear me of your own accord and free grace, without any merit of mine, goeth far beyond the reach of any price or value. It transcends all weight, all number, all measure; it is endless and everlasting; therefore, should I offer to commensurate and adjust it, either to the size and proportion of your own noble and gracious deeds, or yet to the contentment and delight of the obliged receivers, I would come off but very faintly and flaggingly. You have verily done me a great deal of good, and multiplied your favours on me more frequently than was fitting to one of my condition. You have been more bountiful towards me than I have deserved, and your courtesies have by far surpassed the extent of my merits, I must needs confess it. But it is not, as you suppose, in the proposed matter. For there it is not where I itch, it is not there where it fretteth, hurts, or vexeth me; for, henceforth being quit and out of debt, what countenance will I be able to keep? You may imagine that it will become me very ill for the first month, because I have never hitherto been brought up or accustomed to it. I am very much afraid of it. Furthermore, there shall not one hereafter, native of the country of Salmigondy, but he shall level the shot towards my nose. All the back-cracking fellows of the world, in discharging of their postern petarades, use commonly to say, *Voila pour les quittes*, that is, For the quit. My life will be of very short continuance, I do foresee it. I recommend to you the making of my epitaph; for I perceive I will die confected in the very stench of farts. If, at any time to come, by way of restorative to such good women as shall happen to be troubled with the grievous pain of the wind-colic, the ordinary medicaments prove nothing effectual, the mummy of all my befarted body will straight be as a present remedy appointed by the physicians; whereof they, taking any small modicum, it will incontinently for their ease afford them a rattle of bumshot, like a sal of muskets.

Therefore would I beseech you to leave me some few centuries of debts; as King Louis the Eleventh, exempting from suits in law the Reverend Miles d'Illiers, Bishop of Chartres, was by the said bishop most earnestly solicited to leave him some few for the exercise of his mind. I had rather give them all my revenue of the periwinkles, together with the other incomes of the locusts, albeit I should not thereby have any parcel abated from off the principal sums which I owe. Let us waive this matter, quoth Pantagruel, I have told it you over again.

CHAP. VI.

𝔚𝔥𝔶 𝔫𝔢𝔴 𝔪𝔞𝔯𝔯𝔦𝔢𝔡 𝔪𝔢𝔫 𝔴𝔢𝔯𝔢 𝔭𝔯𝔦𝔳𝔦𝔩𝔢𝔤𝔢𝔡 𝔣𝔯𝔬𝔪 𝔤𝔬𝔦𝔫𝔤 𝔱𝔬 𝔱𝔥𝔢 𝔴𝔞𝔯𝔰.

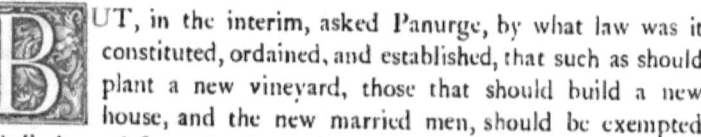UT, in the interim, asked Panurge, by what law was it constituted, ordained, and established, that such as should plant a new vineyard, those that should build a new house, and the new married men, should be exempted and discharged from the duty of warfare for the first year? By the law, answered Pantagruel, of Moses. Why, replied Panurge, the lately married? As for the vine-planters, I am now too old to reflect on them; my condition, at this present, induceth me to remain satisfied with the care of vintage, finishing and turning the grapes into wine. Nor are these pretty new builders of dead stones written or pricked down in my Book of Life. It is all with live stones that I set up and erect the fabrics of my architecture, to wit, men. It was, according to my opinion, quoth Pantagruel, to the end, first, that the fresh married folks should for the first year reap a full and complete fruition of their pleasures in their mutual exercise of the act of love, in such sort, that in waiting more at leisure on the

production of posterity and propagating of their progeny, they might the better increase their race and make provision of new heirs. That if, in the years thereafter, the men should, upon their undergoing of some military adventure, happen to be killed, their names and coats-of-arms might continue with their children in the same families. And next, that, the wives thereby coming to know whether they were barren or fruitful—for one year's trial, in regard of the maturity of age wherein of old they married, was held sufficient for the discovery—they might pitch the more suitably, in case of their first husband's decease, upon a second match. The fertile women to be wedded to those who desire to multiply their issue; and the sterile ones to such other mates, as, misregarding the storing of their own lineage, choose them only for their virtues, learning, genteel behaviour, domestic consolation, management of the house, and matrimonial conveniences and comforts, and such like. The preachers of Varennes, saith Panurge, detest and abhor the second marriages, as altogether foolish and dishonest.

Foolish and dishonest? quoth Pantagruel. A plague take such preachers! Yea but, quoth Panurge, the like mischief also befall the Friar Charmer, who, in a full auditory making a sermon at Pereilly, and therein abominating the reiteration of marriage and the entering again in the bonds of a nuptial tie, did swear and heartily give himself to the swiftest devil in hell, if he had not rather choose, and would much more willingly undertake the unmaidening or depucelating of a hundred virgins, than the simple drudgery of one widow. Truly I find your reason in that point right good and strongly grounded.

But what would you think, if the cause why this exemption or immunity was granted had no other foundation but that, during the whole space of the said first year, they so lustily bobbed it with their female consorts, as both reason and equity require they should do, that they had drained and evacuated their spermatic vessels; and were become thereby altogether feeble, weak, emasculated, drooping, and flaggingly pithless; yea, in such sort that they in the day of battle, like ducks which plunge over head and ears, would sooner hide themselves behind the baggage, than, in the company of valiant fighters and daring military combatants, appear where stern Bellona deals her blows and moves a bustling noise of thwacks and thumps? Nor is it to be thought that, under the standard of Mars, they will so much as once strike a fair stroke, because their most considerable knocks have been already jerked and whirrited within the curtains of his sweetheart Venus.

In confirmation whereof, amongst other relics and monuments of antiquity, we now as yet often see, that in all great houses, after the expiring of some few days, these young married blades are readily sent away to visit their uncles, that in the absence of their wives reposing themselves a little they may recover their decayed strength by the recruit of a fresh supply, the more vigorous to return again and face about to renew the duelling shock and conflict of an amorous dalliance, albeit for the greater part they have neither uncle nor aunt to go to.

Just so did the King Crackart, after the battle of the Cornets, not cashier us (speaking properly), I mean me and the Quail-caller, but for our refreshment remanded us to our houses; and he is as yet seeking after his own. My grandfather's godmother was wont to say to me when I was a boy,—

> *Patenostres et oraisons*
> *Sont pour ceux-la, qui les retiennent.*
> *Ung fiffre en fenaisons*
> *Est plus fort que deux qui en viennent.*

Not orisons nor patenotres
Shall ever disorder my brain.
One cadet, to the field as he flutters,
Is worth two, when they end the campaign.

That which prompteth me to that opinion is, that the vine-planters did seldom eat of the grapes, or drink of the wine of their labour, till the first year was wholly elapsed. During all which time also the builders did hardly inhabit their new-structured dwelling-places, for fear of dying suffocated through want of respiration; as Galen hath most learnedly remarked, in the second book of the Difficulty of Breathing. Under favour, sir, I have not asked this question without cause causing and reason truly very ratiocinant. Be not offended, I pray you.

CHAP. VII.

How Panurge had a flea in his ear, and forbore to wear any longer his magnificent codpiece.

ANURGE, the day thereafter, caused pierce his right ear after the Jewish fashion, and thereto clasped a little gold ring, of a ferny-like kind of workmanship, in the beazil or collet whereof was set and enchased a flea; and, to the end you may be rid of all doubts, you are to know that the flea was black. O, what a brave thing it is, in every case and circumstance of a matter, to be thoroughly well informed! The sum of the expense hereof, being cast up, brought in, and laid down upon his council-board carpet, was found to amount to no more quarterly than the charge of the nuptials of a Hircanian tigress; even, as you would say, 600,000 maravedis. At these vast costs and excessive disbursements, as soon as he perceived himself to be out of debt, he fretted much; and afterwards, as tyrants and lawyers use to do, he nourished and fed her with the sweat and blood of his subjects and clients.

He then took four French ells of a coarse brown russet cloth, and therein apparelling himself, as with a long, plain-seamed, and single-stitched gown, left off the wearing of his breeches, and tied a pair of spectacles to his cap. In this equipage did he present himself before Pantagruel; to whom this disguise appeared the more strange, that he did not, as before, see that goodly, fair, and stately codpiece, which was the sole anchor of hope wherein he was wonted to rely, and last refuge he had midst all the waves and boisterous billows which a stormy cloud in a cross fortune would raise up against him. Honest Pantagruel, not understanding the mystery, asked him, by way of interrogatory, what he did intend to personate in that new-fangled prosopopœia. I have, answered Panurge, a flea in mine ear, and have a mind to marry. In a good time, quoth Pantagruel, you have told me joyful tidings. Yet would not I hold a red-hot iron in my hand for all the gladness of them. But it is not the fashion of lovers to be accoutred in such dangling vestments, so as to have their shirts flagging down over their knees, without breeches, and with a long robe of a dark brown mingled hue, which is a colour never used in Talarian garments amongst any persons of honour, quality, or virtue. If some heretical persons and schismatical sectaries have at any time formerly been so arrayed and clothed (though many have imputed such a kind of dress to cosenage, cheat, imposture, and an affectation of tyranny upon credulous minds of the rude multitude), I will nevertheless not blame them for it, nor in that point judge rashly or sinistrously of them. Everyone overflowingly aboundeth in his own sense and fancy; yea, in things of a foreign consideration, altogether extrinsical and indifferent, which in and of themselves are neither commendable nor bad, because they proceed not from the interior of the thoughts and heart, which is the shop of all good and evil; of goodness, if it be upright, and that its affections be regulated by the pure and clean spirit of righteousness; and, on the other side, of wickedness, if its inclinations, straying beyond the bounds of equity, be corrupted and depraved by the malice and suggestions of the devil. It is only the novelty and newfangledness thereof which I dislike, together with the contempt of common custom and the fashion which is in use.

The colour, answered Panurge, is convenient, for it is conform to that of my council-board carpet; therefore will I henceforth hold me with it, and more narrowly and circumspectly than ever hitherto I have done look to my affairs and business. Seeing I am once out of debt, you never yet saw man more unpleasing than I will be, if God help me not. Lo, here be my spectacles. To see me afar off, you would readily say that it were Friar [John] Burgess. I believe certainly that in the next ensuing year I shall once more preach the Crusade. Bounce, buckram. Do you see this russet? Doubt not but there lurketh under it some hid property and occult virtue known to very few in the world. I did not take it on before this morning, and, nevertheless, am already in a rage of lust, mad after a wife, and vehemently hot upon untying the codpiece-point; I itch, I tingle, I wriggle, and long exceedingly to be married, that, without the danger of cudgel-blows, I may labour my female copes-mate with the hard push of a bull-horned devil. O the provident and thrifty husband that I then will be! After my death, with all honour and respect due to my frugality, will they burn the sacred bulk of my body, of purpose to preserve the ashes thereof, in memory of the choicest pattern that ever was of a perfectly wary and complete householder. Cops body, this is not the carpet whereon my treasurer shall be allowed to play false in his accounts with me, by setting down an X for a V, or an L for an S. For in that case should I make a hail of fisticuffs to fly into his face. Look upon me, sir, both before and behind,—it is made after the manner of a toga, which was the ancient fashion of the Romans in time of peace. I took the mode, shape, and form thereof in Trajan's Column at Rome, as also in the Triumphant Arch of Septimus Severus. I am tired of the wars, weary of wearing buff-coats, cassocks, and hoquetons. My shoulders are pitifully worn and bruised with the carrying of harness. Let armour cease, and the long robe bear sway! At least it must be so for the whole space of the succeeding year, if I be married; as yesterday, by the Mosaic law, you evidenced. In what concerneth the breeches, my great-aunt Laurence did long ago tell me, that the breeches were only ordained for the use of the codpiece, and to no other end; which I, upon a no less forcible consequence, give credit to every whit, as well as to the saying of the fine fellow Galen, who in his ninth book, Of the Use and Employment of our Members, allegeth that the head was made for the eyes. For nature might have placed our heads in our knees or elbows, but having beforehand determined that the eyes should serve to discover things from afar, she for the better enabling them to execute their designed office, fixed them in the head, as on the top of a long pole, in the most eminent part of all the body—no otherwise than we see the phares, or high towers erected in the mouths of havens, that navigators may the further off perceive with ease the lights of the nightly fires and lanterns. And because I would gladly, for some short while, a year at least, take a little rest and breathing time from the toilsome labour of the military profession, that is to say, be married, I have desisted from wearing any more a codpiece, and consequently have laid aside my breeches. For the codpiece is the principal and most especial piece of armour that a warrior doth carry; and therefore do I maintain even to the fire (exclusively, understand you me), that no Turks can properly be said to be armed men, in regard that codpieces are by their law forbidden to be worn.

CHAP. VIII.

Why the codpiece is held to be the chief piece of armour amongst warriors.

ILL you maintain, quoth Pantagruel, that the codpiece is the chief piece of a military harness? It is a new kind of doctrine, very paradoxical; for we say, At spurs begins the arming of a man. Sir, I maintain it, answered Panurge, and not wrongfully do I maintain it. Behold how nature, having a fervent desire, after its production of plants, trees, shrubs, herbs, sponges, and plant-animals, to eternize and continue them unto all succession of ages (in their several kinds or sorts, at least, although the individuals perish) unruinable, and in an everlasting being, hath most curiously armed and fenced their buds, sprouts, shoots, and seeds, wherein the above-mentioned perpetuity consisteth, by strengthening, covering, guarding, and fortifying them with an admirable industry, with husks, cases, scurfs and swads, hulls, cods, stones, films, cartels, shells, ears, rinds, barks, skins, ridges, and prickles, which serve them instead of strong, fair, and natural codpieces. As is manifestly apparent in pease, beans, fasels, pomegranates, peaches, cottons, gourds, pumpions, melons, corn, lemons, almonds, walnuts, filberts, and chestnuts; as likewise in all plants, slips, or sets whatsoever, wherein it is plainly and evidently seen, that the sperm and semence is more closely veiled, overshadowed, corroborated, and thoroughly harnessed, than any other part, portion, or parcel of the whole.

Nature, nevertheless, did not after that manner provide for the sempiternizing of [the] human race; but, on the contrary, created man naked, tender, and frail, without either offensive or defensive arms; and that in the estate of innocence, in the first age of all, which was the golden season; not as a plant, but living creature, born for peace, not war, and brought forth into the world with an unquestionable right and title to the plenary fruition and enjoyment of all fruits and vegetables, as also to a certain calm and gentle rule and dominion over all kinds of beasts, fowls, fishes, reptiles, and insects. Yet afterwards it happening in the time of the iron age, under the reign of Jupiter, when, to the multiplication of mischievous actions, wickedness and malice began to take root and footing within the then perverted hearts of men, that the earth began to bring forth nettles, thistles, thorns, briars, and such other stubborn and rebellious vegetables to the nature of man. Nor scarce was there any animal which by a fatal disposition did not then revolt from him, and tacitly conspire and covenant with one another to serve him no longer, nor, in case of their ability to resist, to do him any manner of obedience, but rather, to the uttermost of their power, to annoy him with all the hurt and harm they could. The man, then, that he might maintain his primitive right and prerogative, and continue his sway and dominion over all, both vegetable and sensitive creatures, and knowing of a truth that he could not be well accommodated as he ought without the servitude and subjection of several animals, bethought himself that of necessity he must needs put on arms, and make provision of harness against wars and violence. By the holy Saint Babingoose, cried out Pantagruel, you are become, since the last rain, a great lifrelofre, — philosopher, I should say. Take notice, sir, quoth Panurge, when Dame Nature had prompted him to his own arming, what part of the body it was, where, by her inspiration, he clapped on the first harness. It was forsooth by the double pluck of my little dog the ballock and good Senor Don Priapos Stabo-stando— which done, he was content, and sought no more. This is certified by the testimony of the great Hebrew captain [and] philosopher Moses, who affirmeth that he fenced that member with a brave and gallant codpiece, most exquisitely framed, and by right curious devices of a notably pregnant invention made up and composed of fig-tree leaves, which by reason of their solid stiffness, incisory notches, curled frizzling, sleeked smoothness, large ampleness, together with their colour, smell, virtue, and faculty, were exceeding proper and fit for the covering and arming of the satchels of generation—the hideously big Lorraine cullions being from thence only excepted, which, swaggering down to the lowermost bottom of the breeches, cannot abide, for being quite out of all order and method, the stately fashion of the high and lofty codpiece; as is manifest by the noble Valentine Viardiere, whom I found at Nancy, on the first day of May—the more flauntingly to gallantrize it afterwards—rubbing his ballocks, spread out upon a table after the manner of a Spanish cloak. Wherefore it is, that none should henceforth say, who would not speak improperly, when any country bumpkin hieth to the wars, Have a care, my roister, of the wine-pot, that is, the skull, but, Have a care, my roister, of the milk-pot, that is, the testicles. By the whole rabble of the horned fiends of hell, the head being cut off, that single person only thereby dieth. But, if the ballocks be marred, the whole race of human kind would forthwith perish, and be lost for ever.

This was the motive which incited the goodly writer Galen, *Lib.* 1. *De Spermate*, to aver with boldness that it were better, that is to say, a less evil, to have no heart at all than to be quite destitute of genitories; for there is laid up, conserved, and put in store, as in a secessive repository and sacred warehouse, the semence and original source of the whole offspring of mankind. Therefore would I be apt to believe, for less than a hundred francs, that those are the very same stones by means whereof Deucalion and Pyrrha restored the human race, in peopling with men and women the world, which a little before that had been drowned in the overflowing waves of a poetical deluge. This stirred up the valiant Justinian, *L.* 4. *De Cagotis tollendis*, to collocate his *Summum Bonum, in Braguibus, et Braguetis.* For this and other causes, the Lord Humphrey de Merville, following of his king to a certain warlike expedition, whilst he was in trying upon his own person a new suit of armour, for of his old rusty harness he could make no more use, by reason that some few years since the skin of his belly was a great way removed from his kidneys, his lady thereupon, in the profound musing of a contemplative spirit, very maturely considering that he had but small care of the staff of love and packet of marriage, seeing he did no otherwise arm that part of the body than with links of mail, advised him to shield, fence, and gabionate it with a big tilting helmet which she had lying in her closet, to her otherwise utterly unprofitable. On this lady were penned these subsequent verses, which are extant in the third book of the Shitbrana of Paltry Wenches.

> *When Yoland saw her spouse equipp'd for fight,*
> *And, save the codpiece, all in armour dight,*
> *My dear, she cried, why, pray, of all the rest*
> *Is that exposed, you know I love the best?*
> *Was she to blame for an ill-managed fear,—*
> *Or rather pious, conscionable care?*
> *Wise lady, she! In hurlyburly fight,*
> *Can any tell where random blows may light?*

Leave off then, sir, from being astonished, and wonder no more at this new manner of decking and trimming up of myself as you now see me.

CHAP. IX.

How Panurge asketh counsel of Pantagruel whether he should marry, yea, or no.

TO this Pantagruel replying nothing, Panurge prosecuted the discourse he had already broached, and therewithal fetching, as from the bottom of his heart, a very deep sigh, said, My lord and master, you have heard the design I am upon, which is to marry, if by some disastrous mischance all the holes in the world be not shut up, stopped, closed, and bushed. I humbly beseech you, for the affection which of a long time you have borne me, to give me your best advice therein. Then, answered Pantagruel, seeing you have so decreed, taken deliberation thereon, and that the matter is fully determined, what need is there of any further talk thereof, but forthwith to put it into execution what you have resolved? Yea but, quoth Panurge, I would be loth to act anything therein without your counsel had thereto. It is my judgment also, quoth Pantagruel, and I advise you to it. Nevertheless, quoth Panurge, if I understood aright that it were much better for me to remain a bachelor as I am, than to run headlong upon new hairbrained undertakings of conjugal adventure, I would rather choose not to marry. Quoth Pantagruel, Then do not marry. Yea but, quoth Panurge, would you have me so solitarily drive out the whole course of my life, without the comfort of a matrimonial consort? You know it is written, *Væ soli!* and a single person is never seen to reap the joy and solace that is found with married folks. Then marry, in the name of God, quoth Pantagruel. But if, quoth Panurge, my wife should make me a cuckold—as it is not unknown unto you, how this hath been a very plentiful year in the production of that kind of cattle—I would fly out, and grow impatient beyond all measure and mean. I love cuckolds with my heart, for they seem unto me to be of a right honest conversation, and I truly do very willingly frequent their company; but should I die for it, I would not be one of their number. That is a point for me of a too sore prickling point. Then do not marry, quoth Pantagruel, for without all controversy this sentence of Seneca is infallibly true, What thou to others shalt have done, others will do the like to thee. Do you, quoth Panurge, aver that without all exception? Yes, truly, quoth Pantagruel, without all exception. Ho, ho, says Panurge, by the wrath of a little devil, his meaning is, either in this world or in the other which is to come. Yet seeing I can no more want a wife than a blind man his staff—[for] the funnel must be in agitation, without which manner of occupation I cannot live—were it not a great deal better for me to apply and associate myself to some one honest, lovely, and virtuous woman, than as I do, by a new change of females every day, run a hazard of being bastinadoed, or, which is worse, of the great pox, if not of both together. For never—be it spoken by their husbands' leave and favour—had I enjoyment yet of an honest woman. Marry then, in God's name, quoth Pantagruel. But if, quoth Panurge, it were the will of God, and that my destiny did unluckily lead me to marry an honest woman who should beat me, I would be stored with more than two third parts of the patience of Job, if I were not stark mad by it, and quite distracted with such rugged dealings. For it hath been told me that those exceeding honest women have ordinarily very wicked head-pieces; therefore is it that their family lacketh not for good vinegar. Yet in that case should it go worse with me, if I did not then in such sort bang her back and breast, so thumpingly bethwack her gillets, to wit, her arms, legs, head, lights, liver, and milt, with her other entrails, and mangle, jag, and slash her coats so after the cross-billet fashion that the greatest devil of hell should wait at the gate for the reception of her damned soul. I could make a shift for this year to waive such molestation and disquiet, and be content to lay aside that trouble, and not to be engaged in it.

Do not marry then, answered Pantagruel. Yea but, quoth Panurge, considering the condition wherein I now am, out of debt and unmarried; mark what I say, free from all debt, in an ill hour, for, were I deeply on the score, my creditors would be but too careful of my paternity, but being quit, and not married, nobody will be so regardful of me, or carry towards me a love like that which is said to be in a conjugal affection. And if by some mishap I should fall sick,

I would be looked to very waywardly. The wise man saith, Where there is no woman—I mean the mother of a family and wife in the union of a lawful wedlock—the crazy and diseased are in danger of being ill used and of having much brabbling and strife about them; as by clear experience hath been made apparent in the persons of popes, legates, cardinals, bishops, abbots, priors, priests, and monks; but there, assure yourself, you shall not find me. Marry then, in the name of God, answered Pantagruel. But if, quoth Panurge, being ill at ease, and possibly through that distemper made unable to discharge the matrimonial duty that is incumbent to an active husband, my wife, impatient of that drooping sickness and faint-fits of a pining languishment, should abandon and prostitute herself to the embraces of another man, and not only then not help and assist me in my extremity and need, but withal flout at and make sport of that my grievous distress and calamity; or peradventure, which is worse, embezzle my goods and steal from me, as I have seen it oftentimes befall unto the lot of many other men, it were enough to undo me utterly, to fill brimful the cup of my misfortune, and make me play the mad-pate reeks of Bedlam. Do not marry then, quoth Pantagruel. Yea but, said Panurge, I shall never by any other means come to have lawful sons and daughters, in whom I may harbour some hope of perpetuating my name and arms, and to whom also I may leave and bequeath my inheritances and purchased goods (of which latter sort you need not doubt but that in some one or other of these mornings I will make a fair and goodly show), that so I may cheer up and make merry when otherwise I should be plunged into a peevish sullen mood of pensive sullenness, as I do perceive daily by the gentle and loving carriage of your kind and gracious father towards you; as all honest folks use to do at their own homes and private dwelling-houses. For being free from debt, and yet not married, if casually I should fret and be angry, although the cause of my grief and displeasure were never so just, I am afraid, instead of consolation, that I should meet with nothing else but scoffs, frumps, gibes, and mocks at my disastrous fortune. Marry then, in the name of God, quoth Pantagruel.

CHAP. X.

How Pantagruel representeth unto Panurge the difficulty of giving advice in the matter of marriage; and to that purpose mentioneth somewhat of the Homeric and Virgilian lotteries.

OUR counsel, quoth Panurge, under your correction and favour, seemeth unto me not unlike to the song of Gammer Yea-by-nay. It is full of sarcasms, mockeries, bitter taunts, nipping bobs, derisive quips, biting jerks, and contradictory iterations, the one part destroying the other. I know not, quoth Pantagruel, which of all my answers to lay hold on; for your proposals are so full of ifs and buts, that I can ground nothing on them, nor pitch upon any solid and positive determination satisfactory to what is demanded by them. Are not you assured within yourself of what you have a mind to? The chief and main point of the whole matter lieth there. All the rest is merely casual, and totally dependeth upon the fatal disposition of the heavens.

We see some so happy in the fortune of this nuptial encounter, that their family shineth as it were with the radiant effulgency of an idea, model, or representation of the joys of paradise; and perceive others, again, to be so unluckily matched in the conjugal yoke, that those very basest of devils which tempt the hermits that inhabit the deserts of Thebais and Montserrat are not more miserable than they. It is therefore expedient, seeing you are resolved for once to take a trial of the state of marriage, that, with shut eyes, bowing your head, and kissing the ground, you put the business to a venture, and give it a fair hazard, in recommending the success of the residue to the disposure of Almighty God. It lieth not in my power to give you any other manner of assurance, or otherwise to certify you of what shall ensue on this your undertaking. Nevertheless, if it please you, this you may do. Bring hither Virgil's poems, that after having opened the book, and with our fingers severed the leaves thereof three several times, we may, according to the number agreed upon betwixt ourselves, explore the future hap of your intended marriage. For frequently by a Homeric lottery have many hit upon their destinies; as is testified in the person of Socrates, who, whilst he was in prison, hearing the recitation of this verse of Homer, said of Achilles in the Ninth of the Iliads—

"Ἡματί κε τρίτατῳ Φθίην ἐρίβωλον ἱκοίμην,

We, the third day, to fertile Pthia came—

thereby foresaw that on the third subsequent day he was to die. Of the truth whereof he assured Æschines; as Plato, *in Critone*, Cicero, *in Primo, de Divinatione*, Diogenes Laertius, and others, have to the full recorded in their works. The like is also witnessed by Opilius Macrinus, to whom, being desirous to know if he should be the Roman emperor, befell, by chance of lot, this sentence in the Eighth of the Iliads—

Ὦ γέρον, ἦ μάλα δή σε νέοι τείρουσι μαχηταὶ,
Σὴ δὲ βίη λέλυται, χαλεπόν δὲ σε γῆρας ὀπάζει.

Dotard, new warriors urge thee to be gone.
Thy life decays, and old age weighs thee down.

In fact, he, being then somewhat ancient, had hardly enjoyed the sovereignty of the empire for the space of fourteen months, when by Heliogabalus, then both young and strong, he was dispossessed thereof, thrust out of all, and killed. Brutus doth also bear witness of another experiment of this nature, who willing, through this exploratory way by lot, to learn what the event and issue should be of the Pharsalian battle wherein he perished, he casually encountered on this verse, said of Patroclus in the Sixteenth of the Iliads—

Ἀλλά με μοῖρ' ὀλοὴ, καὶ Λητοῦς ἔκτανεν υἱός.

Fate, and Latona's son have shot me dead.

And accordingly Apollo was the field-word in the dreadful day of that fight. Divers notable things of old have likewise been foretold and known by casting of Virgilian lots; yea, in matters of no less importance than the obtaining of the Roman empire, as it happened to Alexander Severus, who, trying his fortune at the said kind of lottery, did hit upon this verse written in the Sixth of the Æneids—

> *Tu regere imperio populos, Romane, memento.*

> *Know, Roman, that thy business is to reign.*

He, within very few years thereafter, was effectually and in good earnest created and installed Roman emperor. A semblable story thereto is related of Adrian, who, being hugely perplexed within himself out of a longing humour to know in what account he was with the Emperor Trajan, and how large the measure of that affection was which he did bear unto him, had recourse, after the manner above specified, to the Maronian lottery, which by haphazard tendered him these lines out of the Sixth of the Æneids—

> *Quis procul ille autem, ramis insignis olivæ*
> *Sacra ferens? Nosco crines incanaque menta*
> *Regis Romani.*

> *But who is he, conspicuous from afar,*
> *With olive boughs, that doth his offerings bear?*
> *By the white hair and beard I know him plain,*
> *The Roman king.*

Shortly thereafter was he adopted by Trajan, and succeeded to him in the empire. Moreover, to the lot of the praiseworthy Emperor Claudius befell this line of Virgil, written in the Sixth of his Æneids—

> *Tertia dum Latio regnantem viderit æstas.*

> *Whilst the third summer saw him reign, a king*
> *In Latium.*

And in effect he did not reign above two years. To the said Claudian also, inquiring concerning his brother Quintilius, whom he proposed as a colleague with himself in the empire, happened the response following in the Sixth of the Æneids—

Ostendent terris hunc tantum fata.

> *Whom Fate let us see,*
> *And would no longer suffer him to be.*

And it so fell out; for he was killed on the seventeenth day after he had attained unto the management of the imperial charge. The very same lot, also, with the like misluck, did betide the Emperor Gordian the younger. To Claudius Albinus, being very solicitous to understand somewhat of his future adventures, did occur this saying, which is written in the Sixth of the Æneids—

> *Hic rem Romanam magno turbante tumultu*
> *Sistet Eques, &c.*

> *The Romans, boiling with tumultuous rage,*
> *This warrior shall the dangerous storm assuage:*
> *With victories he the Carthaginian mauls,*
> *And with strong hand shall crush the rebel Gauls.*

Likewise, when the Emperor D. Claudius, Aurelian's predecessor, did with great eagerness research after the fate to come of his posterity, his hap was to alight on this verse in the First of the Æneids—

> *Hic ego nec metas rerum, nec tempora pono.*

> *No bounds are to be set, no limits here.*

Which was fulfilled by the goodly genealogical row of his race. When Mr. Peter Amy did in like manner explore and make trial if he should escape the ambush of the hobgoblins who lay in wait all-to-bemaul him, he fell upon this verse in the Third of the Æneids—

> *Heu! fuge crudeles terras, fuge littus avarum!*

> *Oh, flee the bloody land, the wicked shore!*

Which counsel he obeying, safe and sound forthwith avoided all these ambuscades.

Were it not to shun prolixity, I could enumerate a thousand such like adventures, which, conform to the dictate and verdict of the verse, have by that manner of lot-casting encounter befallen to the curious researchers of them. Do not you nevertheless imagine, lest you should be deluded, that I would upon this kind of fortune-flinging proof infer an uncontrollable and not to be gainsaid infallibility of truth.

CHAP. XI.

How Pantagruel sheweth the trial of one's fortune by the throwing of dice to be unlawful.

IT would be sooner done, quoth Panurge, and more expeditely, if we should try the matter at the chance of three fair dice. Quoth Pantagruel, That sort of lottery is deceitful, abusive, illicitous, and exceedingly scandalous. Never trust in it. The accursed book of the Recreation of Dice was a great while ago excogitated in Achaia, near Bourre, by that ancient enemy of mankind, the infernal calumniator, who, before the statue or massive image of the Bourraic Hercules, did of old, and doth in several places of the world as yet, make many simple souls to err and fall into his snares. You know how my father Gargantua hath forbidden it over all his kingdoms and dominions; how he hath caused burn the moulds and draughts thereof, and altogether suppressed, abolished, driven forth, and cast it out of the land, as a most dangerous plague and infection to any well-polished state or commonwealth. What I have told you of dice, I say the same of the play at cockall. It is a lottery of the like guile and deceitfulness; and therefore do not for convincing of me allege in opposition to this my opinion, or bring in the example of the fortunate cast of Tiberius, within the fountain of Aponus, at the oracle of Gerion. These are the baited hooks by which the devil attracts and draweth unto him the foolish souls of silly people into eternal perdition.

Nevertheless, to satisfy your humour in some measure, I am content you throw three dice upon this table, that, according to the number of the blots which shall happen to be cast up, we may hit upon a verse of that page which in the setting open of the book you shall have pitched upon.

Have you any dice in your pocket? A whole bagful, answered Panurge. That is provision against the devil, as is expounded by Merlin Coccaius, *Lib.* 2. *De Patria Diabolorum.* The devil would be sure to take me napping, and very much at unawares, if he should find me without dice. With this, the three dice being taken out, produced, and thrown, they fell so pat upon the lower points that the cast was five, six, and five. These are, quoth Panurge, sixteen in all. Let us take the sixteenth line of the page. The number pleaseth me very well; I hope we shall have a prosperous and happy chance. May I be thrown amidst all the devils of hell, even as a great bowl cast athwart at a set of ninepins, or cannon-ball shot among a battalion of foot, in case so many times I do not boult my future wife the first night of our marriage! Of that, forsooth, I make no doubt at all, quoth Pantagruel. You needed not to have rapped forth such a horrid imprecation, the sooner to procure credit for the performance of so small a business, seeing possibly the first bout will be amiss, and that you know is usually at tennis called fifteen. At the next justling turn you may readily amend that fault, and so complete your reckoning of sixteen. Is it so, quoth Panurge, that you understand the matter? And must my words be thus interpreted? Nay, believe me never yet was any solecism committed by that valiant champion who often hath for me in Belly-dale stood sentry at the hypogastrian cranny. Did you ever hitherto find me in the confraternity of the faulty? Never, I trow; never, nor ever shall, for ever and a day. I do the feat like a goodly friar or father confessor, without default. And therein am I willing to be judged by the players. He had no sooner spoke these words than the works of Virgil were brought in. But before the book was laid open, Panurge said to Pantagruel, My heart, like the furch of a hart in a rut, doth beat within my breast. Be pleased to feel and grope my pulse a little on this artery of my left arm. At its frequent rise and fall you would say that they swinge and belabour me after the manner of a probationer, posed and put to a peremptory trial in the examination of his sufficiency for the discharge of the learned duty of a graduate in some eminent degree in the college of the Sorbonists.

But would not you hold it expedient, before we proceed any further, that we should invocate Hercules and the Tenetian goddesses

who in the chamber of lots are said to rule, sit in judgment, and bear a presidential sway? Neither him nor them, answered Pantagruel; only open up the leaves of the book with your fingers, and set your nails awork.

CHAP. XII.

How Pantagruel doth explore by the Virgilian lottery what fortune Panurge shall have in his marriage.

THEN at the opening of the book in the sixteenth row of the lines of the disclosed page did Panurge encounter upon this following verse:

Nec Deus hunc mensa, Dea nec dignata cubili est.

The god him from his table banished,
Nor would the goddess have him in her bed.

This response, quoth Pantagruel, maketh not very much for your benefit or advantage; for it plainly signifies and denoteth that your wife shall be a strumpet, and yourself by consequence a cuckold. The goddess, whom you shall not find propitious nor favourable unto you, is Minerva, a most redoubtable and dreadful virgin, a powerful and fulminating goddess, an enemy to cuckolds and effeminate youngsters, to cuckold-makers and adulterers. The god is Jupiter, a terrible and thunder-striking god from heaven. And withal it is to be remarked, that, conform to the doctrine of the ancient Etrurians, the manubes, for so did they call the darting hurls or slinging casts of the Vulcanian thunderbolts, did only appertain to her and to Jupiter her father capital. This was verified in the conflagration of the ships of Ajax Oileus, nor doth this fulminating power belong to any other of the Olympic gods. Men, therefore, stand not in such fear of them. Moreover, I will tell you, and you may take it as extracted out of the profoundest mysteries of mythology, that, when the giants had enterprised the waging of a war against the power of the celestial orbs, the gods at first did laugh at those attempts, and scorned such despicable enemies, who were, in their conceit, not strong enough to cope in feats of warfare with their pages; but when they saw by the gigantine labour the high hill Pelion set on lofty Ossa, and that the mount Olympus was made shake to be erected on the top of both, then was it that Jupiter held a parliament, or general convention, wherein it was unanimously resolved upon and condescended to by all the gods, that they should worthily and valiantly stand to their defence. And because they had often seen battles lost by the cumbersome lets and disturbing encumbrances of women confusedly huddled in amongst armies, it was at that time decreed and enacted that they should expel and drive out of heaven into Egypt and the confines of Nile that whole crew of goddesses, disguised in the shapes of weasels, polecats, bats, shrew-mice, ferrets, fulmarts, and other such like odd transformations; only Minerva was reserved to participate with Jupiter in the horrific fulminating power, as being the goddess both of war and learning, of arts and arms, of counsel and despatch—a goddess armed from her birth, a goddess dreaded in heaven, in the air, by sea and land. By the belly of Saint Buff, quoth Panurge, should I be Vulcan, whom the poet blazons? Nay, I am neither a cripple, coiner of false money, nor smith, as he was. My wife possibly will be as comely and handsome as ever was his Venus, but not a whore like her, nor I a cuckold like him. The crook-legged slovenly slave made himself to be declared a cuckold by a definite sentence and judgment, in the open view of all the gods. For this cause ought you to interpret the afore-mentioned verse quite contrary to what you have said. This lot importeth that my wife will be honest, virtuous, chaste, loyal, and faithful; not armed, surly, wayward, cross, giddy, humorous, heady, hairbrained, or extracted out of the brains, as was the goddess Pallas; nor shall this fair jolly Jupiter be my co-rival. He shall never dip his bread in my broth, though we should sit together at one table.

Consider his exploits and gallant actions. He was the manifest ruffian, wencher, whoremonger, and most infamous cuckold-maker that ever breathed. He did always lecher it like a boar, and no wonder, for he was fostered by a sow in the Isle of Candia, if Agathocles the Babylonian be not a liar, and more rammishly lascivious than a buck; whence it is that he is said by others to have been suckled and fed with the milk of the Amalthæan goat. By the virtue of Acheron, he justled, bulled, and lastauriated in one day the third part of the world, beasts and people, floods and mountains; that was Europa. For this grand subagitatory achievement the Ammonians caused draw, delineate, and paint him in the figure and shape of a ram ramming, and horned ram. But I know well enough how to shield and preserve myself from that horned champion. He will not, trust me, have to deal in my person with a sottish, dunsical Amphytrion, nor with a silly witless Argus, for all his hundred spectacles, nor yet with the cowardly meacock Acrisius, the simple goose-cap Lycus of Thebes, the doting blockhead Agenor, the phlegmatic pea-goose Æsop, rough-footed Lycaon, the luskish misshapen Corytus of Tuscany, nor with the large-backed and strong-reined Atlas. Let him alter, change, transform, and metamorphose himself into a hundred various shapes and figures, into a swan, a bull, a satyr, a shower of gold, or into a cuckoo, as he did when he unmaidened his sister Juno; into an eagle, ram, or dove, as when he was enamoured of the virgin Phthia, who then dwelt in the Ægean territory; into fire, a serpent, yea, even into a flea; into Epicurean and Democratical atoms, or, more Magistronostralistically, into those sly intentions of the mind, which in the schools are called second notions,—I'll catch him in the nick, and take him napping. And would you know what I would do unto him? Even that which to his father Cœlum Saturn did—Seneca foretold it of me, and Lactantius hath confirmed it— what the goddess Rhea did to Athis. I would make him two stone lighter, rid him of his Cyprian cymbals, and cut so close and neatly by the breech, that there should not remain thereof so much as one ———, so cleanly would I shave him, and disable him for ever from being Pope, for *Testiculos non habet.* Hold there, said Pantagruel; ho, soft and fair, my lad! Enough of that,—cast up, turn over the leaves, and try your fortune for the second time. Then did he fall upon this ensuing verse:

Membra quatit, gelidusque coit formidine sanguis.

His joints and members quake, he becomes pale,
And sudden fear doth his cold blood congeal.

This importeth, quoth Pantagruel, that she will soundly bang your back and belly. Clean and quite contrary, answered Panurge; it is of me that he prognosticates, in saying that I will beat her like a tiger if she vex me. Sir Martin Wagstaff will perform that office, and in default of a cudgel, the devil gulp him, if I should not eat her up quick, as Candaul the Lydian king did his wife, whom he ravened and devoured.

You are very stout, says Pantagruel, and courageous; Hercules himself durst hardly adventure to scuffle with you in this your raging fury. Nor is it strange; for the Jan is worth two, and two in fight against Hercules are too too strong. Am I a Jan? quoth Panurge. No, no, answered Pantagruel. My mind was only running upon the lurch and tricktrack. Thereafter did he hit, at the third opening of the book, upon this verse:

Fœmineo prædæ, et spoliorum ardebat amore.

After the spoil and pillage, as in fire,
He burnt with a strong feminine desire.

This portendeth, quoth Pantagruel, that she will steal your goods, and rob you. Hence this, according to these three drawn lots, will be your future destiny, I clearly see it,—you will be a cuckold, you will be beaten, and you will be robbed. Nay, it is quite otherwise, quoth Panurge; for it is certain that this verse presageth that she will love me with a perfect liking. Nor did the satyr-writing poet lie in proof hereof, when he affirmed that a woman, burning with extreme affection, takes sometimes pleasure to steal from her sweetheart. And what, I pray you? A glove, a point, or some such trifling toy of no importance, to make him keep a gentle kind of stirring in the research and quest thereof. In like manner, these small scolding debates and petty brabbling contentions, which frequently we see spring up and for a certain space boil very hot betwixt a couple of high-spirited lovers, are nothing else but recreative diversions for their refreshment, spurs to and incentives of a more fervent amity than ever. As, for example, we do sometimes see cutlers with hammers maul their finest whetstones, therewith to sharpen their iron tools the better. And therefore do I think that these three lots make much for my advantage; which, if not, I from their sentence totally appeal. There is no appellation, quoth Pantagruel, from the decrees of fate or destiny, of lot or chance; as is recorded by our ancient lawyers, witness Baldus, *Lib. ult. Cap. de Leg.* The reason hereof is, Fortune doth not acknowledge a superior, to whom an appeal may be made from her or any of her substitutes. And in this case the pupil cannot be restored to his right in full, as openly by the said author is alleged in *L. Ait Prætor, paragr. ult. ff. de minor.*

CHAP. XIII.

How Pantagruel adviseth Panurge to try the future good or bad luck of his marriage by dreams.

NOW, seeing we cannot agree together in the manner of expounding or interpreting the sense of the Virgilian lots, let us bend our course another way, and try a new sort of divination. Of what kind? asked Panurge. Of a good ancient and authentic fashion, answered Pantagruel; it is by dreams. For in dreaming, such circumstances and conditions being thereto adhibited, as are clearly enough described by Hippocrates, in Lib. Περὶ τῶν ἐνυπνίων, by Plato, Plotin, Iamblicus, Sinesius, Aristotle, Xenophon, Galen, Plutarch, Artemidorus, Daldianus, Herophilus, Q. Calaber, Theocritus, Pliny, Athenæus, and others, the soul doth oftentimes foresee what is to come. How true this is, you may conceive by a very vulgar and familiar example; as when you see that at such a time as suckling babes, well nourished, fed, and fostered with good milk, sleep soundly and profoundly, the nurses in the interim get leave to sport themselves, and are licentiated to recreate their fancies at what range to them shall seem most fitting and expedient, their presence, sedulity, and attendance on the cradle being, during all that space, held unnecessary. Even just so, when our body is at rest, that the concoction is everywhere accomplished, and that, till it awake, it lacks for nothing, our soul delighteth to disport itself and is well pleased in that frolic to take a review of its native country, which is the heavens, where it receiveth a most notable participation of its first beginning with an imbuement from its divine source, and in contemplation of that infinite and intellectual sphere, whereof the centre is everywhere, and the circumference in no place of the universal world, to wit, God, according to the doctrine of Hermes Trismegistus, to whom no new thing happeneth, whom nothing that is past escapeth, and unto whom all things are alike present, remarketh not only what is preterit and gone in the inferior course and agitation of sublunary matters, but withal taketh notice what is to come; then bringing a relation of those future events unto the body of the outward senses and exterior organs, it is divulged abroad unto the hearing of others. Whereupon the owner of that soul deserveth to be termed a vaticinator, or prophet. Nevertheless, the truth is, that the soul is seldom able to report those things in such sincerity as it hath seen them, by reason of the imperfection and frailty of the corporeal senses, which obstruct the effectuating of that office; even as the moon doth not communicate unto this earth of ours that light which she receiveth from the sun with so much splendour, heat, vigour, purity, and liveliness as it was given her. Hence it is requisite for the better reading, explaining, and unfolding of these somniatory vaticinations and predictions of that nature, that a dexterous, learned, skilful, wise, industrious, expert, rational, and peremptory expounder or interpreter be pitched upon, such a one as by the Greeks is called onirocrit, or oniropolist. For this cause Heraclitus was wont to say that nothing is by dreams revealed to us, that nothing is by dreams concealed from us, and that only we thereby have a mystical signification and secret evidence of things to come, either for our own prosperous or unlucky fortune, or for the favourable or disastrous success of another. The sacred Scriptures testify no less, and profane histories assure us of it, in both which are exposed to our view a thousand several kinds of strange adventures, which have befallen pat according to the nature of the dream, and that as well to the party dreamer as to others. The Atlantic people, and those that inhabit the [is]land of Thasos, one of the Cyclades, are of this grand commodity deprived; for in their countries none yet ever dreamed. Of this sort [were] Cleon of Daulia, Thrasymedes, and in our days the learned Frenchman Villanovanus, neither of all which knew what dreaming was.

Fail not therefore to-morrow, when the jolly and fair Aurora with her rosy fingers draweth aside the curtains of the night to drive away the sable shades of darkness, to bend your spirits wholly to the task of sleeping sound, and thereto apply yourself. In the meanwhile you must denude your mind of every human passion or affection, such as are love and hatred, fear and hope, for as of old the great vaticinator, most famous and renowned prophet Proteus, was not able in his disguise or transformation into fire, water, a tiger, a dragon, and other such like uncouth shapes and visors, to presage anything that was to come till he was restored to his own first natural and kindly form; just so doth man; for, at his reception of the art of divination and faculty of prognosticating future things, that part in him which is the most divine, to wit, the Νοῦς, or Mens, must be calm, peaceable, untroubled, quiet, still, hushed, and not embusied or distracted with foreign, soul-disturbing perturbations. I am content, quoth Panurge. But, I pray you, sir, must I this evening, ere I go to bed, eat much or little? I do not ask this without cause. For if I sup not well, large, round, and amply, my sleeping is not worth a forked turnip. All the night long I then but doze and rave, and in my slumbering fits talk idle nonsense, my thoughts being in a dull brown study, and as deep in their dumps as is my belly hollow.

Not to sup, answered Pantagruel, were best for you, considering the state of your complexion and healthy constitution of your body. A certain very ancient prophet, named Amphiaraus, wished such as had a mind by dreams to be imbued with any oracle, for four-and-twenty hours to taste no victuals, and to abstain from wine three days together. Yet shall not you be put to such a sharp, hard, rigorous, and extreme sparing diet. I am truly right apt to believe that a man whose stomach is replete with various cheer, and in a manner surfeited with drinking, is hardly able to conceive aright of spiritual things; yet am not I of the opinion of those who, after long and pertinacious fastings, think by such means to enter more profoundly into the speculation of celestial mysteries. You may very well remember how my father Gargantua (whom here for honour sake I name) hath often told us that the writings of abstinent, abstemious, and long-fasting hermits were every whit as saltless, dry, jejune, and insipid as were their bodies when they did compose them. It is a most difficult thing for the spirits to be in a good plight, serene and lively, when there is nothing in the body but a kind of voidness and inanity; seeing the philosophers with the physicians jointly affirm that the spirits which are styled animal spring from, and have their constant practice in and through the arterial blood, refined and purified to the life within the admirable net which, wonderfully framed, lieth under the ventricles and tunnels of the brain. He gave us also the example of the philosopher who, when he thought most seriously to have withdrawn himself unto a solitary privacy, far from the rustling clutterments of the tumultuous and confused world, the better to improve his theory, to contrive, comment, and ratiocinate, was, notwithstanding his uttermost endeavours to free himself from all untoward noises, surrounded and environed about so with the barking of curs, bawling of mastiffs, bleating of sheep, prating of parrots, tattling of jackdaws, grunting of swine, girning of boars, yelping of foxes, mewing of cats, cheeping of mice, squeaking of weasels, croaking of frogs, crowing of cocks, cackling of hens, calling of partridges, chanting of swans, chattering of jays, peeping of chickens, singing of larks, creaking of geese, chirping of swallows, clucking of moorfowls, cucking of cuckoos, bumbling of bees, rammage of hawks, chirming of linnets, croaking of ravens, screeching of owls, whicking of pigs, gushing of hogs, curring of pigeons, grumbling of cushat-doves, howling of panthers, curkling of quails, chirping of sparrows, crackling of crows, nuzzing of camels, wheening of whelps, buzzing of dromedaries, mumbling of rabbits, cricking of ferrets, humming of wasps, mioling of tigers, bruzzing of bears, sussing of kitlings, clamouring of scarfs, whimpering of fulmarts, booing of buffaloes, warbling of nightingales, quavering of mavises, drintling of turkeys, coniating of storks, frantling of peacocks, clattering of magpies, murmuring of stock-doves, crouting of cormorants, cigling of locusts, charming of beagles, guarring of puppies, snarling of messens, rantling of rats, guericting of apes, snuttering of monkeys, pioling of pelicans, quacking of ducks, yelling of wolves, roaring of lions, neighing of horses, crying of elephants, hissing of serpents, and wailing of turtles, that he was much more troubled than if he had been in the middle of the crowd at the fair of Fontenay or Niort. Just so is it with those who are tormented with the grievous pangs of hunger. The stomach begins to gnaw, and bark, as it were, the eyes to look dim, and the veins, by greedily sucking some refection to themselves from the proper substance of all the members of a fleshy consistence, violently pull down and draw back that vagrant, roaming spirit, careless and neglecting of his nurse and natural host, which is the body ; as when a hawk upon the fist, willing to take her flight by a soaring aloft in the open spacious air, is on a sudden drawn back by a leash tied to her feet.

To this purpose also did he allege unto us the authority of Homer, the father of all philosophy, who said that the Grecians did not put an end to their mournful mood for the death of Patroclus, the most intimate friend of Achilles, till hunger in a rage declared herself, and their bellies protested to furnish no more tears unto their grief. For from bodies emptied and macerated by long fasting there could not be such supply of moisture and brackish drops as might be proper on that occasion.

Mediocrity at all times is commendable; nor in this case are you to abandon it. You may take a little supper, but thereat must you not eat of a hare, nor of any other flesh. You are likewise to abstain from beans, from the preak, by some called the polyp, as also from coleworts, cabbage, and all other such like windy victuals, which may endanger the troubling of your brains and the dimming or casting a kind of mist over your animal spirits. For, as a looking-glass cannot exhibit the semblance or representation of the object set before it, and exposed to have its image to the life expressed, if that the polished sleekedness thereof be darkened by gross breathings, dampish vapours, and foggy, thick, infectious exhalations, even so the fancy cannot well receive the impression of the likeness of those things which divination doth afford by dreams, if any way the body be annoyed or troubled with the fumish steam of meat which it had taken in a while before; because betwixt these two there still hath been a mutual sympathy and fellow-feeling of an indissolubly knit affection. You shall eat good Eusebian and Bergamot pears, one apple of the short-shank pippin kind, a parcel of the little plums of Tours, and some few cherries of the growth of my orchard. Nor shall you need to fear that thereupon will ensue doubtful dreams, fallacious, uncertain, and not to be trusted to, as by some peripatetic philosophers hath been related; for that, say they, men do more copiously in the season of harvest feed on fruitages than at any other time. The same is mystically taught us by the ancient prophets and poets, who allege that all vain and deceitful dreams lie hid and in covert under the leaves which are spread on the ground—by reason that the leaves fall from the trees in the autumnal quarter. For the natural fervour which, abounding in ripe, fresh, recent fruits, cometh by the quickness of its ebullition to be with ease evaporated into the animal parts of the dreaming person—the experiment is obvious in most—is a pretty while before it be expired, dissolved, and evanished. As for your drink, you are to have it of the fair, pure water of my fountain.

The condition, quoth Panurge, is very hard. Nevertheless, cost what price it will, or whatsoever come of it, I heartily condescend thereto; protesting that I shall to-morrow break my fast betimes after my somniatory exercitations. Furthermore, I recommend myself to Homer's two gates, to Morpheus, to Iselon, to Phantasus, and unto Phobetor. If they in this my great need succour me and grant me that assistance which is fitting, I will in honour of them all erect a jolly, genteel altar, composed of the softest down. If I were now in Laconia, in the temple of Juno, betwixt Œtile and Thalamis, she suddenly would disentangle my perplexity, resolve me of my doubts, and cheer me up with fair and jovial dreams in a deep sleep.

Then did he say thus unto Pantagruel: Sir, were it not expedient for my purpose to put a branch or two of curious laurel betwixt the quilt and bolster of my bed, under the pillow on which my head must lean? There is no need at all of that, quoth Pantagruel; for, besides that it is a thing very superstitious, the cheat thereof hath been at large discovered unto us in the writings of Serapion, Ascalonites, Antiphon, Philochorus, Artemon, and Fulgentius Planciades. I could say as much to you of the left shoulder of a crocodile, as also of a chameleon, without prejudice be it spoken to the credit which is due to the opinion of old Democritus; and likewise of the stone of the Bactrians, called Eumetrides, and of the Ammonian horn; for so by the Æthiopians is termed a certain precious stone, coloured like gold, and in the fashion, shape, form, and proportion of a ram's horn, as the horn of Jupiter Ammon is reported to have been: they over and above assuredly affirming that the dreams of those who carry it about them are no less veritable and infallible than the truth of the divine oracles. Nor is this much unlike to what Homer and Virgil wrote of these two gates of sleep, to which you have been pleased to recommend the management of what you have in hand. The one is of ivory, which letteth in confused, doubtful, and uncertain dreams; for through ivory, how small and slender soever it be, we can see nothing, the density, opacity, and close compactedness of its material parts hindering the penetration of the visual rays and the reception of the specieses of such things as are visible. The other is of horn, at which an entry is made to sure and certain dreams, even as through horn, by reason of the diaphanous splendour and bright transparency thereof, the species of all objects of the sight distinctly pass, and so without confusion appear, that they are clearly seen. Your meaning is, and you would thereby infer, quoth Friar John, that the dreams of all horned cuckolds, of which number Panurge, by the help of God and his future wife, is without controversy to be one, are always true and infallible.

END OF VOLUME I.

www.ingramcontent.com/pod-product-compliance
Lightning Source LLC
Chambersburg PA
CBHW051245300426
44114CB00011B/895